ON OUR BEST BEHAVIOR

ON
OUR BEST
BEHAVIOR

THE SEVEN DEADLY SINS
AND THE PRICE WOMEN
PAY TO BE GOOD

ELISE LOEHNEN

THE DIAL PRESS | NEW YORK

Published in the United States by The Dial Press, an imprint of Random House, a division of Penguin Random House LLC, New York.

THE DIAL PRESS is a registered trademark and the colophon is a trademark of Penguin Random House LLC.

Library of Congress Cataloging-in-Publication Data
Names: Loehnen, Elise, author.
Title: On Our Best Behavior: The Seven Deadly Sins and the Price Women Pay to Be Good / Elise Loehnen.
Description: First Edition. | New York: The Dial Press, [2023]
Identifiers: LCCN 2023005017 (print) | LCCN 2023005018 (ebook) |
ISBN 9780593243039 (hardcover) | ISBN 9780593243046 (ebook)
Subjects: LCSH: Women—Religious life. | Women—Religious aspects—Christianity. |
Women—Psychology. | Women—Social conditions. | Psychology, Religious. | Sins.
Classification: LCC BV4527 .L63334 2023 (print) | LCC BV4527 (ebook) |
DDC 248.8/43—dc23/eng/20230309
LC record available at https://lccn.loc.gov/2023005017
LC ebook record available at https://lccn.loc.gov/2023005018

Printed in the United States of America on acid-free paper

randomhousebooks.com

2 4 6 8 9 7 5 3 1

First Edition

Book design by Jo Anne Metsch

*For Peter, who had faith in me long before
I had faith in myself, and whose death gave me faith
in something much larger than myself.*

CONTENTS

AUTHOR'S NOTE

THIS BOOK IS ABOUT HOW WE'RE CULTURALLY PROGRAMMED. I, too, of course, am a product of the culture in which I was raised. I am a white, straight, married mother, born in the United States to two heterosexual parents who are still married. I was raised in an upper-middle-class family and I am upper middle class today. I identify as a woman, and other people, for the most part, identify me as a woman. I am fortunate that these identities feel accurate and that I can easily claim words to describe my experience. For many, the language we have to define who we are falls painfully short.

I use the words *women, woman,* and *we* liberally in the following pages. But it's important that I state clearly: These words are shortcuts for *an idea of what it means to be a woman*—an idea that can be reductive and essentialist. My use of these terms is also framed by my own point of view, as a woman born in a female body. On these pages, I've attempted to interrogate our culture and the lives of as many women as possible, but it is not my intention to speak for *all* women, nor do I presume that I can. Yet I do believe our culture corrals all people who identify as women in universal ways; my hope is that this book will illuminate those ways.

I've recounted events in my own life to the best of my memory's ability, and I've asked friends and family to fact-check me. I've anonymized some people, per their request, throughout this book, and changed some details to preserve identities.

INTRODUCTION

Genesis

IN LATE 2019, I HYPERVENTILATED FOR AN ENTIRE MONTH. I could not take a deep, complete breath without yawning because, ironically, my lungs were oversaturated with oxygen. Hyperventilation is a classic mix-up between the body and the brain that I had been experiencing on and off since I was in my twenties. The first time it happened, I went to the emergency room thinking I had hours to live before I asphyxiated and that I needed to be intubated, stat. The doctor advised me it was all in my head and sent me home with a pat on the back and a Xanax prescription. This recent spell was different. I couldn't nap it away. Cutting out caffeine offered no relief. I struggled and suffered, yawning and sighing through meetings, interviews, and meals. It's a strange experience—to appear to the world as calm and sedate, sleepy really, while contending inside with consuming anxiety. I felt a bit like a duck, paddling frantically beneath the surface, while appearing to glide with little effort on top.

I sat in my therapist's office that month, in exhausted tears.

"I feel like I can't breathe," I said.

"I know," he answered.

"It's like I'm suffocating, like I've been buried alive."

"Where is it in your body?"

"It feels," I said, "as if something is sitting on my chest and no matter what I do I can't get it off."

"That sounds really scary."

We sat, quietly.

"I'm just so tired. I don't understand. I try to do it all right, to be perfect, to be everything for everyone." I paused to breathe before rushing out, "Why isn't that enough to give me some space? What more can I do to push this thing away?" I stopped, then asked: "Do you know what it is?"

"I don't," he offered. "But I understand why you feel urgency to figure it out."

"Is it the weight of my unreasonable expectations?" I asked. "Am I putting too much pressure on myself? Neither of those statements feel true to me, but you know me well."

He looked at me. "I think you are trying to live up to some sort of saintly ideal, yes. But I think it's deeper, that if you feel like you're good enough, you'll be safe from judgment, loved."

This observation hit, right in my clenched heart.

"So, what is sitting on my chest exactly?" I asked.

"Whatever tells you that you're not."

After our session, I sat in my car, head resting on the steering wheel. I could feel something primal and angry, something rebellious and pissed, break free. I was trying to be good. I had always been trying to be good. I ran myself ragged; cared dutifully for my family, friends, and colleagues; punished my body so that it stayed a certain size; kept my temper in check. What would happen if I just . . . stopped? I didn't know the answer, but in my parked car that day, I resolved to find out. I planted a tiny seed, an inquiry that became the germ of this book—its unfurling would cost me a lot, but it would give me back my life.

.   .   .

I WISH I COULD report that this revelation in my therapist's office was enough to break the spell, to unlabor my breathing, to provide relief. Sadly, admitting that I felt pinned down by *something* didn't disappear the phantom in the way that flipping on the lights when one of my kids sees a strange shadow at bedtime dissipates the threat. But acknowledging the specter's heft and weight did give shape to my investigation: Where did this beast come from, how did it get its power, and why was I so willing to submit? I began to trawl through history to locate the early murmurs of when goodness and acceptability were conjoined for women—and I revisited my own childhood to trace when this programming had first caught me in its maw.

I've always liked asking questions. I was a precocious and curious child, probably a little annoying in my insistence to understand: *Why? Why? Why?* Fortunately for me, my mother used the library as a babysitter. I always had my face in a book. I looked for answers in novels, history, science—anywhere they might be hiding. And on the long drive to and from town every day (we lived in the woods up a valley outside of Missoula, Montana), my parents played NPR's *All Things Considered,* so I listened as masterful radio journalists like Cokie Roberts, Nina Totenberg, and Susan Stamberg used *their* questions to make the world more comprehensible. Now I realize I was trying to impose logic on a society that felt chaotic to me: I could sense an underlying structure, a code of behavior, a way life is *supposed* to be done. I needed to discern this map's contours— the boundaries of acceptance, belonging, and goodness—so I could pick the right path, one that might ensure my own safety, success, and survival.

When I became an adult, I took jobs writing and editing, positions where I was paid to pursue my interests, to parse how systems work and why we do what we do. I've interviewed hundreds of deep thinkers and cultural influencers—doctors, scientists, theologians, therapists, activists, politicians, historians, healers, actors, poets, and journalists—about what it means to be human. In the past decade, I've spoken to Bryan Stevenson, the death row defense attorney who argues that we are better than the worst thing we've done, that no one deserves to be someone else's executioner. I've spent time with Laura Lynne Jackson, a famous psychic medium whose ability to channel the dead suggests we are part of a much larger energetic story—that we don't vanish but endure, that we are here in "Earth School" to learn, evolve, and grow. I've chatted with legendary historian Mary Beard about the silencing of women in literature throughout history; physician Gabor Maté about how intergenerational trauma drives addiction; U.S. surgeon general Vivek Murthy on the epidemic of loneliness; historian Isabel Wilkerson about our unseen but pervasive racial caste system; marriage therapists John and Julie Gottman about why some couples are destined to divorce; and many, many more authors, philosophers, artists, and academics. If someone can offer an insight or clue into the human condition, I'll collect it, add it to my web.

As I've reflected on these conversations, I've come to realize that, on some level, everyone is saying the same thing: We all struggle to be known, to express the truest, most tender parts of ourselves, to feel safe enough to bring our gifts to bear. We wonder: Who am I? What do I want and need? How do I find my purpose and serve? Our greatest imperatives are to belong, to love and be loved in return. Yet life gets in the way. Sometimes interference comes from tangible constraints that are outside our control—traumatic childhoods, systemic injustice, natural disasters—but more frequently, the barriers that keep us from full expression of our potential are intangible. These are whisperings of self-doubt, limiting beliefs, or social constructs of roles and responsibilities: What's appropriate for each of us to want, and to do? These gossamer threads tie us up or pull us along like marionettes. They are the long tails of cultural programming, a legacy that clings to us as we move throughout the world.

The late visionary anthropologist Ashley Montagu talks about humans as having "first nature" and "second nature." Our first nature is who we are, at our root and most whole: our unique genetic design and natural instincts. Our second nature, according to Montagu, is the way society informs this biology and how it shapes *our beliefs* about who we are. As he explains:

> The forms of behavior that characterize us as human beings are determined by the socialization process we undergo, the cultural conditioning in which we are molded, the customs by which we are all made. And there's the rub, for we are the most educable of all the creatures on this earth. . . . Everything we come to be, to know, and to do as *human beings* we have to learn from other human beings. Indeed, educability is our species' trait. And that is why to be human is to be in danger, for we can easily be taught many wrong and unsound things.

When I first encountered this quote, it left a pit in my stomach. I had spent my early life leaning into this "species trait" of educability, trying to understand who I was according to who I'd been told I should be—and how a girl who wanted to belong should behave.

But in the past decade I approached all of the conversations I had with our culture's thought leaders with a subconscious agenda: I wanted all those thinkers, healers, and guides to help me unwind and reverse-engineer this education. I wanted to know how to replace it with something truer. Many of those conversations helped. But they also revealed to me that we are *all* stuck in a web. Every one of us is conditioned and caught in a system that we cannot see—but its effects are suffocating and deadening. We are so used to functioning in this structure that it's only when we attempt to break free that we can feel just how tightly we've been restrained. It became my journey to understand these fibers and their hold, to feel out their dimensions and complexities. In this process, I realized all is not lost: Once you discern the web and its perverted construction, you can begin clipping strands one by one, letting falsehoods about who we are blow away.

This book is about the "wrong and unsound things" we've been taught, how we've internalized those ideas as beliefs, rooted them in our societal structures, and passed them on to future generations, perpetuating our own confused oppression. I'm specifically interested in how this legacy shows up in the lives of women, and the ways our subordination across millennia came to be seen as normal and natural. Montagu again: "Our biology does not decree that one sex shall rule over the other. What determines that sort of thing is tradition, culture." Well, our tradition and culture have decreed that women are inferior in all ways: physically, spiritually, and morally. This social mythology has kept us desperate to prove our basic goodness and worthiness.

Adhering to the dictates of the web and suppressing our natural instincts is learned behavior. And it is relatively recent. The devaluation of the feminine can be traced to the emergence of monotheism; its demonization of the goddess and a maternal, nature-oriented worldview; and the rise of Christianity. This system of God-the-Father religion supposes an eternity beyond our mortal lives and mediates who is or is not worthy to ascend to the heavenly realms someday. Women—the instigator for the fall of men—are at a notable disadvantage as a result: We are compelled to prove our *virtue,* our moral perfection. But we will never be able to prove our virtue, as the word itself is out of reach for women: Its etymology is Latin (*vir*), for *man.*

We all know the story of curious Eve and the apple, the serpent, and the Tree of Knowledge. Many of us can recite the Ten Commandments and some of the six hundred–plus other laws (*mitzvahs*) in the Old Testament. But there are more subtle scripts about bad behavior that have taken firm root in our culture, continuing to circumscribe our lives. When it comes to a mythology that has kept women from the truth of who we are, there is no better map than the set of vices that are considered the gateway to immorality: the Seven Deadly Sins. The attempt to avoid these sins corrals women and diminishes the potential fullness of our lives. These sins are woven into society and our concepts of selfhood in profound ways. They are primary threads of this sticky web.

Really? you might ask. *But I'm not religious. I don't believe any of this.* Even if you consider yourself an atheist, or agnostic, or opposed to organized religion, the moral codes directed by the Seven Deadly Sins have influenced you. They are not solely the provenance of the church; the sins have permeated culture. The Seven Deadly Sins aren't even in the Bible; they were posited by a desert monk as "Eight Thoughts" in the fourth century, a few decades after the codification of the New Testament. The Eight Thoughts included sadness, though several centuries later sadness was dropped, and they were refined into the list we know now—pride, sloth, greed, envy, anger, gluttony, lust. The church worked hard to mainstream them as a guideline for confession. The sins became a punch card of trespasses requiring penance: Anyone who indulged in them needed to atone.

THE QUALITIES OF CULTURE

While there are those who take the Word of God and his commandments literally, there are many today for whom religion is less about dogma and more about collective values. And religious or not, the tenets of what it means to be "good" flow through every faucet, regardless of faith. This code of behavior washed into me, even though I grew up in a world largely absent of religion. I didn't need to hear about sin from a priest to worry about my goodness and lovability. As a child, I felt out with my hands in the dark to find the boundaries of acceptable behavior: Is this OK? And this? How should I act? How should I look? What should I want? We can denounce religion and reject its beliefs at a literal level, but its traditions, these tenets of "good" and "bad," are woven into the fabric of society. They don't need our approval or subscription to hold us captive. They operate in us on a subconscious level.

After all, culture is contagious: We pass it on to each other like a virus. It permeates everything. No one wholly invents themselves. Culture is whispered into us, transmitted through almost every interaction. "Nature" and "culture" are conflated and debated—the question of whether culture drives behavior or behavior creates culture will never be answered. What is apparent, though, is how twisted many of us feel, like a snake eating its own tail: What's me, versus the me I think I'm supposed to be?

For millennia, culture *was* religion. Its programming revolved around redeeming ourselves from our base human appetites and desires and proving ourselves worthy of heaven. The Seven Deadly Sins became a kind of CliffsNotes on how *not* to be. Easy to remember, they lend themselves to visual and allegorical representation. They are also unavoidable in daily life: To be alive is to engage with them. The sins became the perfect mechanism through which the church could maintain power and control and could pressure the public to repent continually and stay permanently on their knees.

While the Old Testament's Ten Commandments are concrete, the Seven Deadly Sins are amorphous, ripe for interpretation, which may have something to do with their continued potency. They are not about objective, tangible bad actions (you stole, you killed, you cheated); they are about human qualities where one crosses an imperceptible yet defining line (you *are* slutty, greedy, lazy!). And because they are subjective, they are easy to brandish like a whip. It's impossible to pinpoint the moment when you've transgressed. How much food is gluttonous? When does meeting your needs morph into greed?

Badness is in the eye of the beholder, the vested authority, society. Because these values are subjective and arbitrary, it's so easy to damn someone, to accuse them of falling short.* As a corollary,

---

* Notably, this happened to women all the time: The etymology of wicked is *Wicca*, i.e., witch.

then, "goodness"—virtue, belonging—cannot be claimed. It must be granted by some authority "out there." Sinning is a disempowering concept. Centuries ago, the people mediating between supplicants and God were priests. Now, in our secular culture, we turn to parents, critics, partners, bosses, even strangers on Instagram. We are easy to shame, eager to prove our worthiness, to seek validation from some power outside of ourselves. And this tendency often shows up in the shadow of the Seven Deadly Sins, which have been an impressively brilliant tool for ensuring good behavior across millennia. Their fingerprints are everywhere, particularly in the lives of women: We have been trained for goodness. Men, meanwhile, have been trained for power. While this might sound like a better deal—power is something women are currently being coached to assume and then sanitize with our femininity—we see the dangerous implications of this programming everywhere. Men are persecuted by the patriarchy as well; it poisons everyone. I believe, and will argue, that sadness—with its corollary, weakness—haunts us all. While officially dropped from the list of the Seven Deadly Sins, it must be examined as well.

WOMEN AND OUR "GOODNESS"

While the Seven Deadly Sins traveled through time and culture as a set—see Hieronymus Bosch's paintings, Dante's *Purgatory,* Chaucer's *Canterbury Tales,* Marlowe's *Doctor Faustus,* Bertolt Brecht and Kurt Weill's ballet *The Seven Deadly Sins,* the movie *Seven*—they also became recognizable as stand-alone concepts. They're all over our fairy tales, and they are embedded in the language and "wisdom" of our culture, such as the common sayings many of us heard as the chorus of childhood: You can sleep when you're dead (sloth). Jealousy is the green-eyed monster (envy). Pride goeth before a fall (pride). Nothing tastes as good as skinny feels (gluttony). Money is the root of all evil (greed). Good girls go to heaven, bad girls go everywhere (lust). Hell hath no fury like a woman scorned (anger). There is a lot of stigma attached to each of these ideas, which are ingrained, specifically, in the minds of women.

These concepts control us and keep us small. When we overindulge at a meal, we condemn ourselves as "bad" and promise to be "good" the next day. When we spend a Saturday morning binge-watching Netflix rather than cleaning the house, we chastise ourselves for being lazy. We routinely stop ourselves from exulting in any moment of permissiveness because doing so feels like a transgression, as if a rubber band has been stretched and will snap back in our faces.

Once I saw how deeply embedded the Seven Deadly Sins were in my understanding of what it means to be "good," both as a woman and for myself in particular, I couldn't unsee their influence. When I made a list of the ideas and behavior I correlate with being good, these traits mapped perfectly onto them:

I want to be seen as professionally successful, and I want to be seen as someone who cares for and nurtures her family lovingly and effortlessly; to get it all done, I wake up early, go to bed late, and am constantly busy. **Good women are tireless and hardworking with no professed interest in or requirements for rest, either at work or at home.**	**SLOTH IS A SIN**
When I see a woman doing something I dream of doing myself, I look for reasons to fault or criticize her. If she appears unassailable, I disengage or look away, finding it too painful to study or celebrate her accomplishments. **Good women do not want or strive for more than they have; they do not openly covet the skills or achievements of others.**	**ENVY IS A SIN**

I work hard to be unassuming and modest and to look like I'm not seeking acknowledgment or praise. Instead of celebrating my gifts, I have spent most of my career hiding behind other people. **Good women are not too intimidating or confident; they work hard to appear modest, minimizing, and focused on finding other people who can champion their ideas.**

PRIDE IS A SIN

I berate myself regularly for the baby weight I still haven't lost and chastise myself for finishing my kids' (unhealthy) food but still probably don't eat enough calories to support my frame. **Good women strive to be thin, really as small as possible.**

GLUTTONY IS A SIN

I feel guilty about how much money I have relative to others, yet anxious that I don't have enough. I worry about appearing stingy, and spend and give money away compulsively even as I worry I can't afford to. **Good women don't negotiate on their own behalf, never ask for more, appear grateful for what they've been given, and avoid talking about money. They often spend faster than they save and strive to be generous "to a fault."**

GREED IS A SIN

I've never dressed provocatively or like "I want it," as it's my job to patrol the borders of my own physical safety. I see myself as a vessel for male desire rather than the operator of my own body. **Good women want to be seen as sensual, warm, and inviting of sex but not overtly interested.**

LUST IS A SIN

I am ashamed of my impatience and irritation. I stuff all feelings of resentment and frustration when my needs go unmet or my boundaries are crossed because I'm worried I'll appear mean, selfish, or unhinged. If I get visibly angry, I apologize and backpedal immediately, fearful of repercussions. **Good women are assertive only on behalf of other people. They are quick to forgive and nonconfrontational, content to sacrifice their needs and embrace discomfort to preserve the peace and maintain the status quo.**

ANGER
IS A SIN

This list gives me chills. I hate it. I see it and feel, viscerally, how tired I am of controlling my own behavior, of bending myself to abide by cultural expectations. I recognize that the ways in which I want to be seen do not align with who I *know* myself to be. There is a deeper, more real me. I keep her largely hidden, mediate her through these filters, make sure she remains in check. I always believed it was dangerous to let her out. But now I've come to understand that it's more dangerous to keep her bound: If I don't unshackle her from these oppressive ideas of goodness, that part of her will slowly asphyxiate and I will never know what it will feel like to live fully as myself—not diminished, not bound, not scared.*

THE TRAGIC CONSEQUENCES

When we overlimit ourselves, we become complicit in denying ourselves a full existence. We force ourselves to lead narrow lives.

---

* As a white woman with privilege, just a few theoretical steps removed from power, I've often wondered if women like me are most attached to the system, convinced we have the most to lose. But I've also spoken to many marginalized women who feel mired in "good girl" programming, too. These beliefs are in all of us, deeply internalized.

We fear crossing a line we can't see. We don't want to be perceived as wanting too much, or *being* too much; we equate "self-control" with worthiness.

In worrying about everything we do not want to be, in suppressing our instincts and impulses out of fear or shame, in attempting to be "good," we've forgotten who we *are*—all special, all "divine" in our own individual ways. We've gone unconscious and, oddly, *unnatural*. We are so consumed with the doing—and the *not* doing—that we have forgotten how to *be*. We are so fixated on an authority "out there," we're missing the miracles inside, all the moments that illuminate our connection to something bigger within ourselves. We are giving away our power and accepting exhaustion, resentment, despair, and disconnection instead. We deny ourselves joy, our rightful inheritance. Meanwhile, *the world needs us, just as we are.*

The saddest part is that in accepting the restrictions of the Seven Deadly Sins—subconsciously or not—we've trained ourselves to separate our true nature (our first nature, the essence of who we are) from how we act in the world. We sever ourselves from the deepest parts of our souls, the pulse of life that feels right, resonant, and, perhaps not ironically, a truer definition of *good*. We've become disconnected from our intuition, that inner knowing that many would identify as our connection to the divine. We have been led to believe that something primal and essential, our relationship to the universal force—God, nature, true self, whatever you want to call it—must be forced through the prism of an interpreter. And so we go there for approval, rather than trusting in ourselves.

Placing faith in our own sovereignty is critical. Even those who don't believe in a larger spiritual or religious construct seem to agree that developing and making use of your unique gifts—finding and fulfilling your individual, true purpose—is the primary work and point of life. But we can't focus on that when we are spending our mental, emotional, and spiritual capital contorting ourselves, pulling ourselves out of balance, and using an abundance of energy to punish ourselves for the very qualities that make us human. Rather than following our instincts, we have been taught to deny them. This denial prevents us from crediting ourselves (pride), pleasuring ourselves (lust), feeding and securing ourselves (gluttony, greed), releasing our emotions and asserting our needs (anger), relaxing (sloth), and desiring . . . really anything at all (envy). This denial keeps us from celebrating abundance, personal accomplishment, and fulfillment. And for those who think that there is *more* (heaven, an afterlife, reincarnation, the beyond), fixating on proving ourselves worthy of it prevents us from recognizing that maybe *this is the thing,* and *this is the place.* There is no need to pay for passage through the pearly gates with asceticism because *we are already there.* But we are so consumed with staying in bounds, we're missing it.

THE REWARDS OF BALANCE

Many religious scholars believe that sin denotes a separation from God—the word *sin* in Hebrew (*chatta'ah*) and Greek (*hamartia*) translates to "missing the mark." I love this concept when it speaks to integrity, or wholeness, or the idea of achieving full humanness: when we think of "the mark" as an alignment with oneself and, theoretically, the divine. If sins are intended as an *internal* compass, this directional guide is for our own use—nobody can or should decipher it on our behalf. If we follow the needle, the goal is not to numb ourselves through overindulgence and not to sever ourselves from desire. The path to connection is balance, the middle: being aware of our wants and needs and acknowledging, modulating, and meeting them while being conscious of the wants and needs of others. If we can come into balance within ourselves, we can come into balance in the world. This is the feeling I crave, the freedom I want to create for myself.

The naturalist E. O. Wilson said about the problem of humanity: "We have Paleolithic emotions, medieval institutions, and godlike technology." This idea reminds me of what one of my great spiritual teachers, Carissa Schumacher, says: "We have had much progress without evolution." They both mean that we've created a world that's changing at a speed beyond our ability to keep up. We're trying to construct a new era of peace and equity from tired and worn-out materials, methods, and energy. But we cannot get to where we need to go by using the same old ideas. We must open our eyes to the ways in which old stories and outdated science imprison us, and to the fear and shame that get stuck in both our subconscious and our bodies and hold us at the throat.

Life is hard, full of pain, suffering, death, decay; it's also beautiful, magical, renewing, and meaningful, replete with bright sparks of wonder and transcendent joy. We too often forget that balance is the goal—fulfillment *and* restraint, eating *and* excreting, "light" *and* "dark," "good" *and* "bad," masculine *and* feminine. Many of these are false binaries. Perfect goodness, as an absolute state, is not achievable; to be alive requires participation in some harm—after all, we must kill plants and animals to sustain life. We are not pawns in a battle between the dark and the light. We are human, a bridge between matter and spirit; we can find the middle and hold the line. We can sense that we are on a seesaw that's bending out of control and that unless each of us comes into balance we will struggle to survive.

I'VE BEEN WRITING THIS book amid a pandemic, a racial reckoning, climate instability, and war. It's scary out there, but it also feels like a hopeful, albeit strange, time. I think of the past several years of disruption as the turmoil required for the change we need: We were woken up, startled out of complacence, and made to look at what we didn't want to see, at what festers beneath the surface. Only through cleaning these old wounds can we break the cycle and repair the world. We must look beyond the symptoms to heal what's ill at the root. And while we must still contend with gross injustice, inequity, and an increasingly unstable, overtaxed, and angry planet, it seems that increasing numbers of us recognize it's time to push toward and fight for a more balanced future. Hopefully, the hurdles that bar our progress will continue to fall.

If we can get over ourselves.

I recently interviewed Loretta Ross, who has spent her career in the human rights movement advocating for marginalized people and fighting abusive systems of power. When she teaches activism, she asks of her students: "Are you programmed? Or are you self-determined?" I hear her. It's time for us to self-determine, to detach from the trap of goodness and unwind these patterns so we can create new ones. It's time to stop perpetuating—and believing— "wrong and unsound things" and to teach—and walk—a path to inner truth instead.

We need to process the ways in which the legacy of "goodness," defined as purity and abnegation, continues to both limit and torment us. Until we learn how to give ourselves and each other grace, we'll struggle to dismantle the parts of society that are toxic and to do the work of building it back anew. Wise therapists often counsel that you can't heal what you can't feel; well, you can't address what you can't see either. It's my hope that this book makes visible an insidious system of beliefs that have, for too long, curtailed our lives—and that once they are revealed, we can drive these damaging fictions from our minds.

ON OUR BEST BEHAVIOR

I

A BRIEF HISTORY
OF THE PATRIARCHY*

TO UNDERSTAND HOW THE SEVEN DEADLY SINS INFLUENCE OUR
lives, even to this day (even if we don't consider ourselves religious), we must understand the system that produced them: the
patriarchy, which has defined Western culture for millennia. Its
forefathers adopted and shaped early Christianity to enforce behavior in ways that continue to affect us. I struggled to understand how
someone like me, even with all my privileges—white, cis, heterosexual, upper middle class, agnostic/spiritual—still feels prisoner to
these Judeo-Christian ideas of "goodness." Why do I feel bound to
keep from committing these "sins"? To answer that question, I
need to examine the story about who we are, a story we've been
telling each other through history. A warning: This chapter is the
book's densest and most academic—skip it if you're inclined—but

---

* I'm going to move through this (laughably) fast—there are notes and further reading
suggestions at the end of the book for those who want to go deeper. A reminder: We
have no written records for a majority of our history, though as more and more evidence
emerges from the Paleolithic and Neolithic periods, we can recognize how varied, socially creative, and fascinating our ancestors were. They were certainly not a monolith.
But per anthropologist David Graeber and archaeologist David Wengrow, authors of *The
Dawn of Everything,* social theory requires simplification, which I'm attempting here: "Essentially, we reduce everything to a cartoon so as to be able to detect patterns that would
be otherwise invisible. . . . One must simplify the world to discover something new about
it."

to imagine something new, it's important to understand where we've been.

ORIGINALLY PARTNERS

While we tend to think of the patriarchy as an inevitable reality, this conception is wrong. For most of human existence—from 2.5 million years ago to 10,000 B.C.—we were nomads, ranging across the planet in small collectives that were partnership societies, dependent on what many disparate bands thought of as the "Great Mother," the creative force behind all life. In these partnership societies, women were revered for their generative powers—after all, birth is a miracle.

This is not to say early tribes were matriarchies—that would have still insisted on an arbitrary hierarchy, where women were perceived as superior to men. Paleolithic societies were primarily affiliation based, rather than predicated on continual oppression. In these first *millions of years* of our existence, there was no private property in the way we'd define it today—no resources to hoard, no generational wealth to sock away under the mattress, no land or titles to pass to biological children. Our ancestors were focused on the collective—a "we" rather than an "I," where all would have been dependent on the group, and nature, for survival.

Throughout the Stone Age, our ancestors planted small gardens and foraged for fruit, vegetables, and small animals like snails and frogs, with only the occasional big game prize; anthropologists assert we were gatherer/hunters, not the opposite. As much as 80 percent of our food supply was generated, and processed, by women. And though hunting has been significantly overstated as *the* way of life, where it did occur, some women participated. In settlements like central Turkey's Çatalhöyük (7500–6400 B.C.), men and women were the same size, received equivalent calories, and spent an equal amount of time inside. I can't be the only one who was startled to read in *The New York Times* that a recent examination of nine-thousand-year-old graves in the Andes revealed that ten of the twenty-six bodies buried with hunting tools were the bodies of women, or to discover that a recent reassessment of pre-historic cave drawings, long held to be hunting scenes painted by men, concluded that the handprints were primarily female.

There are many theories for what changed some ten thousand to twelve thousand years ago, when we started practicing agricul-ture on a wider scale, and between 8000 and 3000 B.C., when farming became the norm. Most historians seem to agree that re-source scarcity *or* opportunity—changing temperatures around 5000 B.C. revealed uber-fertile lands around rivers throughout Eurasia—pushed humans to migrate, bringing discrete groups into conflict with each other. Waves of Proto-Europeans invaded the existing "Old Europe" planting culture—overwhelmingly male Indo-Europeans from the North* and Akkadian and Semitic tribes from the Syro-Arabian desert in the South. These warring tribes raped, pillaged, and subordinated those they conquered, creating hierarchical cultures that elevated some and oppressed others. While Paleolithic and Neolithic societies had acknowledged their dependence on nature, those in agrarian society thought of nature as something to dominate, control, and order. When we became agrarian—over a protracted period, variably around the globe—everything changed, particularly for women, children, domestica-ble animals, and whoever and whatever could be marginalized, co-opted, and enslaved for the benefit of others.

If conflict begat chaos, the fallout demanded a reorganization of society into structures through which order could be imposed. Be-

---

* This sweeping theory is the primary legacy of the late archaeologist, anthropologist, and UCLA professor Marija Gimbutas. Yet after her death in the nineties, fellow academ-ics destroyed her reputation, in part because her work had been co-opted by New Age feminists who argued that all Neolithic cultures were matriarchal (they weren't, and Gimbutas never said this). This didn't stop Gimbutas's name from becoming a type of kryptonite, and her work from being trashed (even as it was clear her critics hadn't read it)—*until* recent DNA evidence vindicated her assertions. It appears she was right: Those Indo-Europeans from the North—called Kurgans because of their burial style—wiped out the local population in the third millennium B.C.

tween 3000 B.C. and 1300 B.C. we see the advent of such systems; a broader array of rules and laws became essential as society became more complex. Yet power almost always perverts, particularly when scarcity and security are in play.

WOMEN AS FIRST PROPERTY

Women and children conquered in conflict and taken as slaves, servants, and concubines were the first property of the patriarchy: Men practiced their dominance on them and learned its possibilities. This became the foundation of slavery, the economic engine for many cultures. Over time, the oppression of women came to seem natural, normal, the way it had always been. "Otherization," creating socially acceptable power distinctions, has been used broadly since—against Jews, Muslims, Black people. Women simply went first.

One of the mechanisms of the patriarchy was to force adherence to a vertical family structure. Because strong, even primary bonds between women had persisted over time in communal-living cultures, the push toward vertical family structures was intended to shift women from interdependence among each other to dependence on men. Even married women were essentially enslaved. While we think of marriage now as a mutually elective (and ideally romantic) partnership, that's a *very* modern interpretation. In marriage's earliest incarnations, women connected families, concentrated assets and status, and produced children; effectively, women were owned by their husbands, purchased through marriage or sold into the arrangement.*

Before monotheism became standard (it appeared first in 1300 B.C. in Egypt, though millennia later in the Greco-Roman world),

---

* The first *record* of marriage dates to 2350 B.C. in Mesopotamia, which is early days of the patriarchy—and about eight thousand years after the Paleolithic period. From there it began to evolve and take hold in other cultures. It's very possible that something akin to marriage is much older; there's just no written record.

women *did* maintain active roles in temple life as priestesses, prophets, and healers—the goddess, and her power to give life, continued to be worshipped among other deities, perhaps as primary. But in civil society, day-to-day, there was little reverence for mortal women. Even women who were more proximate to power were in permanently tenuous positions: A wife could easily, without warrant or reason, be demoted to concubine or slave. This ever-present threat coerced dependence and good behavior and ultimately was codified into law.

Around 3000 B.C., when the Semitic tribes emerged from an inhospitable desert—where they'd been shepherds rather than planters, with little concept of a creative and generous planet—they effectively put an end to the goddess traditions that had persisted for so long. Previous invaders had co-opted the local mythologies and integrated belief systems: This is why we see the same deities with different names across various regions, and male divinities marrying female divinities or taking on roles as protectors. Because local culture was not completely stamped out, these deities survived and reemerged. But according to Joseph Campbell, these early patriarchal cultures had long found nature cruel and harsh, something to battle and subjugate. They were also misogynistic and violent, with perverse double standards. Hammurabi (1792–1750 B.C.)—best known for "an eye for an eye"—developed the first legal code to survive for our study: Of the 282 mandates Hammurabi codified, 73 revolve around marriage and sex and almost exclusively delimit women. Where a man might pay a fine for adultery, a woman would be drowned. Or if a man killed a pregnant woman, his own *daughter* was to die as compensation.

And then, of course, there's the Hebrew Bible, otherwise known as the Old Testament (written in parts, between 1200 and 165 B.C.), full of laws that are not generous to women. One of Judaism's distinguishing features is its sacred books: It was the first religion where laws and rituals were written down, many of which were collated from existing myths and belief systems. Judaism's most pronounced distinction, though, was that the law now had divine sanction: This wasn't Hammurabi's preference, this was *patriarchy directed by God*. Judaism's official patriarchs were Abraham, his son Isaac, and Isaac's son Jacob, followed down the family tree by Moses, who took dictation on Mount Sinai and delivered the Ten Commandments. God made deals almost exclusively with men—and confirmed women's role as property.* Ishmael, Abraham's other son, became the father of Islam.

Men were shown preference in all ways. With the advent of monotheism, we also see the creation of an all-powerful, male deity: For the first time, there was no goddess, either as primary divinity or a consort. Genesis, the Bible's creation story, is a retelling of a Sumerian myth from 2500 B.C. that includes the goddess (i.e., the Divine Mother), a tree, and a serpent. In the original, the serpent, in its skin-shedding, represents death begetting new life, not evil, and there is no eviction from paradise. But in the Old Testament version many of us hold sacred (scholars believe Genesis was written between 950 and 500 B.C.), God the Father replaces the goddess as the lone creator, and a woman becomes the symbol of sin and the cause of man's fall. Meanwhile, the snake, a symbol of the fertility goddess as well as of Isis†—who had her own cult and dedicated temples across Egypt and the Greco-Roman world (360 B.C.–A.D. 536)—is the instigator of her transgression. In this ancient Creation story, common to all Judeo-Christian cultures (about one-third of the world's population today), women are not only disempowered but spiritually depraved.

---

* Here's Exodus 20:17, for example: "Thou shalt not covet thy neighbor's house, thou shalt not covet thy neighbor's wife, nor his manservant, nor his maidservant, nor his ox, nor his ass, nor any thing that *is* thy neighbor's."

† Isis, a major Egyptian goddess, was believed to be the sister and wife of Osiris. She was worshipped throughout the Greco-Roman world in temples and mystery rites. Some historians argue she was the precursor to Mother Mary. The writer Lucius Apuleius (A.D. 125) explains that "Queen Isis" is the true name of the goddess, who has gone by many other names: Minerva, Venus, Diana, Ceres, Hecate, and more. There was significant temple life devoted to Isis where women ruled and initiated men into the sexual mysteries.

THE (NOT QUITE WHOLLY) NEW TESTAMENT

In its first emergence, Christianity was not the organized, religious arm of the patriarchy: In fact, it's easy to find textual evidence of Jesus's feminism. Yet early church fathers conveniently ignored this, eventually creating a canon that ensured the second-class status of women. In its early years, Christianity was a small, fledgling, widely persecuted cult. It had no formal center or official documents, only "gospels"*—individual recountings of Jesus's teachings and experiences—recorded long after his crucifixion. Preached and proselytized, the gospels were passed on by mouth and ear, and then written down and copied by scribes for generations, with varying and unknown accuracy. Original versions—if there even were any—did not survive.

In A.D. 325, Constantine—the emperor of the Holy Roman Empire who had recently converted to Christianity—convened a council at Nicaea to establish agreement about the canon: Which of the gospels—there were many more than the four contained in today's New Testament—were to be ordained as "orthodox," or "right," and which were "wrong"? The decision came down to preference for a specific narrative. The gospels deemed "right" confirmed a male apostolic tradition and the central role of a church. The council marked gospels that ran counter to their mission as heretical (the etymology of which is, tellingly, "to choose"), and ordered them destroyed (including the Gospel of Mary Magdalene, which recounts Christ's teachings after his resurrection). While historians today assert that women were critical to early Christianity—as leaders, teachers, and believers—the early church not only minimized and erased this legacy but cast women as progenitors of sin, containers for moral turpitude. Later that century, Christianity became the official religion of the Roman Empire,

---

* *Gospel* means "good news."

complete with an all-male apostolic tradition carried forward by the "first apostle," Peter.

While the creation of the Old Testament nearly wiped out the fertility cults, organized Christianity and the New Testament—with the vast political power of Rome at its back—managed to extinguish goddess worship almost completely. Byzantine emperor Justinian I formally eliminated the cult of Isis in A.D. 536, and the Inquisition took care of other heretical sects, many of which were feminist.

The irony, of course, is that if you go back to Jesus's teachings, an all-male apostolic tradition was never the point—nor was an organized religion. And Jesus himself did not write. The Bible is the product of a centuries-long game of Telephone, edited by men according to their preferences. This might sound silly and obvious, but when I realized that, I felt a door had been wrenched open in my mind. What has been lost? And what did we get wrong?

The recent discovery of several long-lost gospels gives us a sense of what did not make the cut at the Council of Nicaea. A great many ancient, "heretical" codices were buried by concerned monks in the desert and were not recovered and translated until modern times—in many cases, we have only fragments of what was exhumed. There were more than fifty such texts recovered in Egypt in 1945 (though they weren't translated and published until 1983). Together with the Gospel of Mary, discovered in 1896 and first translated from Coptic in 1955, these sacred texts are now known as the Gnostic (meaning "to know" or "knowledge") Gospels. While each piece is different, the consistent theme of Gnosticism is that the experience of the divine is personal and direct, mediated only between you and God. There's no priest, no physical church.

When it comes to women in the patriarchy, Mary Magdalene—her role in the New Testament, her "heretical" gospel, and her cultural reputation—proves pivotal. For many religious scholars, the rediscovery of the Gnostic Gospels was an aha moment, an explanation for the absence of a feminine voice in the Bible—a textual legacy that we were taught was a comprehensive survey or understanding of God. The early church was fixated on the idea of an exclusively patrilineal lineage: Jesus came to earth from God in heaven, assembled an all-male team of disciples, and, upon his ascension, anointed them as his priests, end of story. That the church deemed the Gnostic Gospels (and their followers) heretical and then hunted them says it all about the church's desire to assert itself as the sole authority, the mediator of God's will, and the enforcer of behavior required for salvation.

The Gnostic Gospels prompt us to ask: How might a world work in which we recognized a direct connection to the divine, no translator or middleman required? Had Christianity survived as a direct-experience religion that required no church or priest—just a deep, inner knowing—our culture might look quite different.

THE ROOTS OF THE SEVEN DEADLY SINS

A few decades after the Council of Nicaea, a Greek-speaking monk named Evagrius Ponticus (A.D. 345–99) exiled himself to a monastery in the Egyptian desert to battle demons in his mind (he had fallen in love with a married woman). In Greek, the word *dīmon* translated to a life energy that wouldn't obey the rules—that part of ourselves that's impossible to control—so Evagrius was not so much imagining literal, fire-breathing demonic beings as battling with his own natural inclination toward emotion or passion, passions that might distract him from prayer. In response to these human instincts, Evagrius created a book of sayings, called *Talking Back,* that circulated among other monks: It's a collection of short pieces of scripture to be used as exhortations against these (inner) demons, like a spell book of sorts, so that the passionate thoughts (*logismoi*) they plant do not blossom into sinful actions. *Talking Back* is arranged into eight "books," which identify the demons and address them in this order: (1) Gluttony, (2) Fornication, (3) Love of Money,

(4) Sadness, (5) Anger, (6) Listlessness, (7) Vainglory, and (8) Pride. Other desert fathers translated and disseminated Evagrius's teachings.*

Two centuries later, Pope Gregory I (A.D. 540–604) crystallized Evagrius's list into the Capital Vices in his six-volume *Moralia on Job*. According to Gregory, pride is the cardinal or head vice, as it defines the moment when man turns away from God, and from pride spring the rest: vainglory, envy, anger, melancholy, avarice, gluttony, lust. While this list morphs again (vainglory and pride are conflated, and sloth replaces sadness, although, as you'll see, I have a lot to say about sadness's excommunication), Pope Gregory's version became the Seven Deadly Sins we know today.

When Pope Gregory preached about the Seven Deadly Sins for the first time, he assigned these vices to Mary Magdalene and branded her a whore, conflating Mary Magdalene with the "sinful woman," the presumed prostitute who appears in Luke 7 and anoints Jesus's feet with oil. In that commingling, Pope Gregory made Mary the embodiment of the Seven Deadly Sins. As he sermonized in the fateful Homily 33: "She whom Luke calls the sinful woman, whom John calls Mary, we believe to be the Mary from whom seven demons were ejected according to Mark. And what did these seven demons signify if not all the vices?" By condemning Mary, Gregory condemned all women.

Why, you might ask, would religious authorities at the time insist that Mary, Jesus's best student and potential lover, was the embodiment of all sin? Episcopalian priest Cynthia Bourgeault explains, "Feminist scholars are inclined to see a deliberate plot here: In an emerging church hierarchy founded on the assumption of a male-only and celibate succession from the original apostles, Mary Magdalene's apostolate was clearly an anomaly and threat." If she had been rightfully recognized as primary and essential, the church

---

* In an ironic twist, Evagrius's followers were persecuted as heretics only months after he died, but his work found a larger audience regardless.

would look very different. What's more important than intent, though, is the cultural wake her disparagement created. (The Magdalene wore her reputation as a whore until 1996, when the Catholic Church acknowledged Pope Gregory had made a mistake; in 2016, Pope Francis made Mary the "Apostle to the Apostles." But the damage was done.) Mary is still perceived as ignominious and base, a suggestion to all women that we will never be worthy, never fully redeemed—in part because we will never be men. It's almost impossible to assess how insidious these ideas are, how they seeded our collective consciousness with an idea of the "natural" inferiority of women and the primacy—spiritually, morally—of men.

THE PURSUIT OF REDEMPTION

Women may be condemned to perpetual depravity, but we have been encouraged to pursue redemption. In the original Christian tradition, one confessed and repented sins directly to God, and did so publicly and communally because such sins were perceived as an affront against your neighbors. But in the centuries after the Roman Catholic Church accrued power, confession—the means to absolution—became a private affair between penitent and priest. This change imbued clergy with even more authority to sanction morality (and capture parishioners' darkest secrets), as penitents were no longer appealing straight to God but allowing a mediation or intervention in their relationship with the divine. In 1215, more than a thousand bishops and abbots decided to put confession on a schedule—they stipulated that all mortal, or grave, sins (those that lead to a separation of the offender from God's grace) must be confessed within the year. These bishops and abbots then went on a mission to educate the public about the transgressions that necessitated this type of absolution.

The Seven Deadly Sins were a useful tool for illustrating to the public what those transgressions were. Few people could read, manuscripts were precious and rare,* and the Seven Deadly Sins were grisly, clear, and easy to illustrate. Incidentally, while the Old Testament's Second Commandment prohibits any iconography, Pope Gregory lifted that edict, and a rush of religious art emerged, frequently highlighting the Seven Deadly Sins. They became cemented in the church's teaching, including in Thomas Aquinas's fifteenth-century *Summa Theologica* (Summary of Theology), a three-thousand-plus-page text that serves as a primary curriculum for priests. They are embedded in the Catholic catechism used to this day. Even though they weren't in scripture, or uttered by Jesus, they linger, ensconced in confessionals around the globe. This is how history is made and then remade, how it seeds ideas about what's natural, what's right, and how it's always been—at its essence, because some men said so.

The sins soon emerged in the literature of the age. They're a central theme of Dante Alighieri's *Inferno* (ca. A.D. 1300), and they were popularized even more by "The Parson's Tale" in Geoffrey Chaucer's *Canterbury Tales* (ca. A.D. 1387–1400). It makes sense that they captured the public's imagination while proving a useful teaching tool for the church. They became the whip with which to coerce behavior, providing an uneducated population with a very simple bargain: If you committed one of these seven sins, you were damned and destined for hell until you confessed, repented, and paid an indulgence,† by which you earned your spot in heaven. This was a very dark and scary time in history, where death and the threat of hell were particularly present. It was the era of the Inquisition, which began in 1184; then the bubonic plague, from 1347, which decimated the population; and finally, the witch hunts, which began in 1450. (Both the Inquisition and witch hunts went

---

* The Gutenberg Bible—the first book printed on a press with movable type—didn't emerge until A.D. 1454. Even then, fewer than two hundred very precious copies were made.

† Indulgences, or payments to the church to lessen the punishment for sin, were formally outlawed by the Council of Trent in 1563, though never stamped out. This type of mercenary corruption became one of Martin Luther's primary focuses in the Reformation.

on for centuries across Europe and America; in some parts of the world, like Africa and the Middle East, the latter continue today.) Those inclined toward the church became desperate for a path to assured redemption, or at least a way to avoid censure. Repenting their sins was an easy remedy.

WITCH-HUNTING

The Inquisition first focused on heretics, those who refused to adhere to the established biblical canon and held to the Gnostic Gospels or other religions instead. The Catholic Church persecuted anyone who questioned its authority or criticized its corruption, squelching dissent and the free flow of ideas. Punishment was grisly, public death or expulsion. (The church would also claim possession of a heretic's property, thereby dispossessing antagonists while amassing more money and power for itself.) The Inquisition is also remarkable in that it created and cemented a precedent for holocaust: that is, the persecution and destruction of entire groups of citizens, a turning against one's own.

While women weren't the original focus of the Inquisition (it was primarily other, more powerful groups of religious men), they came into focus as the bubonic plague ravaged the world, escalating fears of damnation. The plague, which killed between twenty-five and fifty million people, was presumed to be a curse or punishment from God for the sins of humanity. This interpretation motivated believers to behave in ways they thought would assure salvation and access to heaven. Those who were deemed "other" were blamed for the outbreak, along with additional social ills like overpopulation, inflation, and food scarcity, which were escalating in Europe in the mid-sixteenth century: The ruling class was looking for not only scapegoats but worthy, morally suspect targets.

When the government ran out of others to blame, women became the primary focus of frustration and fear. While the witch trials were theoretically secular, they followed a formula established by the Inquisition, which included forcing confession and the naming of conspirators through torture, along with horrific public punishments, like being burned at the stake. The witch hunts targeted women (and some men) of all ages, as well as children, but the first hunted were the "crones," the wise women, the elders, typically widows who refused to remarry or had no options to do so. These older women had long been the keepers of powerful traditions— they were the culture's healers, prophets, and midwives; they initiated young girls into the rites of womanhood; they mentored mothers; and they carried intergenerational stories and wisdom. But beginning in the middle of the fifteenth century (dramatically peaking from 1560 to 1760), these women, too old to be seen as sexual objects, and possessing knowledge and skills the church viewed as threatening, were persecuted as witches.* We can see their rejection to this day: Our culture has little tolerance for or interest in women past their procreative prime, and certainly we have no reverence for them. While we have sanctified old men and propped them up as the ultimate authorities—the priests, lawmakers, judges—we have exiled their counterparts.

In 1487 a Dominican monk named Heinrich Kramer wrote a treatise on hunting, identifying, and torturing witches called *Malleus Maleficarum,* ultimately sanctioned by Pope Innocent VIII.† The primary crime of these witches was their lustfulness (cue Mary Magdalene), although in the fifteenth, sixteenth, and seventeenth centuries witch-hunters persecuted women for completely pedes-

---

* A wizened woman clutching a cauldron and broom is who we commemorate in our Halloween costumes: Both artifacts are symbols of a housewife. Per Joseph Campbell, the presence of a black cat is a nod to the goddess, typically portrayed in art accompanied by a feline, like a lion, panther, tiger, or leopard.

† While some historians assert that the *Malleus Maleficarum* never became an official court-sanctioned document, its ideas spread everywhere: Fifty years later, in 1532, Emperor Charles V approved the "Carolina" code, which made judicial torture permissible and crimes like witchcraft punishable by death.

trian "crimes," like talking to neighbors and sharing remedies for common ailments.

The result was a terror campaign that isolated women through fear. Women had always traded information, support, friendship—they *did* life together.* Those female friendships were specifically targeted by the witch hunts; when witches were tried, accused women were forced under torture to denounce each other. It is unknown how many women were persecuted, tortured, and killed under this banner, a "gendercide" that went on for centuries. On the basis of trial data, historians today believe that the number of actual executions in Europe was between eighty thousand and one hundred thousand—but the propaganda and hype machine stoked fear in the nervous systems of women across the globe. For context, only twenty-five were murdered in the witch trials in Salem, Massachusetts, an event so terrifying that it continues to capture our imaginations today.

THE LEGACY OF FEAR

Under extreme torture, women betrayed each other—friends turned in friends, daughters their mothers. We came to learn that glancing contact can be dangerous; it's best to keep to your own. I have to wonder if the emotional sediment of this is one of the reasons women today can be wary of each other and are often willing

---

* Professor Silvia Federici reminds us that *gossip* originally meant *god-parent*. It was a positive term, suggesting a close, emotional bond. But in the fifteenth to seventeenth centuries, gossip became a negative, reason enough for murder. She writes, "In 1547, 'a proclamation was issued forbidding women to meet together to babble and talk' and ordering husbands to 'keep their wives in their houses.' " Professor Maria Tatar elaborates in *The Heroine with 1,001 Faces*, "What is gossip's greatest sin? One possibility is that gossip knits women together to create networks of social interactions beyond patriarchal control and oversight. It can be seen as counter-discourse that operates against prevailing communal norms, a strategy for collecting talk in the form of compelling stories that can be parsed and analyzed to turn into useful sources of wisdom and knowledge."

to watch each other get cut down: This trauma is in our DNA. I suspect this fear is one of the reasons we self-restrict. We continue to hold the line, enforce our own smallness, and struggle with the idea that we'll be called out, put back in our rightful place, blamed.

While the ways we are hunted and policed are arguably less explicit now, make no mistake that implicit rules about the behavior of women are woven into the fabric of society. The rights and very sovereignty of women continue to be on the line: There is horrendous legal inequity, certainly, but the most insidious attacks are the questions that circle and poke at our morality. What exactly constitutes a good woman? The patriarchal paradigm of femininity—selfless, physically perfect, nurturing, obedient, compliant, modest, responsible, self-effacing—persists. Women are expected to "know their place"—firmly outside, yet supporting circles of power—and abide by it. This is so programmed into our behavior that we even uphold it unwittingly: We scold, shame, and "cancel" women who deviate, and we also do this to ourselves.

This book is not about blaming the victims. It's about understanding from what our current culture was born, and how it holds us in its sway, so we can see how artificial its restrictions are.

It's hard to believe we would willingly collaborate to enforce a system that oppresses us. But so much of this is beyond our conscious awareness. The professor Gerda Lerner, who created the first graduate program for women's history in the United States, argued that women have participated in our subordination because we've been psychologically shaped to see our inferiority as natural. This perception of inferiority becomes a shadow, difficult to strike out. The need to prove our goodness as the price for protection and upward mobility has been coded into how we behave; it's hard to recognize because we are inside the structure itself. Lerner writes, "The system of patriarchy can function only with the cooperation of women. This cooperation is secured by a variety of means: gender indoctrination; educational deprivation; the denial to women of knowledge of their history; the dividing of women, one from the other, by defining 'respectability' and 'deviance' according to women's sexual activities; by restraints and outright coercion; by discrimination in access to economic resources and political power; and by awarding class privileges to conforming women."

All this programming, which we have absorbed unconsciously, must be deconstructed. We must understand where it comes from so that we can recognize that this is patriarchy in action. We must unyoke ourselves from its constraints. Only then can we find our way back to something that looks closer to our "first" nature, to who we truly are. Only then can we reject this paradigm of "goodness" foisted on us by a society that would prefer for us to be obedient and obliging servants providing care. And only then we can we stop policing each other for behavior that we've been coded to condemn in ourselves. This is a variation on philosopher and professor Kate Manne's definition of misogyny. As she writes in *Entitled,* "Misogyny should not be understood as a monolithic, deep-seated psychological hatred of girls and women. Instead, it's best conceptualized as the 'law enforcement' branch of patriarchy—a system that functions to police and enforce gendered norms and expectations, and involves girls and women facing disproportionately or distinctively hostile treatment because of their gender, among other factors." Men certainly engage in this type of behavior, but we also do this to ourselves. Instead, we must shake this off and do as the definition of Gnosticism suggests: return to our first nature and tap into our knowing. We must remind ourselves that this knowing, this instinct, has been there all along and that rejecting it keeps us separate from our deepest and truest desires, desires that are pure and worthy of exploration.

THE REEMERGENCE OF THE FEMININE

To unwind the patriarchal paradigm of goodness, we must locate within ourselves the ways in which we police our own behavior, the way we've been coded by the Seven Deadly Sins. While each sin has its own essential quality, the appetites of the body and its perceived carnality define many of them. Historically, there seem to be two camps of thinkers on this subject: those who believe the body is *the* sacred vessel, and those who believe the body must be subjugated and overcome. Thomas Hobbes (1588–1679), Charles Darwin (1809–82), and Sigmund Freud (1856–1939) believed that the body is abhorrent. They argued we are beasts who are slowly evolving and civilizing ourselves over time, engaged in the ongoing and difficult work of transcending the base desires of our physical selves to inhabit our minds. The flesh is lowly; the intellect is the only part that counts. And for some in this camp, we might some-day transcend the depravity of the human experience to access the spiritual realms of a place called heaven, but only if our dirtiness is surmounted and cordoned off by the higher mind, our "better" nature.

On the flip side, there are those who believe we are spiritual beings having a physical experience, that the divine is in every-thing, including our naughty bits, and that the denseness of the body and its pleasures is what keeps us from floating away, back into the energetic force field from which we came and to which we will return. This camp holds there's no place to "go" in the afterlife and nothing to overcome; being in the body, with its manifold plea-sures, in this 3-D world, is the main event. To touch and be in physical relationship is beautiful. This group would argue that we are not depraved animals but that we make a hell in our own minds by repressing our natural urges.

Those in the first camp, who believe the body must be con-trolled, overruled, and dominated, attribute much of the body's baseness to its "feminine" qualities. After all, physical matter (or *mater*, i.e., mother) represents the potential of life, the magic and sometimes chaos of creativity. Rather than recognizing that what runs through our bodies is sacred, holy, and even divine, people in this first camp are in battle with themselves, looking outside for approbation and approval. They desire to dominate nature, to control it, to sanitize and separate the human experience from that of other living creatures. You can see how this ideology manifests from the macro to the micro, and still does today: man in dominance over nature, man in dominance over woman, and then within each of us—male or female—the desire to subject the body and its "feeling" states to the primacy of the mind and its thinking states. This is patriarchal thinking, and it doesn't affect only women. Men, too, are victimized by this need to repress and suppress emotions and creative chaos.

The good news for all of us is that the feminine, the goddess in all her forms, does not enjoy suppression. She invariably rises. We are feeling this now. Patriarchy taught us to valorize the masculine, to see it as the redeeming force, as divine. These qualities in our culture have been horribly overdeveloped, with devastating consequences for us all. It is imperative that women reclaim our precious energy so we can bring forward the feminine principle, the Divine Feminine, with the full force required to rebalance society's ills.

The Divine Masculine and the Divine Feminine might sound like woo-woo concepts, and it's easy to conflate these ideas with being a man and a woman, as we have long been socially conditioned to embrace the energy associated with our assigned sex, but they have nothing to do with gender and everything to do with consciousness. We know what toxic masculinity looks and feels like—it's the dominance and aggression that define our current culture. But when balanced, or "Divine," the masculine is the energy of direction, order, and truth, the container that gives creation (a feminine quality) *structure*. Balanced, or "Divine," femininity is creativity, nurturance, and care, the energy of bringing things into being. It also represents the ability to hold many things at once without jumping into action. Toxic femininity is chaos and overwhelm, emotional disturbance and despair.

We recognize each of these energies in ourselves. We all have the capacity and need to express both. Almost every woman I know already extends herself in both directions; men are behind, though it feels like it's becoming more publicly permissible for them to show their feminine side, to caretake, nurture, and create. In a balanced version of the world, masculine and feminine energy would be present in equal parts within each of us—and therefore would be present equally in the world. When we tip into either extreme, we veer off course and become stuck, addicted, scared. Right now, the resurgent energy of the feminine is required to bring our culture's toxic masculinity into balance: It's an energy dedicated to nurturing and tending what's already been created, rather than extracting more and more.

It is incumbent on all of us to release the feminine from its strictures, to venerate those impulses and sacred parts of ourselves once again. Only then can we take our rightful place as *part* of nature, rather than maintaining the delusion that it's outside of us and ours to dominate.* When we come into balance, when we relinquish our instinct to tamp down and control, we can kick up our feet and savor this experience, rediscover freedom and joy.

Those who subscribe to the belief that the patriarchal structure is the safest and best path have had their way for millennia, and I get the attraction. Life is terrifying, full of uncertainty. Why wouldn't we want to establish a scientific language and framework to explain away every miracle and to force the body and nature to adhere to how we believe they should be? Of course we want to identify the laws that govern the universe and our place within it. That feels much more powerful than submitting to the idea that we are merely bit parts of the natural world and that there are mysteries at work that we cannot grasp, much less control. But coming into balance requires acknowledging our appropriate position: not as dominators but as responsible stewards and partners.

* This delusion is underlined by the definition of *nature,* which specifically excludes humans: "the phenomena of the physical world collectively, including plants, animals, the landscape, and other features and products of the earth, as opposed to humans or human creations" (*Oxford Reference*).

The body is the mechanism by which we experience the world. We are supposed to use it as a means for understanding, transmuting, and bringing ourselves and our world into balance. We are not supposed to badger it into submission with our minds, in the same way we are not supposed to subvert and overwhelm nature. The body and nature are both metaphors for the feminine: We must allow it to emerge, to reinstate it in a place of respect if not reverence.

Author and philanthropist Lynne Twist told me of a Bahá'í Faith prophecy about the twenty-first century, the moment we're in. She explained that the belief is that humanity has two great wings—a male wing and a female wing—and the male wing has become so muscular and developed, it's too strong and powerful. Meanwhile the female wing has not yet been extended. Twist described how the male wing has become almost violent in its attempts to keep the bird of humanity in the air. Like a spinning boat, we've been flying in circles for hundreds, if not thousands, of years. According to the prophecy, in the twenty-first century the female wing in each one of us will finally fully extend, and the male wing will relax and come into balance. *This* story—about the potential of humanity grounded in our ability to flex all parts of ourselves equally—is one worth keeping and passing on to our children. It feels, to me at least, like a truer place to start anew.

The patriarchy has run its course. It is time to usher it out and replumb society's structure with organizing principles that are more appropriate to this era. We must identify the patriarchy's practices and tactics so we can pull them out by the roots and then investigate the holes they've left in our psyches, the way they've perverted some of our most natural instincts. Only then can we redress these wrongs.

This transition to balance will feel scary, perhaps chaotic. Achieving it will require loosening our grip, allowing that we are not wholly in control. But so we must, for otherwise the patriarchy will endure, as both a ghost and a bogeyman. And haunt us it does. As for its enduring and insidious reverberations in our lives today? That's what the following chapters are about.

SLOTH

Believing Sloth to Be Sinful,
We Deny Ourselves Rest

ADDICTED TO WORK

Through most of the pandemic, I huddled in the corner of my bedroom, in a makeshift home office that was, in before times, just a small table where my husband and I parked books and bills. Now it's my five square feet of a wall-less she-cave/office. It's Labor Day, and I'm here, working. I'm aware of the irony. Clickety-clack. I should probably take some time to relearn the history of this day, to read about how it became a holiday after the working class revolted against oppressive, unsafe conditions and unlivable wages. I feel ashamed that this morning I complained about needing to work. Honestly, when it comes to work or pleasure, for me, work has always been an easy choice.

My kids are not outside because it's approaching one hundred degrees, and my husband, Rob, is approximating time in nature by sprawling on the couch with them and watching *Blue Planet*. Yesterday, we locked eyes after the sixth round of *Z-O-M-B-I-E-S 2* and knew that today needed to be different, even if only by the subtle insistence on Nat Geo over the Disney Channel. Or that was the plan. If I'm honest, my son Max is probably playing *Grand Theft*

Auto (he's eight), while his younger brother, Sam, inhales the inane *Ryan's Mystery Playdate* on an iPad and Rob watches a movie. But I am choosing not to know because it's painful to feel that this dual tide of parental workaholism and laziness is failing my kids. I should stop writing and take them somewhere, anywhere. But, deadlines. And a husband whose butt has worn grooves into his preferred spot on the couch, whose old-fashioneds leave sweaty rings on the side table. He is a masterful relaxer. I clickety clack.

I cannot pull myself from my desk, from my blinking cursor, from the rows of books above my head that might offer the perfect example. I'm driven by an ever-present fear: If I don't do enough, I won't be enough. Effort is my best self-protection, my coping mechanism. Work is what distracts me from anxiety. In my world-view, "making it" means putting my shoulder to various boulders, like a multitasking Sisyphus—it doesn't mean I know where I'm pushing them, only that should I stop, I'll be crushed. I work all the time, I rarely sit down, and I don't think I've watched more than twenty minutes of a movie with my full attention in a decade.

I am not unique. In fact, my privilege means I have it better than many: Marginalized folks are even more overwhelmed.* Yet according to a long-term study, women of all variations report higher levels of stress than men, and the gap is widening. We're all living in burnout nation, certainly, but it seems to me that women are propelled forward by a different form of overwork, by an invis-ible Taser. As a white woman, I know I am close to the wheels of power, but I feel compelled to demonstrate my value, well, compulsively—a tendency I recognize in my fellow women, par-ticularly in other moms. We are a cast of synchronized swimmers,

---

* As Devon Price, a trans professor and psychologist, writes of their fellow queer friends in *Laziness Does Not Exist,* "We feel insecure about living on the fringes of society and recognize that what acceptance we do receive could be taken away at any moment—and so we work as hard as we possibly can to protect ourselves. We take second jobs, pull long hours, get reports in early, and take on responsibilities that exhaust us, wanting to believe that our trophies, savings accounts, and satisfied managers will protect us from igno-rance."

our feet pedaling frantically below the surface, arms held high, teeth clenched beneath smiles plastered across our faces. My two little boys never act pressured; nor does my brother, Ben; certainly not my husband.

I learned young how to keep "doing." I was raised beyond the ambit of the cable company, on a rutted dirt road that needed to be plowed all winter. We received only a few basic channels, no *90210*, no MTV. My parents parked the TV in the corner of our basement, amid a detritus of exercise equipment, where it was cold and dark. The idea was that we should use our time more productively.

I grew up in the era of benign neglect, which translated to being turned out of the house and told to come home when we heard the dinner bell—literally. My mother didn't believe in boredom. She would meet that refrain with frustration and fierceness. "Life is boring!" she would bark. "I am not here to entertain you! Go outside! Find a book!" And so my brother and I would. While it wasn't a popular concept back then, perhaps our mom realized that boredom is the crucible of creativity.

We had the luxury and privilege of growing up in the woods. No prospect of playdates or idling time on downtown streets or in city parks. We had to make our own fun. I remember my mom drawing with me once and marveling that we were sharing the experience. Mostly we engaged in parallel play. She worked—household bills, cleaning, gardening, making dinner, organizing, always moving, doing. To be in her orbit required sitting in the kitchen and chatting while she julienned vegetables. If she was working at her desk in her bedroom, I would find the squares of nearby carpet lit up by the sun to lie in like a cat while I watched her. She spent her leisure time with books and *Ms.* magazine, which she read upright at the dining room table with a glass of wine.

My mom did not know how to play, and it would never occur to her to relax, or even to try. There was always something in her hands. For her—as indeed for many of us—an endless to-do list was her form of therapy, the measure of her time, the record of her productivity, a way to suppress whatever else might have been fermenting below. When you don't stop, you don't have to feel.

My dad would sweep into the house at 5 or 6 P.M. after a day at his medical practice or at the hospital tending to patients. We would all eat together, talking about my father's patients and prognoses and who was in the hospital—a clinical undressing of the body and its functions over dinner.

And then we would disperse. My dad watched black-and-white movies with me and my brother in the basement—running down a list he pulled out of *Time* that we knocked off one by one like a punch card—while my mom escaped into dishes and public radio. I felt bad throughout my childhood that she was always left with the mess, but she resisted offers to help. Now I find a similar compulsive satisfaction in cleaning the kitchen, wiping down every surface, being alone with skillets and soap bubbles. Putting everything in its right place is its own kind of meditation. My mom would join us in the dark basement and sit in a rocking chair, her mind turning over everything yet to be done. If I sat between her feet, she would play with my hair.

My mom is the eldest of seven children, raised in a poor Catholic household in Iowa. Her dad was a contractor, while her mother, in my mom's memory of her, did nothing. "She was very lazy," my mom explained, "and I wanted to be nothing like her." She was also cruel and abusive to my mother and her sisters, though when I knew her as a child she seemed to me like a fellow preadolescent, trapped in the body of an aging woman who wore Disney sweatshirts and slept with curlers in her thinning hair. My grandmother collected dolls (which were not to be played with, sadly), chain-smoked cigarettes, and spent most of her time sipping lukewarm instant coffee and going to Bingo with colorful daubers stashed in her bag. She loved doing "the warsh," though I never saw her make a meal. When I knew her, she had mellowed, but the long shadow of her emotional absence touched my entire extended family—she created a through-line of neglect for my mom and her siblings, which consisted of food insecurity, coldness, and an emptiness of soul in my grandmother that everyone struggles to explain.

The effect of my mom's childhood was that my brother and I were mothered by a woman who was never mothered herself. She did not have the playbook, nor did she know what being a kid was supposed to look like. She learned on the job, with a nagging resentment that nobody had ever done the same for her. She shored us up with everything she believed would keep us safe in the wider world: namely, a devotion to work, academic excellence, and an aversion to laziness. If we were always going, we would never get stuck. If we contributed—had important jobs—then we could anchor ourselves to some bigger idea of belonging, of security. To this end, we could do anything we wanted with our lives, so long as we did something, and did that something with unyielding insistence. If we stopped moving, perhaps she feared, we would get used to the stillness, turn lazy.

MY MOTHER'S WORK, MY FATHER'S REST

My dad did not bear equal responsibility for the work of parenting. He was the fun parent, the chocolate mousse to my mom's broccoli. That said, he knew how to land his words. I remember one summer afternoon when he came home early and found me and my brother watching TV downstairs. "I'm so disappointed that you're not outside," he said. His tone was unmistakable, as he could wield judgment like a whip. While my mom's anxiety was general and unbounded, my dad subscribed to the now-outdated idea that criticism was the antidote to failure, that excellence could only be prompted by admonishment. According to Kristin Neff, who studies self-compassion, this approach fits a common worldview: the belief that being kind to ourselves is the gateway drug to indolence, that we will become lazy or self-indulgent unless we propel ourselves forward through hate and judgment.

In short, my dad wanted his effort justified by our own. From his perspective, his primary commitment to the family was to provide, and this contribution was confined to his hours in the office with patients and his hours in the hospital attending to those in the ICU. Except for weekend call, which none of us envied, nothing else came home with him. Home was supposed to be his reprieve—he cared about his patients, but he had enviably firm boundaries. All the hours outside of his time doing patient care were his alone for leisure. What his commitment earned, he felt, was a house that was well tended and children who appreciated the sacrifices made on our behalf. It was our "job" to return on his investment by maximizing every opportunity, achieving excellence, and pitching in gratefully. While my brother and I both needed to be hardworking and academically perfect, there was a critical difference when it came to his expectations of me: I needed to be emotionally considerate to him, to *care*. For me and not my brother, others should come first.*

And in my family, not unusually, my dad came first. We were my mom's baggage. She would wake us at 5:30 A.M. and pile us in the car so she could play tennis before school started, and on our way home from my dad's office, or swim practice, she would park us in the car while she grocery shopped and ran errands. We witnessed how the invisible work of life fell on her, the thankless and unacknowledged tasks of weaving our disparate needs together. Besides running my dad's medical practice, sitting on the local Planned Parenthood board and the school board, and working as an administrator at the hippie alternative school we attended, she cooked,

---

* There's a reason that daughters are also typically the ones who tend to aging parents and that we outpace men in volunteering despite the other binds on our time. Per a Pew Research Center report, "Women (13%) are more likely than men (8%) to have already cared for an aging family member." When it comes to volunteerism, according to the latest report from the Bureau of Labor Statistics, 27.8 percent of women volunteer compared with 21.8 percent of men. Married people volunteer more than those who have never married (29.9 percent of women to 19.9 percent of men), and parents more than those without children (31.3 percent of women to 22.6 percent of men).

cleaned, planned, scheduled, paid bills, and booked our trips and extracurriculars. It was a lot, but she did it with a zealous competence, rising at 4 A.M. And I realize now, it gratified her. Throwing herself into this work proved the value of her time outside of being a mother, a title for which she did not have much reverence or respect—nor, it should be said, did our culture. My mother could have been "somebody." Perhaps our presence reminded her she was not: She was just another invisible cog in the wheel of raising the next generation.

WHEN MY BROTHER AND I were in our early twenties, my parents took us to Zihuatanejo for a vacation. They rented a lovely little house on a cliff, and then, with Ben, proceeded to wake up well before dawn every day to go out with local bird guides in search of finds for their "life lists." While they crept through the jungle with binoculars, I would sleep until 8 A.M., then take a stack of books down the hill to a nearby hotel on the beach, rent a chair, and spend the day eating guacamole, drinking margaritas, and alternating my attention between naps and novels. It seemed like a great solution to me: I was a tired New Yorker and my family took the car for the day, in this era before Uber. But the way I spent my time that week irked my dad, who had paid for the vacation and clearly wanted me to be *doing something* with my days. It wasn't entirely clear *what* he wanted me to do while they were away, but my idleness chapped his hide. Maybe it was the afternoon dozing, maybe it was the profligacy of paying to rent a piece of furniture. It did not help that—gasp—my mother opted out of the birding adventures one day to sleep in past 4 A.M. and sit at the beach with me instead. As we sipped our second round of cocktails, protected from the midday sun by the shade of a giant beach umbrella, she looked at me over the salted rim of her margarita glass.

"This is really nice. I get why you come here. It is *so* relaxing." I looked back at her for a long moment, clocking a revelation.

Wow, it's as if this lady has never experienced a vacation before. Then I realized, she hadn't.

WHEN SLOTH BECAME THE ULTIMATE SIN

In her 2020 book, *Do Nothing,* journalist Celeste Headlee traces the history of work in our culture and reveals how it became all-consuming, a treadmill that won't shut off. She puts much of the blame on Martin Luther and what would eventually become the idea of the Protestant work ethic, that labor can be a salve for suffering, a form of penance. As Headlee writes, "We have been deluded by the forces of economics and religion to believe that the purpose of life is hard work." And this hard work doesn't necessarily have to happen in the office: People like my mother measured her sloth-less existence by a pristine home and high-achieving children. My fellow moms who also work outside the home feel compelled to deliver excellence in both spheres, to prove we can do it all, without shirking any of it.

Headlee also points to another essential turning point in the way we began to quantify labor and how it came to be attached to virtue. With the Industrial Revolution, time became money. Instead of being paid per task, or bushel, workers were put on the clock. As Headlee writes, "Even our vocabulary reflected this change. In the 1600s, the word *punctuality* meant 'exactness.' Somewhere around 1777 or so, people began to use the word to mean 'on time.' For centuries, the word *efficiency* meant 'the power to get something done,' from the Latin verb *efficere,* which means 'to accomplish.' But in the 1780s, we see it used as a synonym for *productive work,* and in 1858, an article first used *efficiency* to mean 'the ratio of useful work done to energy expended.' *Time well spent* began to mean 'time during which money was earned.'" Another side effect of the Reformation for women, per religious historian and professor Beth Allison Barr, is a doubling down on the belief that the hard work of good Christian women *must* be spent in the home.

Over the years, most cultural leaders have contributed to the idea that your sense of self should match the value of your output. While the Seven Deadly Sins are now largely thought of as a remnant of the Catholic confessional, Martin Luther's efforts in the sixteenth century and the Reformation, which resulted in a break with the dominance of the hierarchical Roman Catholic Church and the emergence of Protestant Christianity in its many forms, kept an idea of sloth as sinful at the center of Protestant ideology. Early Protestants believed that grace, which would ensure salvation, came from hard and diligent work. Economist Max Weber credits this idea as being the foundation of capitalism. A timecard-punching "working class," supervised by salaried, managerial overlords, defined early capitalism, but these days almost all of us participate in an economy that measures us by output. The computers of white-collar VPs are increasingly surveilled with "productivity tools" that track desktop activity and moments when the mouse lies dormant. Your time belongs to your employer. The early promise of technology was to improve efficiency to liberate us from constant toil. In reality, it's done the opposite. The idea of fallow time, creative time, time for sitting and thinking or for visiting with an office mate suggests that you're not maximizing your yield, that there's room to give or do more.

And you should do more, we're told, because through the grace of work, you'll climb a mountain built from your talent and then be able to look back and survey the summation of your life, your worth. This ascent rests on several myths. One is the myth of meritocracy, of the power of the individual, of personal responsibility where application of effort is the most consequential metric. The other myth, of course, is that this climb is the most important part of the journey, the best use of our time. So many of us recognize that we toil in silly and fruitless ways—that in "making it" we make nothing at all. For in determining the value of our minutes, capitalism also determines our values. A CFO gets $300 an hour, a graphic designer's talents may earn $50, and the enrichment of the minds of future generations through teaching guarantees . . . a nonlivable minimum wage.[*] And if you've opted out of "work" entirely to take care of your kids, then the value of your contribution is nothing—or maybe it's negative when you sum up lost wages over a lifetime. None of it makes any sense.

Of course, what we've missed in the equation that time is money is that time is a nonrenewable resource. It's insane to put a price on something so valuable. We can ideally influence its arc—eat well, exercise, avoid the perils of free climbing or skydiving—but it is out of our control and relentless in ticking forward. Perhaps that's why we are eager to mark its passing with our production, to leave a measure of our time, to try for permanence in a world that is anything but permanent.

I think sometimes of my friend who took a job as a bankruptcy attorney. Since she was a lawyer who billed by the hour, her time unequivocally equaled money, which naturally encouraged her to devalue any activity where she wasn't getting paid. Was going to the bathroom worth $125?

"The pace was so intense I would go from a call to a meeting to the next meeting until suddenly it was the end of the day and I had disassociated from my body," she recalls. And she hadn't gone to the bathroom. On her first vacation in two years, she was sitting on a tour bus and looked down to discover she had peed her pants. She hadn't felt a thing. After a battery of tests—they thought she had bladder cancer—doctors told her she had weakened her bladder walls. She had worked so hard, she blew up her thyroid and induced incontinence (no childbirth required!). She needed months of physical therapy—and a different job.

While my friend could account for her every minute, the rest of

[*] According to the Bureau of Labor Statistics, in 2021 childcare workers earned a median of $27,490 per year. The median annual wage for an elementary school teacher was $61,400.

us still feel we're working all the time. We often estimate that we work sixty or eighty hours a week, but studies reveal that people with full-time jobs "work" much less than that. We aren't working 24/7—it just feels that way because we've lost control of our days. Work feels relentless because it follows us to the gym, to the bedroom, to dinner, to the bathroom at 2 A.M. Work has become a sprawl, something we do, and think about, all the time, instead of being relegated to the confines of an office or the outlines of a traditional workday. Through technology, our work pervades and invades every corner of our lives, zapping us with endless anxiety. There is no distinction between home and work anymore, which is why, when I sit in front of Netflix with my husband, I'm inevitably hammering away at online bills, to-do lists, memos, emails to teachers and friends, thank-you cards, presentations, and scheduling of meetings until he reprimands me. "Can't you just relax? Can you just sit here and do nothing with me?"

No, unfortunately, I can't. I carry a subconscious conviction that dialing back the anxiety will flatline my productivity—and we'll end up homeless and adrift. My husband does not share my (irrational) perspective, I suspect, simply because as a man he's immune from the programming that he should be proving his worthiness by doing more. He feels no compulsion to make all his time have redeemable value. For him, once he's done his day job and the boys are asleep, it is enough. I will forever be apprehensive about my adequacy, plagued by the idea that I could, and should, do more. I am not alone.

My youngest son, Sam, went to a co-op preschool, where they required us to work at the school two mornings a month. When I was serving snacks one Monday, sneaking looks at my work emails, one of the teachers approached "to tell me a funny story." Sam's best friend's parents were divorcing, and this child had reported to the class that he now had two houses.

"How many houses do you have?" she asked Sam.

"I have one house," he replied. "I sleep there with my daddy.

My mommy sleeps at her office." Ouch. I had always maintained a reasonable schedule when I worked full-time—I typically beat Rob home and walked in the door by seven. But I did travel a lot. And earlier that year, when we had to evacuate from a wildfire in the middle of the night, I took the boys to my office so I could figure out which hotel would welcome our two furious and frantic cats. (Rob stayed behind to wake and help our elderly neighbors—yes, for all my shit-talking he's a wonderful guy.) That night, I tried to get Sam to fall back asleep on a couch in my office. As his teacher reported that my son thinks I sleep at work, I told myself he was confused because he had recently slept at my office. But the idea that I'm not as present as I want to believe lingered. Or perhaps, what was really happening was that when I *was* home, I was so preoccupied with the litany of tasks that needed to be done, Sam barely noticed I was there.

THE EXISTENTIAL ANXIETY OF BEING A MOM

If anything, my children are the only ones capable of pulling me away from my desk, but through them I find myself adrift in another sea of *Am I doing enough because I should probably do more.* After all, there is no A/B test for raising a person, no assurance that everything will be OK: How many hours are required to raise a perfectly parented child? When do you know you're done? Asking for a friend, but how do you avoid careening from feeling entirely and abjectly negligent to pathologizing your kid on the basis of what you were apparently too busy to see? I wonder if my eight-year-old has ADHD, or dysgraphia, or if he struggles to spell because I haven't put in the hours, tugging him along on the path to academic excellence. I don't know where he ends and I begin, what's my responsibility or his fate. I don't know who to blame or credit. What's more confusing is how alone I feel swimming in this anxiety soup of parenthood. My husband doesn't seem similarly anxious, and while I know my fellow "mom friends" feel this way too, we're all so consumed by the needs of our own families that there's not much left for us to be able to support each other's angst. I ping-pong between knowing I can help my children chart their course and acknowledging that their future is largely out of my control. It's a nebulous uncertainty where no amount of effort or resources can engineer an outcome. But that doesn't stop me—or any of the women I know—from trying.

It is easy in the outside world to "do" things, to measure days by what you've completed and achieved. My workaholism is *somewhat* of an antidote to existential anxiety. I've worked for safety and security, I've worked to prove my value, that I matter, that I make an impact in the world. The effort keeps fear at bay. Before I had kids, this tireless application of energy to jobs seemed without downside. But now I don't know what my efforts *out there* are costing my kids *right here*. I don't know what has more value. Our patriarchal society would dictate that my focus should be on my children, that a career can only be gravy. Our capitalist culture has me believing that the summation of a valuable life is in a checking account: what we earn, create, and monetize. But my soul argues that it's not an either/or, that my children's goodness should not be used as a measure of my own and that my contribution is not supposed to be so fixed.

Perhaps I find so much comfort in career because it's easier to demonstrate value there relative to contribution. With children, effort can't guarantee a good outcome. The anxiety of this uncertainty, the realization that making money, paying bills, and buying opportunity is what is within control is probably why I hold it so tightly as an antidote to the fear that my kids won't be OK. For there is no end to the mothering, no finish line to cross. I cannot stop or rest; there's always more to be done, that *could* be done. It's a terrifying pursuit. Until recently, being a mother was framed as everything, the extent of ambition—though the housewives of the fifties, specifically white middle-class ones, did less parenting than we do now. Today, there seems to be underlying anxiety for women who don't have to work, which can sometimes lead to full-throated mothering: perfect bedrooms, pancakes, birthday parties. These moms professionalize the art, yielding Excel skills and JD degrees for school fundraisers and after-school schedules that look like *American Ninja Warrior* obstacle courses. We are all trying to show the world that we have done enough; we are all searching for safety, security, an expression of our value. We work, strive, and perform from a defensive position, trying to prove to the world that we're earning our keep, that by doing enough we are enough. Nobody can quantify what a "good mother" even looks like these days; most of us just swim in the shame of certainty that we wouldn't qualify.

THE BURDEN OF BUSYNESS

I was the mother of a one-year-old in the spring of 2014. I was also newly at a start-up, working part-time for another start-up, and spending my weekends ghostwriting a book for a celebrity. Then Pulitzer Prize–winning journalist Brigid Schulte wrote a *New York Times* bestseller called *Overwhelmed* that put words to an experience I couldn't articulate but felt acutely. I knew I was struggling, and, like everyone around me, when asked how I was, I'd reflexively respond, "Busy," as if it were a badge of honor. And I *was* busy. But *overwhelmed* was more accurate.

Recently, I sat down with Schulte and we talked about whether anything had changed in the years since her book came out. She admitted that beyond awareness about debilitating factors for women and families—like the fact that we *still don't have paid parental leave*—progress has been slow, in part because of the ongoing battle against the mythology that women belong at home. She points to our affiliative, alloparenting heritage, a community style of living that went poof with the patriarchy.

Alloparenting is a concept widely in play across the animal kingdom. It's the idea that in many species of animals individuals work together in extended clans to care for children and secure needs for survival—this approach includes primates and humans as well. Anthropologist and primatologist Sarah Blaffer Hrdy pushed the prevailing parenting style of our ancestors into contemporary consciousness. Her view, now widely accepted, is that we were never supposed to do this work alone, sequestered in a nuclear family structure where the well-being of everyone, including the children, rests solely on the parents, and often primarily on the mom. We are natural cooperative breeders. Just as we collected, grew, hunted, and processed food together as nomadic tribes, we tended children as a group.

But that's not what we've been taught. For millennia, though even more insistently in recent centuries, we've been told that the health of our children depends on whether mothers are there to provide care. As women working outside of the home became possible in recent decades, more emotional complexity emerged, but the reality is that women have always worked. Many women—particularly lower-class women and women of color—worked for others *and* for their own families. Enslaved Black women not only worked "for free" but paid for this work with their lives. Meanwhile, before the Industrial Revolution, white women's work supported their families. Women grew and prepared food, made clothes, brewed beer—they just weren't part of the capitalist market. But as it became possible to buy goods rather than grow and make them, the world began to change. Then when world wars took most men into conflict, women stepped into the paid workforce, and many didn't want to leave. It was only in the 1950s that the fantasy of the working dad and stay-at-home mom emerged, an arrangement that was specifically the prerogative of white, middle-class families. While we look back at this period with nostalgia, this was the reality in America for *only* ten years. A mere decade has come to represent "the good old days" for millions of Americans. TV was right in time to capture it for posterity.

While a lot of credit goes to the women's rights movement of the sixties and seventies for enabling options for women, Schulte points to the primary yet oft-overlooked factor that drove most women into the workforce, a factor unrelated to the provocations of the feminist revolution: In the seventies it became impossible for one person to earn enough money to support a family. "Women entered the workforce just to maintain the same standard of living," Schulte explained to me, citing the work of economist Heather Boushey. "If women didn't go into the workforce—you know, the conservative *dream* that women stay home—a significant number of American families would have fallen into poverty. We had a choice, but we also didn't have a choice."

In 1971, President Richard Nixon vetoed the Comprehensive Child Development Act (CCDA), a bill with significant bipartisan support that would have implemented a high-quality, government-funded national daycare program, providing a significant boost to working families and a lifeboat for single parents.* He labeled it a threat to the traditional family structure—and likened it to communism. As economist Heather Boushey writes, "American businesses used to have a silent partner. This partner never showed up at a board meeting or made a demand, but was integral to profitability. That partner was the American Wife. She made sure the American Worker showed up for work well rested . . . in clean clothes . . . with a lunch box packed to the brim with cold-cut sandwiches, coffee, and a home-baked cookie. . . . This unspoken business contract is broken." The reality of trying to make a living in the United States broke that contract, not the ambitions of

---

* Conservative icon Phyllis Schlafly, who began to accrue power in the seventies and was part of a wave of Republicans who pressured Nixon to veto the CCDA (most of the credit goes to Pat Buchanan), described the bill as a "radical piece of legislation" that "was really for the government to take over the raising of children." Ironically, Schlafly was the daughter of a mother who earned the family wage. Her dad lost his job during the Great Depression, so her mom took a job as a librarian and teacher to keep them afloat, to give young Phyllis a middle-class existence. The battle she stoked between "housewives" and "women's libbers" still reverberates in society today, as if one choice precluded or negated the other.

women. Families couldn't swing it on one paycheck. Many women certainly *wanted* to work, and in most cases they also *had* to.

What was most remarkable, or perhaps insidious, about this shift was that while women's roles changed, the roles of men largely stayed the same. While dads are arguably more involved at home than they were a generation or two ago, their new (extra-credit) contributions do not match the level of output in both spheres required of women. As activist and writer Soraya Chemaly explains, "In the United States . . . men engage in relaxing and entertaining activities 35 percent of the time that women are doing chores. For women, that number is almost half, 19 percent. . . . [On weekends] fathers engage in leisure 47 percent of the time that mothers are taking care of kids. . . . A [UK] survey . . . found that women have five hours less leisure time a week than men do. Furthermore, since 2000, men's downtime has increased, while women's has shrunk."* According to a Gallup poll that tracked the roles of men and women in U.S. households from 1996 to 2019, while the gap between women and men is tightening, the gender roles are as entrenched as ever: Women are more likely to do laundry (58 percent to 13 percent), prepare meals (51 percent to 17 percent), clean house (51 percent to 9 percent), grocery shop (45 percent to 18 percent), and wash dishes (42 percent to 19 percent). Both sexes are equally likely to pay routine bills. And then men take over when it comes to decisions about money (31 percent to 18 percent), keeping the car in good condition (69 percent to 12 percent), and performing yardwork (59 percent to 10 percent). It's depressing.† These statistics

---

* What's surprising is that in countries known for being more egalitarian, the same trends hold. Chemaly reports that men do just over a third of unpaid work in Norway, Sweden, and Denmark, adding, "In Ireland, Italy, and Portugal, women do 70 percent. Italian women continue to do more work than women in other European countries. Gaps in paid, unpaid, and leisure time are greatest in Arab and sub-Saharan African countries."

† What's more disturbing is that Chemaly reports that many millennial men hold neo-traditionalist views, writing of those without children that "35 percent believe women should 'take care of the home and children,' a nine-point increase above Gen Xers and a fourteen-point jump above men older than forty-five." She continues with the research

check out for my marriage, and I'm an upper-class married white woman who spends more than my monthly mortgage on exceptional full-time help. Even with the support of my children's nanny, I feel as though I do the equivalent of two jobs, while my husband does just one. By contrast, 23 percent of families in America are headed by single moms, and 29 percent of families are not in the middle class. We're all drowning.

With all of my privilege, it feels bad to complain that this is hard, that I'm tired and often sad, irritated, and frustrated. I know there are many, many women who do not have the support I do. But the comparative pain scale is part of the problem we find ourselves in: Our knowledge that it could be worse keeps many of us from putting words to the overwhelm and from fighting against it. We need to acknowledge that the way we're functioning now is no way to live, and we need real systemic solutions for all families, including paid family leave and government-funded childcare. Absent that, women have no chance.

One extra piece of baggage that women carry around is the idea that we're somehow responsible for destroying the sacred family structure, that by shirking parenthood as our sole objective, we're not doing our *real* jobs, that despite the stark economic reality of America, those of us who work are choosing to put children second and should be penalized for our selfishness. We are still struggling to liberate ourselves from our profoundly patriarchal past, the flames of which were fanned in the seventies when women needed to bring home a paycheck.

Brigid Schulte told me that she had once made a long list of all the work at home that fell on her shoulders, outside of her parenting and her job (her husband is also a journalist).

---

of Yasemin Besen-Cassino and Dan Cassino, who explain that there is a masculinity backlash. "In what they note is an American phenomenon, one study they conducted reported . . . men do one-third the amount of work of what women do at home. Contrary to what might seem sensible, men whose wives earned more did even less than those whose wives did not."

It went something like this: Pediatrician: me. Dentist: me. Child-care: me. Carpool: me. Grocery shopping: me. Bills: me. Summer camp planning: me. Vacation planning: me. And on, and on, and on. My husband and I would even talk about it every now and then, but it wasn't very productive. He'd get angry and defensive and say my standards were too high, and I'd seethe and accuse, and then we'd get back to where we were: Stalemate. It was really poisonous for me, for our marriage, and for our kids. I felt like I was a perpetual nag. He'd help, but only if I asked him, or pointed something out.

This invisible labor kept my mother toiling, and it's what all my friends contend with when they slip out of their work clothes and into their sweats. Typically, the daily load of keeping milk in the fridge, a schedule in motion, and clean underwear on butts con-sumes women's time; their husbands might take the children to a weekend sports class, where they sit on the sidelines and watch, venerated for being great dads. For women, not only is sloth *not* an option—our work and overwhelm are compounded by the belief from ourselves, each other, and society that we should always be doing *more*.

THE MYTH THAT MOTHERS MATTER MORE

Many people look at the unequal division of labor in households and say something like "Women are naturally just better caregiv-ers." Well, in addition to the sticky myth that men are valiant while women are meek, there's a pervasive idea that women are the only ones who are hormonally changed by pregnancy and parenthood to bond with newborns. This is false. According to biological an-thropologist Lee Gettler, testosterone drops in new fathers, in part, they believe, so that oxytocin can soar. Men are biologically de-signed to be right there with us, hunched over nappies and dodging vomit. Instead, we have bought into a cultural idea that women instinctively must know best. Keeping men at arm's distance is called maternal gatekeeping: that you must rush in because your husband is too doltish to change the diaper *just right.* In upholding this concept, we fulfill a false prophecy, guarding gender roles defined by culture, not nature.

When Max, my first child, was born, I was exhausted. (In a not intentionally ironic move, I read Sheryl Sandberg's *Lean In* while waiting for the Pitocin to kick in and then shoved a nine-pound baby out of my body.) On our way to the hospital that morning, my husband, Rob, confessed he was worried he would feel . . . nothing. I assured him that would be normal, that his feelings would come, and that I didn't know if I would feel much either, except for relief to be able to sleep on my stomach again. Late that night, when my work was done and I passed out, Rob stayed up with Max, sucking amniotic fluid out of his mouth with a bulb syringe, making videos, and crying. The nurses taught Rob how to swaddle and how to put on a diaper. Rob was in charge. My good friend Liz had instructed me to *let this happen because a more equitable marriage would be the result,* and I tried to follow orders.

Liz is a now well-established TV writer, but she fought to get into her first TV writer's room on *Nurse Jackie,* after a long and painful slog through a career in magazines. She wasn't planning to get pregnant, but she accidentally *did*—right after getting this job. (As they say, man plans and God laughs. Use protection, kids!) Three weeks after she gave birth, she needed to be back in that writer's room. She and her husband, Jeff, a fellow screenwriter, panicked, but he pushed her out the door, assuring her he had their baby's care under control. He told us months later that he surely *did not have it under control,* but he figured it out. Not only did they all survive, but the situation cemented Jeff's status as a formidable co-parent; he is as competent as his wife, if not more so. (And their children—plural, they did it again!—are delights.) While the story is "lunacy," to quote Liz, "particularly when I had mastitis and spiked a 103 fever by the time I hit midtown," this forced shift in gender roles ended up being a boon for both of them.

Unfortunately, couples like Liz and Jeff are rare: Only 23 percent of workers, and fewer than 20 percent of men, are eligible for leave in the United States, and men are less likely to take the full amount (62 percent of men take parental leave versus 93 percent of women, according to a 2019 study).* The reality is, when men have access to paternity leave but refuse to take it, they're reinforcing the enduring story that babies need their mothers and not their fathers. This myth is insidious: Not only does it shortchange the bonds between fathers and children, asserting that fathers will never be the *most* primary, but it piles additional pressure onto moms. And it is a disservice to gay partner parents too. Babies need warm, loving bodies to attach to, regardless of gender.

Liz and Jeff's story was on my mind when I was at the hospital after giving birth to Max. I thought if I could resist micromanaging Rob, I'd be at an advantage—I'd have a more competent and confident spouse at my side. And that's what happened, at least for a while. Max preferred Rob for the first three years of his life. It hurt my feelings, and sometimes my pride, but I was grateful I wasn't the one-and-only who could attend to his cries. Vicky, our nanny, soon supplanted me as well. When she came over to meet us, Max was fresh off his first round of vaccinations and wouldn't stop crying. I put him in her arms and he fell asleep. She's been our third parent ever since, the one who takes care of all of us, the conductor who keeps the train on the tracks. We are so lucky, as being able both to afford her and to pay her well and with benefits is a privilege and has been one of the motivators of my career. Our relationship is one of the most important in my life: Her tenderness for my family is what allows me to write and do my work. And every day, she teaches me how to accept her anchoring support. If her kids

---

* In one dismaying study, "1 in 3 male respondents claim their position could be in jeopardy" if they were to take advantage of paid parental leave benefits.

weren't already grown, I would feel unrelenting guilt about pulling her away from her own family to take care of mine—even though, like us, she's one-half of a two-income home and needs the paycheck and health insurance. Even as I do what I know intellectually is good, and practically required—creating a community of care for my kids and showing them that other adults will love them too—guilt and shame linger, reminding me that I could always do more. The emphasis is on *I:* My kids have every opportunity, they're healthy and happy, yet that's still not enough to banish the specter of inadequacy that haunts me.

HOW PARTNERSHIP IS SUPPOSED TO FUNCTION

Nearly a decade ago, I interviewed a tantra expert named Michaela Boehm for a story on partnership. I girded my loins for what I thought would be a conversation about seven-hour orgasms, as popularized by Sting and his apparently patient and well-lubricated wife, Trudie. But tantra, Boehm said, is not really about sex; it's about intimacy and the cultivation of sexual tension, because, over time, couples become too similar, too *friendly.* Friendliness is not the polarity required for magnetic attraction, it's difference. One partner must be in their "masculine," while the other must be in their "feminine"—both types of energy, receiving and directing, must be represented, regardless of the gender of the participants. It doesn't matter who chooses which, but per Boehm, when it comes to good sex, one partner must "animate one end of the spectrum, while the other partner goes as far to the other end as possible."

Creating this type of sexual tension is essential: Too much sameness is not sexy. A 2013 study seemed to prove this point and caused an uproar by finding that men who do more work around the home, like laundry and dishes, have sex 1.5 fewer times than guys who don't. As a hetero woman who wants a 50/50 partner or better, I wanted to disagree with the finding, but on some level I couldn't. When I asked Boehm about it, she understood. "For many women, the idea of coming home from work and being greeted at the door by a smiling, apron-clad husband actually feels disconcerting—even though the idea of a husband who makes dinner is very appealing. However, with a subtle shift—coming home to a husband who directs you to have a glass of wine while he finishes up dinner prep suddenly sounds quite sexy. . . . The direction—the assumption of the masculine aspect—is a subtle but essential necessity," Boehm told me.

This distinction clicked for me. Yes, it would be kind of sexy to be "bossed" around by my husband in the kitchen. This wasn't just resonant in the context of my own home life and conflicting desires there; it also helped me realize that in my "outside life" I am often in my masculine. I direct work, make decisions, tell others what to do. My mother is the same, as are many other women. The feminine is harder for me. I struggle to *receive,* for one, whether that's help, comfort, or support, and I am not a natural homemaker.

Ultimately, each of us, regardless of gender, needs to find the balance between our masculine and feminine, to flex into each capacity at different points of our days, weeks, and lives. Many men seem to reflexively recognize that they are off-kilter, even as the patriarchy insists on confining us to our predetermined gender. There are plenty of guys who want to be nurturing, creative fathers and partners, who want to do their share.

To some extent, as for many of my peers, my marriage is a re-creation of my parents', despite my best intentions to modernize the institution. In my household, unlike my parents', I am the primary breadwinner, which I thought would mean that Rob's and my gender roles would be reversed. I did not grasp how much pressure I would still feel to conform—from my own programming, from the culture at large—and to gun for both mom and wife of the year, even as I was outearning my husband.

Even when my husband *says* he will take on more at home and with the kids—as he said he would give me time to write this book during the weekends when I wasn't tending to my full-time job, consulting, and, in the age of COVID, teaching Zoom school to a second grader—it's not much more than a vocal gesture. All activities require my prep and then typically my ongoing participation, even if only by constant text updates and question fielding. This is a type of learned helplessness, born out of the idea that if Rob makes it onerous enough for me by needing a lot of direction, I'll just do it myself. It works. The other night, I asked him to heat some tortillas and cut up an avocado while I finished dinner prep (turkey tacos). After he asked me for guidance on which avocado was ripest and how long he should heat the tortillas, I shooed him out of the kitchen.

Rob and I had a conversation the other weekend about our plans. Mine, unsurprisingly, was to fold in time between Costco and the grocery store to work.

"What are you going to do with the kids?"

"We're going to spend the first half of the day being lazy," he replied, without any apparent irony.

That sentence galled me—and that is a problem. Yes, it's not good for my kids to be sucked into a vortex of screen time, but "sitting around doing nothing" wouldn't have been the worst skill for me to have learned as a child. I am exhausted—I need that week back on the beach in Zihuatanejo with my mom, some margaritas, and a stack of novels. Why would I ever, ever wish this state of perpetual unrest and depletion on my own kids? It is no way to live. I want to try something different. And different might require letting my husband dictate the day without feeling as if I need to be the cruise director. Different might mean addressing the feelings of guilt that subsume me as a patriarchal hangover that I need to flush from my system. Perhaps I don't need to "*do* parenting" and instead need to find peace and grace in just *being* a parent, as amorphous and immeasurable as that activity might be.

Celeste Headlee reports that "according to the US Bureau of Labor Statistics, working moms spend eighty minutes longer than dads every day taking care of kids and households, while dads spend almost fifty minutes more than moms watching TV or doing other enjoyable activities." According to Headlee, men are more likely than women to take it easy at the office too. As she writes, "Even when they're at work, women tend to put more pressure on themselves. Data collected by the Captivate Network shows men are 35 percent more likely to take a break while on the job, 'just to relax.' Men are also more likely to go out to lunch, take a walk, and take personal time during working hours."

The other evening, I went to a neighboring mom's house to talk about after-school extracurriculars for our kids—notably, no husbands were present. And while we sat outside, the French doors were open, and I could see that her house was . . . a spectacular disaster. This woman has three kids and runs her own business, but I still marveled at both the mess and her being completely unfazed by it. And I also noted that *I not once attributed the mess to her husband,* even after he wandered out to say hi in his pajama pants (his wife was fully dressed). As I drove home, I recognized I was judging her in an unhelpful way. If I could do it again, I would toast her freedom from housekeeping and ask for tips on how I might untether myself from my own unachievable expectations.

THE BENEFITS OF REST

That chill dad in his pajama pants has the right idea. So do the men who take breaks at work to go for a walk or relax. Srini Pillay, a psychiatrist and Harvard professor, has written several books about the power of rest for the brain. Downtime is obviously a concept we grasp when it comes to our bodies—nobody can run a marathon at the pace of a sprint, we know we need sleep—but we struggle to let our minds off the leash. When we chatted, Pillay explained that as a young medical student he had been relentlessly intent on putting in the hours. And his advisors chastised him for it: "We are really worried because we're not here to develop robotic thinkers. We want to develop people who are going to change the world, and you are never going to change the world if you don't build in these periods of unfocus into your life," they told him. These periods of unfocus look like doodling, midday naps, meandering walks. This feedback changed Srini's life, and he began to study the unconscious mind, which, incidentally, is the brain's most powerful state: The conscious brain can process sixty bits per second, while the unconscious brain can process *eleven million bits per second*. We are so busy trying to focus, to do everything that needs to be done, that we not only leave our full potential untapped but burn ourselves out.

"A lot of people think a lot of important breakthroughs have come through focus only," Srini explains. Then he adds:

> Think about Albert Einstein when he describes how he discovered the theory of relativity. He says it was a musical perception. He doesn't say it was the result of his focus on mathematics and physics. . . . Steve Jobs . . . has said, "You cannot join the dots moving forwards, you can only join them backwards." In his words, he said, you've got to use something else like gut, karma, destiny, whatever—that there is some other forward moving force that takes us somewhere. . . . Recently, when somebody asked Jeff Bezos, "Well, how do you make your decision about the new places for Amazon?" he said, "We collect a lot of data and then we make the final decision intuitively." There are a lot of people who I think recognize that intuition, the unconscious, this is that intelligence we really need to access.

I don't think it's a coincidence that Srini pointed only to powerful white men as people who've been able to use rest and intuition to harness the power of the unconscious mind. In our society, they are the ones who take breaks, call on others for support and care, and don't beat themselves up for taking a walk around the block.

What's perhaps most compelling to me in Srini's prescription is that women's intuition is more bang-on. There's science to support this idea, that intuition isn't a woo-woo quality but a confluence of shifts in physiology. As Srini explained, women are "complex information integrators. . . . They pick up a lot of subtle variables and then they integrate this information." Imagine what we might create if we built time into our days for gamboling around our neighborhoods and dozing.

Fortunately, sleep, once the domain of losers who couldn't get their work done—"I'll sleep when I'm dead!"—has been reprioritized as an essential state for productivity. Not getting enough hours, particularly for kids and teenagers, is seen as a health crisis—and a key factor in the precipitously rising rates of Alzheimer's disease. When we sleep, the glymphatic system "washes" our brains, clearing out detritus. And researchers believe other modern crises like ADHD are at least partially sleep disorders. We all need rest.

THE NATURAL SUPERIORITY OF WOMEN*

There's another insidious consequence of the hamster wheel women find ourselves on: Because we're so consumed by our busyness, because so much of our attention is trained on living up to society's expectations for survival, it's impossible to find the space to think and plan our way out of these inequities. We're too over-

---

* Did I get your attention? That was the title of an article that anthropologist Ashley Montagu published in *The Saturday Evening Post* in 1952, followed by a book that's been updated over the decades. As he explains, while the term *superiority* feels distasteful to women, it's the truth—on every measure, we are better built for survival. He writes: "My many years of work and research as a biological and social anthropologist have made it abundantly clear to me that from an evolutionary and biological standpoint, the female is more advanced and constitutionally more richly endowed than the male. It seemed to me important to make facts clear. Those are the provable facts. Women, as biological organisms, are superior to men. If anyone has any evidence to the contrary, let them state it. The scientific attitude of mind is not one of either belief or disbelief, but of a desire to discover what is and to state it, no matter what traditional beliefs may be challenged or outraged in the process."

whelmed. We don't have time to fight for our reproductive rights, for equal pay, for paid family leave and reasonable gun laws to keep our children safe. We don't have time to expand. Denying us space and stillness is the most pernicious way those at the top of the patriarchy keep their feet on our necks. I understand their fear. Those who benefit from this system of dominance understand that when women and other marginalized communities rise in righteous anger, pulling each other up into full resistance in the process, their time in power will come to an end. Not only will we outwork them—let the preceding pages be proof of our unfailing industriousness—we will also outperform them.

When Zoom school became an unexpected and uninvited full-time job, it provided an initiation into a knowing most women have long understood: The girls run circles around the boys. In my observations from peering over my son's shoulder at the screen, the girls seemed to be grades ahead—in reading, in math, in sitting still and listening, in putting on their own clothes and combing their hair. As the mother of two sons, I wonder if I should fear for my children's future: They are not primed for a postpatriarchal world.

The work of sociologists Thomas DiPrete and Claudia Buchmann illustrates that girls have outperformed boys in school for a century. But you wouldn't know that from the power stack in society, or the ways in which women feel like they can't win. Women are still widely unrepresented outside school hallways: We're all well aware that there are more CEOs named John (and David) in the Fortune 500 than women with that title. As of 2021, women represented only 27 percent of Congress and held only 18 percent of governors' seats. Fifty-eight percent of jobs that pay less than $11 per hour are held by women, and 56 percent of women live in poverty, particularly women of color.

We know that systemically nothing feels right or balanced. We know that this way of living and doing is not sustainable. While we must be unrepentant in our efforts for *more* than equity in the boardrooms and the courtrooms—after all, you don't get to equal representation (the middle) by aiming for the middle, particularly when things are so unbalanced in our disfavor—focusing on systemic change is not the only work. This isn't simply a numbers game; it requires an energetic shift, an equalization between the Divine Masculine (structure, order) and the Divine Feminine (nurturance, care, creativity) in each of us and in our systems. We need to change the standards of society, and that will not happen while we keep doing it all ourselves. We must drop the ball and force others—men—to pick it up. We must let ourselves off the hook, cultivate deep self-love, and then learn how to turn and reflect it back on other women—unabashedly, fervently, with the full force of our empathy and compassion. We need our rest, our energetic reserves, for putting the world back in order. We need to move past our worry that we're not doing enough and get on side with each other so that we can expand together.

This work requires rest, self-care, and support. It requires boundaries and letting go of perfection, or any expectation that pulls us away from what absolutely needs to get done—and distracts us from what we feel called to do. Our planet and our future depend on our tender care, our capacity—innate or not—to help tend to the messes we've made. It's not that we don't need men—we certainly do—but we need their energy to be focused on easing the burdens of care: The cleaning up of messes in the home and outside of it must be shared.

THE VALUE OF OUR WORK

The pandemic drove millions out of the workforce for myriad reasons—some lost jobs while others quit. But: unequally. In September 2020 alone, four times as many women dropped out of the labor force as men (865,000 versus 216,000). And per *Politico,* "One out of four women who reported becoming unemployed during the pandemic said it was because of a lack of child care—twice the rate among men." The pandemic surfaced the underlying disenchantment so many of us feel about our careers in the context of everything else happening in the world. So many are struggling with the pull of being needed at home but also questions of personal ethics—namely, that it doesn't feel good to be a captain of industry, or work for a captain of industry, when the integrity of what you sling doesn't align with the integrity of your soul. I've watched many women I know turn away from jobs they used to justify because they feel like they are making our teetering world more damaged. They can't tolerate the discomfort anymore—but these women have the privilege of choice.

Many—most—do not. So many women are forced into low-paying jobs where life is an unrelenting struggle. And it must be clearly stated: A disproportionate number of these underpaid women are not white. While some of the pay gap is flat-out bias—women of equal experience earning less than men in the exact same role—the reason the pay gap is so stark is that so many of the jobs of "care" in this country (teaching, nursing and home health-care, food services, housekeeping, and childcare) pay the worst. This essential support is perceived as low-authority, low-status "women's work," of lesser value. (Men in the care categories typically outearn women, a double slap.)* Culturally, we don't think that "women's work" is valuable, productive, or important, and we pay accordingly. Our priorities are backwards. It's also important to

---

* According to a 2021 survey, male nurses (who compose only 12 percent of the nursing workforce) earned an average of $38.61 an hour versus female nurses, who made $35.88—annually, this $2.73 difference adds up to almost $6K a year. Meanwhile, according to a 1996 report, "Male public school teachers earn between 10 to 13 percent more than females, on average. . . . Married females receive lower salaries than nonmarried females, while for males, no difference associated with marital status is identified, all else equal." There are many factors at play here, including the fact that a lack of paid family leave means that many women miss out on wage-earning periods and commensurate pay increases. But there is certainly also cultural bias, which suggests that a job will never be, or should never be, a mother's priority.

note that the women whose wages are most affected by pay disparity are mothers; childless women are neck-and-neck with men in compensation, pointing to a large and insidious "mommy tax."*

It shouldn't be lost on any of us that there is so much pay disparity between different types and "classes" of women. It's hard to win as a group. Intentional or not, the patriarchy managed to put all of us in an eddy, fighting for sovereignty over our own lives, over who has value, over who is meting out their time responsibly and well. This push into perpetual action, this coached fear of sloth—or more practically, the idea that we don't deserve *rest*—has made us frantic, exhausted, depleted, depressed. In the great mythic lie we tell ourselves about who we are, women are supposed to kick back and be protected from tigers, fed by the spoils of the hunt. We've historically been cast as freeloaders and walking wombs. But the reality of patriarchal culture is different. If you're single or childless, your value in the capitalist market approaches that of a man—but socially, you're perceived as broken or selfish. Pick your path. If you're a mother who doesn't work outside the home, you're wasting your potential. If you're a mother who does work outside the home, you're damaging your children. On top of this, the constant drumbeat of our lives is that in at least one of the spheres *you're not doing enough*. Who even has time for sloth?

I believe that this drumbeat, the persistent cattle prod that has women in this terrible double bind, is a patriarchal reverberation that's quite brilliant. The men I know and love benefit from our insistence on doing everything and being everything for everyone. My husband, for one, *can not only rest, but rest easy,* knowing that I'm nailing down the minutiae of our lives, that my hypervigilance ensures nothing essential will be missed. Like other women, I am the bulwark against the storm of life, even as our culture insists that I'm

---

* According to the research of Henrik Kleven, a Princeton University economist, mothers experience a precipitous salary drop after having kids, even in Denmark, one of the most gender-egalitarian countries in the world. He reports Danish mothers earn 20 percent less than men over the course of their careers.

simply protected by the patriarchy and not using my own back to hold it up. It's a kind of gaslighting. The patriarchy outlines the expectations around our performance; we fulfill these every day, ratcheting up the standards as we go. Few of us, unlike my acquaintance with the messy house, feel strong enough to break the mold and say, "Not today. Today, I eat ice cream in my underwear in front of the TV while my kids dump every toy they own on the living room floor." Instead, I have friends who perversely wish for a fever so they will have reason to call in sick and sleep. And for women with no paid leave, no healthcare, and no support, there's no version of time off, or putting anything down.

Let us put our weight into doing better, for ourselves and for each other. For some of us, realignment to something truer and more sustainable will require sorting through our own ambivalence and recognizing moments when we are behaving in patriarchal ways. This patriarchal training shows up when we enforce different standards for ourselves and other women than we do for men, as when we condemn each other's parenting, housekeeping, or contributions at work. We must refuse to level judgment at other women to try to ease our anxiety about not doing enough or our feelings of sadness about decisions we wish we had made. Instead of feeling ashamed, naked, or judged in front of women who have made different choices—in the home or outside of it—we must stand together and rally for what will afford all of us more opportunities and ensure stronger families, villages, and communities, regardless of their heteronormative or nuclear makeup. We need to fix our attitude toward care and begin to worship (or at least respect) those willing to attend to our basic *and* essential needs— across the gender spectrum—while also clearing the path so our children can blaze trails to bring us to the next level of consciousness. This effort includes our sons too, whom we must teach to distinguish between their Masculine and their Feminine qualities, and then teach to cultivate the latter as fiercely as they've been taught to attend to the former.

ENGAGING WITH THE RIGHT STRUGGLE

To plot our next steps as a society, we need to slow our roll, just as COVID forced us to. And at the same time, we must aggressively engage in changing the system. These two statements feel like a paradox. By putting us in the physical penalty box, into a forced time-out, a sacred pause, the pandemic cast a new light on our "busyness" and forced us to look at it more closely. We assessed the quality of our relationships, the products we surrounded ourselves with in our homes, and whether our lives had meaning or were just a swirl of passing days. And we recognized that by rushing around, we'd been hiding from what we didn't want to see.

In my conversation with Brigid Schulte, the journalist who wrote *Overwhelmed,* I copped to a resistance to slowing down. I told her that I worried about what I was missing in my kids' lives; that I felt my output was attached to my self-worth; that I ascribed my perpetual hustle to the quest for financial security. But that's not the whole story. Like any good workaholic, I use work to numb—to cover up hard feelings. I turn to work for succor in moments when I feel emotionally flooded; at work, I feel I can control my fiefdom, hold the reins on my fate. I rush around so I can measure my hours by a carefully crossed-out to-do list, a tidied kitchen, a well-stocked fridge, shelves full of books I've inhaled rather than savored. Getting a lot of stuff done is the count of my days. I want to believe it energizes rather than drains me. I want to believe that *doing,* rather than finding contentment in merely *being,* has been the right choice, and that in my freneticism I haven't missed the point. Schulte went straight to it: "To be a human and to be alive is painful because we're not really quite sure what we're doing here. I know a lot of people have faith, and I think that's wonderful, but we don't know what comes next. The only thing we know is that it's brief, and that we will die, and there is real pain to that. Busyness does cover some of that up."

Busyness will never deliver me into the power and stillness of just being. I recognize that rest does not inherently follow from work unless you make it so, that it's not about *doing all the work so that you can be done*. There is nobody at the finish line, flagging you down with a high-five, a ribbon to crash through, and a big flag that says YOU'VE ARRIVED, NOW REST. I recognize that rather than ensuring I am never lazy, of being vehemently "anti-sloth," I need to reclaim my right to just sit and be.

For when I allow myself space, when I stop filling my days with tasks and instead allow myself the time to really think, to feel, to be creative, I see clearly what needs to be done and how we can do it together. I am not afraid of hard work; *women* are not afraid of hard work. We intimately understand that life is not supposed to be easy. We recognize and acknowledge the necessity of pain and hard work. The type of pain, the ache I experience when I slow down, when I pause from my frantic anti-slothness, brings empathy, understanding, wisdom. It hurts, yes, but it enables me to lean more heavily into moments of unencumbered joy, to fight for all that is wonderful in this world. If there is no yin to the yang, then we lack perspective and our range of feeling becomes limited, partially expressed, unfit for the vagaries of life. It's like that well-worn concept that when someone breaks your heart it doesn't destroy your capacity to love, it tears and builds the muscle so that you can then love stronger. When we resist what's hard, when we are not fully in it, swirling and splashing around in the muck and the mess, we grow tight and small. We atrophy. For many of us, work is the antidote to the pain of life, the clearest path to self-evolution. We can't *be* until we *do*.

But rather than spending all our energy on the doing *out there,* where we can never be *done,* we need to reserve some power for ourselves. We need rest so that we can apply ourselves to what matters to us, whatever that may be in the moment.

There is important doing that needs to be done. We need to put aside some of the busywork, the perfectionistic minutiae that are not worthy of our care, and take up the Work, the battle against entropy that feels like the undertow of our lives. *Apathy,* not sloth, would be the more appropriate "sin," the one against which we should collectively rail. *The Work* is the reason we're here, hurtling around on a rock in space. We need to put aside everything we don't want to consume our time—whether that's doing the laundry, organizing a calligraphic pantry, baking brownies for a party, planning a maximized vacation, or performing an unrelenting and unrewarding job—so that we have the energy, the reserves, and the power necessary to put our shoulders to the boulder to emancipate ourselves and each other.

There is a lot at stake—the possibility of a planet that is no longer lashing us with its death throes; the potential of true equity, where everyone's essential needs are met; the liberation of all of us from drudgery through abundance. The real promise is peace. We need to recognize we're confusing peace with security, believing that by ensuring the latter through unyielding effort we will arrive at the former. This is a fallacy. By working all the time, we are theoretically buying ourselves a momentary break from fear, but this cannot last. Peace will come when we get into the river of life together, when we accept that we are all bound to each other, when we share the burdens—and beauty—of care, for a more balanced future.

Accepting sloth as essential, we can demand support, embrace rest, and reserve our strength for the worthiest work.

ENVY

Believing Envy to Be Sinful, We Deny Our Own Wanting

HOW WE GET ENVY WRONG

"She's just jealous of you." As children, we're often fed this line whenever we complain of mistreatment by another child, usually a girl. It's not you, it's her: "She can't control that green-eyed monster within her that wants to bring you down." I don't remember thinking about the truth of this excuse much when I was young; I was happy to take this leap of logic. That girl who mocked me on the playground probably was jealous of me! While this assessment was never interrogated for accuracy, it did provide an easy emotional Band-Aid.

In our culture, we conflate jealousy and envy, even though there's a critical difference between the two words. Jealousy is not between two people. It requires a third. This might show up as someone in pursuit of the same date to the prom, or a sibling who gets more time and attention from a parent, or a co-worker who has a better relationship with the boss. Jealousy is about fear and threat of loss, and there's typically a reasonable target. It's a word that gets a lot of use—jealousy feels natural and understandable, even respectable. Sometimes we throw it at each other as a loose, passive-aggressive compliment to disguise our own dismay: "Your husband bought you earrings for your birthday instead of a coffee maker? I'm so jealous! You went to Hawaii? I'm *so* jealous! Your kids happily read books without being coerced? *I'm so jealous.*"* Some couples even like the frisson jealousy creates, to be reminded that their partner is objectively attractive and could be swept away by someone else.

Envy, on the other hand, is unsavory; we think of it as malicious and largely unconscious.† It's also intimate and one-to-one: Someone has something, or is doing something, that *you would like for yourself.* Maybe a friend announces her engagement while you've struck out on yet another blind date, or is having a baby after you've experienced a series of miscarriages. Maybe someone else got the job you thought was yours, or is succeeding in a way that minimizes your own accomplishments. Your envy in those situations is painful. And as we learned from fairy tales like "Snow White"— the ultimate, insidious tale of intergenerational envy—envy is so powerful and bad, it might motivate someone to have you killed so they can eat your heart. While we're generally accepting of jealousy in relationships—love will make you do crazy things!—we can barely tolerate the wash of shame that comes from envy. "I'm so envious" doesn't really roll off the tongue. It sounds malevolent.

Brené Brown explains in her book *Atlas of the Heart* that envy is typically armed with hostility and deprecation: "I want that, and I don't want you to have it. I also want you to be pulled down and put down." This might sound extreme, but I believe it's accurate— the way we apprehend envy currently does not make it palatable or acceptable. As Brené contemplates (italics her own), "I wonder if, unconsciously, we don't use the term because it's one of the 'seven deadly sins,' and two of the ten commandments are warnings against

---

* These are actually examples of being envious, but *jealous* just sounds better.
† The etymology of each word gives us clues, too. *Envy*, from Latin's *invidiere,* comes from "regard maliciously, grudge," whereas the root of *jealousy* comes from *zeal.*

envy. *Is it in our upbringing and our culture to feel shame about feeling envy?"*

I think the answer to her question is: Yes. This shame shuts us down from exploring and even identifying envy when it rears its green little head; we ascribe our discomfort to something else—usually to the shortcomings of the person inspiring our irritation. But recognizing our envy can be an act of emancipation, and embracing it fully is one of the most important things we can do.

Because it requires us to own our wanting, envy is the fulcrum, or hinge, for all the other Deadly Sins: To voice desire, to want something, is the first expression of agency. *Want* is an essential verb—this compulsion to get our needs met, to wish for opportunity and excitement, drives us forward. It's the initial step on the path to asserting yourself. While envy is a gateway for the other sins, it also has the honor of being the one that, unlike gluttony, greed, or lust, offers zero sustained pleasure. Envy tests our tolerance for watching other people get what they want—and reminds us of what we've been too afraid to pursue.

DIAGNOSING OUR ENVY

In the spring of 2019, I interviewed psychotherapist and author Lori Gottlieb and asked her about the reasons people come to her for therapy: the malaise, suffering, and confusion that mark our lives, and our use of comparison and competition as benchmarks to mark our progress, and often as excuses for not achieving what we think we should. We talked about how it's easier to train our eyes on what's happening *over there* than it is to address what's within our relative control, the life in front of us *right here*. We also talked about how we perceive scarcity and limitations, how when someone has something we want—a fantastic job, a stable relationship, children—it can feel like a threat to our own security, and our options seem somehow more limited as a result of another's success. You know, that sticky myth of scarcity, that game of musical chairs: If someone else has something, I can't have it too.

"I always say to people, 'Follow your envy. It tells you what you want,'" Gottlieb explained to me. "Instead of sitting there saying, 'Oh, I wish I had what that person has'—and then denigrating them to make yourself feel better—say, 'What is this telling me and how can I get it?'" This conversation was the first time I had heard envy discussed in this way, and my mind stuck on the point, circling it, underlining it, wondering if it was in fact a trapdoor to so much more. I asked if, in her experience, envy was gendered—meaning did women and men experience it differently—and she replied that it was a mixed bag, with a subtle but significant distinction: Envy, for women, was countered by an immediate unregistered wash of shame. Women, she had noticed, "are very cautious about feelings they believe are unacceptable." Gottlieb believes women usually reserve their undiagnosed envy for other women (as opposed to men), and especially those who are most like them. I feel this tendency acutely. Men who are doing big things in the world don't trigger much emotion in me, but women are something else entirely, particularly women who occupy the same lanes I swim in. But it wasn't until my conversation with Gottlieb that I started to acknowledge the truth of this to myself and realized how bad it makes me feel.

I ran through this thought like a car wash over the following months, trying it on whenever I would encounter someone who seemed a little unhinged, who was spinning out about someone else and her choices. Was it envy? When I found myself sending an eyebrow up in my own dismay/irritation/resentment/judgment about another woman's outfit, Instagram post, or parenting, I deliberated: "Is this envy coming out sideways? Is this envy that I'm too embarrassed to acknowledge?"

I also began to contemplate what it meant that envy—so maligned, shameful, hard to admit—could be something good. I could not shake this idea, wondering whether it was some sort of key. I also realized that repression of envy runs so deep that even when I went actively digging for it, I frequently missed its cues; I was oblivious of the ways in which envy operated inside of me. I would find myself telling my husband all the seemingly valid reasons I didn't like someone, only to realize that I had, again, missed the point: Oh, she's not pretentious, I'm envious that her grade schoolers are doing high school–level math and winning art fairs! Oh, she's not a sellout, I'm envious that she's achieving more than me in the world *and* is always on vacation! In romantic, far-flung locales! What. a. bitch.

One afternoon, I asked my friend and mentor Jennifer Rudolph Walsh if she'd ever knowingly felt the emotion. She was someone who had worked with some of the most high-profile cultural influencers of our time, so few doors and opportunities were closed to her. I figured envy would feel foreign to someone so accomplished, but she immediately knew what I meant.

"Oh yeah," she offered.

Envy is often an arrow, pointing me to a breadcrumb on my own path, my future self, tapping me on the shoulder to say, "Pay attention to this." Tina Brown did this summit for a decade called "Women in the World." Tina had always been lovely to me, and she was doing this beautiful, well-intentioned conference that was shining a light on all these incredible people and necessary conversations, including many voices who had never been put on the mainstage. And *yet*, I would sit in that room with my arms crossed, hypercritical, looking for all the reasons why this event wasn't authentic or impactful enough. It was so deep inside me it took me years to realize Tina was pushing on a dream I had for myself. I had to own that. Once I did, I co-created the Life You Want tour with Oprah, then the Thrive conference with Arianna [Huffington], and finally founded Together Live with Glennon [Doyle]. But in that moment, sitting with my arms crossed in judgment, I didn't realize it was envy, coaxing me to step forward into my own dream. I was looking for every reason to criticize Tina rather than owning that feeling. Thinking back, it's wild how blindsided I was by it.

GIRLS WHO ARE ALL THAT

In January 2020 I flew to Florida to interview Glennon, in advance of her soon-to-be-a-runaway-bestseller *Untamed*. I brought up a section of her book that punched me in the gut: She wrote about being at her daughter's soccer game, watching a rival player, a young tween girl, prance on the sidelines, fully full of herself. The girl knew she was drawing the gaze of the mothers on the other side, and she was almost taunting them, daring them to seethe in anger and disgust. They obliged. Glennon describes them asking each other: "How dare she?" and "Who does she think she is?" Like the other moms, Glennon felt a wave of distaste and abhorrence for the girl rise in her body, which, as Gottlieb would have suggested, she checked with a big, fat *Why?* In *Untamed,* Glennon writes: "Strong, happy, confident girls and women are breaking our culture's implicit rule that girls should be self-doubting, reserved, timid, and apologetic. Girls who are bold enough to break those rules *irk* us. Their brazen defiance and refusal to follow directions make us want to put them back into their cage." Our response to women and girls like this is to say things like "I just don't like her." It's reflexive, unconscious, and incredibly vague, yet this is the de facto blanket statement we reach for to cover any woman who makes us feel uncomfortable with her bigness.

Glennon's story invokes Rachel Simmons's 2002 classic about girlhood in America, *Odd Girl Out*. Simmons talks about the damnation implicit in accusing a fellow girl of "thinking she's all that," the underlying assumption being that she must believe she's superior to her peers—or, if not better, then different, and somehow happily so. Simmons explains, "There are rules of femininity: girls must be modest, self-abnegating, and demure; girls must be nice and put others before themselves; girls get power by who likes them, who approves, who they know, but not by their own hand. . . . The girl who thinks she's all that is generally the one who resists the self-sacrifice and restraint that define 'good girls.' Her speech and body, even her clothes, suggest others are not foremost on her mind." She's not concerned with fitting in or staying one with the group, a group defined by its reliance on *not* being all that. Her power doesn't come from indirect sources: It's based on herself, not the approval of others.

But in reality, a majority of girls *are* concerned with fitting in with the group; social exclusion is tantamount to a type of death. From both my understanding of envy *and* the way we attach it to meanness in young girls ("She's just jealous!"), I think most of us did what we needed to do—and likely continue to operate this way in our adult lives—to avoid doing anything that might incur rejection. Pattern recognition formed in our childhoods: Acting like we're "all that" inspires censure, patrolling, exclusion. Act big, and you will be put back in your place. Do not inspire envy.

Simmons writes primarily about teenagers, but her words are true for women of almost any age, as underlined by Glennon's fellow soccer moms. Because we're so unsettled by these expressions of "all that," and because our first instinct is to judge, criticize, and condemn, rather than to explore our own feelings about what a girl who presents herself as "all that" is doing that feels so minimizing and threatening, we miss the lesson. Per Simmons, we "learn to mute feelings of jealousy and competition. . . . Jealousy and competition do not disappear but instead morph into 'acceptable' forms. . . . To remain steadfastly 'good' and 'nice,' girls must resort to hidden codes. They learn, in other words, to express competition and jealousy indirectly." One could argue that competition—our desire to win or get the thing—is an essential, affirming impulse, one that should not be shut down, much less policed. Instead, when we belittle, undermine, or sabotage, we suffer twice: These

actions feel terrible because they also violate all our conflicting desires to be seen as good, to be women who are kind and caring. It's
a Catch-22. And it is deeply human. It wouldn't feel so shameful if
we could acknowledge and then air our envy out, if we could
openly discuss what it brings up for us and then move on: "Ugh, I
get it, she's perfect and it makes me feel inadequate," rather than,
say, "That woman is the fucking worst."

I asked Glennon what drives this reflexive dislike, this instinct to
smack each other down, and told her about Gottlieb's contention
that envy disguised as judgment or rejection is a signpost for what
we want.

"So why can't we identify—and then lift the hood on—our
envy?" I asked. "Why is this so hard?"

"Women struggle to acknowledge what they want," she offered,
"in part, because we've been conditioned to believe we don't actually have wants." Pow.

Glennon has written extensively about how the idea of the
"selfless woman," who sacrifices her own longing for a bigger life
for her spouse, her children, her co-workers, is central to our culture and how unusual, if not controversial, it is to see women who
put themselves first, who strive to realize the dreams they have for
themselves.

I thought about this feeling of wanting opportunities and experiences for ourselves—just because we want them!—and how
deeply we bury it in our subconscious. I thought about how shameful it is for women to express desire, in all parts of our lives—and
how many of us would rather clip the bud of our ambition than
experience the humiliation of being exposed for thinking we're
worthy of adding something meaningful to the world. We recognize that wanting is dangerous, for ourselves and for each other,
because when we disparage the other, it just might be because we
want what she has. But when that longing is not reacted to but
studied, it can be a lighthouse for your heart's desire, shedding its
rays on purpose and potential.

HOW DARE SHE

We are quick to wholesale reject this wanting in ourselves. And we're equally quick to monitor and police it in each other. We do this through ad hominem attacks (She's bad), snide remarks (What did she have to do to get that?), and finger-pointing (She broke the rules). It boils down to the following: Who does she think she is? And: *Why her and not me?* Envy is reflexive—and because we're so ill-equipped to understand it, we fail to identify what it is before it comes out of our mouths. Typically, envy comes out wrapped in cruelty and masked as opinion. It presents in perverted and unconscious ways, disguised in attacks against other women, women who don't seem so constrained. But when a woman acts big and we look to make her small, is it because we don't like her, as we typically suggest? Or is it that we don't like what she's doing? And is she doing something harmful or threatening, or do we not like it because we would never allow ourselves—or trust ourselves—to do the same? Those who have hurdled the barrier wall of reasonable aspirations for women reflect how the rest of us are still confined. We become crabs in the bucket, pulling each other down.

We haven't taught ourselves to pause, to feel, to diagnose. I sat with my friend Emma recently, and we got to chatting about women we've encountered who have irritated us in outsized ways. She told me that when she was in her twenties, she had a co-worker who was so triggering, she had regular fantasies that this woman would get fired. She even admitted to thinking about how to speed that along. She was consumed with her dislike. "It was a big thing for me. I remember my boyfriend at the time telling me I needed to stop talking about her."

"So what was it about her?" I asked, peering over my coffee. "Was she incompetent? Mean? Lazy?"

"No," Emma mused. "It was none of those things, though she wasn't very nice and didn't try to be my friend, which probably made me feel bad. But it wasn't even that. She was just . . . really fucking confident. She always asked for the best assignments and then she got them, which drove me wild with the injustice of it because I thought I was better at the job. But I guess I never really asked—I just thought my work spoke for itself . . . but she spoke for her work. And I resented that I needed to."

Then Emma paused and looked up at me. "Wait, was I just jealous?" As she processed this experience twenty-odd years later, it seemed to lift from her shoulders, releasing a puff of anger and resentment as she distilled this truth. The issue wasn't Emma's co-worker; it was the way Emma's co-worker made Emma feel about herself. Anne Lamott describes a similar epiphany in *Bird by Bird*, as she finally began to process her seething envy toward another, more successful writer: "Sometimes this human stuff is slimy and pathetic . . . but better to feel it and talk about it and walk through it than to spend a lifetime being silently poisoned." Acknowledging we feel envious is enough. It's a testament to the idea that if we equip ourselves to sit with the discomfort that arises when another woman makes us uncomfortable—without reflexively reacting— we could recognize the gifts this chafing brings.* We might see what it paints for us in terms of what our hearts yearn to do or be. It is a call to action, rather than a chastisement. And it is a specific call—the women who grate on our nerves are typically telling us what we want. They are the ones who are holding up a mirror.

SCHADENFREUDE

Identifying our envy is difficult: We will do almost anything to avoid the truth that what's bothering us is a call from inside the house. We would much rather malign the other person. As phi-

---

* Professor Richard Schwartz, who pioneered a powerful type of therapy called Internal Family Systems (IFS), calls these people our "tor-mentors." Only after we've been irritated can we address the revelations our "mentors" have left behind.

losophy professor Gordon Marino wrote in *The New York Times:* "Nietzsche preached that those of us who are called to search ourselves need to go into the inner labyrinth and hunt down the instincts and passions that blossom into our pet theories and moral judgments. In this labyrinth, Nietzsche detected the handwriting of envy everywhere, observing, 'Envy and jealousy are the private parts of the human soul.'" Instead of denying envy, we need to let it be our compass, let it land on those tender spots that point us toward the fulfillment of desire. This isn't an easy path, though, as those "pet theories" and "moral judgments" will always be our first instinct because envy is uncomfortable. It's much easier to blame, to project, than to come to know ourselves more deeply, to bump up against what we want and the possibility that we might not get it.

After all, blame and projection are forms of self-protection. When we begin to feel envious of another woman, we often try to delineate the ways she *deserves* our rancor. We list all our reasons for wishing her ill or wanting to see her fail. By making her bad, we soothe our own panic and pain. This attack seems to start by characterizing the woman in question as being grandiose for daring to want something in the first place: How could she possibly believe she deserves it? We'd rather nobody get the "thing" than feel like it's out of our reach—even though the reality is that very few of us *even want the same things.* Or more markedly, we fail to see that life is not a zero-sum game; it's not true that if one woman "wins" another must invariably lose.

I believe this perceived scarcity is probably why I can find perverse satisfaction in watching a woman get a public spanking— Martha Stewart going to jail for insider trading, for example—even though I want nothing in Martha's life for myself (except her talent with a pastry bag). Her success has denied me no opportunities. In fact, it enabled and helped my own career: She turned "lifestyle" into a multifaceted business. She broke out of a single corralling box—caterer—and transformed herself into a titan. Where she went, so many of us have followed. And yet, I remember the wash of glee I felt when her arrest made headlines. *Serves her right.* Culturally, it was clear she was being penalized for her perfection, not her white-collar crime. In my mind, I had decided she must be uppity and ambitious, and what she had achieved in homemaking was an affront to us all. It's far easier to hate Martha for her success—and to laugh at her jail time—than to acknowledge I have similar dreams of my own: I want to grow, expand, and share everything I've learned. I want to be an example of excellence. And I'm happy to be paid for it.

Finding perverse joy in watching each other fail, fall short, or be taken down a notch has a name. It's *schadenfreude,* originally a German word that translates to "damage, harm" and "joy," and means, colloquially, the delight we feel when bad things happen to other people. It runs rampant in our culture, as it has across time. We want to see other people brought down to their appropriate size; we would rather feel superior to our peers than inferior. We don't want to see them *die* or anything, just put in their rightful place, right below us. (Interestingly, research suggests schadenfreude is more common in men, though that might mean it's more easily expressed, as women likely feel ashamed about acknowledging it.) Regardless, schadenfreude rooted in envy is profoundly human. We don't want others to have what we want so badly. We feel better about ourselves when they fail to get what they want too—or when they lose it.

WHEN GIRLS LOSE THEIR VOICE

Therapists and academics hold up psychologist Carol Gilligan's *In a Different Voice* as a defining text about the cultural and moral development of girls. Gilligan traces a series of social experiments gauging the ways boys and girls perceive morality and develop psychologically—and, most chillingly, the ways in which a male-dominated world sows the first seeds of self-doubt in girls. The research documents "the coming not to know what one knows, the difficulty in hearing or listening to one's voice, the disconnection between mind and body, thoughts and feelings, and the use of one's voice to cover rather than to convey one's inner world." Gilligan focuses on what happens to girls in adolescence as they conform themselves to fit within the expectations of the culture. Her work illuminates the moment of suppression, when girls stop saying what they feel and start saying what they think they're supposed to feel.

Gilligan acknowledges how this self-silencing continues to show up for women in adulthood, how we modulate what we say and how we say it, suppressing what we "know" to cater our words to our audience, to preserve connection and comfort. Eventually, through the literal and figurative throttling of our voice, we lose connection with that knowing, and what we want is never given air. It suffocates inside us. She writes,

> Women's choices not to speak or rather to dissociate themselves from what they themselves are saying can be deliberate or unwitting, consciously chosen or enacted through the body by narrowing the passages connecting the voice with breath and sound, by keeping the voice high in the head so that it does not carry the depths of human feelings or a mix of feelings and thoughts, or by changing voice, shifting to a more guarded or impersonal register or key. Choices not to speak are often well-intentioned and psychologically protective, motivated by concerns for people's feelings and by an awareness of the realities of one's own and others' lives. And yet by restricting their voices, many women are wittingly or unwittingly perpetuating a male-voiced civilization and an order of living that is founded on disconnection from women.

This disconnection Gilligan writes of is required to exist and thrive within patriarchy. It persists because our world is defined by the voices and experiences of men—one look at *recorded* history suggests women were barely present. Speaking our truth, honoring our stories, saying what we feel and want, is a relatively new experience, and we're still learning how to share and receive other women's stories without judgment.

Though Gilligan's book came out forty-odd years ago, when the onus of parenting rested on mothers, not much has changed today. As boys grow, they learn they are different from their mothers and are taught to define their masculinity in opposition to the feminine; girls, on the other hand, struggle to distinguish themselves from their moms—*even* as fairy tales and Hollywood movies instruct girls that mothers are threatened by, and thus threatening to, younger generations. Gilligan explains that girls perceive danger in separation, in standing out from the crowd at the threat of exclusion. She writes, "The danger men describe in their stories of intimacy is a danger of entrapment or betrayal, being caught in a smothering relationship or humiliated by rejection and deceit. In contrast, the danger women portray in their tales of achievement is a danger of isolation, a fear that in standing out or being set apart by success, they will be left alone." What's more, Gilligan's research describes how boys shape their morality around *being someone* in the world, adhering to logical and legal codes, whereas girls are conditioned to see their morality as *being in service* to the world. Gilligan asserts that to achieve full women's rights, which we still haven't done, we must enable "women to consider it moral to care not only for others but for themselves." This means we must begin to prioritize and assert our own wants and needs, to give them a voice, to let others hear our desires.

THE IMPORTANCE OF KNOWING WHAT YOU WANT

Wanting, in many ways, is humiliating. For one, it suggests you think you're deserving, that you're worthy. It connotes arrogance, or *pride*. There is no reliable model for women to understand what it looks like to know what you want and to go after it without slamming into the assignation of "selfishness." We are conditioned to believe that selfishness is bad, immoral, wrong; that we must step back, serve through compliance. A symptom of this is that we ascribe any good fortune or success to something outside ourselves, as if it's *not our fault* we're successful, smart, attractive. This minimizing through effort is the way to be self-protective. The striving must be imperceptible, a slight kick beneath a still screen of water. We know that we can't get away with much—sex (see chapter 7: Lust), money (see chapter 6: Greed), eating and looking how we want (see chapter 5: Gluttony)—without social blowback. The most insidious form of misogyny can be found in the ways we shame and slam each other. As the witch hunts illustrate, we've been at it for centuries, and we're still doing it. As Carol Gilligan and Naomi Snider write in *Why Does Patriarchy Persist?,* "We can believe in a woman's equality and yet, as women, feel guilt when we put our own needs forward or uncomfortable when other women do the same." And in answer to the question the title of their book poses, they remind us that patriarchy's dominance depends on the complicity and compliance of women and on the way *we* enforce these rules with each other, training our children to be obedient to this system as well. As they point out, children come to insert the word *don't* before critical words: For boys, it becomes *I don't care;* for girls, it is *I don't know.*

This is the way we've been programmed, and our mothers and grandmothers before us. This stunning revelation is an intergenerational pattern, and breaking it is hard. Doing life differently feels disloyal—many of our mothers abided by the cultural dictate that caring for us was their primary destiny. Rejecting this as too small of an ambition for our own lives feels ungrateful at best.

Many of our mothers cared for us compulsively, following the dictates of a society that decreed that taking care of children should be the *only* job a "good" woman wants. Our mothers were supposed to be selflessly devoted to our advancement and safekeeping, ministering to our needs, encouraging us to suck them dry. Society hasn't evolved much. Our culture still insists that women's ambitions should be at least partially crowned by children, that not wanting a family suggests something is wrong with you. This reality continues to put daughters in a double bind: You are supposed to be your mother's greatest achievement, her jailer and her joy, and then you're supposed to pass the honor on to the next generation. In addition, as a girl, when you are dependent on your mother to attend to all your pressing needs, to initiate you into society and culture, to teach you what it is to be a woman, you integrate her programming. Your ability to thrive is in some ways defined by the bounds of whether she herself felt that she was allowed to thrive. Most women of a certain age weren't allowed to thrive at all. Or they felt forced to make a choice not to. As the patriarchy endures— even as it seems to be loosening its grip—we are still made up of generations who have been raised by tired moms, who likely put their own desires on hold in exchange for our safety, security, and comfort. Many of these women couldn't prioritize their own wants and ambitions to model for us what it means to live fully free. To move forward in a different direction requires a break with this past.

Which brings us to our tenuous relationship with our own mothers, what it means to leave them behind, how it feels to use their devotion as a springboard to do our lives differently. This push-pull is captured in Jia Tolentino's brilliant essay collection *Trick Mirror,* where she writes, poetically and painfully, of the "complicated, ambivalent, essential freedom that a daughter feels when she looks at her mother, understanding her as a figure that she simultaneously resists and depends on; a figure that she uses, cruelly and lovingly and gratefully, as the base from which to become something more." This heartbreaking truth points to the unspoken tension between mothers and daughters, that what you choose to do with your life has the potential to impugn what your mother did with hers. While rivalry between generations has frequently been portrayed by Hollywood and other media as predicated on beauty and sexual desirability—cue the mom who envies her daughter's youth, who dresses like her and tries to seduce her boyfriend—that's a harmful and mocking stereotype. The real rivalry between mothers and daughters goes unspoken: It's predicated on a mother watching the girl she cherishes achieve something outside the mother's reasonable ambition and live a life that wasn't necessarily available to her. It's possible to want this for your daughter fervently while also experiencing envy, particularly because there's no cultural avenue for exploring this ambivalence. It's shameful and unsavory.

Meanwhile, when it comes to knowing what we want, few women today had mothers who could initiate them into the concept, who could model for them how this sacred act is done. Most of our mothers were not allowed to fully express themselves. How could they possibly teach us how to do it? For our mothers, often their desires, their wants, were stuffed into suitcases and stowed in the basements of their subconscious.

Carl Jung said that nothing is more influential in a child's life than the unlived life of the parent, an idea that Jungian psychotherapist Marion Woodman expands on as a component in many mother-daughter relationships, writing: "The mother . . . is often the one who gave up her hopes for her own creative life, and in her disappointment projected her unlived life onto her child. Spoken or unspoken, the grief and frustration of that sacrifice weigh heavily on the child. The mother felt locked in a cage of marriage, the bars of the cage being not her husband, whom she had already realized was not Prince Charming, but the child in her womb. The guilt that the child feels for the crime it never committed has its etiology then in the very fact of its existence." Many girls carry the weight of this burden, their perception of their mother's sacrifice, not understanding the full historical context in which it was made: My mother, probably like your mother, felt that she had little choice about who she could be. And my mother has subtly, yet perceptibly, struggled with this sacrifice for the length of our relationship.

It was only when I became a mother myself that I realized that my mother's sometimes obvious frustration with parenthood was nothing personal, just a function of the time and place we find ourselves in now.*

After all, we are still only a few generations from there being any choice at all. We are still shaking this out of our system, working out how it needs to go, what it looks and feels like to compete with your mother in the same way that boys have been culturally primed to succeed their fathers, to outperform them in the corner office and to school them on the basketball court. They've been celebrated for doing so, pressured to excel. It's a venerated part of the code of patriarchal masculinity. For women, dunking on your own mother feels like usurpation, unnatural somehow—unfair, gross, and wrong, as if the game is rigged.

My mother and I try to speak candidly now about her deep ambivalence about becoming a mother, her sometimes envy of the opportunities she worked so hard to provide for me, the way she quietly berates herself for her wasted potential. My mother grew up in a turbulent household without real financial security. While she felt she had no options, she acknowledges now that she has female friends who came from equally or more impoverished backgrounds who went on to become successful lawyers, professors, doctors. My mom was born in 1950 and lived through the women's liberation movement. If she had pushed hard enough, had bet on herself, had not met and been seduced by my charming doctor dad with his suave South African accent and the promises of the life he could afford her, who knows what she might have achieved? In her mind,

---

* There is another sinister undertone to the ways our society insists that care be the primary function of mothers, because when mothers are not equipped for this function—mentally, emotionally, socially, physically—there is no safety net for children. (And mothers are invariably blamed.) Psychotherapist Galit Atlas, who studies the transmission of intergenerational trauma, explains that this gap in care frequently shows up in her practice, writing: "It is not unusual for mothers who didn't have mothers themselves, or those who had abusive mothers, to resent their daughters for having the mother they never had. In therapy, the mother often explores feelings about her daughter having more than she had; she envies her daughter for having her as a mother."

she made the reliable, smart, safe, and secure choice: playing the doctor's wife. In that decision, as with many decisions that feel like stark forks in the road, she lost what-could-have-been. When I struggled throughout my twenties—broke, single, miserable, trying to hatch a job into a career—she seemed to come to a greater acceptance and appreciation for her own choices. By living through me vicariously, she understood that big-city dreams aren't always what they're cracked up to be. Her envy faded.

A friend of mine, a popular TV personality whom we'll call Jill, echoed my experience. When she was working small-town news circuits and eating ramen for dinner, her mom was her champion, rushing in to fill voids in her closet and fridge. But once Jill "made it" to national TV, resentment grew. Jill believes that once she was standing on her own, not just struggling to, her mom felt unneeded and stripped of the only identity she'd ever known. (Jill's mom had stayed home to care for Jill when she was growing up.) She struggled to relate to Jill in any other way. Jill also decided not to have kids, which exacerbated the difference between them. By distinguishing herself so fully, Jill has widened the gap between herself and her mother.

DESIRE AS AN ACT OF INDIVIDUATION

We are parenting—and being parented—in an unprecedented time, at a moment when women can theoretically be, and do, anything we want. Yet we're still feeling the reverberations of a backlash against our ambitions. Yes, we clamor for more women to celebrate in the C-suite, while continuing to harshly judge these women for the toll their success (must) take on their families. Most important: We harshly judge ourselves. The choices women face—none of which feel assured, or great—are not something that women of my generation discuss. Nor do we dwell on the intergenerational turbulence of doing it differently. We've refused to acknowledge the survivor's guilt so many of us feel—our existence curtailed the lives of our mothers, required the sacrifice of their own ambition so they might doula our own. It has seeded in us ambivalence about everything we've achieved, and an uncertainty about what we lose when we take a different path and abandon the women who gave us everything. It feels like judgment, and it's painful.

The therapist Kim Chernin masterfully explored the struggle for daughters to separate and individuate from their mothers against a backdrop of newly won possibility in her eighties classic *The Hungry Self*. Forty years later, we are still trying to acknowledge, wrap our arms around, and process its impact:

> And so this mother of the modern day, with her emerging, frustrated, ambivalent sense of self and her silenced sense of failure, cannot become her daughter's co-conspirator and join forces with her against a tyrannical, patriarchal system that has done so little to articulate or to solve the dilemma of the mother-as-woman, a person with an imperative need for life and development beyond marriage and maternity. To become her daughter's co-conspirator she would have to admit her conflict and ambivalence, acknowledge the nearness or actuality of breakdown, become fully conscious of her discontent, the hushed, unspoken sense of her life's failure. She would need to reach back for that moment in her life when she too struggled with these issues and turned around to brood about her mother's life. She would need a great deal of political knowledge and a vast amount of courage and no small store of cunning, and above all she would need permission to tell the truth about her envy and resentment of her daughter.

She would need permission to tell the truth about her envy and resentment of her daughter. Wow. I'm confident that with every generation of daughters we are working this out more, more fully understanding the glory of expression and *choice* and all it affords: stay home with your kids, work more than full-time, adopt later in life, choose otherhood, pick a partner willing to do more than half the work at home. We are trying to get to a place where we can assess our lives without feeling triggered by the ways in which our needs subjugated the lives of those who were required to tend to them. We are trying to get to a place where our desires, and our wants, are championed, not as a reproach to the generations before us, but as an extension of what it is to be a girl or a woman today. As parents, this pursuit requires moving past our reflexive judgment of other women to make it clear that whatever our daughters want to do is supportable, achievable, wonderful—that they're not living our agendas and that they are not an expression of our unfulfilled dreams but are on missions uniquely their own. It will require examining whether we feel, or not, that their choices somehow reproach us. The underlying concept is revolutionary: Help them figure out what they want, and then push them to attempt exactly that, without exterior pressure to play it out differently. (And guess what? What they think they want might change, too—and that's OK.)

I believe that as we become better at voicing what's in our hearts, we will become more conscious of the way we monitor other women for expressing what's in theirs. Wanting things for ourselves is an essential act of individuation. We must learn how to express our desires truthfully, prioritize their expression, and normalize this action for girls in the way we do for boys. And then we need to become conscious of our tendency to swat this instinct down in other women, and instead identify with and applaud them, rather than chastise. It may have been the yoke around our necks for eons, but it is actually not a woman's job to make everyone else happy. It's not our job to serve the needs of others at the expense of our own. It's not our job to stifle and suffocate our own desires out of fear that we'll offend or lose connection to those we most love. Clearing the path for this possibility requires a new level of honesty and a clarity of voice, one that's connected to the deepest parts of ourselves.

PUSHING INTO THE RIVER

One antidote for short-circuiting conversations about what we want is to pretend we're enlightened—that we've transcended the baseness of desire and are content to embrace whatever life gives us, as if the solution to all this wanting is to unhook from wanting anything at all, to stop engaging with the struggle. We ascribe a lot of high-mindedness to this idea: After all, Zen monks, who have abandoned the messiness of life, are a cultural and intellectual ideal. According to psychiatrist and practicing Buddhist Mark Epstein, though, the Buddha's Second Noble Truth is mistranslated as "The cause of suffering is desire." He argues this has led to a misguided assumption about Buddhism that asceticism is mandatory, that one of its foundational premises requires us to detach from wanting, that to *want* is diametrically opposed to the whole concept of Buddhism. According to Epstein, this is an incorrect interpretation: The Buddha did not teach asceticism. He tried it for a period on his path to becoming the chubby Buddha we revere now, but as his flesh wasted away he recognized he would cease to live should he deny all his physical urges. And self-denial to the point of self-abnegation was *not* the point. Instead, the Buddha taught people how to walk the line between self-expression and attachment— how to know who you *are* and what you *want* without clinging to a certain *outcome*. You are responsible for your part, your blooming lotus from the mud beneath, as it were—but how the world relates to you is beyond your control or provenance. In the interim, you must do your best to express your gifts—you must put yourself out there.

Owning our desire, this bid for wholeness, also requires taking responsibility for our reactions, particularly in those moments when we find the behavior of others threatening. We need to study how our irritation might be reflecting our own, unrequited desire. If this other woman is doing something we would never allow ourselves to do, instead of swatting at her we must unshackle ourselves. This effort requires grace, particularly as we reflect back on ways we might not have been generous or kind to other women. We must emerge out of the contraction of the patriarchy. We must shake it out of our systems as a destiny. We can choose something different. While this transition is painful and hard, while we have *all* been wounded on some level by the journey, we belong to each other in these horizontal bands of society, as sisters. And together we can expand the conception and idea of what is possible for all of us, including generations to come.

We might also need some reverse mentorship, because younger generations are a bellwether of possibility: Many *are* doing it differently, conceiving of envy as something good, as a motivational force for action. In the past few years, I've noted that the word *expanders* is taking off like a grass fire—I see it weekly, if not daily, on my social media and in my email. I've heard it at coffee shops while I've typed out this book. It's primarily used by women to describe other women: "You are one of my expanders." Let me explain.

Lacy Phillips, a manifestation expert, coined (and trademarked) the term as part of her process, which she calls To Be Magnetic. I first heard about Lacy years ago from friends who found her work alternately therapeutic and effective—as they dug into her workshops, relationships and opportunities began to shift. As one friend told me, "I feel like I'm in a coven, but it works." Lacy, a onetime preschool teacher/wannabe actress, tried to use the old-school manifesting approach—Think positive! Ban all negativity! Experience that Malibu house of your dreams!—and found that it not only didn't deliver her fantasies but made her feel paranoid, worried that one wrong thought would bring disaster. Lacy is woo-woo as hell, but to her, manifesting felt superstitious. So she got to work and developed her own approach, which she says is steeped in basic psychology and neuroscience. She leads a program that puts you in dialogue with your subconscious and all its limiting beliefs. We have these limitations in part, she explained to me, because we've been conditioned to think that satisfaction, abundance, safety, and security aren't possible. If you've never seen it, you can't believe it. In Lacy's view, to make the impossible possible, to make all our wanting plausible, we must journey deep into our own minds to remove blocks—and then replace those blocks with concrete examples of people who represent our biggest dreams for ourselves. These people serve as our "expanders," shedding light on a realizable path. It's a process diametrically opposed to how so many of us have been conditioned to think: It's her or me, there's room for only one of us, scarcity, scarcity, scarcity. In Lacy's world, it's *She has it, and so I can have it too.*

Per Lacy, there are expanders and fragment expanders. Here's Lacy's checklist for an expander, all conditions required:

1. They've been in the exact place you're in now, whether it's struggling, or lack, or limit, or not having what they want.
2. They've gone on to become successful in, own, or embody what you're calling in.
3. Their success track feels believable and obtainable to you.
4. They give you an aha moment that sounds egotistical, but it's not. You know you've been expanded on a subconscious level when you have an aha moment where you go, "Oh . . . oh my gosh, if they accomplished that, then I can do that too."

Fragment expanders might be holding one piece of your dream—like buying their first home while freelancing, or getting a TV pilot sold—but there might not be any other part of their life that appeals to you. Both the big kahuna expanders and the fractional ones are useful. Lacy also speaks of "reality expanders," who can help minimize pining or impatience by showing us the harder side of a dream (e.g., you think you really want to own a restaurant, find an expander living that life, and realize by studying her that being a chef is very difficult—you might not lose the dream, but you might ground it more in an awareness of the challenges). I love

Lacy's checklist and the concept: expansion in lieu of envy, a reclamation and re-languaging around this essential need, and then a way of using each other to get bigger and bigger. This support and abundance is the model of a sisterhood.

THE BIGGEST GIFT WE can give all women—our mothers, sisters, daughters, and friends—is a new paradigm for expressing desire, one that untethers it from the shame, embarrassment, and judgment that too typically come as the backwash for daring to have a dream for yourself. Of course, we won't all get what we want—but we will never come closer to it when we're too ashamed to admit what's in our hearts, when we restrain ourselves from speaking openly and candidly about the complexities of what it is to be a woman. We need to do that with each other, and for each other, in the way we gathered historically: to share information, resources, and secrets; to hold space; to wish the very best for each other in the hope that if *you* achieve what *I* want for myself, it only outlines our potential. Rather than serving as a reproach, or a retort, envy can be a light of possibility: an invitation for each of us to fully express in this next era.

Before we misapply our envy and use it to point a finger in judgment, looking for reasons to justify our discomfort in the actions and behavior of other women, we need to explore whether that predilection to shame comes from opportunities and experiences we want for ourselves and from fear that another person will take from us something we feel we rightfully own, or from things we hold against ourselves. And we need to remind ourselves of this other inviolate fact: As Brené Brown explains, shame is a tool of the oppressor. This shame is wrapped up with the morality of the sins and baked into our culture, invisible to our eyes. I believe envy is at the crux of woman-on-woman conflict, the leashing that pulls us back from expression. It may seem unyielding, but it's a spell we can break: We need to examine the instinct, then unbuckle the col lar and let it fall to the ground. When we shame another woman for dreaming and acting "big," for daring to think she's something special, we oppress our own potential. May we stop reflexively condemning, so that we may birth what we want for ourselves as well.

Accepting envy as essential, we can open the door to every possibility and invite our wanting to enter.

PRIDE

Believing Pride to Be Sinful,
We Deny Our Own Talents

THE SPECTER OF LIKABILITY

"It came true."

Three small, ill-fated words, uttered by Anne Hathaway as she looked down at the Oscar statuette cradled gently in her hands. It was 2013, and she had just won Best Supporting Actress for her turn as Fantine in *Les Misérables.* She then addressed the audience in a trembling voice, carefully thanking and acknowledging a long list of people. She had clearly practiced her speech. For the occasion, she wore a long, pink columnar dress by Prada, which happened to have two darts at the chest, creating the subtle illusion of cone boobs. The wider world couldn't abide these offenses: the earnest acknowledgment of a long-held dream, the suggestion she thought it could happen and prepared for the possibility, and a poor fashion choice. The self-titled "Hathahaters" spun into action, slamming her for being an overly enthusiastic, excited theater dork and "tryhard." It didn't help that the other female winner of the night—Jennifer Lawrence for *Silver Linings Playbook*—tripped on the stairs and laughed it off with the audience before bumbling through her speech, shocked at her win. Lawrence at the beginning of her ascent to stardom was just so funny, "real," unwitting, and lovable, while Hathaway, who was becoming old hat (she'd already been nominated in 2009), expressed in her composed delivery that she'd *known* her dream could come true. She believed in her gifts; the award acknowledged what she already recognized about herself.

After her dress and speech were criticized, Hathaway lamented that she had learned the night before the Oscars that another actress was wearing a similar dress and so made a last-minute swap to avoid being lambasted for *that* faux pas: "I really needed a dress, *and everybody hates me,* and I just really needed a dress." And as for that speech, Hathaway claimed that she was actually miserable about accepting the award—playing Fantine had been depleting and hard and she was still recovering. Instead, she had feigned enthusiasm, and she suggested that for that she deserved to be shamed: "I tried to pretend that I was happy and I got called out on it, big time." Forced contortions to redeem herself for no crime, all in response to a hard-won, crowning achievement. And she continues to contort herself: All these years later, every media appearance for her acting still includes questions about why people hate her. As she tries to shine and share her gifts, she's continually told not to.

Hathaway's downward slide in public opinion had begun a few years earlier, when she was asked to co-host the 2011 Academy Awards with a clearly stoned and smug James Franco. She tried to overcompensate for his not-charming highness by acting, in her words, "slightly manic and hyper cheerleadery." She was panned for being a "chirping," "relentlessly peppy," attention-seeking dork, while the same critic described Franco as a "sleepy-eyed multi-hyphenate." This wasn't the first time a woman had taken the fall for her male co-star's poor judgment during a live performance: Cue Justin Timberlake stripping Janet Jackson at the 2004 Super Bowl, for which *she* alone was censured and ultimately blacklisted by CBS's Les Moonves.* Jackson was slut-shamed and accused of

---

* Fourteen years after "Nipplegate," Les Moonves was forced into retirement from CBS Corporation after multiple allegations of sexual harassment and abuse.

staging a publicity stunt for self-promotion. Meanwhile, *People* called Timberlake the "Teflon man": He didn't take accountability, continued to perform, and complained that his own image had been tarnished. Like Hathaway, Jackson endured endless press about the event, and it derailed her career.

Sadly, we know this cultural cycle well. It's the story of Icarus, the boy who flew too close to the sun: His waxen wings melted and he dropped to his death. His story is a parable about hubristic overreach; it shows what happens to those who fly too high. While the specter of Icarus hasn't prevented men from taking literal moonshots—three billionaires privatized space travel during the pandemic—women seem to have gotten the message to keep their heads down, to lie low. Or the public, it would seem, will lay them low, especially the most visible women of all: famous ones.

Journalist Sady Doyle wrote a book on this topic called *Trainwreck: The Women We Love to Hate, Mock, and Fear . . . and Why*. In it, Doyle presents many case studies of women who succeeded in the public eye and were initially loved and lauded—and were then gunned down for flying too high. As most women have come to understand, our flight plans must be dialed into a perfect trajectory, one that's for the most part below the radar. Otherwise, we're bound for a crash landing, from which we can only *very* occasionally rise from the ashes (#FreeBritney), or perhaps be venerated after our death, like the late Amy Winehouse, Billie Holiday, Princess Diana, or Whitney Houston. Many of the women Doyle discusses as "trainwrecks" are women we once held up as paragons of purity and goodness, and then watched (with glee) as they joined the annals of women deemed slutty, wack, *crazy*, bad.

In 2013, *Star* released their annual "Most Hated Celebrities" list. Of the twenty, only seven were men. *The Cut* collated them into three offenses: Tries Too Hard (all women); Doesn't Try Hard Enough (primarily women); and Crimes Against Other Celebrities (primarily men). This was before #MeToo, so the "crimes" were largely cheating or being mean (e.g., Jay Leno to David Letterman), but the list included notables like Chris Brown, Jesse James, Shia LaBeouf, and Matt Lauer. Not one of the women on the list has ever been accused of actual wrongdoing.

For all the women who were once powerful, accepted by the establishment, and then publicly ousted, the biggest crime they committed was putting themselves out there. They welcomed us all to appraise and adjudicate their talents and gifts, and they basked in our transitory admiration. The public censure they've received is a warning. As Doyle writes, "Women who have succeeded too well at becoming visible have always been penalized vigilantly and forcefully, and turned into spectacles. And this, I would argue, is a none-too-veiled attempt to push women back into the places we've designated as 'theirs.'" The place that's historically been ours is shut away, out of sight, in the home. It's dangerous to cross the threshold, to live a public life, to attempt something significant, to dare to be seen.

Our dislike of strong, visible women—even when our aversion evades our conscious awareness—doesn't reflect views held only by men. Women are right there, willing ignominy on other women's heads (see chapter 3: Envy). It's culture-wide and systemic. Like other women, I know better than to behave big. We must be likable and unthreatening *enough* to ensure everyone else feels comfortable—our power must be cushioned. *Who, me? Don't look at me.* It's an impossible balancing act to parent any young girl to be both strong and universally adored. Strength is partnered with respect; love, with sweetness, obedience, and care. Girls who excel must walk a high wire and still risk banishment and exclusion. My experience of this tempering as a child was the admonition to, above all, be *humble*. Nobody likes a braggart. Nobody likes a show-off. When you win or stand out, be modest, even embarrassed, ideally a little ashamed. Then deflect. A girl who is "full of herself" will have no friends. This idiom, which dates to the 1600s, suggests someone who is so bloated on self-regard, so full of the false and empty calories of self-love, there's no room for anyone or anything else. If you're too full, you can't consume the expectations of what's required to fit into our society either. A girl who is full of herself will be separate, shunned, cast out. She may be "the best," but she will celebrate alone. We are coached, above all, to prioritize our likability as the surest path to safety and survival.

This call to being liked as a woman is coded into all parts of culture, which makes it actually revolutionary when the mandate is rejected. In a conversation with her longtime producing partner, Betsy Beers, legendary television creator Shonda Rhimes explains that for twenty-odd years she's been getting the note: *But can you make this female character more LIKABLE?* "Nobody has ever asked us to make a man more likable . . . and since when is being likable the goal? That's like saying, 'Can you make her more bland? Can she be a little more blah?' Why is likable a thing for women?" Shonda refuses to deliver on the note, shaking an intractable norm. After all, likability offers security within the patriarchy—it means you offer no disturbance to the status quo, you are just getting along with everyone and everything, exactly as it is. Every time Shonda and Betsy refuse the trap of likability, though, when they portray and celebrate complex female characters, they liberate more women off-screen to relax into reality. It's one chip off the patriarchal parapet. But this note that Shonda's been getting from television executives—even in her strong feminist fare—says a lot about how we are expected to perform likability as the way to acceptability, how softness and humility are the ways to win an audience. (Rhimes also rightly bristles at the way critics laud her for writing "strong women"—"I don't know any women who are not strong!"—and points to the fact that we never modify our descriptions of men by appending adjectives like *strong* or *smart*.)

FEELING PROUD OF OURSELVES

The "big-headedness" associated with pride is not a new turn of phrase. When Pope Gregory officially codified the Deadly Sins, he named pride *the* cardinal vice, the "head" one, from which all the others sprang. He deemed pride most terrible because it implied you felt you didn't need God. To be prideful suggested you could do it alone, or thought you had done it—and that you believed you deserved glory reserved only for the Divine. A few centuries earlier, Evagrius Ponticus established a similar sentiment, writing in *Patrikos:* "The demon of pride is the cause of the most damaging fall for the soul. For it induces the monk to deny that God is his helper and to consider that he himself is the cause of virtuous actions. Further, he gets a big head in regard to the brethren, considering them stupid because they do not all have this same opinion of him." Ultimately, pride undermines right relationship—to God and to other men. The irony should not be lost on any of us that today (supposedly) "self-made" men are admired, while women are shamed for taking any credit at all.

And so women don't, working hard while not overtly seeking praise. In the push for power, we have prioritized competence, convinced that effort and excellence are our best path: We raise our hands and speak up only when we're sure of the answer; we keep our heads down and put in the hours at work; we hope to be recognized for our value, rather than needing to state it on the record. This hasn't gotten us particularly far in this capitalist system. We continue to be underrepresented and underpaid (see chapter 2: Sloth). Academics and business-book gurus state a confidence or ambition gap as one of the primary reasons for the inequity, urging women to dig deeper for self-esteem; to raise their voice; to demand promotions, pay increases, and votes. The problem is with us, it would seem, for lacking the confidence to assert our value. But we all know better—or should know better—than to accept blame for our own oppression: We've been well-schooled in what happens to women who go big, who dare to ask for more.

In one frequently cited study, 156 subjects assessed two fictional CEOs—one man, one woman—who both talked a lot, or a little. Participants expected the powerful man to speak up and rewarded him for dominating the conversation, whereas the woman received backlash for talking more than others. Both the male and female respondents judged the female CEO harshly. What's especially troubling, to me, is that women know they'll be penalized for the *performance* of confidence. When I ask friends if they think they have a confidence problem, they assure me they don't: They acknowledge that they know they're better prepared and more competent than most of the men with whom they work; they just know better than to show it.

Reticence to express confidence is borne out in research by Christine Exley and Judd Kessler, who found that even when women knew they performed equally to men, they were loath to profess it: We have been trained not to. *And* it backfires: One study confirmed that women's influence is so pegged to warmth and appearing caring and prosocial that the "performance plus confidence equals power and influence" formula that's so effective for men blows up in women's faces. The study's author concludes: "Self-confidence is gender-neutral, the consequences of appearing self-confident are not." Portraying confidence does not work for women, so telling women to simply *be more confident* is twisted.

Can you recall the last time you heard a woman say she is proud of herself? Proud of her partner, child, co-worker, and friends—sure! But proud of herself? Maybe in the context of finishing a marathon or completing some other physical trial—pride in the *overcoming*—but rarely do you hear a woman give voice to pride in herself for a singular achievement. There are always others to thank—all the people who got her there and are co-responsible for her achievements—instead. When I say I'm proud of myself I almost choke in embarrassment. I'm much more comfortable caveating, minimizing. "I can be proud of myself when . . ." or "It's not a big deal." I've only met expectations. I had supportive parents, a pedigreed education. I have white skin, made a career for myself with brand-name companies, and did so with the added benefit of a financial safety net. In this society engineered for people like me, it feels perverse to take pride in my accomplishments. But should I take no credit?

A few years ago, I interviewed Arlan Hamilton, a Black, queer venture capitalist focused on BIPOC founders. She spent much of her thirties homeless and on food stamps, struggling to lift herself out of poverty. She worked tirelessly, *while homeless,* to raise her first fund,* yet even she chafes at the idea that she is self-made. Being a lone creator is a myth that men cling to readily, but Hamilton maintains that her mother, her brother, her teammates, and the community of friends who bought her meals when she couldn't afford to feed herself all deserve credit too. And in the face of what she has accomplished, despite her unabating modesty, critics are eager to suggest she is full of herself; they are desperate to strike her down. The headline of an *Inc.* magazine article about her reflects that impulse: "The Hype Has Always Been Ahead of Arlan Hamilton, and It Finally Caught Up." (It didn't; she's thriving—and helping other founders of color thrive too.) But Hamilton's caveating makes sense—women must be stealthy on the road to survival and success.

THE ANXIETY OF WINNING AND STANDING OUT

My family is competitive. My brother's husband, Peter, used to joke that my family could turn a restaurant breadbasket into a competition. He would watch us from the sidelines of the dinner table or hiking trail and laugh, shaking his head when we tried to drag him into whatever sport or nonsport we were up to. My parents often

---

* Ninety-eight percent of venture capital money goes to men, according to Crunchbase data. Barf. Not incidentally, the authors of "Male and Female Entrepreneurs Get Asked Different Questions by VCs—and It Affects How Much Funding They Get" in the *Harvard Business Review* evaluated 140 Q&A interactions at TechCrunch Disrupt between VCs and entrepreneurs, writing: "They tended to ask men questions about the potential for gains and women about the potential for losses. We found evidence of this bias with both male and female VCs." They also found that men's funding was seven times women's.

measured "winning" not by trophies but by output—pages read, ski days logged, resolutions kept—to underline that a work ethic was more important than awards. This combo—most excellent, most effortful—confused me. I came to hate playing to win, preferring instead to focus on how much I worked. There was humility and virtue in trying hard—glory, on the other hand, made me uncomfortable. And my parents confirmed this. While I'm pretty sure they were proud of me and my ribbons, they were loath to tell me this, for fear "I would get a big head." This was the refrain I had on repeat as I trained, studied, excelled. As I got older, when things got intense close to victory, I was not steely. I often folded and imploded. I self-sabotaged. But I also, more frequently, did win, despite my deep discomfort. I knew how to do my best, to work hard, to train my body and my mind, to prove my worthiness through performance, to be impeccable. This did pay off with trophies.

I competed at a lot of endeavors—tennis, swimming, horseback riding, math. I prevailed most dramatically in mogul skiing, for which I was ranked first in the country when I was ten.* I am a great skier. Even writing that, I want to equivocate and say "very good." I'm precise with every turn, legs pinned together, fast, and likely to take the fall line straight to the bottom. I spent more time skiing than doing anything else. I went to the mountain, a family-owned two-lift operation just up the road from our house, ninety days a year—both weekend days, half-day Wednesdays, every available hour of my holiday breaks. And when I got off the chairlift, I worked: Turn, turn, turn. Repeat. I skied by myself often, training to keep myself company, training to not feel awkward when I ate in the lodge alone. I went to ski camp in the summers. I did my dry

---

* Without irony, my dad cautioned me when he read a draft of this chapter that perhaps I was overstating my achievements, and was I first in the country, or only in the region? (I was first in the country when I was ten, at a time when there were admittedly few girls in the sport—the rankings were assembled through meet points, not direct competition. I probably accrued more points because I had less competition in the Northwest.) See what we're doing here?

land training. Before I went to boarding school when I was fifteen, I had a choice: try to make the national team, or head east for a better education. Perhaps I could have made it all the way to the Olympics, but my body decided for me. My hip flexor started snapping back and forth over my hip bone, and I ended up pulling myself out of the Nationals competition the first year I made it that far. I was in pain and unhappy, far from having fun. The moguls were huge and pounding. I went home in relief, grateful for the out. My body said no because my throat wouldn't open to say it for me.

Kate Fagan, an author, former WBNA player, and ESPN commentator, grew up with a dad who played professional basketball and recently passed away from ALS. She wrote a love-letter memoir about him that is a study in the way Fagan and her father crafted their relationship over decades on the court—a relationship complicated over time by puberty, her desire for space and independence, her anxiety about coming out of the closet, and her increasing dissatisfaction with the game. Kate, who no longer plays, even for fun, was a great basketball player, but despite her prowess, her dad insisted she downplay her skill. She writes, "One of my dad's core life philosophies was: Don't tell people you're good; let them figure it out for themselves. . . . Even at a young age, I recognized bragging of any kind as an unattractive quality." For Fagan, basketball was her primary early identity, and I wondered if her burnout and disavowal could in some way be attributed to the fact that she was shamed from exulting in her talent, from celebrating herself, even just a little. There's a certain amount of terror that comes with the spotlight, I've found. It dulls the joy.

I have come back to skiing as an adult, prioritizing it for myself and my children. And I've found pleasure in it again, with no one to mark my form, my flailing airs, my time to the bottom. But it still makes me uncomfortable when people notice my skiing. I will stand and wait, tempting my frostbitten toes to freeze over, until other skiers are out of the frame of my goggles. This is conflicting:

I want to be recognized as a good skier because it's probably the thing I do best, and at the same time I can hear my dad in my ear warning me about the size of my head. I remember one family ski trip to Jackson Hole. It was foggy and I was about ten and bombing down Toilet Bowl, famous for its minicliffs, when I accidentally flew straight off one. I was fine, I landed in soft powder, but my parents, though laughing and relieved to find me intact on the other side, reminded me that that's what happens to show-offs: You plunge to your death, Icarus-style.

As a child, I skied almost exclusively with boys, their quiet shadow as they did everything possible to draw attention to their prowess—360s off roads under the chair, whooping, chasing each other to the point of recklessness. The boys never refrained from beating their chests, unrepentantly pulling eyes to their skills. I don't recall anyone admonishing them for showing off, maybe just yelling after them to slow down, as they could have easily killed an erstwhile snow-plower who veered into their path. I loved being in the company of the boys. They pushed me to be better, dragging me under ropes, through the trees, and sometimes over cliffs—and they also created the camouflage in which I could conceal myself, easy with my short hair. They were all faster and stronger than me. I worked to keep up—and accordingly, I was unthreatening, a kind of pet. We also never directly competed against each other. There was freedom there—and so much more joy.

My parents were not wrong to feel anxious that my success would go to my head, because then, in the eyes of society, I would become intolerable, unlikable, alienated from the other girls. This teaching—be excellent, but be unseen, don't reach for credit or attention—followed me throughout my life. It was reflected by a culture obsessed with "scouting," the prevailing idea that a talent agent who knows best would discover you, pluck you out of obscurity. Cultural stories abound with tales of being spotted in suburban malls or in the wild: Rosario Dawson sitting on a stoop, Kate Moss on a plane, Cindy Crawford shucking corn at a farm stand in

Illinois. The idea that in the meritocracy of America talent naturally rises trained us into passivity. If you build it, they will come; if you've got it, you'll be found. To push for attention or avowal is unseemly at best.

I was recently chatting with a near-Olympian, the last woman cut from a team that went on to win gold in Tokyo. Though they'd all been training together for three years, she had heard from only one team member and none of the coaches after being clipped. As we watched a bunch of kids play softball one night, she told me the story beneath the story. Yes, she felt a little hurt her teammates hadn't called, but she felt more betrayed by herself. She had bought into the fantasy that team trumps all, that personal ambition should come second to the glory of what you achieve together.

"I have more steely resolve for next time," she offered. "I will be more self-driven and focus on being my best instead of focusing so much on everyone else's happiness and how people perceive me." She then retracted: "But I will of course keep my team and my teammates in mind." We sat in silence for a while before she continued. "God, it's funny to think about. In female sports, we get uncomfortable talking about ourselves and *always* bring it back to the team, no matter what. Coaches always tell us to respond to the media by bringing it back to the team. Always bring it back to the team. I have no clue if they do that to the men."

As she worked through her ambivalence in front of me, there was sadness in the revelation and a little bit of anger. Though she seemed resolved to prioritize her own desire to prevail, *to win for herself,* she acknowledged that even saying that felt shameful. "I know I can't win without the team." Yes, and she can't win if she's not on the team. That's the game sometimes, that is part of life, even as we instruct women that it's not. Instead of being coached to use competition as a whetstone for our desires, as a mechanism for sometimes winning and someone losing but *always trying,* we are implicitly told by the cultural narrative that if you can't sublimate your own desire to the greater good, it's better to sit it out;

then you don't have to take something from someone else or feel anger at them for snatching it from you. When we see someone achieve what we want for ourselves, heckle each other for hubris, or cover each other with shame for daring to prevail, it keeps many of us from stepping onto the field at all.

THE DESIRE TO BE SEEN

My good friend Jane appears almost daily on morning TV. Naturally vivacious and infectiously appealing, she's been the face and talking head for many magazines. America loves her. But as comfortable and practiced as she should be with the spotlight, Jane can't hold a compliment—the deflection is so intense you'll be in the middle of expressing adoration when she'll push it back on you.

"You look great, Ja—"

"*No, you* are so pretty!"

One night when I was visiting New York, we stayed out late at a restaurant overlooking Central Park, lingering long after other diners had gone home. I pushed her to explain her anxiety about attention when she's so fun to watch and so worthy of our interest. And she gets booked on TV *all the time*! She acknowledged that producers call her back every week, then caveated, "I make it easy for them!" (That's not why.) When I asked her why it's so hard for her to acknowledge her own talent, she thought for a minute and then offered that she had been a child actor/model when she was young and had booked some ads. Jane's burgeoning stardom created a tremendous amount of unease for her mother, who warned her not to make her sister or the other girls in her class feel bad. Jane internalized this lesson so thoroughly that she became perceptibly ashamed about who she naturally is. There's no joy or validation in the attention—instead, she spends an inordinate amount of energy trying to show the world she doesn't think she's "all that." It's a loss for all of us: It's a waste of Jane's time to dim her own light, and we lose a public example of someone celebrating her own gifts. I want her to be *proud of herself.* But I also understand her inclination to keep her head down low—so it doesn't get chopped off. Her compliment deflection and refusal to accept praise are ways we know how to simultaneously shine and survive. I understand this, because I'm scared to be seen too. Most of us are.

I entered the job market as an editorial assistant at *Lucky* magazine—doing assistant-level things like packing and shipping samples, writing small uncredited blurbs for the pages, and then editing and writing multipage sections. But I would never have dared to call myself a writer—even though that's what I was doing, and I was a published one at that! I started ghostwriting books for celebrities and other "experts" as a side hustle. The extra cash was essential to my survival in New York City, but I also felt comfortable being the voice for someone else, as if I wasn't a faker because I was taking no credit. I was eagerly pointing to the public reach of the people for whom I wrote, their capacity to spread ideas that I could not. Why not write for someone with a platform? I knew words flowed out of me, yet there was safety in filtering them through the "authority" of others and then standing offstage, tucked into the side curtains, to see how it all might land. I've ghostwritten or co-written a dozen books, and I don't care whether I'm even acknowledged in the back. It feels safe to let words pass through me without ego, to be detached from outcome, to feel unjudgeable, untraceable, unseen.

In all of my jobs, I've been thrilled to hide behind the brands and their famous founders. I've reveled in anonymity. But in my last role, when we launched a podcast, I came out of hiding; and when we did a Netflix show I became visible, and not just a ghost whispering in people's ears. Anxiety gripped my throat in the months before the show premiered, not because I didn't think it was a good series, but because I was terrified of handing over my invisibility cloak. I recognized that I would become fodder for critics and internet trolls, that by being seen I could easily be destroyed. And my parents reconfirmed for me that I was right to be afraid, simply by not acknowledging it was happening. At one point, maybe after I was in *The New York Times* or *The Wall Street Journal,* my dad texted me, teasing but with a spear-like point: "With all of this attention, are you going to get a big head?" And then, on the day the TV show aired, nothing. My parents didn't comment. Either they didn't think it was a big deal, or they didn't want *me* to think it was a big deal. (Option 3: They were terrified to watch me get eaten by the wolves, to watch my big head get lopped off, so they manufactured amnesia.)

It is perhaps no accident that the day the Netflix show came out is the same day I interviewed the psychologist Craig Malkin, an expert in narcissism. We all know the story of Narcissus, the boy who fell in love with his own reflection in a spring—so entranced by his own beauty, he pined away and died. We hear less about Echo, the wood nymph who fell in love with Narcissus. Echo's unflagging desire to give herself over to him meant she was cursed to live her life without a voice of her own, echoing only other people's thoughts. Narcissus and Echo have come to represent two ends of a cultural spectrum: those who are dangerously self-obsessed and those who are completely self-negating.

Official narcissistic personality disorder, which requires a medical diagnosis, is typified by grandiosity, a need for admiration, a sense of entitlement, a tendency to monopolize and dominate conversations, sensitivity to any criticism, and other similar factors. It sounds an awful lot like Evagrius Ponticus's description of pride. It's interesting that while women are damned for an inflated sense of self, there's no penalty for men—you can even be president.*

Malkin's practice focuses primarily on echoists, or those with a

---

* According to Columbia Business School professor Ernesto Reuben, who coined the term *honest overconfidence,* men benefit from self-aggrandizement, particularly when it comes to recruiting and promotions. When MBA students were asked to recall their past performance, "men consistently rated their past performance about 30 percent higher than it really was."

lack of healthy narcissism, a term he did not coin but did popularize. Unsurprisingly, more women than men struggle with echoism. As Malkin explained to me, "Echoists live by the rule: The less room I take up, the better. They are afraid of being a burden. And in our research, what we found is that the *core defining feature was a fear of seeming narcissistic in any way.*" And then Malkin went more directly to the point: "People end up conflating pride with arrogance, right? And they punish or they shame moments of pride, particularly in girls, but also in boys. But when those normal feelings of pride are shamed, people cut them out, they cut off from them, and they learn to connect by leaving pride out entirely. That is a recipe for echoism right there." Malkin's description reminds me of my friend Jane, and of so many women I know: We are so afraid of being perceived as prideful that it limits our full self-expression—and sometimes any self-expression at all. Malkin works with his patients to get them to the middle point between echoism and narcissism in a zone called "healthy narcissism." Feeling pride is an essential and important component of healthy self-esteem: It suggests that you recognize your gifts, your specialness, your uniqueness, and that you feel empowered to use your talents in the world.

Malkin and his peers in the field of self-esteem and psychology believe these feelings of specialness—whether justified or wishful thinking—are not only positive but essential. Malkin notes, "For the past twenty-five years, psychologists have compiled massive amounts of evidence that most people seem convinced they're better than almost everyone else on the planet. This wealth of research can only lead us to one inevitable conclusion: The desire to feel special isn't a state of mind reserved for arrogant jerks or sociopaths." Humans need to feel special, even if we only feel safe enough to admit our specialness to ourselves.

But what if it's more than that? What if this feeling of specialness—what if pride—is an imperative of humanity? What if it's the point of it all? We desire equality: equal rights, equal opportunities, equal funding for schools. And those are admirable, critical goals. But we must recognize that we are not all the same: We each have our own design, makeup, talents, and gifts. We are each here to contribute, do our share, give and receive. These are our egoic qualities, nothing to shame. Is our ego not what gives us our sentience and our distinction as animals that can understand and give breath to "I am"? The ego—as a hallmark of unique identity and purpose—encompasses the self. It must express. When I sat with Malkin, the day I found myself exposed to an audience of millions on Netflix, it would have been helpful to hear from my parents: that they were proud of me for being brave and letting myself be seen, that come what may, it was more important to use my gifts than to hide away. In an ideal world, I would have been able to give that assurance to myself. But that's also the point: Our talents are significant insomuch as they touch other people and serve their needs. It's a call and response. We all are, whether we like it or not, one collective. The ego as a point of distinction is essential, because it's what makes us a global community of humans, not an efficient hive of honeybees. Women are primed to serve the whole—it's how we're conditioned. Our ultimate survival as a species revolves around the imperative that women bring their gifts to bear—in every sphere. And that they're echoed back to us.

HOW WE COME TO UNDERSTAND OUR SPECIALNESS

The problem with specialness comes when we wield it as a tool of oppression or dominance—better than, superior to. The distinctness itself is not the problem. Our true self, that tiny seed of potential, needs to be shielded, protected, and nurtured from birth so that it can stay a little wild and natural. The problem with ego or self comes when we let it become an illusion, divorced from the reality of who we are. Ego becomes an issue when it surges toward primacy and dominance rather than communion and co-creation.

After all, we are not intended to all be good at the same things; this is the biodiversity of humanity. And just as the trees and the fungi have a codependent and complex relationship—one reaching its branches toward the sky, the other extending its mycelium network below the surface of the soil—who is to judge which contribution is more essential or important?

Our instincts urge us to leave our mark, burn our legacy into the world, make our impermanent lives permanent. The divinity in each of us yearns to be seen, acknowledged, ratified, and passed down. As Malkin writes, "Slightly outsized ego has its benefits. In fact, numerous studies have found that people who see themselves as better than average are happier, more sociable, and often more physically healthy than their humbler peers. The swagger in their step is associated with a host of positive qualities, including creativity, leadership, and high self-esteem, which can propel success at work. Their rosy self-image imbues them with confidence and helps them endure hardship, even after devastating failure or horrific loss." This is healthy narcissism. It's where we feel engaged, feel appropriately appreciated, and see how our presence *matters*. This faith in our own specialness is critical so that we stay attuned to doing and being better. It's essential for us to believe that we can improve the world, that we can overcome hurdles that often feel overwhelming.

Healthy narcissism, or healthy ego, is different from self-esteem, though the concepts are often conflated. Like all concepts of "self," they are slippery—and ultimately barely cousins. After all, extreme narcissists tend to be saddled with low self-esteem—the grandiosity and swagger is what papier-mâchés over feelings of inadequacy and self-doubt.* An instinct to barricade oneself against reality is learned

---

* In his 2021 book, *Us,* therapist Terry Real caveats against this as a blanket assessment, writing, "Research shows that about half of all people classed as narcissistic are driven by inward shame. The other half simply think that they are better than everyone else. Grandiose traits of superiority may be an escape from feelings of inadequacy, but they may also simply be the legacy of false empowerment."

in childhood, typically planted by parents who are *also* narcissists and not capable of holding a mirror for their kids to behold themselves accurately. Instead, the kid becomes a screen for the projections and expectations of the parent. On the other side of the scale, echoism results when nobody sees you—when you are paired with an abusive parent or when your version of reality is too uncomfortable to be held. It is perhaps one of the most foundational wounds of childhood if your parents, the first people you idolize and revere, do not see or celebrate your true self. As toddlers and then young children, we rely on our parents to give us a grounded accounting of who we are, to help us make sense of our essence before we're able to. It doesn't get us all the way to our final identity, but it's a fundamental first step. As Malkin explains, "Young children only feel like they matter—only feel like they *exist*—when their parents make them feel special. Parents who pay attention to their children's inner lives—their hopes and dreams, their sadness and fears, and most of all their need for admiration—provide the 'mirroring' necessary for the child to develop a healthy sense of self."

My parents did a great job—truly, well done—though as with everyone I know, you can get a lot from your parents and still not get everything you need. Like many others, my parents were preoccupied, busy, opposed to "spoiling" us with attention, being too interested in what we were up to, or celebrating what we had achieved. My parents were not wrong to prepare us for a world that would not reverberate with constant and consistent admiration, but as a child you need validation. You will look wherever you can to find assurances you're OK, and you'll figure out what you need to do to get love, to feel secure attachment. I have close loved ones who had the opposite experience—who were gaslit about their excellence, the high quality of their writing, the exquisiteness of their art, what they must be feeling. "You're great, honey. Everything is wonderful, honey. There's nothing wrong, honey." It's not that this hot air set my friends up to fail when they emerged into the real world and discovered they weren't necessarily as talented as they'd been led to believe—it seems, though, to have undermined their ability to trust their own reality. As children, we know: We know when our painting of an apple looks like a sad turd; we know when we're sad, or scared, or lonely—and to be told that's not true is at best confusing. At worst, it means you lose faith in yourself to know yourself. We crave accuracy of assessment—we want our perception of ourselves in the world to be in lockstep with how we're perceived by the world.

For many of the women I know, it feels safer and more secure to be underestimated, overlooked, and not valorized in any way. I don't think we minimize ourselves because we're naturally afraid of pressure; I think it's because we've been coached to lead with our worst qualities or to undermine ourselves through caveats: "This may be a stupid question, but . . . ," "I'm *just* wondering . . . ," "Sorry if you've thought of this before . . . ," "I could be wrong, but . . ." We also rush to point out all our potential shortcomings to others before they're pointed out on our behalf. After all, you can't hurt us when we've hurt ourselves first.

We find safety and security in not believing in ourselves—not only because there's a world that tells us we shouldn't but also because there's less to lose this way. So we remain tight and confined, even slapping down other women who attempt to rise. How dare she, we think, when I am down here, in a defensive crouch?

THE TRUE SELF VERSUS THE ILLUSION SELF

When we "cut off those normal feelings of pride," we create a separate self. We bury those parts of ourselves that feel more tender and true, and we choose the safe version instead, the one that's distinct from who we really are. This instinct was brought home to me in October 2020, when I sat in a convention center in Utah on a weeklong journey with sixty other seekers. We were there to listen to a full-body channel for Yeshua (yes, Jesus), named Carissa

Schumacher, and a full-body channel for Mother Mary, named Danielle Gibbons, as they led us through a series of talks and meditations about the true self versus the "illusion self," or the self we create as a projection.* At that point, I had spent seven years of my life on these sorts of work-sponsored missions, trying *everything*. Still, this week was something different; it offered a series of wholly new and wholly profound revelations. On the second day, Carissa spoke at length about the illusion self, the space most of us occupy, where we spend most of our days. We do this unconsciously, acting out of a deep belief or understanding that living apart from who we really are will prevent our authentic selves from getting hurt. It is the perch of hypervigilance, a shield against the presumption of pain, rejection, and not getting our needs met. As Carissa said, "As children, many of us had to leave our true selves because it was not safe. Naturally, the child assumed an identity based on what it saw was 'safe.'"

In short, we will do almost anything to avoid embracing the reality of who we are, if only because getting still, looking inward, and sitting with ourselves is so much harder than letting others do the defining for us. As Carissa explained, "Your service is to be *just as you are*, fully seen and held *by yourself.*" In that process, we are asked to put down the armor of the illusion self—armor that protects us from exactly nothing—and assume the divine armor of our authentic self instead. It requires a deep act of faith and vulnerability, but it is the narrow gate to freedom and joy.

We need to find a way to rest easy within ourselves—to show ourselves exactly who we are and celebrate that. By embracing our true selves, we can better support other women as they celebrate themselves too. And perhaps for our children, we can find the way to be the doulas of their purpose, rather than the foretellers of how they need to conform themselves to society for the assurance of

---

* In a way, it was an echo of the anthropologist Ashley Montagu's version of first self (biology) and second self (culture).

safety. How nice it would be to exist in a system where we value people not by how well they fit in but by what they uniquely contribute, how accurately they achieve the work of being who they are meant to be. As Carissa explained: "The less you need to be to the world, the more you can be to yourself." Sit with that for a minute, particularly fellow women who feel that their value is mediated by whether they're *doing,* and therefore *being,* enough to the wider world. What if we each gave to ourselves first? What if we learned to love ourselves before turning to love others? What if we came to know and embrace ourselves so we could feel more secure in offering those gifts to the world? What if instead of begrudging other women for reveling in their uniqueness, we held up the mirror for them instead? What if instead of "Am I worthy?" we learned, "I give, and in turn, I receive"? It would be remarkable if we could behold and celebrate our specialness without the accompanying wash of shame that seems to follow any gestures of self-love. I was designed to be me. You were designed to be you. It is a betrayal of self to live out someone else's destiny. We need to surrender to who we are and not who we think we should be. By skirting the insinuations of being "prideful," by hiding ourselves from the world, we've missed out on discovering true self-knowledge.

DISCOVERING AND SHEPHERDING OUR UNIQUE GIFTS

Because of our inclination to think in linear ways, always reaching for more, we've forgotten that life comes in cycles and seasons, not ranked and hierarchically ordered, as the patriarchy would have us believe. Sure, nature has its food chain, but it is determined in the wild by strength *in the moment* and not by a system of oppression where power is hoarded and wielded according to arbitrary law. In the natural world, the ecosystem comes into balance—and some plants and animals give their lives to ensure it. Poet and biologist Robin Wall Kimmerer goes deep into the cycle of reciprocity according to a Native American framework in her bestselling book *Braiding Sweetgrass.* One example she gives is the Three Sisters— corn, beans, squash—and why Indigenous communities planted them, not in discrete, manicured, and monocrop rows, but always bundled together. In this way, each plant ensured the other two sisters could get their needs met; together they flourished. The corn provides the scaffolding; the "curious" bean meanders in many different directions but cannot overwhelm the space the corn has marked for herself. The squash provides shade and a microclimate with her big leaves. The soil thrives, ensuring a healthy environment for the next season.

While we love stories of self-reliance and personal responsibility and have siloed ourselves away from our proverbial—and literal— sisters in our own homes, on our own private property, there is a lesson here for all of us. It lives in our individual and communal indebtedness for the gifts of the planet and in our profound reliance on each other. The mechanism behind the cycle of reciprocity is to recognize and employ our individual talents to serve the collective whole. As Kimmerer writes, "The way of the Three Sisters reminds me of one of the basic teachings of our people. The most important thing each of us can know is our unique gift and how to use it in the world. . . . Being among the sisters provides a visible manifestation of what a community can become when its members understand and share their gifts." We need pride in our unique talents to deliver them to the world; when we feel shame in developing our powers, they die on the vine.

Our culture does not seem to understand this. Rather than reveling in cultural sisterhood, we pay endless tribute to male alpha dogs. We love men who are leaders, winners, first-place finishers— we herald those who prevail visibly, regardless of what they might have done to get there. We are eager to place our faith in systems and their figureheads, in those who seem to be arbiters of their power—presidents, priests, professors. We often disown our own agency in the process. We let others tell us how to be, we let them dictate our value, we adhere to what they say, regardless of its resonance in our hearts. In her bestselling book *Caste*, Pulitzer Prize–winning journalist Isabel Wilkerson talks about the science of wolf packs and our misunderstanding of what keeps the dogs together: She discovered that while the alpha gets the attention and acclaim, it's the omega who functions as the group's heartbeat, the most essential canine, the most mourned when lost. This indicates to me that our obsession with the ones who stand in front means we miss the gifts of everyone else—we're failing to recognize how the work gets done, who does it, and the essential role every one of us plays.

Everyone's part is critical: We cannot afford for women to stand back. We need their leadership, their wisdom, their understanding of the whole. I recently met with CNBC reporter Julia Boorstin and Jasmina Aganovic, a young female founder/CEO. Jasmina, an MIT grad with one successful company already behind her, was confessing her imposter syndrome, even though she had just finished a massive Series A fundraise in the beauty biotech space. Boorstin, who has profiled most of the women who are global leaders in business, advised her to look at the research of cognitive psychologist Therese Huston, who suggests that the best leaders are able to modulate their confidence: They dial it down when they need to take in information and consider other perspectives, and then, when they move into making and executing a decision, they dial it back up. Boorstin, who wrote a book called *When Women Lead,* about the superlative leadership skills of women, believes that confidence modulation is one of the reasons women-led companies deliver results. As Boorstin writes, "Exaggerated self-confidence often stood in the way of rational decisions," continuing, "Male CEOs scored higher on typical measures of CEO confidence, whereas female leaders were found to be more accurate in assessing their own abilities and were much more sensitive to different types of feedback. There's also evidence that when faced with negative news and in anticipation of negative outcomes, women respond more decisively than men." Jasmina was visibly comforted by this news that her best chance at business success was to be herself, rather than assuming the mantle of a more assertive, masculine persona.

After all, women are much better at listening to other people, acknowledging what they don't know, and not interrupting. When it comes to the sin of pride and what might be a more appropriate representation, I turn to the idiomatic expression "swallowing your pride." The saying suggests you should move from a position of certainty to one of not knowing, in which you can apologize for getting something wrong and acknowledge that in relation to someone else maybe you didn't get it perfectly right. There is certainly wisdom there, particularly when it comes to fixity of belief, or anytime any of us cling to certainty. "I don't know" and "I was wrong" are powerful mantras. Like most of the women I know, I look forward to the day when we are led by people—male or female—who are balanced in their self-regard, who prioritize preparation, question asking, listening, and the power of community rather than the "rugged individualism" that is the mark of so many narcissistic and grandiose men. In our patriarchal society, the behavior of (white) men is perceived as normal, while anything else is deviant: I chafe against the idea of pushing girls and women to behave more like men. Society should evolve to normalize itself and balance against qualities of the feminine, to prioritize and reward collaboration, hard work, and care with as much ardor as it supports "honest overconfidence."

In our desire to adulate only the most visible leaders, we often overlook the people who matter most in our lives. Aren't they ourselves and our neighbors, the mayor, the teachers at our children's school, the people who work alongside us? Whom would we miss the most: the person who collects the garbage from the curb, the person who harvests the summer crops, or the CEO down the street? It's no mystery who has a greater impact on our collective health and well-being. Prioritizing the wrong roles and functions, we avoid the question of when we will take our agency and autonomy back and when we will begin to study the ripples that extend from the pebbles we, ourselves, throw. We cannot deny our participation in the ecosystem, our varied roles as cogs that move the wheel of life around. It's imperative that we lean into what makes us special, what makes us unique. Not to sound like your preschool teacher, but this is the point of it all, that we each show up for our part. The call is distinct for each of us, beckoning us forward into a role predesigned for us. It is a denial of source, or the universe, when we try to be something *less* than what we are.

THE ROOTS OF HUMILITY

My therapist told me that women bring Glennon Doyle's bestselling book *Untamed* to their sessions and read earmarked sections out loud to him. It's a book of deep resonance, speaking truths we did not quite know how to articulate before Glennon gave us the language. When I met Glennon, she told the story, which she recounts in the book, of meeting Oprah for the first time, where she minimized the response to her writing, downplaying its impact. In response, Oprah said: "Playing dumb, weak, and silly is a disservice to yourself and to me and to the world. Every time you pretend to be less than you are, you steal permission from other women to exist fully. Don't mistake modesty for humility."

That mistake sounds familiar: Few women understand how to thread this needle. Not many of us hit the "healthy narcissism" target, the Goldilocks zone of proper and accurate self-regard. We don't know what we can take credit for and what belongs to our genetic ancestors, our mentors, the universe—what's us, and what's the result of our upbringing, our luck, our privilege, our opportunity. It's a cycle too. Just as our parents didn't always know how to hold our hands with steadiness while we figured out who we are, they can hardly be blamed. Most likely, nobody held their hand either. It's hard to give someone the path to self when you're also lost in the woods. Just as we cannot leave others to define us, value us, grade us, and validate us, we cannot look to other people and conditions of society to be responsible for our happiness.

I think back to those early admonishments from my dad to be humble at all costs. He wasn't wrong, per se, but I think the tweak I'd give it would be to not marry my ability to achieve to the assumption that it would make me arrogant. He was telling me not to become something before I had the chance to even try. That if I felt I was "done" or had crossed some sort of finish line, I was wrong to stop going. He put me in a double bind: be impeccable, be of service, maximize your potential—and don't feel proud. He cut me off with a danger sign, made me feel as if expanding further into self-expression would surely lead to my destruction. He cautioned me by preemptively shaming me, so the shame wouldn't instead be at the hands of someone who didn't love me.

Glennon writes in *Untamed,* "The word humility derives from the Latin word *humilitas,* which means 'of the earth.' To be humble is to be grounded in knowing who you are. It implies the responsibility to become what you were meant to become—to grow, to reach, to fully bloom as high and strong and grand as you were created to. It is not honorable for a tree to wilt and shrink and disappear. It's not honorable for a woman to, either." Humility doesn't mean hiding in the side curtains, it just means you should keep your feet planted while you reach for the sky. Your gifts, after all, belong to the earth: humility, humus, the soil beneath our feet. Robin Wall Kimmerer takes her students out into the field so they experience nature and the fecundity of its offerings, the lavishness with which the earth provides. She notes of her young protégés: "The gifts they might return to the cattails are as diverse as those the cattails gave them. This is our work, to discover what we can give. Isn't this the purpose of education, to learn the nature of your own gifts and how to use them for good in the world?" Wouldn't we all hope.

We frequently hear what the world might look like if women

unleashed their potential, their full creative powers. What might happen if each one of us wielded our gifts and supported every other woman in the deliverance of hers as well? It seems as if we could create a more perfect, more integrated and whole world. We know and feel this promise. In 1992, Marianne Williamson presaged Oprah's advice to Glennon Doyle, writing: "Our deepest fear is not that we are inadequate. Our deepest fear is that we are powerful beyond measure. It is our light, not our darkness that most frightens us. We ask ourselves, 'Who am I to be brilliant, gorgeous, talented, fabulous?' Actually, who are you not to be? You are a child of God. Your playing small does not serve the world. . . . As we let our own light shine, we unconsciously give other people permission to do the same. As we are liberated from our own fear, our presence automatically liberates others."

I believe the antidote to fear is faith. It's a belief in something greater, some system of alignment that asks us to balance the wonders of the natural world with the unleashing of our own divinity. We were designed for balance, for reciprocity, for a bountiful give-and-take. This is deeply personal work. It is not systems work, structural work, or work that we can do for each other. This isn't work that can be done for us by elected officials, or CEOs, or community leaders. It can't be done for us by our mothers, fathers, sisters, or brothers. I cannot liberate you; you cannot liberate me. But if you liberate yourself, perhaps I can model my freedom after yours. We can show each other what it would look like to live in a state of loving ourselves, celebrating ourselves, living in service of purpose, and delivering on our own unique prophecy, fully bringing ourselves to the world in pride.

---

*Accepting pride as essential, we can
develop and embrace our unique gifts.*

GLUTTONY

Believing Gluttony to Be Sinful,
We Deny Our Own Hunger

WHAT WE THINK WE CAN CONTROL

My parents met at the Mayo Clinic in Rochester, Minnesota. My dad was a dashing South African Jew completing his pulmonology residency; my mom, a striking, short-haired nurse in the psych ward. A story as old as time. When they married, they tried to solve two common marital plagues in one swoop: They would each get the same annual allowance, to spend as they pleased, without censure or commentary. To earn it, they weighed themselves every January and needed to be within five pounds of their thirty-year-old baseline. This idea was my dad's, unusual for a man—I don't know many men who police their bodies in this way. In his practice, he described patients slipping into obesity as a surprise attack. His patients experienced a weight creep so subtle, suddenly they were fifty pounds overweight and overwhelmed by the prospect of trying to lose it. My dad was determined to stay active into old age.

These weigh-ins have worked for my parents—in their seventies, they are, compared to most Americans, fit and active. But my dad's preoccupation with weight created a sniper-like vigilance in our home, made all the more frustrating by the fact that my father is one of those people who can, and does, eat whatever he wants. Despite his five-foot-eight, 150-pound frame, his friends call him "Bubba," because of what appears to be an elastic gut. He's like Pac-Man, a human trash compactor—always looking for a snack, a piece of fruit, a go at whatever is left on everyone's plate. His most irritating maneuver is to abstain when dessert menus are passed, only to ambush anyone who does order something with his hovering fork and hoovering mouth. He is, ironically, the glutton in our midst, the one with little self-control but the blessing of a big metabolism. My mom, meanwhile, maintains her weight by vacillating between indulgence and restriction. Long before intermittent fasting became a thing, my mom was working it as a way of life, just in reverse: a full-fat latte and cinnamon roll for breakfast, followed by abstention.

Despite his lack of struggle, or perhaps *because* of his lack of struggle, my dad is judgmental about fat* people, not understanding that for most of us, weight maintenance requires effort, and often deprivation. My dad has no understanding of what it's like to engage with food as a normal person—or as a woman. I have friends who say that if they smell a pastry they'll put on a pound; as I age, I'm becoming one of them. In my father's defense, the five hours of medical education on nutrition he received five decades ago—even at Mayo—has been outdated for some time. My dad, like

---

* I'm using *fat* here per the instructions of Aubrey Gordon, @yrfatfriend on Instagram, host of the *Maintenance Phase* podcast, and author of *What We Don't Talk About When We Talk About Fat.* She writes that *fat* is "a neutral descriptor for predominantly plus-size people. While *fat* is frequently used to insult people of all sizes, many fat activists—those of us who are undeniably, indubitably fat by any measure—reclaim the term as an objective adjective to describe our bodies, like tall or short. . . . Fat stands in contrast to an endless parade of euphemisms—*fluffy, curvy, big guy, big girl, zaftig, big boned, husky, voluptuous, thick, heavy set, pleasantly plump, chubby, cuddly, more to love, overweight, obese*—all of which just serve as a reminder of how terrified so many thin people are to see our bodies, name them, have them." Gordon explains that the term *obese,* which I do use in this book because it is still the prevailing medical term, is felt by some fat activists to be a slur. (Its etymology is Latin for "having eaten oneself fat.") Similarly, describing people as overweight is deemed problematic by fat activists because it suggests that there is one normal weight and everyone else is deviant.

most people today, assumed fat people were miscounting, over-loading their plates, sneaking candy bars and French fries while sleepwalking. He attributed their heaviness to nutritional illiteracy, lack of self-control, and a refusal to exercise (you know, gluttony and sloth).

My dad's is the typical medical view—fatphobic, certainly—and now we are learning where we've oversimplified and where we've been wrong. We've overlooked how individual each body is. It's funny we assume we have as much control as we do when we're helpless over our skin color, our eye color, the gradients in our hair, our height, the size of our feet, the scope of our private parts. When babies are born and measured on the CDC's growth curve charts for weight and height, we don't insist that all infants track the same—in fact, the singular expectation at every weigh-in is that they stay on their own curve.

The variance shows up on a chemical level too, as we can't even control how we react to pharmaceuticals, often presented as pana-ceas. For some a drug might be effective, while for others it might be a dud. Side effects are always a mixed bag. Despite the looseness of the reins we hold on our health, we've been convinced that we should have dominion over the scale, that, like alchemists, we can each turn matter into matter in a reliable way, we can make our parts grow or disappear on command. If we don't look the way society would prefer, it's our fault: We've failed at some essential mandate, to please and conform, to express our goodness through obedience to expectations of our size. Yes, something alarming is happening to us collectively as we continue to expand—but it's not as simple as we've been led to believe.

OUR FAT-PHOBIC CULTURE

Culturally we despise fat people. Fat-phobia is the last bastion of acceptable bias, disguised in the morality of health. Our rejection of large bodies continues even as the body positivity movement has taken hold. Body positivity does not translate to fat acceptance, according to the famous Harvard University implicit bias test. Analyzing data from 2007 to 2017, researchers documented that explicit antifat bias changed the slowest of all stated attitudes, while implicit bias—of the six that they evaluated—got worse. This finding doesn't surprise me. I've spent most of my professional life working at women's magazines and within the wellness industry—where I acknowledge and admit that I participated in promoting unrealistic body size. Whenever we published a story that challenged the idea that obesity is a reliable measure of health (it's not always), I would get blown up on social media by women who felt that by suggesting thinness shouldn't be the ultimate goal, I was promoting a dangerous lifestyle: "Fat kills and obesity is an epidemic, what are you doing?!? This is not healthy!!!" they'd write to me.

We shudder and sometimes protest when fat people sit next to us on planes, stare when they dare to reveal their bodies, shake our heads at them as they pass in the grocery aisles, laugh as they continue to be the butt of so many jokes on TV. Don't believe me? Just look around. And start listening to fat people, who detail the daily abuse they suffer as they navigate the world—along with structures and systems that are not built to contain them. It's still perfectly legal to discriminate based on weight.* Aubrey Gordon, fat activist, @yrfatfriend on Instagram, host of the *Maintenance Phase* podcast, and author of *What We Don't Talk About When We Talk About Fat,* weighs 350 pounds. She endures what she calls "thinterrogations," otherwise known as "concern trolling," where people remove food from her shopping cart with gentle admonishments ("Fruit has sugar") and suggest diets she should try. As she writes, "Concern trolls lament our size, offering compliments only with judgmental caveats attached. *You've got such a pretty face. If only you'd*

---

* Michigan is the *only* state with explicit laws on the books stating that you cannot discriminate on the basis of body shape or size.

lose some weight. Their eyes follow our fork from our plate to our mouth and back again, sometimes even freely commenting on what we eat, whether we eat, and how much." Gordon believes that her size provokes fear in the people she encounters. She explains, "The ways that thin people talk to fat people are, in a heartless kind of way, self-soothing. They are warnings *to themselves from themselves.* I am the future they are terrified of becoming, so they speak to me as the ghost of fatness future."

While internationally, childhood obesity is more prevalent in boys than girls,* as adults more women qualify as obese than men— and a majority of fat people are also people of color and of lower economic means. Per Gordon and other experts like Paul Campos, who wrote *The Obesity Paradox,* antifat bias has become a "dog whistle that allowed disdain and bigotry aimed at poor people and people of color to persist, uninterrupted and simply renamed." It's a mechanism for racism, sexism, and classism wrapped up as "healthism." Gordon cites attorney Fall Ferguson, a former president of the Association for Size Diversity and Health, who explains that healthism "includes the idea that anyone who isn't healthy just isn't trying hard enough or has some moral failing or sin to account for."

Fatness is so feared in our culture that according to a survey conducted by the Yale University Rudd Center for Food Policy and Health, 46 percent of the 4,283 respondents (of whom 83 percent were women) would give up a year of their life rather than be obese. Fifteen percent would sacrifice ten years to avoid this fate. Thirty percent would rather be divorced, 14 percent would choose alcoholism, 25 percent would give up the ability to have children, and 15 percent would prefer severe depression. Let's just pause here: 15 percent of respondents would rather die ten years early than be

---

* Despite the stats that suggest the reverse, in Jessica Nordell's book *The End of Bias,* she reports that parents google "Is my daughter overweight?" at twice the rate that they search "Is my son overweight?" Chillingly, she also reports that parents search "Is my son gifted?" at two and a half times the rate that they search "Is my daughter gifted?"

fat.* Gordon points to a UNC-SELF study that's tracked body dissatisfaction across women's lifetimes, writing, "Women of all ages report astronomical levels of body dissatisfaction, ranging from a low of 71.9 percent of women ages seventy-five and up, to a high of 93.2 percent of women between the ages of twenty-five and thirty-four." Effectively, you need to be close to death before this "normative discontent," as researchers call it, begins to fade. These statistics reflect how bad it is to be perceived as having a deviant, or not ideal, body in today's society. It makes me sad, and perversely grateful, that I don't have daughters. As Gordon writes, "Most of us take up our expected roles as disciples in the gospel of thinness. In it, bodies like mine are venal sins. Fat people are morality tales, our bodies feral prophets of the fatness that would follow any pious thin person who abandoned their vigilance even briefly." Describing fatness as an "epidemic" makes it sound like something you can catch—or to hear my dad preach, if you stop fighting the battle, you'll slip into obesity's reaches like quicksand, never to return.

THIN AS THE CULTURAL STANDARD-BEARER FOR BEAUTY

No man will ever experience anything as insidious as the way women's bodies and appearances are rated and judged.† Our "beauty" is social currency, a ticket to adoration and acceptance, along with fidelity from our partners (don't let yourself go, you'll be traded in for a younger model!) and better pay and career opportunities.‡ Maintaining our physical desirability is one of our

---

* When you double-click into the data, this antifat bias was most extreme for the respondents who qualified as underweight (33.4 percent would give up ten-plus years of life). Ten to 11 percent of those who were obese or extremely obese were willing to make that trade-off.

† This judgment extends to the courtroom: A study revealed that male jurors were more likely to find an obese woman guilty of check fraud. Women did not extend this bias.

‡ According to one landmark study, a sixty-five-pound increase in a woman's weight was associated with 9 percent lower pay.

jobs. We love to judge the worthiness of women on the basis of factors we can apprehend with our eyes, and, in my lifetime at least, that worthiness has been pegged to litheness, a body under control. We equate goodness and purity with beauty: This is how health and vanity become intertwined, when we find a shield behind which to shame others for existing outside of what's acceptable. And we equate thinness with obedience, with being someone who cares—about acceptance, desirability, discipline. When women are too large, we chastise them for being burdens on the collective, warn them that they'll never be valued when they clearly don't value themselves.

Women and food, a story as old as stories. It's the mythological tale of Eve, whose single bite of an apple evicted us from the garden and opened a trapdoor of condemnation beneath our feet. Every time we eat, we're judged—by our dinner mates, our parents, ourselves. Instead of listening to what hunger signals, we condemn and shame it, deny its existence, refuse to consider what it's trying to express.

Every generation produces new tools for comparison—from the painter's brush (and the male gaze behind it) to Photoshop, Facetune, and "beauty" filters on TikTok. It's impossible to get a grip on what's real. We live in a funhouse of comparison. Until the middle of the twentieth century, women made dresses by hand—they were sewn from patterns and tailored to fit each woman's body shape. It wasn't until the fifties that clothes started to be mass-produced and the sizing chart by which we could all compare ourselves came into fashion. And this chart shifted in the eighties, which created even more confusion. While people like to reminisce that Marilyn Monroe was a size 12 sex symbol, hourglass curves and all, she would have been a size 2–4 by today's standards. At five foot six, she weighed only 120 pounds and had a twenty-two-inch waist, which she apparently maintained by having two raw eggs in milk for breakfast and a broiled steak or liver with raw carrots for dinner. Very keto.

Like Marilyn, the models and actresses who represent beauty in Western culture have always been *tiny*—at times incomprehensibly thin. I was a tween when Kate Moss emerged—staging a subtle body coup on the "healthier" supermodels like Cindy Crawford and Claudia Schiffer who came before her. At fourteen, I read in the pages of *Vogue,* with a wash of shame, that at five foot seven Moss weighed 105 pounds. I was of equivalent height at the time but already had 20 pounds on her—it was my first revelation about weight and women, the moment when I realized that maybe I wasn't *that* thin and I was still growing. This realization scared me away from the scale for at least a decade, which was probably good for me. Looking back, it's funny that Kate created such a stink, earning censure from President Clinton for ushering in "heroin chic." The cover girls today are Kate Moss, but stretched. Somehow, they are taller and skinnier, the curves that distinguish them as women even more ironed out. But then again, most of them aren't women yet—they're typically teenagers, yet they're heralded as paragons of mature female beauty.

While almost everyone is concerned about the signals skinniness sends to young girls—that desirability is the prerogative of the ultrathin and that it's normal to talk about and judge women's bodies—I've always found it more harmful that models, celebrities, and other exemplars of beauty push the messaging that litheness comes without effort, without deprivation—that they're born this way. Sure, they've been blessed with genetics—long legs, arms, height—but hovering underweight requires exerting tremendous will over your body's natural needs, even if you have a speedy metabolism. I understand it's a paradox. If these women acknowledge that their svelteness requires going hungry and taxing their bodies, they will be accused of setting unhealthy standards. But if they can't adhere to the standards, they don't work, and don't get to set the beauty standards in the first place. Rinse and repeat. This cycle is not empowering. It requires battling your measurements with restricted eating, or no eating at all, and a shit ton of gym time. It's whisper circles of diet tricks, like weekly shots of Ozempic, a drug for diabetics used off-label, and appetite suppressants. It's plastic surgery. It's a full-time job. It requires extreme self-obsession. And yet: The *only* part that feels fair to judge is the lack of transparency and honesty. The impulse to be small at any cost is understandable in our culture. I just wish it were stated, that the means were clarified. We see images of these women with their tiny, toned bodies and we're told they eat "what they want," but we are not told that what they "want" is only a side salad, twelve almonds, and a chicken breast in between Pilates and a six-mile run. We wonder why we too can't eat what we want and look like that. We want to know where we've gone astray, why our math does not add up. It would be so much more reassuring to know we are in a room full of distorted mirrors. Ah, you look like an hourglass because you froze your fat away, went under the knife, or didn't eat for two weeks. Perhaps "I eat whatever I want" does not feel dishonest if you're trying to disprove the reality of your hunger to yourself.

HOW GLUTTONOUS ARE WE?

Pope Gregory I, who codified the Seven Deadly Sins in the sixth century, defined gluttony as eating "too daintily, too sumptuously, too hastily, too greedily, too much." How are we to know when we're getting it just right? Gregory effectively suggests we are to eat for sustenance alone, to support but not pleasure the body—after all, per the thinking at the time, the body is base, and giving precedence to its appetites breeds immorality. Today, we do not equate gluttony with daintiness, sumptuousness, haste, or greed; we believe it applies only to *too much,* with obesity as its obvious, visual result. But as we all know, we can eat in perfect opposition to Gregory's list—strongly, cheaply, slowly, liberally, scantily—and still not look the part. An obliging body is difficult to control and deliver.

While our society's increasing levels of obesity are concerning, it's difficult to assess what's going on: Is it gluttony and sloth? Or is it a veritable stew of genetic and environmental factors? Lee Kaplan, the director of the Obesity, Metabolism and Nutrition Institute at Massachusetts General Hospital, has identified almost sixty varieties of obesity. And researchers from Cambridge have found more than two dozen genes where a single mutation guarantees obesity. The title of a *New York Times* story from 2016 sums up the conundrum: "One Weight-Loss Approach Fits All? Not Even Close." Research suggests that weight loss is an individual maze, not a one-size-fits-all possibility.

We also love any narrative around personal responsibility, preferring to damn those who don't fit the parameters prescribed by society. And while we do describe obesity as an epidemic, we don't treat those affected as if they're victims of a chronic disease. We blame them for poor choices. We may call it a public health crisis and talk about how taxpayers will bear the considerable medical costs of obesity's implications, yet in a few short decades, at this rate, about half of taxpayers will *be* obese, as many lawmakers already are. Meanwhile, we are collectively loath to acknowledge that science does not fully support the narrative that all who qualify as obese are about to drop dead or that everyone must want to be thin. Google "The Obesity Paradox," and you'll find a confluence of studies showing that while obesity is a risk factor for the development of vascular and cardiovascular diseases, obese patients may do better and live longer than those of "normal" weight—particularly after interventions like surgery or cancer. They also do better than those of "normal" weight when it comes to chronic hypertension. Essentially, we've jumped to a lot of conclusions based on our own biases.

We're culturally obsessed with this idea that we've become more sedentary, that sitting is the new smoking. But evolutionary biology doesn't bear this out. While we love to romanticize our ancient forefathers and foremothers as rock-climbing triathletes, perpetually on the move, it wasn't so. As animals, we've always been programmed to conserve calories for reproduction, to limit unnecessary movement, to stay still. We're not built to crave exercise—if anything, the opposite. Despite the CrossFit craze sweeping the nation, those of us who walk a few miles a day are as active as our hunter-gatherer ancestors. They, too, spent a lot of time sitting and resting. According to Daniel Lieberman, PhD, an exercise biologist and Harvard professor who wrote the tome *Exercised,* the average physical activity level (PAL, which is the total expenditure level divided by basic metabolic rate) of a hunter-gatherer was 1.9 for men and 1.8 for women; an American who sits at a desk all day is typically between 1.4 and 1.6. It doesn't take much effort to beat our ancestors. Yes, moving our bodies is good for us and we should try to do it every day; but we need to accept that running a quick 5K before breakfast will never be—and has never been—our natural instinct.

Professor Bruce Blumberg, who studies obesogenic chemicals— environmental factors that might be making us fat—points out that the "obesity epidemic" has swept America in tandem with a boom in health clubs. We are unquestionably more conscious about exercise than we were in prior generations. And the preponderance of diets and diet aids suggests we're more weight-conscious too. Yet we weigh 10 percent more. A typical American guy, just north of five foot nine, weighs 200 pounds, up from 181 pounds in 2001; a typical postadolescent American woman, just shy of five foot four, weighs 171 pounds, up from 152. Meanwhile, the weight loss market in 2019 was north of $70 billion, up from $34.7 billion in 2001. In 2000, there were 32.8 million members of health clubs and fitness centers; by 2019, that number had almost doubled. People seem to be fighting harder for less payback on the scale. Why are we going in the wrong direction?

Our weight is scaling *with* our awareness and hypervigilance.

There's compelling research to suggest that weight stigma drives weight gain—and worse health outcomes. As Gordon writes,

> A study called "The Ironic Effects of Weight Stigma" revealed that weight stigma *increases* the likelihood of eating caloric foods like candy and chips. . . . Another study, published in 2018 in the journal *Body Image,* found that the fatter a woman was, the more likely she was to internalize antifat stigma, to harbor guilt and shame about her own body, and to avoid healthcare. . . . Research has also linked internalized weight bias to prediabetes and "a conglomerate of cardiovascular disease risk factors that strongly increases the risk for diabetes, heart disease and stroke." That is, what we think of as health risks associated with being fat may in fact be health risks of experiencing discrimination and internalizing stigma.

Diet is one of the remaining frontiers in medicine, in which clinicians and doctors really have no definitive answers: The adage of calories in and calories out is clung to but woefully outdated and overly simplistic. Tell any woman that the simple math of burning more calories than she consumes should correlate with her experience on the scale, and she'll laugh. We are tired of this lie, this idea that our bodies are machines equivalent to cars, unaffected by hormones, history, and other complex systems we still don't understand. The body diversity around us is a testament to the fact that no two of us are alike—we don't carry weight in the same way, and we don't metabolize the same foods at the same rates either. We are not a homogenous mass. Women who have gone through any hormonal shift—adolescence, monthly ovulation, pregnancy, nursing, menopause, even just changing birth control brands—recognize the impact that evolving levels of estrogen, testosterone, and cortisol have on our waistbands. And these are just the main hormones. Throw a lifetime of stress and dieting in the mix, and watch as metabolisms distort even more.

DIET CULTURE IS A LIE

When it comes to bodies and food, we are never done. If the legions of pills, drinks, powders, and programs available delivered the slimming effects they promise, they would have put themselves out of business. Instead, the onus is on us for failing, for not having enough discipline. People are lifers, repeat users, never delivered to goal weights and graduation. There is no magic dust, no quick fix, no material way of assuring that you can calcify your body in its ideal form, forever. Beyond that, we all know the basic truth that slenderness does not ensure happiness: There's no salve or solve to guarantee that you'll look how you want to look in perpetuity. We have to question why smallness is the goal in the first place.

Marisa Meltzer, who wrote a book about Jean Nidetch, the founder of Weight Watchers, describes her own life as a perpetual diet and its rebellions. Her parents started obsessing about her weight when she was a little kid. She writes,

> The most magical way of thinking is one I can't seem to give up: that it's going to be different this time. Dieting is asking you to control something wild and ungovernable, like the body, with your brain, only slightly more under our control. . . . The average weight loss in behavior-modification programs is only about a 5% reduction in weight over six months and most participants will regain one-third of that weight back after two years. . . . I'm aware that the house always wins! And in this case the house is both diet companies and my fat body. I'm cynical as they come, and yet I also think, over and over, this could be the one time the diet sticks. . . . I still think I'm not thin because I don't want it bad enough, that I'm not dedicated enough, that I'm simply not trying hard enough.

Meltzer is right: The house does always win. A UCLA team carefully scrutinized decades of studies on calorie-restricting diets and found they do not work: 83 percent of people who dropped weight gained back more than they had originally lost. Yet we continually subscribe to the fantasy that this time will be different.

Fixating on our diets, on thinness, on whittling ourselves down, takes up a huge amount of our finite, creative energy. It takes us out of life, focuses us on the wrong thing—to put it plainly, it fixates us on the outside, rather than the inside. As therapist and author Geneen Roth explains in *Women Food and God,* it's Sisyphean: "You always have something to do. As long as you are striving and pushing and trying hard to do something that can never be done, you know who you are: someone with a weight problem who is working hard to be thin. You don't have to feel lost or helpless because you always have a goal." The promise here is that if you get the thighs you want, you'll finally be happy, safe, accepted, over some invisible safety line of belonging.

The scale obsession distracts us from the real work of being in our bodies and understanding our hunger. Our bodies are not machines we could master if only we had the proper manuals. They're our soul's home, and when there's dissonance, when energy and emotion aren't properly directed or expressed, they become blocked, stagnant, stuck. That blockage is then reflected in how we do, or do not, show up in the world. If we could stop ourselves from numbing these "bad" emotions, we could, perhaps, come to understand how our bodies feel—and what they're trying to tell us.

THE SPECTRUM OF DISORDERED EATING

When I was fifteen, I went to boarding school. At the time, I thought two bagels—smothered in butter and cinnamon sugar— was an appropriate breakfast. And a pint of Ben & Jerry's before dorm check-in was the perfect capstone to an intensive day of school. I did not have a weight problem and I was active, so I ate this way until I realized how different my habits were from those of my new girlfriends, who hovered around the salad bar and frozen yogurt machine or skipped meals, arguing the food was "gross." Nobody said anything to me, but I had a revelation because of what these beautiful, thin, well-heeled girls said about themselves— moments when they complained they were fat, or would be fat imminently, and grasped at imaginary love handles. I remember hearing this editorializing for the first time with a real "Oh fuck." Because if this wisp of a girl across the table from me thought she was too large to deserve dessert, or carbs, what did that say about me? The compulsion to make conversation through self-criticism is not specific to boarding school; it's secret code in girl world for "Don't rush to talk shit about me because I'll do it first." This is the language we use when we don't want others to think we think we're full of ourselves (see chapter 4: Pride). As Rachel Simmons explains in *Odd Girl Out,* "Girls use 'I'm so fat' to short-circuit the possibility of getting labeled 'all that.' The researchers found that if a girl didn't say she thought she was fat, she would imply that she was perfect." Essentially, if you weren't on a diet, the presumption was that you thought your body didn't require work. It's telling that in our culture we equate thinness with perfection, with impeccability, as the definition for satisfaction with who we are.

But doesn't feeling sated require being full? The word *satisfaction* suggests that you believe you deserve to have enough, you deserve to stop trying so hard, managing every morsel, every step, every minute. Yet even when a slender body is in our possession, we refute its existence: We demur, we suggest we can do better.

In boarding school, eating disorders seemed more contagious than strep, though now, having more context in life, I might categorize them differently. Overly disciplined eating, or "stylish anorexia," to quote Jungian psychotherapist Marion Woodman, is not always of the same dimension as a full-blown, compulsive food disorder. What I learned in boarding school is what I've witnessed at work lunches and dinners with friends in the years since—not complete abstention but a hypervigilance about food akin to a perpetual diet of *can'ts* and *won'ts*. Now, among fellow mom friends in our metabolism-waning forties, we've gone beyond an annual diet or cleanse to permanent restriction or orthorexia. And even that doesn't stave off gut creep. Nobody looks ill; it's just an obsession that's not about health and is only tenuously about vanity. It's really about the fear of losing control.

One of my most beloved friends in high school explained she knew she was at her goal weight when she could put both hands in between her legs when she lay on her side at night—without touching flesh. After she passed this test, she would shiver herself to sleep, relishing all the extra calories burned by her body's need to vibrate for warmth. When she made this confession, I did not know how to respond, whether I was supposed to try for concave thighs as well or drag her into therapy. Was I supposed to call her mother, the woman who helped her pack and dropped her off in the New Hampshire woods, who perhaps rejoiced in her daughter's hard-won wisp of a silhouette? At the time, I didn't know what my friend was after. Now, after acquainting myself with therapists who work with eating disorders, I think I understand that any compulsive disorder—whether of starvation or overeating, often a combination of the two—is an act of resisting life, a refusal to be in the body, with all its rumblings, desires, needs.

Marion Woodman, in her Jungian framework, believed that anorexics want to be light, to be untethered to matter, to feel empty and clean, as though they've been scrubbed inside with a bottle brush. On the other side, those who eat compulsively want to be buried alive, to concretize themselves in mass. Both are avenues to numbing, to dissociation—and at the same time a battle for control. Geneen Roth, the author of *Women Food and God,* came close to killing herself after gaining and losing one thousand pounds over the course of her early life. She argues we are all on the spectrum of restricting and permitting. While "Permitters" use food to bail on their bodies, eating to unconsciousness, "Restrictors" believe in control. She writes: "Whenever possible, they'd also like to control the entire world. Restrictors operate on the conviction that chaos is imminent and steps need to be taken *now* to minimize its impact. . . . If I limit my body size, I (believe I can) limit my suffering. If I limit my suffering, I can control my life. I make sure that bad things don't happen. The chaos stays away." In Roth's experience, the same body will vacillate between the two—restricting until collapsing into a binge, at which point the individual tries to annihilate herself with food. It's like pulling the ball back on a Newton cradle—once it's put into motion, the cycle begins. For some of us, it's a small click between the strange moralizing of "I was bad last night, I'll be good today." For others, it's a catastrophe. How can we get these balls to stop clacking?

THE BODY AS INTERMEDIARY BETWEEN THE SOUL AND THE WORLD

Being in a body is hard. It's the prism through which we work out our relationship to the world. It is the home for our feelings and our soul, from which we are often so disconnected, choosing to live up high, in our minds, instead. Spiritually and energetically, we don't know where we end and others begin. We struggle to understand exactly how much space we deserve to take up. We recognize we're always changing, yet we want to live in something imperturbable: a home that doesn't age, creak, expand, bust a leak. And what is the appropriate size?

The choice to use food as defense is sometimes the outcome of trauma, from experiencing the body and world as unsafe. Recent research about adverse childhood events (ACEs) and obesity is damning: Emotional, physical, and sexual abuse; neglect; mental illness; incarcerated relatives; divorce; and addiction all increase the risk of physical and mental health problems, including obesity.

Writer Roxane Gay describes in her spare and shattering memoir *Hunger* how she was gang-raped by a group of boys when she was twelve. She carried this searing, shameful secret in herself for decades, a secret she buried by eating compulsively until she hit 577 pounds. As she writes, "Some boys had destroyed me, and I barely survived it. I knew I wouldn't be able to endure another such violation, and so I ate because I thought that if my body became repulsive, I could keep men away. Even at that young age, I understood that to be fat was to be undesirable to men, to be beneath their contempt, and I already knew too much about their contempt." Gay turned herself into armor to protect that twelve-year-old child, whose own little body had failed to fend off a group of attacking boys.

The body is the way that we contact the world and each other. Food is simply a medium through which many of us express ourselves, almost as an antidote to the poisonous expectations that are projected onto us about what we should look like and how we should be. When we eat beyond our hunger or override our hunger instinct entirely, we seem to be saying: I cannot metabolize my feelings and emotions, I deserve no pleasure, I want to disappear, I want to die.

The Seven Deadly Sins are about toeholds of control—if we can excise all our human impulses, we will be safe, if not divine. Gluttony, like lust, lands in the body as its battleground; under its banner we commit acts of war against ourselves, judging ourselves as good or bad, too much or just right. We idolize control—particularly self-control—especially when it comes to women. We are initiated into restraint, self-consciousness, awareness of other people before ourselves, from a young age. Eating in any way that is punishing is unkind, certainly, and it's also an abnegation of who we are and who we're trying to be. It is a profound rejection of self. We treat ourselves like prisoners who must be punished with solitary confinement, who must be wrestled into their cells. We don't trust ourselves enough to let ourselves be.

When you're told you can't have something, or shouldn't be trusted with something, it only makes you want it more. By restricting ourselves when it comes to what we eat, we are setting ourselves up to be at war with our very nature; we are trying to snuff out the parts of ourselves that have wants and desires. Particularly when we moralize: I was good all week, now I can be bad. Goodness has lost all relativity. Good compared to what? Or perhaps more appropriately, to whom? When we look at the causes of our global weight creep, we need to factor in our increasing self-consciousness. There is a psychic toll to comparing ourselves with every swipe of the phone. We used to have minimal opportunities for comparison, but now they are everywhere. It is too much: It stokes our self-hatred and apparent lack of discipline, perhaps enough to create an inverse reaction from the scale. In my own battles with our digital scale, I've clocked that the more I fixate on my weight, the more it seems to squirm out of my control. Thinking about it has never helped, nor has willing it to change, even with fasts and cleanses and counting my bites. After I had my second son, I hovered fifteen pounds over my baseline. And there I've stayed, despite a valiant effort to erase the motherhood rite of passage from my body, "to get my body back." Whenever I attempt deprivation, I can feel my body revolt, as though it's flipping me the middle finger by gaining a few pounds. It's asking for freedom from restraints and restrictions. It's asking me to allow that I have changed—and to love myself anyway.

RECONNECTING TO OUR HUNGER

A few years ago, I filmed an episode for a show on Netflix in which I lay facedown on a table while John Amaral, a chiropractor, held his hands above my body and manipulated my energy field like a puppeteer. Reflexively and without control, my body responded with movement—it wanted to go in a wave but consistently got stuck at my lower back, with my butt stuck up in the air. It was painful and I couldn't force my body to relax. "Make sound," he coached me. "You have to make sound. Let *go!*" I couldn't. What emerged from my mouth sounded like a weird, extended fart. I could not release, nor could I convince my body—arms undulating like a lunatic—to let the clench go. As cameras moved around us on the tables, I stayed contorted, wondering when it would end, what I needed to communicate to my body to make it go flat again. This was a reminder of a lesson I had only recently learned: I don't have control over my body.

A few weeks prior, I had done an all-day MDMA-assisted psychotherapy session with an underground therapist. The idea is to take two doses of medical-grade Ecstasy—spread out over two hours—put on an eyeshade and headphones, and go inside your body. The entire session lasts eight hours, though it feels much faster. It is a therapy marathon, and many people who have done it equate it to years spent on a couch. The MDMA mutes your amygdala, which controls the fear response, so you can access subconscious memories without feeling triggered or retraumatized. The therapist sits quietly, holds space, and lets you talk, writing things down to be processed later—there is no prompting. The first sensation I felt was loving warmth, moving from the top of my head slowly down. "I think this is the first time I've ever been in my body," I called out, eyeshades on. That was the sensation. It felt like an overwhelming truth. It made me cry. Then, after recalling an early sexual trauma, my body began to move—my legs would shake up and down, my hips would vibrate quickly, and then my back would arch, and my shoulders would roll furiously. This happened on a loop, for hours, like a great unwinding. The therapist helped me stretch, but the motions returned, taking over my whole body as I released whatever was trapped inside. I felt passenger to the motions—the "I" of me was powerless over their expression. While it felt good to get it out, it was strange to not know where it came from, or what it even was; what was unraveling, uncoiling, loosening inside of me felt like years of trying to control and silence my body. It was as if the cork had popped out of the champagne bottle, or as if, like a gazelle, I was shaking tension out after narrowly escaping a cheetah. To the therapist, I kept repeating the mantra: "I'm me, I'm not my biology." In that moment, it felt like the wisest and truest understanding I'd ever had.

Part of the trauma I had suppressed in my body involved feeling pleasure when I consciously didn't want it. I realized I had always felt betrayed by this, deeply ashamed by these mixed signals—a voice saying no, a body saying yes. But in that moment on MDMA, when I was both loving and holding myself, I connected on a deeper level to the fact that my body was its own entity, not fully under my dominion. It would do what it would do. It had its own language. Yet I had never tried to talk to it, or to listen. I had ignored its attempts to communicate for years, leaving it stuffed with shame and other bad feelings.

After several hours of unabated movement, my therapist helped me stretch again, and this time he asked me to attach what was happening in my hips to sound. And for the first time, I was able to let out a minor—yet long—noise. It sounded like the angry mewl of a newborn baby—not from my voice box but from somewhere deeper inside. As I let it out, the movement in my body slowed. But I knew that was just the beginning. Years later, I'm still working with my body, trying to understand what it's saying when I feel pain, upset, hunger. I sit quietly until it speaks. Before, I didn't know to listen, so I ignored the distress, letting it crouch in my hips, my jaw, my lower back, my heart. Sometimes, when I'm quiet—meditating, in yoga class, asleep at night—my body starts to move. I just let it happen, let it unspool. "Sorry, sometimes my body just does its own thing," I offer to the strangers on the mat next to me. The other night, my husband was startled awake and jumped out of bed, thinking there was an earthquake: nope, just my legs going nuts next to him.

I know that my body will express itself, whether I will it to or not. And I know that when it comes to what my body wants and needs, I should do a better job listening. I still don't know how to properly feed myself. I often catch myself skipping meals because I get busy or stressed, or I stand over the kitchen sink, hoovering chips into my mouth because I'm starving and running late. I'm only now learning to talk to my body, to understand where we're the same and where it has its own intelligence. My body tells me I need to slow down, or sit and chew. I'm often in such a rush I forget to taste, missing one of life's greatest pleasures: being present at a meal and holding flavor on the tongue—letting the body smell and savor. Therapist and physician James Gordon has worked all over the world helping groups address trauma. He has a tool kit for addressing trauma locked in the body, from soft belly breathing to drawing, to chaotic breathwork, to shaking and dancing. All these practices allow long-ignored emotions to emerge so they can be metabolized, integrated. He talks about the impact of trauma on digestion, how when we eat compulsively and quickly, enzymes don't have time to break down our food and we swallow air, leaving us bloated and uncomfortable. To slow down, he recommends putting a piece of fruit and a piece of dark chocolate on a plate and then meditating. As you breathe, he instructs you to notice what comes up—memories, prejudices, where your eyes are drawn, your feelings about the food. Then you bring whichever piece you choose to your nose. You smell it, touch it, close your eyes, roll it around your mouth, and then chew very, very slowly. "Time after time people realize how little they taste, or appreciate, or are even aware of the food they're eating, and how fast they ordinarily eat. Many people who've been traumatized become aware of the anxiety that has accelerated their eating and denied them a full portion of pleasure," he offers. The practice becomes a map for how to eat every meal: slowly, mindfully, while attending to what you feel—particularly what feels good.

THE REJECTION OF THE FEMALE BODY

Gordon believes that everyone has trauma—sometimes with a big *T*, sometimes little—and that we're all working through something. And in a country that struggles so clearly with weight, it's not hard to argue that one of the ways this expresses itself is food; almost all of us are disordered about our eating. Our anxiety and unease about our bodies is its own type of trauma, regardless of other factors. While clinical diagnoses of anorexia and bulimia might be low, a majority of us qualify as disordered: 75 percent in fact, across racial and ethnic lines, according to a 2008 survey from University of North Carolina and *Self* magazine.

All good feminists understand that objectifying our bodies is another symptom of an oppressive culture that pushes us to control ourselves, our appetites, and our weight. We recognize that the admonishment to maintain smallness is fucked up; we really do believe we should take up as much room as we want. Yet we can't seem to break the cycle. If we stop controlling ourselves, how will this patriarchal structure ensure we stay controlled?

The counter is an argument for body positivity, for loving our handles and curves at any size, for reveling in our strength rather than our size. To me, that feels hollow as well, because it still dictates how we should feel: positive! And it still focuses on the body as the standard-bearer for our identity and our values. As Roxane Gay writes in *Hunger*, "I hate my body. I hate my weakness at being unable to control my body. I hate how I feel in my body. I hate how people see my body. I hate how people stare at my body, treat my body, comment on my body. I hate equating my self-worth with the state of my body and how difficult it is to overcome this equation. . . . I hate that I am letting down so many women when I cannot embrace my body at any size." Body positivity feels like an edict: Loving our bodies is not something that comes naturally to many of us, even if we are deemed to have a "good" one. Our bodies are containers for so many of our traumas, many of which are unprocessed, many of which we try to keep locked inside. As someone with a body that conforms, that sits smack dab in the middle of "normal" on the BMI chart, I still relate to Gay's words, because it's not about the scale. The body is just the means through which we project our own anguish. As Geneen Roth offers, "Being thin does not address the emptiness that has no shape or weight or name. Even a wildly successful diet is a colossal failure because inside the new body is the same sinking heart. Spiritual hunger can never be solved on the physical level." Instead of positivity, we need neutrality. The charge to feel a certain way, any way, must come out, be equalized, be balanced.

In subscribing to the belief that we can change the standards and solve the problem by showing a diversity of shapes and sizes on the pages of magazines, we are just shifting the target. Feeling positive about our bodies is more primal and profound than not feeling bad about the *Sports Illustrated* swimsuit issue. For one, the more diverse images are still about the body, the exterior, not the hard work required on the interior. Pushing people to rush to embrace themselves at any size suggests there's no need to look under the hood, to know themselves, to begin the work of listening and perhaps healing. We can't skip those steps when our bodies are literally dying to speak, to tell us what they've been unable to digest after all these years.

When we contemplate the sins, and all of society's exhortations to conform, to secure safety through belonging, it's important we don't use "inclusivity" as a rebrand on a construct that will never be anything other than exclusive by nature. We must consider the consequences of establishing *any* social norms. As we push to make society more "inclusive" by enforcing language, this still comes at the cost of alienating people who don't understand what that means. These new rules might be more accepting, they might be better, but they do not solve the problem inherent in prescribing social values in the first place. We need a structure in which we can all find ourselves, one where there are no body standards at all, where we're free to just be, exactly how we are, no comment or label required.

Freedom feels like the opportune word, for it suggests a path to peace. Perhaps the goal is really a point of truce or homeostasis with our bodies, where we can live as friends. The science is still out as to whether we have a set point—a preferred weight to which our body will return, when left to its own intelligence. We will probably never know. There is no road map, no way, with precision, to know what we're supposed to look like, every year of our life: where our skin should sag; where we should carry some extra heft; or where our bodies have turned toxic, encouraging our extinction. My parents' approach—submitting to the scale for an annual face slap—feels like one method for denying the gravity that comes with time. Or we can find a different allowance: We can eat what we want until we're satisfied, we can let our bodies wander, we can let them lead us into our futures, relinquishing control to what they want to be.

Accepting gluttony as essential, we can metabolize our emotions and sate our deepest hunger.

GREED

Believing Greed to Be Sinful,
We Deny Our Own Security

THE ROOTS OF ASCETICISM

Before Evagrius Ponticus was a monk, he was a man about town in Ibora (modern-day Turkey): He had money, property, and slaves. His biographers claim he gave up his worldly possessions and fled to the desert after he fell in love with a married socialite; once there, he determined to spend the rest of his days controlling his passions. He embraced extreme asceticism, exposing himself to the winter cold all night while standing in a well of water, and subsisting only on small amounts of bread and oil. Evagrius and his fellow monks lived hand-to-mouth, refusing to store coins for the future, insisting that they could rely daily on God. Perhaps they understood the slippery slope of possession: Once you start with the idea of *more,* it's hard to know when you have *enough.*

Though you can theoretically hoard anything, for Evagrius, avarice or greed revolved around the hoarding of money. In *Talking Back,* Evagrius titled the chapter on avarice "Concerning the Love of Money." And in his guidebook specifically for monks, called *Practices (Praktikos)*, he warned that love of money would pull monks out of the present moment, out of faith: "Avarice suggests to the mind a lengthy old age, inability to perform manual labor (at some future date), famines that are to come, sickness that will visit us, the pinch of poverty, the great shame that comes from accepting the necessities of life from others." In Evagrius's view, achieving a state where you were not enslaved to the emotional demons of the mind required *complete* dependence on God.

When it came time for Pope Gregory I to concretize Evagrius's thoughts into the Seven Deadly Sins a few centuries later, his alterations showed accommodation to life in the wider world. Pope Gregory pushed for massive donations from the elite to provide charity, arguing that the church was a steward of wealth, as its monies really belonged to the destitute. An astute administrator, he organized the Vatican into the government we would somewhat recognize today. The classification of greed as a Deadly Sin became a very useful exhortation for getting wealthy citizens to give the church money; a lack of generosity came to be the sin's most pronounced dimension, *not* the accumulation of wealth. Gregory further argued that the vice could create criminality, writing, "From avarice there spring treachery, fraud, deceit, perjury, restlessness, violence, and hardnesses of heart against compassion." Yet he was careful to distinguish between this spiritual dimension of greed and the practical. This made it possible for the Vatican to later accumulate dramatic wealth. And in kind, Gregory allowed the wealth of individuals so long as they funneled some cash to the church.*

Jesus famously said, "It is easier for a camel to get through a needle's eye than for a rich man to enter the realm of heaven!" (Matthew 19:24). This aphorism has understandably created a lot of controversy and consternation within Christianity: What is an appropriate amount of material wealth? Theologians who were con-

---

* It's hard to get a handle on the wealth of the Catholic Church. The Holy See, the Roman Catholic Church's central administration, controls an estimated 177 million acres of land alone, not to mention churches, monasteries, art, and other priceless objects. According to a 2020 report released by the Vatican in an attempt at transparency, its net assets are about 4 billion euros.

scious of the church's own wealth worked around Jesus's teaching by explaining it was the *attachment* to money that created avarice or greed—the energy of clinging—rather than wealth itself, particularly if that wealth was continually given away. Professor Rebecca Konyndyk DeYoung writes of Thomas Aquinas, "Aquinas opposes the vice of greed to the virtue of generosity, except that he uses this virtue's Latin name: 'liberality,' which comes from the same Latin root as the English word 'liberty.' The linguistic connection gives us a hint: generosity concerns *freedom*—in this case, freedom from attachment to money and the promise of what money can buy. The liberal person's free and open attitude contrasts with the greedy person's preoccupation with possessions and tightfisted grip on money as 'mine.'" So wealth is OK, so long as you are only its steward and not its jailer.

But the church subsequently lost its way, or that was the argument of Martin Luther when he sparked the Reformation in 1517. Luther's primary objection was that the church had come to accept and even require indulgences for salvation: In effect, they were encouraging the congregation to *pay* for the remediation of sins. Confession and penance were no longer sufficient. Luther felt this was not only avaricious on the part of the church but immoral— that faith and the grace of God were the only path to salvation. He also believed that greed had come to be perceived as a virtue, sermonizing in 1535 that "greed nowadays has come to be viewed as talented, smart, careful stewardship." He felt that the market encouraged people to steal and cheat under the name of respectable commerce, that it put them in violation of the commandment "Thou shall not steal." He also felt that in profiting off fellow citizens, some people were committing brazen theft and calling it business acumen.

Luther also took umbrage with the enduring idea that wealth is a sign of God's favor and poverty a justified punishment for baseness. He was careful to distinguish between spiritual and material wealth, arguing that the latter had little to do with the former—

that wealth was a gift from God, intended to be shared, not pursued or held. While Luther obviously believed in work, he did not believe wealth was attached to merit—or had any spiritual value. Luther's belief lands strangely today because of the "prosperity gospel," an offspring of Protestantism made popular in the 1980s: Its famous—and wildly wealthy—televangelists promise that "Wealth and Health" are God's rewards to good people.* If you don't have either, it's because of your own moral failing.

In our current culture, wealth is firmly aligned with opportunity and access, and, accordingly, power. We live in a time of extreme disparity between the haves and have-nots, where the middle ground between the two is disappearing. Even further, we are a culture characterized by greed and avarice: a hoarding of assets† funded by overwhelming consumerism, which the planet cannot support. Men, typically white ones, who were trained for the pursuit of cash, dominate lists of rich people: On the *Forbes* global "Real Time Billionaires" list, which tracks the worth of people *daily,* only six women figure in the top forty (ranging from $33.5 billion to $232.7 billion). And they are heirs to fortunes amassed by men. They are Françoise Bettencourt Meyers (heir to the L'Oréal fortune), Alice Walton (heir to the Walmart fortune), Julia Koch (widow to David Koch, of Koch Industries), MacKenzie Scott (Jeff Bezos's ex-wife), Beate Heister (heir to the German Aldi supermarket chain), and Jacqueline Mars (heir to the candy and pet food company).‡

Bill Gates and Warren Buffett sit at the top of the list. Famously, they started the Giving Pledge in 2010 to encourage other billionaires to pledge 50 percent of their wealth to philanthropy. (This sounds nice, but questions linger: Is it appropriate for *anyone* to

---

* Prosperity gospel preacher Joel Osteen, who is estimated to be worth north of $50 million, found himself in a bit of a pickle when photos of his $300,000 Ferrari emerged online.

† Interesting, the etymology of *assets* is "enough": It implies that you have a sufficient estate.

‡ According to a 2022 story in *Forbes,* only 327 of the world's 2,668 billionaires are women—and of those, 226 inherited their wealth.

have that much money, even if halved? Should a few white, largely male people be self-appointed to attend to the world's most complex and intransigent problems? And how does it figure that most of these billionaires are way richer than they were a decade ago?) Meanwhile, only about 10 percent of the world's two thousand billionaires have signed on for the pledge. Our wealthiest citizens, who have inarguably extracted the most, do not believe in redistributing wealth.* The exception, of course, is Bezos's ex-wife, MacKenzie Scott, who earned half of her and her ex-husband's Amazon equity at the time of their 2019 split. She has already managed to give away a reported 18 percent of her fortune, noting that she will be writing checks to worthy institutions until her safe is empty. Meanwhile, her ex-husband gave away 1 percent of his wealth during the same time span, added $130 billion to his pocket during the pandemic, and is flying penis-shaped jets to space. Elon Musk—who joined Bezos in the personal space race—gave away $150 million during the first four months of 2021, which is equivalent to . . . eight-hundredths of a percent of his total net worth.

Culturally, we not only allow this overweening greed but venerate these men for being good at business, regardless of its cost to others. We expect men to provide and we commend their professional success; meanwhile, we expect women to give. Research suggests that high-net-worth women are significantly more otherminded than their male counterparts: According to a report in Barclay's, women give away nearly twice as much as men. And per research from the 1980s, wealthy female socialites—typically the wives of barons of business—were the ones making donations and volunteering, though they were doing it behind their husbands' names, burnishing their spouses' legacies rather than their own.

---

* There is a lot of interesting research on generosity and gender differences, as well as studies correlating wealth and empathy. Chillingly, per several studies from Berkeley professors Paul Piff and Dacher Keltner, richer people have less compassion. This might also partially explain the gap in charitable giving. According to a 2020 report on giving, women were responsible for nearly two-thirds of total online gifts and between 53 and 61 percent of the dollars donated.

Historically, women did not have wealth. Until the mid-1970s, married women could not get credit under their own names—not a bank account, not a mortgage. Women were an extension of the property of men, celebrated for being passive and resplendent trophies, show ponies for a husband's success, billboards for his financial prowess. He made it, she spends it—and then she wears it in good taste, a visual reflection of *his* worth. What a weird legacy. Within this construct, there's little room for women to create an unmediated relationship with wealth. We are then persecuted doubly by greed: We are trained away from money, taught it's not really for us, and we are, at the same time, programmed by our cultural messaging to believe it's our job to drive the economy by buying stuff. Society champions our consumerism. The women I know are deeply ambivalent about money: We're attracted to its promise of security and power and repelled by the inequities it perpetuates.

HOW WOMEN ARE ENCOURAGED TO CONSUME

I have a bloodhound's nose for gift shops. A blanket on a street corner, a stall, a national park souvenir shop, a boutique laced with crystal chandeliers and the requisite bowl of candy-hued, rolled-up Hanky Panky thongs at the cash register . . . it doesn't matter, I've always been an equal-opportunity consumer. After all, I spent my twenties at *Lucky,* a magazine devoted to shopping and personal style, writing guides to the best boutiques in Paris, Montreal, Los Angeles, Atlanta. I could find something worth buying in a medical supply store. One of my favorite memories is making Rumaan Alam, then a co-worker and now a revered novelist, carry a taxidermied deer head through Staten Island; I had "rescued it" from a pawnshop wall.

As a child, I filled a wooden jewelry box with earrings I made from pine cones and seed beads. None of them were wearable; I just wanted stuff, as much of it as possible. Whenever I accrued $10 from my allowance, I begged for a ride to the mall so I could spend it at the Spencer's gift shop.

As an adult, when I had the chance to travel—typically on a work-sponsored press trip—I would clear out my bag to bring home anything I felt I'd never have the chance to own again. These souvenirs didn't look like they had much value, but they would hook into my mind as must-haves: stacks of fabric, vintage blouses, little hand-embroidered hearts that I hunted in a fever dream in an outdoor market in Laos. The acquisition is the thing. When I get home, the spell breaks. Nothing works in situ. It turns out I don't wear exotic textiles to the office, and the promise of so many throw pillows never materializes.

I don't know if this urge to hoard came from advertisements or whether it was a reaction to parents who refused to indulge any of my whims outside of a little bit of annual back-to-school shopping. When I was "grown-up," I blamed it on my Condé Nast job. I made early-morning TV appearances in bright silk blouses and wobbly high heels, and I consumed an inordinate amount of vintage, sale, and fast fashion: $200 at J.Crew here, $150 at H&M there, $100 at ZARA, $250 at the Neiman Marcus outlet. I rationalized that I needed to be "on-trend" for work, and that if you're buying polyester/rayon clothing it smells terrible by 10:30 A.M. Though I grew up cherishing nature, it did not connect for me that I was polluting the planet with every purchase, that my money would be better spent on a few well-made pieces of clothing I'd wear for a long time. I was violating a rule I've come to hold dear: good, fast, cheap, pick two. Nothing I bought was good, in the real sense of the word. But that wasn't the point. The sheer quantity of stuff in my color-coordinated closet made me feel comfortable, safe, *affluent*.

Now I can look back and see that there was a deeper, subconscious story encouraging me to shop. It's been ingrained in me that it's my patriotic duty to consume, to prop up the economy—I'm the household CEO after all. Even the etymology of the word *economy* translates to "home": In Greek, it's *oikos* (house) *neimein* (manage). Perhaps it's having lived through 9/11, the Great Recession, and COVID, but my panic response to any assault on the American economy is to assume I'll *lose everything* if I don't in turn *spend everything* to keep the market going. Women have been programmed to believe the thrumming economy is *our* responsibility, not the responsibility of policy makers in D.C. This drumbeat is so unconscious as to be insidious, but when I poll my girlfriends they feel the same, as if it's on each of us to spend beyond comfort to ensure the safety of our families and our own jobs.

In *The Soul of Money,* philanthropist Lynne Twist recalls the immediate social impact of 9/11: how the country rallied to help, to donate blood, to grieve. We stopped the busyness of our lives to come together and mourn—until the economy faltered, at which point President George W. Bush exhorted us to do our patriotic duty by heading to the malls, rather than signing up to fight. His call resonated with me. Twist writes, "Shopping was portrayed as an expression of patriotism, a way to show the terrorists that they could not destroy our economy, our consumerism, the American spirit, or the American way of life." This work of patriotism was carried out by women: We spend more.[*]

Twenty years later, this response carried over to COVID. Like many, I had an energetic reaction to the pandemic, forged from watching my fellow countrymen fight over toilet paper and canned goods at Costco and, more directly, from being stuck at home with all my stuff. I could feel the energy of everything I'd chosen to surround myself with vibrating from my closets and walls. Yet, as much as I wanted to get rid of all of it, to sit with myself and my family alone, I still felt prodded to hoard essentials and also to buy more to

---

[*] According to the report *Buying Power* from Catalyst, "On average, 89% of women across the world reported controlling or sharing daily shopping needs, compared to only 41% of men."

forestall economic collapse. Clearly, companies—and their soon-furloughed employees—needed my support more than my own retirement account.

We live in Los Angeles, adjacent to fire country, and in the past few years we've had two near misses. In 2018, we lived for several days under prepare-to-evacuate orders. I readied the tote bags for the cats, along with a go bag of important documents. I packed a small duffel of clothing and put my jewelry in the car with a few pieces of art. We sent our children to stay with their nanny, Vicky, in Riverside, far from the flames. Rob and I sat at home and hammered away at our laptops with the local news on in the background. We talked about packing more but determined everything was replaceable—or not something we would buy again. It was just stuff. Did I need my wedding dress? Did Rob need his collection of Air Jordans? We opted to let it all burn if that came to pass. One year later, when we did have to evacuate in the middle of the night, our dry run had prepared us well. We took our boys, cats, and papers, and fled. As we watched coverage of the fire from the hotel room—our house in the bottom left corner of where the flames reached—we could only hold hands and shrug. Weirdly, in that hotel room at 3 A.M., there was peace. We talked about what we had unconsciously subscribed ourselves to, who we were apart from the trappings of our lives, whether our life fit us, and whether we would choose it anew. Our house, miraculously, survived, dusted in a layer of toxic ash. We cleaned what we could, tossed the rest, and reverted to normal . . . the grind of two working parents, two kids who want and need stuff. More, more, more.

THE TROUBLE WITH WOMEN AND MONEY

It makes sense that women, specifically, feel scarcity—it's core to our identity within the patriarchy, and it feeds the illusion of our dependence on men and authority structures. When men (specifically: white, cis, heterosexual men) are starting out, they are not cultured to believe there's room for only a few of them. They're liberated by the abundance of chairs at the conference room table, the well-trodden path into the executive suite. This still feels like their birthright. It's "natural" for men to want money, to go after it, to discuss it freely without shame. It's expected that a guy will negotiate for himself—if he offends the hiring manager, there will be more opportunities. Men do not have to play by the same rules: They're instructed to not only play the game but play to win it. For men, greed and ambition are good—or if not a virtue exactly, then expected—respected and admired.

Sallie Krawcheck, a onetime lone queen of Wall Street, now has a start-up called Ellevest that's focused on helping women achieve financial freedom. Sallie wants to change the stories women tell themselves about money, and she wants to get us talking about it more openly. "Women have shame when they make or have too little money," she noted to me, "and shame when they have or make too much." The knife's edge of balance is impossible when we careen around like Goldilocks. Our yearly take, our "worth"— determined for the most part by authorities outside of us, particularly since so few of us sit at the top—is the perfect Venn diagram between greed, sloth, and pride: Do we deserve it? Does it mirror our value? Did we work hard enough for it? You don't see women bragging about their day trader secrets, their bitcoin investments, or their bonuses. You don't hear women talking about the money they intend to make for the down payment on a home, or a rare painting. Even married women who happen to be primary breadwinners downplay this capacity, looking for opportunities to rebalance their relationships toward male dominance, to make their husbands feel more "like men."

Sallie told me that someone who invested $1,000 in 1900— despite everything that's happened in the intervening years, including wars, recessions, and depressions—would have $57 million to show for it today. "We always talk about the gender pay gap: 82

cents on the dollar, which is so frustrating," she explained. "But do you know what the gender wealth gap is? It's 32 cents on a man's dollar. The gender pay gap at least is moving slightly in a positive direction. The gender wealth gap is going the wrong way. Part of that reason is that men have invested more than women have, and wealth compounds—even with tough markets." Part of this inequity is the lack of discourse around money for women: We are less financially literate and more pressured to spend on consumer goods rather than stocks. I think it goes even deeper than that, though. I believe women don't participate in the market to the same extent as men because women feel it's wrong to make money materialize without effort. If we view money as a balancing agent, as finite, boundaried, exchanged for goods or employment, the idea of passive income feels sinful. If we did engage, we'd likely make up ground: Women outperform men when we invest, both professionally and within our own brokerage accounts.* But too few of us have the resources to be in the market, or the foundational confidence or willingness to engage. It seems as if it will never be the first instinct of women to conjure money by doing . . . nothing. For us, wealth is grounded in the material, not a magical illusion attached to no output, talent, work.

Over drinks a few years ago, Sallie commented on the childhood programming for girls that it's impolite to talk about money. She then asked me pointedly: "How much money do you make?" She has a commanding presence and so I answered her directly and immediately: After all, I thought, we were practicing talking about cash. In response, she almost fell out of her chair. "You're the first woman to answer that—I didn't expect you to. Typically, we demur with either 'Too much' or 'Not enough,' and then we change the subject." This reticence costs us, a lot. In essence, we've agreed to be valued for less because we've been sold a story of shame around

---

* Researchers believe it's because we do more research, trade *less,* and don't have as much testosterone fueling overconfidence.

money, and we don't know how to ask for it, get comfortable with it, or demand it. We lack the data to assess whether we're being paid appropriately and fairly, regardless of gender. We feel embarrassed we want money at all. We don't know if we deserve it. And because we've been urged to spend rather than save, we've missed out on the opportunity to accrue wealth, to ensure we won't be undone by a cataclysmic event in our lives. That is what the economy needs—sufficiency for all of us, for everyone. Because our society does not want to provide a safety net, it is on each of us to provide it for ourselves.

THE STORIES WE TELL OURSELVES ABOUT MONEY

My mother grew up in a money-stressed home, which imprinted an enduring fear of scarcity. Despite my dad's earning power—by Montana standards, we were wealthy—it never felt like enough. My mom remained hypervigilant, prepped for imminent financial disaster. She would ricochet between lack and abundance, back and forth—a bit like binge eating, followed by abstention. She's incredibly generous and would give regularly to worthy causes, but then the rubber band would hit her in the face. We had the money. She just worried that it would evaporate someday, somehow. I could sense her calculating and obsessing. To buy the latte? Or not? And she was so averse to owing *anyone* money that if we were late to return a movie, she'd make me walk it inside to pay the $1 fine (they thought I was bananas—everyone knew you paid your late fees with the next rental!). While I mocked her to reassure myself she was the one who was crazy, my mom's anxiety was not only palpable but contagious. For the first few years of my marriage, I put my husband through similar paces. We'd go out for a nice dinner, and then I would spend the drive home feeling anxious about the bill. "I'm so confused," he would confess, "because that was your idea." Indeed, it was. I was like my mother in that the reality of a healthy bank account balance couldn't counteract this feeling that letting go, having fun, being a little indulgent would destroy the promise of security.

In an unlikely turn of events, my mother went on the *Donahue* TV show in the eighties as a "relatively wealthy housewife" to discuss her phobias around money and her fear of penury, or, to use the phrase of the time, "becoming a bag lady." The audience heckled her: The white wife of a doctor, they felt, was not close enough to poverty to claim fear of that state. Though I was only about eight at the time, I felt a deep wash of shame. How dare my mother give voice to scarcity when she had so much relatively? The audience didn't see, at least when looking at my mother, that anxiety is often irrational—tethered to a future that is uncertain—and that many of us swim in it, frantically scanning the horizon for our next lifeboat. It doesn't matter if we're "rich" by the standards of others, the anxiety is there.

In 2019 I met Gloria Steinem, who had also been a guest on *Donahue* that day. Not only did she remember the episode, but she was emphatic about its importance—and the well-founded phobia to which my mother gave voice. She told me how crucial it was at that time for women of all socioeconomic levels to talk about their fears of poverty, how traumatizing it was to feel dependent on others for subsistence when money in our world equaled safety. Dependence on a spouse for money is terrifying, and this dependence is the root of the patriarchy's power. In my mother's experience, then, it was a cultural rule that women did not hold the purse strings, did not control their futures. Steinem also remarked how revolutionary the episode was because women were conditioned to not talk about money, to hide their wanting it, to silence their real fears of being ditched for a younger model and left with nothing— and accused of freeloading in the interim. The invisible work inside the home has never counted toward the GDP. In the past thirty-five years, not much has changed.

These factors, and others, ensure that women rarely feel the luxury of security that comes from self-determination. Our value is full of contingencies. We are used to not only taking less but taking it with the message that earning it requires good behavior, staying in line, doing our parts. Only then can we justify the paycheck, the allowance, the social aid. We should be grateful. We'd best not fuck it up. We have been brought up and trained in the world of "if, then" statements. If I marry the right guy, I'll get an assured retirement. If I work hard, I'll get that promotion. If I'm a good person, my kid won't get sick and my parents will achieve immortality. If I make enough, save enough, spend enough . . . I'll be OK. I'll be safe.

Like other children, my brother Ben and I received a small weekly allowance from our parents for chores like feeding the horses and mowing the lawn, but I always "worked" too. I filed charts and prepped exam rooms at doctors' offices, wrapped my head in a hairnet and delivered meal trays in the hospital, filed grants in the psychology department at Yale. When I graduated from college in 2002—despite indulging in the promise of a liberal arts degree by not majoring in anything practical—I knew that paying bills needed to be the primary focus of my job search. I thought gainful employment was assured because in the years before I graduated, Wall Street was so desperate for Ivy Leaguers they offered jobs to anyone who could multiply 16 x 16. Beneficiaries of this open-mindedness included my comparative religion–majoring brother, Ben, who worked in mergers and acquisitions for two years before transitioning to book publishing. Despite majoring in English and fine arts, I had assumed a job like that would keep me in groceries while I figured out what to do with my life. Instead, in 2001, when 9/11 gutted the country and economy, the first internet bubble burst. The top bank, Goldman Sachs, rescinded all entry-level job offers, even for finance majors. The job market was dismal; I couch-surfed, sent out hundreds of résumés, pled for informational interviews, and panicked about my ballooning cell phone bill that netted no callbacks. After four scary, depressing months, I landed an entry-level freelance gig at *Lucky* magazine doing basic administrative work for a handful of editors. Terrified of being jobless again, I found every available avenue to make myself indispensable.

Over the following years, I transmuted a series of jobs in magazines into a career—I wrote, for the most part, about shopping, with a tinge of travel mixed in to make me feel like less of a sellout, and I moved around a bit within the industry to milk a tiny bit more salary out of what is not a well-paying field. I hustled on the side ghostwriting books. As is the way for almost everyone who tries to make it in New York City, I lived paycheck to paycheck, on the precipice of falling into debt, often refusing on the weekends to leave the apartment I shared with strangers, above the Burger King on Canal Street, because I knew I couldn't go outside without spending $25—on groceries, coffee, a book, a subway ride home.

I thought I wanted to be rescued until I realized that I did not— that dependency would only feed my insecurity and that I needed to stand on my own two feet. I wouldn't have my career today if it weren't for a number of men I dated in my twenties who inadvertently did reverse psychology on me. I was bait for Trustafarians, bored corporate lawyers, and hedge funders who loved my educational pedigree and Condé Nast résumé but thought my subtle weirdness and outlier Montana roots made me quirky enough to annoy their grandmothers in Quogue. They referred to my job as just that, a job—or more like a "jobby"—something I'd surely give up once married unless I wanted to keep it "for walking-around money." One even offered me—*and* the friend who set us up—a Birkin bag if it worked out. Even as I struggled financially, I realized I preferred the slow slog to self-sufficiency, with or without a high-end leather purse, over the idea of putting my fate in someone else's hands. I was not interested in feeling owned. Being financially stable and independent became the most important thing. I made a promise to myself that the money I made myself would matter.

I met my husband, Rob, when I was twenty-nine. We fell in

love fast, and because neither of us was making much, we moved in together quickly—in *New Jersey*. We had an 1,800-square-foot loft with views of Manhattan and a near-equal commute to work, for just slightly more than my four-hundred-square-foot ship's cabin in Nolita. I continued to shop and struggled to save money for our future. It felt wrong not to put what I earned back into circulation.

MY ADDICTION TO CONSUMPTION

I knew the sensation I was experiencing as I stood in the soft yellow foyer of Ananda, an Ayurvedic spa at the base of the Himalayas that I was reporting on for a story. The familiar thrill rising in my chest was the scent of commerce. On this first day of panchakarma, the sacred five-day Indian cleanse—on the other side of the globe from my husband and then two-year-old son—I was supposed to hand over decision-making powers to the on-site Ayurvedic doctor, who would expunge my ills. My only mandate was to put on white kurta pajamas, starched and replenished every morning, and pad from my room to Hatha yoga, to the spa, to meditation lessons, to the restaurant. The treatments promised to rid my body of toxins; thanks to multiple enemas (including one for the nose), I would leave everything behind and emerge better, shinier, lighter, certainly emptier. But after my intake consultation where the doctor determined my dosha (Vata—space and air, as compared to Pitta—fire and water, or Kapha—water and earth), I kept finding myself downstairs, behind that reception desk, hovering over cases of jewelry, stocked by Jaipur's iconic Gem Palace. There were diamond slice necklaces, ruby pendants, gold rings in the shape of snakes. These were not impulse prices: I tried them all on. I left. I circled back the next morning.

Then I texted my mom, whose birthday was vaguely approaching.

"Mom, I'd really like to get you this necklace. Or this necklace."

"No, honey, I have many beautiful necklaces I don't wear. It's a lovely thought, but please save your money."

"Mom, what about this ring?"

"No, honey, I won't wear it. Save your money. I don't need or want anything except for you to come visit."

She was right, of course; I didn't need anything in that case either. And I knew, despite my fervent desire to own it all, I wouldn't wear any of it. I'd already accumulated enough jewelry for two lifetimes—too many rings for my fingers, too many dainty necklaces to layer on my collarbone—yet I took pictures of each piece and scrolled through them at dinner, pondering my eventual choice. Pulling out my credit card was a foregone conclusion.

A few days in, a young man (really, very young: he was eighteen) approached and introduced himself as Carlin, the scholar in residence from the Vedanta Institute, a school established in the eighties by Swami A. Parthasarathy in Mumbai. He invited me to join his talk, and since I was facing a schedule free of massages and yoga nidra, I followed him into an adjoining room. Then he changed my life. Vedanta, an ancient Indian philosophy, is based on the conclusion to the four Vedas (a body of religious texts in Sanskrit); it literally means "the end of knowledge." And while it dates to the fifth century A.D., it is shockingly modern. The basic thesis is that we make ourselves miserable because we underdevelop our intellect (not to be confused with intelligence) and let our propulsive minds drive our lives forward. In the Vedanta worldview, a developed intellect comes from meditation and conscious awareness, by which we can separate from our thoughts about something. Our minds are the seat of emotions—our likes and dislikes. Our minds exhaust us and make us crazy. We cannot manage them.

There were three statements Carlin made that I still think about, eight-odd years later:

1) When we let our minds run over with likes and dislikes, we are disappointed when the world fails to meet our prefer-

ences. The only part of the equation that we can control is ourselves and how we choose to react to our environment, yet we insist the world and other people should change, or be different, instead.

2) Our minds use a tremendous amount of energy ruminating on the past and worrying about the future. Unless you train yourself to focus on the present, you will always be tired.

3) The moment right before you acquire something is the moment when it will give you the most delight. As soon as it's in your possession, it depreciates in all ways. The man who bought a fifty-foot yacht now yearns for one that's one hundred feet long. The woman who buys that business-class ticket wishes she were in first. The girl hunting a diamond flake necklace in the gift shop will want something more opulent next. It is the arrival fallacy, grounded in consumerism: What you finally buy never satisfies.

With that, the spell broke. I imagined that necklace, overlooked and languishing in my jewelry case back in Los Angeles, and I didn't want it anymore. I didn't want *anything*. I recognized that shopping sated a momentary yet persistent appetite in me but did nothing to solve an underlying hunger or need. I was buying just to own, to collect. After Carlin's talk, the gift shop lost its pull.

THE DIFFERENCE BETWEEN VALUE AND WORTH

Culturally we equate worth and value. But as I've learned, they are far from synonyms. Worth is an exterior validation: the world deciding what you deserve, your corresponding status. Worth is equivalent to what something costs, including your time. Value, on the other hand, is an internal calculation; it is much more profound, personal. It's the importance of something to you specifically.

It gets even dicier when women set out to define our worth in the market and then must advocate for ourselves. It's embarrassing to state that you believe that your time, your talent, your energy have value—that they should be worth a lot. When I put out the call to headhunters and HR professionals and asked how women negotiate offers and navigate raises, the answers weren't positive. Mori Taheripour, a negotiations expert from Wharton, explained that women are typically excellent at making deals—it's an art predicated on understanding emotion, empathy, and common interests—but *not* when they are negotiating on behalf of themselves. Then we struggle to own our ask. Our tendency is to over-explain, worriedly justify, or fold. (The art of negotiating requires the temerity to sit in uncomfortable silence, a difficult practice for everyone, but especially for women, who are often taught to ensure everyone is happy and at ease.) Taheripour also cited research that suggests that women struggle to be generous with other women, perhaps as part of a hazing cycle.

Another HR executive I spoke to said she is often in the un-comfortable bind of making offers on behalf of companies with the expectation of receiving a counter—and then not receiving one. "Women do not negotiate for themselves," she explained. "It drives me nuts to have the initial offer accepted without a debate, yet be-cause I'm representing the company I can't exactly tell a candidate to ask me for more." Not asking for a better offer establishes a prec-edent that's hard to overcome, as pay compounds over time. She also underlined Taheripour's point about our unwillingness to make it easier for other women. "On the flip side, I've found that women tend to be more stingy and cutthroat when it comes to doling out pay and merit increases. No data, just my point of view, but I think it comes from the sentiment that they had to claw their way to the top, so no easy passes."

If there were any easy passes at all. But I know this is right. Years ago, I made what I thought was a generous offer to a young editor, and she replied with a well-researched, hard-hitting counter that suggested my opening approach wasn't that generous after all. I'm ashamed to admit it, but my first response was, *Who does she think she is?* I wanted to hire this young woman, but I struggled to not reflexively rescind the offer. I pushed past my own knee-jerk reaction and granted what she'd asked, and she became one of our biggest editorial stars. I came to treasure her bravery and willingness to push. I needed to check myself: All she had suggested was that my offer did not match her value. And she was right.

I was thinking about value measured in salary in the context of learning that a man I once worked alongside made twice as much as I did.* Any salary disparity hurts, but regardless of the size of his paycheck, working alongside this person hurt too. He was entirely average—he offered no constructive ideas, produced no consequential work, alienated his team. Yet he was blissfully unaware of his lack of impact: white, straight, middle-aged, he acted like a demigod, as if his presence was a gift to the company. Meanwhile, so grateful to be there, I tripped over myself to show value—to prove it, illustrate it, underline it, and then circle back to make sure it was enough. This has been my impression of most of the women I've worked alongside over the years. We hustle to show we're worthy, every single day (see chapter 2: Sloth). I don't know what was more frustrating—that this man did so little or that I felt compelled to do so much.

In 2017, there was a big push for pay equity among actresses as part of a movement called TIME'S UP, an initiative that fought to end gender discrimination in Hollywood. Several actresses had made waves before the formal movement, notably Jennifer Law-

---

★ Accidentally discovering pay disparities is not an infrequent occurrence. It's happened to me several times in my career, typically through a clerical error—once because the person I reported to at the time let it slip. Point is: This information gets out, so it would be far better for companies to be transparent about compensation, particularly because it should be defendable.

rence after hacked Sony emails revealed she and Amy Adams were paid less than Jeremy Renner, Christian Bale, and Bradley Cooper in *American Hustle*. As she wrote in *Lenny* in 2015, "I would be lying if I didn't say there was an element of wanting to be liked that influenced my decision to close the deal without a real fight. I didn't want to seem 'difficult' or 'spoiled.' At the time, that seemed like a fine idea, until I saw the payroll on the Internet and realized every man I was working with definitely didn't worry about being 'difficult' or 'spoiled.'" As part of her first-person essay, Lawrence acknowledged she felt weird negotiating since she certainly didn't need the money. That was my gut reaction when I first heard about wealthy actresses arguing for equal pay—it seemed as if they were squabbling for millions. *Don't they have enough?* And then I realized how thoroughly this reaction perpetuates the problem. No, Jennifer didn't *need* the money, but she also didn't *need* to be compliant to a system that's not fair by prioritizing an image of herself as a good, grateful girl. It's a terrible precedent for all women, a tendency we need to shake out of ourselves.

And here we land right back in the world of likability and acceptance, because the patriarchy insists that women be conciliatory all the time, that we be obedient, that we keep things nice. As the stakes get higher, as pressures mount, this expectation means that women prioritize the comfort of other people over their own needs. It's a smart survival strategy. It's the patriarchy in action. But it keeps us small and tight and grateful for our slice. While there are millions of systemic issues when it comes to women and money, the insistence that we acknowledge how much we have in comparison to others—the undertones that we're *greedy*—is one of the most insidious swipes. Our culture conditions us to prioritize care, to harbor, to protect, to feed—both inside and out of the womb. This isn't a bad instinct, but it's wrong that it's continually milked, that women take less so that men can take more.

THE MYTH OF SCARCITY AND THREAT OF DEPENDENCE

I know few people who have the self-awareness and the self-restraint to take only what they need and expect to use, whether it's from the produce aisle at the grocery store or in conversations with their hiring manager at work. Screw "Waste not, want not." In today's culture, more is *always* better. This inclination to stockpile and overbuy is not irrational. It's the opposite, trained into our bodies by our earliest days on the planet, when we collected and stored resources to survive long winters and droughts. Our primitive minds haven't caught up with the abundance and availability of grocery stores. When I was in a baby group with my son, the leader, a wise woman named Tandy, listened as a distraught and frantic new mom cried over her dwindling milk supply. "You feel this way," Tandy offered, "because your body doesn't know that there's formula at the corner store. It is making you believe your baby is going to die. She's not. There's plenty of food." And Tandy is right. There's plenty of food if we can afford and access it.* If we share.

In our ancestral heritage, we protected and provided for each other. There was competition, surely, but there was also collaboration, forged out of a recognition that it was the only way to survive. This knowing—and the awareness that in the absence of mutual dependence we could die—lives on in our bodies, our DNA.

We once belonged to communal societies, where all the work supported the family and collective. Everyone's wage was survival, from our own manpower. We foraged and harvested and raised the food we ate, and we made the clothes we wore and the shelters we lived in. We relied on ourselves and each other. Women not only

---

* As the horrific 2022 nationwide baby formula shortage illustrated—pegged to the pandemic, contaminated product recalls, and supply chain issues—families can't always rely on eternally stocked shelves. To not be able to feed your newborn is terrifying and traumatic.

had "jobs" but ensured the security and survival of our families directly. While modern society has liberated us from the demands of subsistence, allowing us to use our own abilities in expanded ways and enabling us to outsource many of the arduous tasks required for staying alive to technology and automation, this dependency has left us vulnerable and disconnected. There was power and security in relying on our own hands. Now our livelihoods— even our health insurance—are attached to our employment, and thus to an economy beyond our grasp. Few of us control any of it. No wonder we feel off-kilter and out of balance. We are at the mercy of other people—obligated to prove our value and worth to them, while simultaneously perceiving everyone beside and behind us as a threat. This is ingrained in our traumatized bodies. We can't metabolize this anxiety, so we pass it to each other as a collective burden. These are hard cycles to break.

Indigenous peoples in North America stewarded the planet and its resources for fourteen thousand–odd years before white people arrived. Throughout *Braiding Sweetgrass,* Robin Wall Kimmerer evokes the Windigo, a mythic and greedy creature who haunted Native American cultures. She writes, "In the old times, individuals who endangered the community by taking too much for themselves were first counseled, then ostracized, and if the greed continued, they were eventually banished. The Windigo myth may have arisen from the remembrance of the banished, doomed to wander hungry and alone, wreaking vengeance on the ones who spurned them. It is a terrible punishment to be banished from the web of reciprocity, with no one to share with and no one for you to care for." In Kimmerer's mind, the Windigo runs amok today. We now live in a world where we feel compelled to get not what we need, but as much as or more than others—otherwise it's *not fair.*

The early days of the pandemic showed that when left to our own devices and judgment—no community rules or structure, no taxes and laws—we cannot deal in the face of scarcity, even when it's just a suggestion. We lose our minds, we become consumed by greed, taking as much as we can get, even if it's far more than we need. Cue the stripped grocery store shelves during COVID and the hall closets soon lined with a dizzying amount of toilet paper. In these moments of presumed scarcity, we betray our higher selves and our values. Scarcity thinking—the feeling, real or imagined, that there's not enough—does something significant to our brains. Economist Sendhil Mullainathan and psychologist Eldar Shafir found that scarcity causes people to "tunnel," a type of hyperfocused, obsessive thinking, and that the resulting constriction in bandwidth has a profound effect on how we function. As they write, "Bandwidth measures our computational capacity, our ability to pay attention, to make good decisions, to stick with our plans, and to resist temptations. Bandwidth correlates with everything from intelligence and SAT performance to impulse control and success on diets." The perception of scarcity puts someone at a thirteen-point IQ disadvantage. When the threat of scarcity disappears, IQ scores recover. The paralysis of not having enough impedes our ability to think, to operate, to make sound decisions.

Women are particularly prone to getting lost in the scarcity tunnel—in time, in money, in opportunity. Systems surrounding us stress there is a finite amount that must be divvied some way somehow, between us, as if we are engaged in the most terrifying game of musical chairs where if you don't secure a seat you are destined to wander in the middle alone.

ZERO-SUM THINKING AND OUR UNDERSTANDING OF ENOUGH

Lynne Twist explains that when authorities "out there" control resources, they introduce what she calls the toxic myth of scarcity: *There's not enough, More is better,* and *That's just the way things are.* It is the zero-sum game where someone wins and another loses. These statements keep us trapped in a "you-*or*-me" world, rather than a world of "you-*and*-me." This is the West in a nutshell, where someone always has it better, someone always has more. In her book *Do Nothing,* Celeste Headlee explains: "Americans don't think someone is wealthy unless their income is about $2.5 million a year. That's thirty times the actual amount an individual needs in order to be classified as upper income in the United States, and thirty times the average net worth of American households." This is crazy, and yet I understand the reasoning. Even though I've earned a decent paycheck over the years, enough to vault me from middle class to upper middle class, I feel impoverished compared to my West L.A. neighbors. I recognize I face few hardships, but context is key. In the United States, far too many of us live leveraged by debt, or from paycheck to paycheck, or worse. America provides little social safety net—no paid leave for maternity or bereavement or to care for an ailing relative. It's a country with little systematized community focus on "we." It's a country that prizes corporate welfare checks, while leaving us to bail each other out with GoFundMe drives. We are all on our own, divorced from the tribe, fending for ourselves while plastering on our smiles because it's too shameful to admit we're terrified.

While the desire for *more* has a masculine energy—the energy of conquering, of taking, of pillaging—women experience it differently. I don't know many women in the West, at least, who feel as though they have *enough:* enough money, enough time, enough support, enough opportunity. And for the most part, this is true. We teeter on the edge, captive to the anxiety of insecurity, and worry that we may be incapable of ensuring we will get what we need. We know enough about the world to understand that nothing is guaranteed—we rarely delude ourselves into believing anything is really under our control. And so we experience a whiplash of shame. First, it's humiliating to give voice to what economic security would feel like—money is gross, base, not spiritual. If you have it, you should give it away—spend it, donate it. And then it's humiliating to express desire for anything beyond basic needs when so many are living in extreme lack. How can I deserve more when

I have more than others? We are conditioned to the concept that what we get invariably means it's coming out of some other deserving person's pocket, or we've left less for everyone else. It's a strange space to occupy, kind of a collective gaslighting—no move feels correct. Am I the only one in a near panic? I think not: These feelings of scarcity are, ironically, abundant.

Women have been programmed to believe money is like a pond, finite and boundaried, whereas men perceive it as a roaring and endless river. Our thinking is problematic for many reasons: Not only are women often stuck in the shallow end, worried about accruing enough money in a culture that defines power by its access to wealth, but we perceive it as a dwindling supply. There's not more where it comes from, it does not expand, it is not plentiful and infinite. As Twist explained to me, "If you think about water when it's moving, when it's flowing, it purifies. It makes things grow, it cleanses. But when it's hoarded or held or stuck, it becomes stagnant and toxic to those who are holding onto it."

It's not insane that we think of money as boundaried. It was once tied to gold, a finite and precious material that needed to be yanked from the earth and panned from streams. It was stolen from nature, at a measurable cost. And yes, we recognize money is energy now, rendered on computer screens in 0's and 1's, rarely counted out in cold hard cash. But it still does not feel wise to imagine it as something that can expand without end—we live in the material world, after all. And while we live on a planet that manages to replenish herself in many magical ways, we know limited resources bind us. We struggle with this paradox in all parts of our lives. Do we treasure what we have, or will there always be more? Save or spend?

It's interesting that women, the ultimate creators, seem to struggle and vacillate the most about spending. Perhaps our anxiety isn't irrational, just an acknowledgment that we're so over budget, so collectively out of balance, we believe it's essential we restrain ourselves from wanting more. We identify with Mother Earth—we know that everything has its end, which then feeds a new cycle of growth. This understanding is in direct contradiction to the market economy—to the right and up, where there's always room for more wealth, more growth. In response to this masculine idea of an exponentiality, perhaps it's incumbent on the feminine in each of us to hold the line, to retract, to turn our backs on the rabidity of incessant accrual.

WANTS VERSUS NEEDS

COVID reminded us of the one inalienable rule: There is no certainty, only the illusion of control. In its early weeks and months, fear of large-scale economic collapse stoked all my existential anxiety about safety, so in response to the waves of fear that came up in me, I did what I always do: I looked for ways to shore myself up, to protect the family, to ensure we would get what we need. I started casting lines: In addition to holding a full-time job, I completed a book proposal and took a board position. And for one entire month, I tasted abundance and what I thought was security. I had put myself into an enviable position. "I want us to live aggressively within our means," I explained to my husband. "I want to experience a feeling of plenty." A month later, I no longer had my full-time job.

Along with a paycheck, the ease of defining myself by a single sentence had vanished. Culturally, being unemployed is one of the most stigmatized states, more than infidelity or divorce. That, and my job had been the container for my creativity for a long time. I mourned the loss of community.

In time, crucially, I realized I was experiencing an inversion that harked back to those agrarian days—I could no longer rely on a structure for support and would need to learn how to be the structure of support for myself instead. To do this, I knew I needed to heal my relationship with money, to learn how to hold it without hoarding it, to spend easily but not rashly or guiltily, to steward it without clinging or attachment. I also wanted to continue to refine and remodel my relationship to the *things* in my life. I needed to figure out the difference between my wants and my needs.

As my financial world shifted, I made a budget with three tabs— *Current, Ideal,* and *5-Year Plan.* It was hard. Writing my needs down and quantifying them in cash was emotional—and it *felt greedy.* Like many women I know, I'm quick to say I don't have enough or don't have what I need—but I had never bothered to articulate what "enough" or "need" look like. It's hard to ask for what you need when you can't express it to yourself. I couldn't quantify what I couldn't admit. In the Ideal tab, I forced myself to list some wants or indulgences. I wrote down five and then was so embarrassed I would have lit my computer on fire if I could have, but I made myself sit with it and allow it. Ultimately, I wrestled myself to the position that while I'll never be enthusiastic about cultivating greed as a virtue, I must get comfortable with the concept of enough: They are not the same thing. It's OK to want things outside of basic necessities.

Even as I contemplate things I may "want" and will likely never be able to afford, I recognize how content, *how joyful* it makes me feel that I'm able to meet my family's needs. It feels like that should be the goal, this standard of sufficiency, the definition of give-and-take, particularly in America, where we carry the foundational belief that our needs won't be met unless we fight for them. In the past forty years, we've defined ourselves as the home of the "I." And the pandemic clarified the implications of what our style of living does to a community: When our economy faltered, that was scarier, it would seem, than losing our grandparents to a suffocating pneumonia. Meanwhile, the countries of community—the "We" countries—many *led by women,* fared much better across every measure. I'm guessing the citizens of those countries felt cared for, as if their needs mattered, even as they might not "want" to stay inside or wear a mask.

What would it feel like to use needs and sufficiency as a balancing tool? Mother Teresa transformed the lives of hundreds of thousands of people simply by helping them, one at a time. She focused on who was in front of her, the needs of that individual, and from there her impact radiated, like a heat lamp. Her organization, which supported four hundred–odd centers around the globe, never operated with a surplus or a cash endowment. For Twist, a career fundraiser, this seemed anathema at worst, at best a puzzle. When asked about it, Mother Teresa offered that when she needed something, she prayed, and her needs had always been met. This is a wild, if not radical, idea—and certainly terrifying to imagine attempting in the face of bills that need to be paid. But what if we wrote our needs down, put them in a little glass bottle, and set them out to sea, trusting they would be received? Perhaps the clarity of the articulation would focus our minds, distilling our needs to their most elementary state. Instead of the nebulosity of "more" and "enough," we could articulate a more precise figure, plus some slack to prepare for all the curveballs life hurls our way.

When scientists from Purdue University and the University of Virginia analyzed data from 174 countries, they found $95,000 a year to be an ideal individual annual income for "life satisfaction" (families with kids need more). North of $105,000 and happiness deteriorates. When people make significantly less than $60,000, they suffer. What might it be like if we could get most families close to this baseline—or ensure access to universal healthcare, quality and affordable childcare, and a livable minimum wage? How many people would be pulled out of the scarcity tunnel— how many people would find the bandwidth and slack to reach for the "American Dream"? Such an American Dream would be expressed not by McMansions with empty formal dining rooms and attics so large they're home to tumbleweed but by a life of safe sufficiency, with room to spare for some joy-making adventures.* Ev-

---

* We have fifty thousand storage facilities in America; as Twist pointed out in a conversation we had in 2019, we have hundreds of thousands of homeless people, yet we pay rent to put a roof over stuff we no longer want to live with.

eryone would have the space, the air, to breathe and dream, to give back, to luxuriate in time, friendships, family, the planet.

We live on a globe of abundance, though we are spending down its resources fast, racking up ecological debt. If we were to halt the excess, the frenzy, and bring it into balance, there would be plenty for us all. We are laboring under the misapprehension that we will run dry—that if we do not shore up a year's supply of toilet paper, we will be left foraging for leaves, and that if we don't have pantries lined with canned food we'll never crack open, we'll starve. These are lies, a function of a market that mediates between us and supply. We need to stop wasting one of the only nonreplenishable sources— our time—trying to control the future and steer our attention back to this moment. We're here, what do we *need*? As Kimmerer writes, "We've accepted banishment even from ourselves when we spend our beautiful, utterly singular lives on making more money, to buy more things that feed but never satisfy. It is the Windigo way that tricks us into believing that belongings will fill our hunger, when it is belonging that we crave." Belonging certainly, and a longing just to be.

Accepting greed as essential, we can clarify our needs and then work with each other to ensure they're met.

LUST

Believing Lust to Be Sinful,
We Deny Our Own Pleasure

OH, I'M DISSOCIATING

It's my freshman year of college and I am in my boyfriend's room. Like other co-eds across the country that night, we are having sex in a twin bed. Romantic. This encounter stands out in my mind because I was wasted—so loose-limbed and plastered, I had a full-body orgasm alongside my boyfriend. What sent me into such ecstasy I can hardly recall, as he wasn't doing anything extraordinary. "Ah," I remember thinking. "This is what it's supposed to feel like." I haven't revisited that state of complete disinhibition since—just that once, delivered via Popov vodka and dining hall orange juice. But the *feeling* stuck in my mind, an elusive state of possibility. For as long as I can remember, with the exception of that one night, whenever I've had sex, I've felt a pervasive self-consciousness and hypervigilance—a "voice" inside objectifying me, pulling me into my head, separating me from my body. Sometimes when I close my eyes I feel like I'm spinning, a process I now understand is called dissociation.

It took me years of being vaguely "elsewhere" during sex to recognize something was wrong—I wasn't just preoccupied with my day, my to-do list. I struggled to acknowledge the issue because (1) I didn't want to think about it, (2) I couldn't find a cultural conversation in which to compare my experience, and (3) sex was not really something my friends and I discussed. A male friend and I were hiking recently, and he offered that sometimes sex with the girls he dated felt like masturbating in the company of a warm body. I was startled, because this was something an ex-boyfriend used to say to me when we fought. And I understood what this friend of mine meant: I've had the reverse experience of feeling like a prop to fellow teenage boys, like only a leg that they attempted to dry-hump into oblivion—the way they would have if they had been overly energetic dogs. These boys didn't seem to care if I was in the room or in my body. And I probably wasn't in there at all.

After nearly twenty years of living this way, I accessed a memory from childhood that I had blockaded behind a door: I realized I had been molested by a friend of a family friend. The revelation was enough for me to think "Aha," and to get me into therapy, where I connected it to a traumatic incident in high school I'd never been able to discuss. (More on that later.) For a long time, I believed that I had brought both experiences on myself. And this fear drove me to "control" my sexual energy, to tamp it way down. Unfortunately, as I've come to learn, suppressing our innate sensuality also means blocking our vitality.

I am not alone. I tell my stories in these pages not because they stand out as particularly devastating—they're not. My stories are unremarkable, "normal" in the context of an adolescent girl's experience of sexuality—and "normal" for many young boys too. As equipped as I may be to therapize them now, for decades they created a wash of shame around sexual pleasure and touch that I'm still trying to shake out of my body. For years, I have worked hard to shush the hypervigilant voice in my head that tells me it's not safe to let go. I've deadened my own desire because I believed it was the price of safety. My fear of lust, my aversion to its call, has harmed and limited me, depriving me of my birthright to pleasure.

WHEN RELIGION FIRST CONDEMNED SEXUALITY

Religion has acculturated us to believe sex is immoral and sinful, but it's not as simple as Genesis. It's how these stories were inter-preted, passed on, concretized in a tradition where celibacy became a mandate. The only sex condemned in the Old Testament is of the homosexual variety, and even that is contested. But in the fourth century, as Christianity became organized, Saint Augustine created the theory of sex-based "original sin," stringing Adam and Eve's awareness of their nakedness to lust. You know, *that* type of "knowl-edge." (This may have been personal. In *Confessions,* Augustine writes of his early life, "Love and lust seethed together within me . . . swept me away over the precipice of my body's appetites and plunged me into the whirlpool of sin . . . floundering in a broiling sea of my fornication . . . a frenzy gripped me and I sur-rendered to my lust.") There's nothing in the Bible to suggest God expelled Adam and Eve from paradise for anything other than eat-ing from the Tree of Knowledge, which opened their eyes to their humanness and introduced them to suffering and mortality. But Augustine maintained that the duo saw something and then *felt* something, like his own feelings of shame around sex. In his view, Adam and Eve noted their nakedness for the first time, and then "they turned their eyes to each other's genitals and lusted after them with that stirring movement they had not previously known." Sounds like a bit of a leap. Augustine mainstreamed the idea that original sin infected everyone except Jesus—thanks to his birth by a virgin mother, a woman who, the church later decided, was also born from a virgin—and though it was sperm itself that transmitted this baseness, it was Eve, of course, who took the fall (literally), for inciting Adam's desire, establishing the precedent of women as the temptresses of men, a crime for which we're still dragged.

Augustine's condemnation of sexuality—our most essential human function—dovetailed with Christianity's role at the time:

that of the moral institution of the Roman state. Institutionalized Christianity set up a system in which people berated themselves, including for this most basic and life-creating impulse, something that had previously been culturally celebrated, even seen as sacred. As cultural historian Riane Eisler writes,

> The Church's "moral" condemnation of sexuality was . . . an integral part of the Church's highly political strategy to impose and maintain its control over a people who still dimly remembered, and clung to, much earlier religious traditions. If the Church was to consolidate its power and establish itself as the one and only faith, the persistence of myths and rituals from an earlier, well-entrenched religious system—in which the Goddess and her divine son or consort were worshiped, women were priestesses, and the sexual union between woman and man had a strong spiritual dimension—could not be condoned. These remnants had to be eradicated at all costs, either through co-option or suppression.

The church succeeded in making sex a dirty thing and marked women as the instigators of this filth; it was in this era that women were understood to be the root cause of human depravity.

Despite the church's efforts to pin an antisex attitude on Jesus, he didn't preach this or talk about sex all that much, which is odd considering the way it's been obsessively discussed and debated in religious circles for millennia. Jesus condemned adultery and suggested that not all men are suitable for marriage; the ardent belief that he advocated celibacy came from a bit of scripture where he mentioned that some men are "eunuchs," focused on the Kingdom of Heaven. Jesus also spoke out against lust, specifically the objectification of women, in his famous Sermon on the Mount: "But I say to you that anyone who looks at a woman and desires her has already committed adultery with her in his heart" (Matthew 5:28). Most famously, when a crowd presented for stoning a woman who had been accused of adultery, he urged the person who had never done anything wrong to "cast the first stone"—and then refused to condemn her.

When it came to sexual union, Jesus referred his followers back to Genesis, where sex itself was God's gift and work: a spiritual and *creative* exercise for the multiplication of the species. "Have you not read," he asked, referring to Genesis, "that at the beginning the Creator 'made them male and female,' and said, 'For this reason a man will leave his father and mother, and be united to his wife, and the man and his wife will become one'? So that they are no longer two, but one. What God himself, then, has yoked together people must not separate" (Matthew 19:4–7). Jesus believed in sexual union—and never condemned sex as sinful.

OUR SLUT-SHAMING CULTURE

Throughout my twenties, I was conscious of the number of people with whom I had slept. It was a mental calculation we all made. My girlfriends and I lived in fear of racking up more than ten partners before marriage. Ten was a tipping point in our minds for some reason: Heading into the teens and definitely twenties signaled sluttiness, looseness, a lack of self-respect, but lower than ten might signal to a potential boyfriend that there was something undesirable about you.

We're still mired in the belief that a vital sex life while single is good for men and bad for women. In 2020, researchers summarized existing studies with a meta-analysis aptly titled "He Is a Stud, She Is a Slut!," where they underlined that these double standards endure. "Traditionally, men/boys are expected to be sexually active, dominant, and the initiator of (hetero)sexual activity, whereas women/girls are expected to be sexually reactive, submissive, and passive. Moreover, traditionally men are granted more sexual freedom than women. As a consequence, men and women can be treated differently for the same sexual behaviors. For example, slut-shaming is experienced by 50% of girls, compared with 20% of boys." This revelation will shock no one, and it confirms that my friends and I were rightly concerned about preserving some semblance of being "hard to get."

When I asked my husband if he would have been alarmed if I had slept with thirty people before I met him, he said no, though he probably knows better than to preach a double standard. But research does suggest we have more to fear about "our number" from our same-sex peers than from our potential partners. According to researchers at Cornell, "A man who has managed to attract many partners is [seen as] particularly successful and assumed to be confident and emotionally secure [by men]. The acquisition of many sexual partners by a woman, on the other hand, is [considered by women] not a difficult achievement and is therefore interpreted as resulting from low self-esteem." I want to emphasize that in this study, the women were judged by other women; men, by other men. The researchers ascribe some of this negativity to "mate guarding," the idea that we don't want to be around other girls who might capture our boyfriend's attention with their magical vaginas. Interestingly, men who cheat are not the focus of women's concern: The fault lies with the siren-like women who would overwhelm their loyalty, flooding them with desire.

These are the ideas that program us about sex, that drive us on a subconscious level. The aversion women feel toward more sexually liberated women is just internalized patriarchy, a reflection of how women have been set up to police each other on rules of morality. If I'm going to confine myself to the cage of purity, you'd best confine yourself too. One of the researchers behind this study later admitted to being surprised by "how unaccepting promiscuous women were of other promiscuous women when it came to friendships—these are the very people one would think they could turn to for support." She also pointed to additional research suggesting that men don't think of promiscuous women as appropriate targets for long-term relationships, which further isolates these women.

Society has long punished women deemed sexually forward. Remember that in Hammurabi's Code, one of the legal artifacts that so clearly codified patriarchy, women could be punished for adultery with drowning, while there was no death sentence for men. And if a woman sought a divorce and her husband refused her request, he could marry someone else and take his previous wife as a slave. While we don't kill women for adultery now, or make them wear giant "A's," Hester Prynne–style, we continue to persecute women whom we deem "too easy to get." The idea of women as agents of sexuality, as subjects of their own desire, is disturbing.

Our culture is more comfortable with women as sexual objects, static receptacles for male lust. First there were "pinups" and "sex kittens" like Marilyn Monroe, Bettie Page, Josephine Baker, Eartha Kitt, and Brigitte Bardot, relegated to cubicle walls and army barracks. The objectification has become more explicit over the years—*Playboy; Penthouse;* the Victoria's Secret Fashion Show (and catalog); and, of course, internet porn—but it serves the same purpose: passive, fetishized women, displayed to ignite men's nether regions. When women started to behave in overtly sexual ways, people freaked out—or laughed. We started to see characters like the beloved Betty White's Sue Ann Nivens, the lustful, outrageous nymphomaniac next door on *The Mary Tyler Moore Show* in the seventies who got great lines like "I was lying in bed last night and I couldn't sleep, and I came up with an idea. So I went right home and wrote it down." White also played the sweet, empty-headed Rose Nylund on *Golden Girls,* in a friendship foursome with Rue McClanahan's Blanche Devereaux,* who got to be the group's nympho. One of Blanche's best zingers: "There is a fine line between having a good time and being a wanton slut. I know. My toe

---

* Blanche was loosely based on Blanche DuBois, a fictional character in Tennessee Williams's play *A Streetcar Named Desire.* Kicked out of her hometown in Mississippi for loose morals—she had a number of relationships after her husband's suicide—Blanche is a profoundly insecure aging beauty who finds herself penniless and dependent on her sister Stella.

has been on that line." These roles were all a precursor, of course, to *Sex in the City* in the nineties and early aughts, in which the person having the most sex in New York City was Samantha Jones, played by Kim Cattrall. One of Samantha's best lines: "If I worried what every bitch in New York was saying about me, I'd never leave the house." Too many of us continue to abide in that opinion prison.

These three women were in comedies, which gave us license to laugh at their raunchiness. Meanwhile, Madonna determined to push all our cultural buttons and blew up the conversation around religion and sexuality, scandalizing the world. First there was her televised performance of "Like a Virgin" at the 1984 MTV VMAs, when her high heel slipped off and she had to retrieve it by writhing around the floor in her wedding dress (she also dry-humped the floor and flashed her underwear). While her agent and publicist were furious with her, fans loved it, inspiring her to go further: There was "Open Your Heart," where she played an exotic dancer (while a young kid tried to get in to see her); the "Like a Prayer" video, for which Pepsi dumped her as a spokesperson (in it, she kissed a Black saint—scandal!); "Justify My Love," with its nudity; her *Sex* coffee table book; the *Erotica* album; and so on. Throughout her career, Madonna was quick to lash out at critics for double standards. As she said during an interview on ABC in the early nineties, "I think MTV should have their violence hour and I think they should have their degradation to women hour. If we're going to have censorship, let's not be hypocrites about it. Let's not have double standards. We already have these videos that have violence and show degradation to women being shown 24 hours a day, but yet they don't want a video playing that deals with sex between two consenting adults." As she underlined, objectifying women was and always has been cultur-ally acceptable; showing them as drivers of their own lust, less so.

Madonna seems almost quaint these days, though other women have picked up the torch. Rihanna, Lady Gaga, Miley Cyrus, Lana Del Rey, Lil' Kim, Nicki Minaj . . . and who can forget the 2020 song "WAP" by Cardi B and Megan Thee Stallion, which had the biggest opening week for a song—ever. Conservatives went nuts. James Bradley, a Republican who was running for office in California at the time, wrote on Twitter that the song made him want to "pour holy water" in his ears and that "Cardi B & Megan Thee Stallion are what happens when children are raised without God and without a strong father figure." People were quick to strike back at Bradley's hypocrisy: After all, this man stood behind Donald Trump, despite Trump's inclination to grab women "by the pussy." Somehow, two Black women celebrating their own "wet-ass pussies" was worse. The culture—and music critics—celebrated this breakthrough, sex-positive hit: It's bawdy as hell, but that's the point. It's an reclamation of the way women have been objectified and described for millennia.* Women, as sexual subjects, stating their lust feels foreign and shocking because it is. Too few of us know what it's like to embody our own desire, and to do so with zero fucks given to what society thinks of us for it.

THE ROOTS OF OUR DYSFUNCTION AND LACK OF BODY LITERACY

It would be so much easier to reconcile with our bodies, to understand and process their intelligence, if we were taught that pleasure is a sacred part of life, if we were coached to understand our desire. Our current culture can claim we're no longer *as* puritanical about sexuality—sex sells, after all—but the teeth marks remain. Here in America at least, we refuse to teach body literacy under the misguided apprehension that if we preach abstinence, if we leave sex as a mysterious and prohibited black box, children will disavow sexual activity. We believe abstinence equates to absence. But that's not how the body, with all its stirrings and hormonal surges, works.

---

* While we think their lyrics are titillating, I wonder if the duo weren't inspired by the Sumerian goddess Inanna, whose myth is the oldest on record (1900–1600 B.C.), who called out: "As for me, Inanna, / Who will plow my vulva? / Who will plow my high field? / Who will plow my wet ground?"

The "absence" starts young, when we teach girls to skip identifying the parts between their shoulders and their knees: That which goes unnamed becomes unspeakable. We acknowledge penises, the exuberance with which boys approach masturbation, their inevitable wet dreams and fantasy worlds. We don't chastise them for touching themselves, which my two sons do all the time—they wag their penises at me, run around the house naked, and hold them like guns every time they pee. But if girls' hands go toward their genitals, they'd better be clutching toilet paper. As a culture, we don't shame or chastise* boys for stashing their hands in their pants while they watch TV. Meanwhile, my friends with young girls are quick to tell them to pull down their skirts, to put on shirts, to remove their hands—all when these girls are clearly preshame, dying to run naked and free.

While boys will be boys, we skip vulvas (I didn't even know that was the term, not vagina, until I was forty, and the famed, renegade sex educator Betty Dodson explained that to me on Netflix), and we don't talk about the clitoris, which was excluded both from the 1948 edition of *Gray's Anatomy* and from the bestselling series *The Care and Keeping of You,* which promises to teach girls about their bodies. Journalist Peggy Orenstein, who studies girls and sex, calls this the "American psychological cliterodectomy." We didn't even understand that the clitoris is just the tip of a vast pleasure network—more nerve endings than the penis!—until the pioneering research of Helen O'Connell in 1998. Yep, just twenty-odd years ago. We don't hear about our sexual organs as pleasure centers; we hear about them as odiferous "boxes" that bleed and seep and will end our ambitions through unwanted pregnancies. And for my generation, Generation X, they could end our lives: We came of age during the AIDS epidemic, which carried with it the idea that sex could and would kill.

---

* The definition of *chastise* is "to censure severely," while its second definition per Merriam-Webster is "to inflict punishment on (as by whipping)." Its etymology is *chaste,* though, from the Latin *castus,* which meant "morally pure." This underlines how that quality has been linked over time with sexual abstinence.

Sex education, so pitiful in the United States, would be laughable if the consequences of its anemia weren't so long-ranging and poisonous in impact. It does little except impart that girls get periods and unwanted pregnancies, while boys get erections and ejaculation. As Orenstein elaborates, "We are more comfortable talking about girls as victims of sexuality rather than agents of sexuality." In America, the prevailing thesis is that sex brings "risk and danger." (Danish parents coach "responsibility and joy.") Our abstinence-minded approach to sex education means we leave children in the cold, with no pleasure map, no language to express desire, and little coaching around the subtleties of consent. Not only does this lack of information leave them without the words to explain what feels good, but it also fails to achieve its desired result: teaching young people that bodies are complicated, like instruments, and that it takes effort and practice to figure them out, to play them well. For all our sex education, no one even seems to be able to define *intercourse*. Our collective definition of *virginity* (never having been penetrated) would mean that many lesbians have never had sex. In spite of all this, teenagers are still having penetrative sex: According to a 2019 report from the CDC, an estimated 38 percent of high school kids have had intercourse. But absent language or even ideas for how to express what feels good, I'm going to guess that most of that intercourse wasn't pleasurable for the girls. Left to our own devices, sex becomes something performed, an objective ideal, rather than something felt in the body: One teenager Orenstein interviewed explained, "My boyfriend always tells me I'm sexy but not sexual." This distinction makes sense. Culturally, we celebrate the former (back to that objectification), while shaming women and girls for being the latter.

After all, we cling to the idea that girls are not *sexual,* they're *relational*. As a society, we preach that good girls should be invested in emotional attachment only, not physical pleasure—to provide sex for his needs and appetite but to be primarily fixated on ensuring his loyalty and affection. This reliance on securing attachment is how we've been conditioned. Sex therapist Ian Kerner defines sex as having three "purposes": procreative, relational, or recreational. For women, procreative sex is socially sanctioned, our duty; relational sex is fine so long as it's requited and committed; but those who are in it for the recreation are "behaving like men." Girls are continually redirected toward love as the only arena for taking off our clothing and giving someone the use of our body. We've been acculturated by fairy tales and rescue fantasies—Sleeping Beauty, the Little Mermaid, Snow White and the Seven Dwarfs, Rapunzel—to believe life begins when a boy chooses us, picks us out of the crowd, anoints us as worthy, redeems us, saves us. These stories present love and marriage but skip right over what happens to get to the baby carriage.*

It's probably not a coincidence that the girls and women of fairy tales are typically royalty—or royalty in the making. Goodness and its claims on chastity have intense class distinctions. After all, the world's oldest profession for women, dating back to that period of Babylonian law in early patriarchy, is prostitution. For millennia, and one could argue this rule still holds, women have been divided into two categories: those who are respectable and those who are not. Respectability is determined by whether a woman is a sexual partner to one man or many. In antiquity, women could occasion-

---

* The earliest versions of these fairy tales—collected and collated from all over Europe—are dark with themes of incest, cannibalism, and rape. There is a lot of kissing passed-out women (i.e., zero consent) in the Disney movies, which are arguably better than how the stories were first told. In the original Sleeping Beauty story the King finds her in a coma and impregnates her. She gives birth to twins; one of the babies sucks on her finger, which removes the splinter left by the spindle, and she wakes up to discover she has children! The King eventually rediscovers her (and his children), and they get married. And these are the (since sanitized) tales that made it into the modern canon. As Harvard folklore and mythology professor Maria Tatar explains in *The Heroine with 1,001 Faces,* Walt Disney "favored tales featuring wicked queens (*Snow White and the Seven Dwarfs*), cruel stepmothers (*Cinderella*), and evil sorceresses (*Sleeping Beauty*) over fathers with designs on their daughters. He and others ignored the many stories about fathers who lock their daughters up in towers, chop off their hands, or sell them to the devil. Tales about abusive fathers and harassing brothers disappeared." Similarly, in the original versions, the evil women were typically mothers—they eventually became "step" to make them less unsavory for modern audiences.

ally gain status but more often would lose it, slipping down from wife to concubine to slave. Some women could claim sexual decency and wear a veil; others were legally barred from telegraphing this level of social station and acceptance. Purity, as defined by class distinction, is one of the focuses of Shonda Rhimes's *Bridgerton,* the most watched TV show on Netflix as of this writing, which is about female sexual awakening and pleasure set against a backdrop of patriarchal high society. The show focuses on debutantes in Regency England, the fresh meat at the seasonal "marriage mart." The sexual innocence of these girls is guarded and policed to ensure that reputations remain intact—all to protect patrilineal property lines. Meanwhile, the rich boys sleep with lots of women, just not "ladies." Lower-class women have sexual knowledge and play concubine to the lords; the ladies, however, can lose all status at the suggestion of impropriety. If caught with a suitor unchaperoned, they are slut-shamed out of society. This double standard is historically accurate, and not only to 1813 London.

We still see this pattern playing out today. In one longitudinal study, two researchers lived with college women for five years (through their first year after graduation) and watched how they navigated the world and their relationships. While the researchers were evaluating many factors as they tracked these girls and their trajectories, they ultimately published a study about their observations around class and the perception of sluttiness. They discovered that while all the women were slut-shamed an equivalent amount in private, the lower-class women faced far more public slut-shaming, *particularly* when they tried to befriend richer girls. As a journalist who covered the study writes, "The rampant slut-shaming . . . was only a symptom of the women's entrenched classism. But more importantly, the allegations of sluttiness had little to do with real-life behavior. The woman with the most sexual partners in the study, a rich girl named Rory, also had the most sterling reputation—largely because she was an expert at concealing her sexual history." The researchers also found that there was absolutely zero consensus about what qualified as sluttiness. It was a nebulous term and identity that all the girls shunned, even as forty-eight of the fifty-three women in the study slapped the label on each other.

It's not an accident that the qualities that make a girl a "slut" are as hazy as what's required to qualify as intercourse. While we're not short on words to describe and objectify "loose" women,* we do lack language and definitions to describe women's desire. We recognize that love and romance begin in the mind and then move to the body. But we never give this voice. There's no honorific title like "boner" for the heat and pressure women feel in our groins and stomachs—it's not something we identify and touch as an expression or response to something we want. It is like a liquid pool, more ephemeral, less centralized—powerful and yet intangible, an unreachable ache. It's visible on men and boys, yet the female equivalent is hidden away. Because of the invisibility of our desire, women are not taught to locate it in our bodies, to give it a name, to study it, or to learn how to express it physically, either alone or in partnership.

When I was eleven or twelve and beginning to crush on boys and experience desire, my thoughts revolved around G-rated kissing at the roller-skating rink to Tiffany's "I Think We're Alone Now." I'd hug myself hard, wishing and praying for someone with whom to tumble to the ground. I didn't focus on what happened after falling to the floor because I didn't know how to connect those experiences in my mind—I had no concept of what sex was. Intellectually, I wanted to be desired and loved—but I also wanted it to be physical, to "French kiss," which I practiced against my hand.

I kept a journal through junior high that was tepid at best. My

---

* Aside from the newly minted *fuckboy,* there's no term for a straight male slut—or harlot, hussy, whore, tart, skank, prostitute, or tramp. (Male prostitutes are called *escorts,* which is so nice for them, and then there's the wonderfully seventies *gigolo,* from *gigole,* which translates to "dancing partner.") In fact, there's barely a male corollary for nymphomania. Who has heard of satyriasis? Meanwhile, in a recent survey, 8.6 percent of respondents reported compulsive sexual behavior—unsurprisingly, men (10.3 percent) outpaced women (7 percent).

crushes were focused on boys I didn't know but maybe saw occasionally on the ski hill or tennis courts. These boys weren't the subjects of sexual fantasies. But I did feel heat in my body, which I recognized because I had also read every book by Jean M. Auel in the Earth's Children series, a predilection I share with many other bookish women of my generation (Maggie Nelson and Roxane Gay, for example). I felt something in my body when I read *Clan of the Cave Bear,* even though I found the descriptions of cave people's sex both terrifying and titillating (there is a lot of "engorged purple manhood"). I'm not sure if it was in those pages that the concept of romance and base sexual desire first fused in my mind, or if I ever made the connection. Certainly nobody explained it that way—that it would be a full-throttled, full-body experience, yes, *and* I would need to advocate for my own pleasure. Like all my friends, I thought buttons were pushed, much like cars were started, and you were in for the ride of a lifetime. I didn't understand that it's so much more complicated than even driving shift, that what you feel physically doesn't always connect with a deeper need, and that sometimes you need an alchemical key. What did seem clear was that romance was a prerequisite for desire, but the desire needed to come from outside of you. A girl was supposed to be a passive object, waiting patiently for the moment a boy parted the crowd to find her, when she was "seen"—always chosen, never choosing.

In many ways, all children are objectified—you belong to your parents, and your fate and future are in their hands—but for girls it's particularly intense. Perhaps it's because boys are pushed to separate from their mothers, to distinguish themselves as men, but they seem to have an easier, clearer path to self-expression. They are expected to know what they want and to go after it, claiming it as their own. There is a penalty for hanging back, for "pussy-footing" around. But girls—even those who hail from the most liberal, feminist, and progressive families—are conditioned by the wider culture into passivity. It is too embarrassing, too unsafe, to blow apart social norms, to ask a guy out and be told no, to be mocked and derided for apparent desperation. Instead, we back-channel our desires, or dump them into diaries with flimsy locks, and then wait until we are picked—a process where our worth is then confirmed. This passivity is problematic. According to gender studies professor and psychologist Deborah Tolman, "Society's dominant cultural construction of femininity encourages girls and women to be desirable but not desiring." She argues that this cuts girls off from full expression. And it seems safer this way, certainly, for we malign girls who we think are made out-of-control by their wanting: We slut-shame them, accuse them of craving attention, blame them for inviting harm.

We need to carve a path for every child in adolescence to figure out how to bring their whole selves into relationship. The whole self includes the part of the self that is physical—their sexuality, knowing what they want, knowing what feels good and what feels bad. This appetite, this lust, is our livelihood, the fountainhead of our vitality. And we must protect our young while they figure out the contours of their sexual power—rather than blaming them for having this power, this life force, in the first place.

THE INTENSITY OF ATTENTION—AND WHOSE EXPERIENCE COUNTS

When I did MDMA therapy for the first time, I had the revelation that I had been molested by an adult, a near stranger, when I was about eight. While I've gone back to the basement in my mind many times, waiting for doors in my memory to open, I've decided that understanding exact events decades later is irrelevant. And in a process Freud called *Nachträglichkeit,* translated to "afterwardness," I recognize that as I age, my memory offers new perspectives. What I've worked with in therapy is dismantling the idea that it was *me* who made *him* lose control, my false sense of power and responsibility. I clearly remember a separate event with this same man at a large Fourth of July party, when he insisted on riding an inner tube with me, dragged by a motorboat across Flathead Lake, again and again. I can still feel in my right shoulder how I tried to pull my slight weight away from his body, and how I would slide down on him as the tube shifted beneath his heft, went vertical and then flipped. We tubed again and again as I waited for an adult to intervene on my behalf. I'm sure I smiled through the entire episode, afraid of hurting this grown man's feelings by honoring my own discomfort.

Looking back, I realize I was Lolita-esque then, with my pixie haircut and precociousness. I remember feeling the attention, the adult male gaze; it was often innocent, I'm guessing, in the way I think many of my kids' friends—with their wild minds and opinions—are fascinating to talk to. But in my memory, I'm not able to sort what was appropriate attention from what was not. It feels as if it all must have been dangerous, tainted by my experience in that basement.

My mother likes to recount how sexual I was as a toddler, my fingers wandering everywhere while she read me books. My parents are liberal hippies, so my mom talks about my penchant for loving my body without intending to shame—she thought it was cute, if distracting. It still sears my ears when she mentions it, as she calls it masturbation, even though, as sex therapist Helen Singer Kaplan explains, boys and girls both explore their bodies intimately as soon as they develop the motor skills. When I tell you I loved to touch my body when I was little, does it not make you shift in discomfort? It's odd to me that we always connect physical pleasure and touch with sexual desire, even when we're describing children. When my cat arches her back toward my hand, purring with her whole body while I stroke her, I don't assume she's sexually aroused. Instead, I think of her as an animal who desires, craves, and enjoys touch, who wants the intimacy of my flesh, who wants to feel good. Why can't I extend that same understanding to myself?

On the basis of my mom's recollections, I always assumed I was a hypersexual child, busy inspiring an "intensity of attention" from old men: Though I didn't know what I was doing to inspire it, I assumed I'd asked for it. "Intensity of attention" is how Mia Farrow and others described Woody Allen's relationship with his daughter, Dylan Farrow, in the HBO Max documentary *Allen v. Farrow*. Watching the show was hard for me, because that's how I would describe my experience when I was young. And it wasn't the culture at the time to notice or stop it. It took decades before anyone believed Dylan Farrow. Even now, people are loath to give up their reverence for Allen or acknowledge how he groomed us through his movies to accept his inappropriate relationships with girls. He mainstreamed a cultural norm for generations of men: coveting the co-ed. In *Manhattan,* a sixteen-year-old Mariel Hemingway plays a seventeen-year-old high school student who dates a forty-two-year-old man (Allen). She had to make out with him on camera; this movie won many awards, and zero what-the-fucks. Everyone loved that movie until the veil lifted on how problematic it is, thirty-odd years later. It was barely acknowledged even when Allen married his own stepdaughter.

One of the great services of the documentary and Dylan's testimony is its spotlight on the "parental alienation" argument, which still has our culture and judicial system in its clutches. Parental alienation is the mechanism by which a father, when charged with abuse, turns it back on the mother and accuses her of implanting stories in the child. The father's next move is to countersue for sole custody. And it works. According to the documentary, "In 98% of cases, when accused fathers claimed Parental Alienation, family courts did not accept the child sexual abuse accusations as true." The film asserts that fifty-eight thousand children have been forced to have unsupervised contact or live with their accused parent. An assumption of parental alienation is what happened to Dylan. I'm older than her, but I remember the terror that coursed through society when Allen stood accused in the early nineties. It wasn't fear that he'd done these crimes; the terror stemmed from the idea that it was easy to convince kids to lie, that they could be gaslit into inventing sexual abuse charges and then being weaponized against innocent adults. In the same way women are presented as unreliable witnesses to their own experience, children have been exiled from a relationship with truth as well. We tell them their memories are so faulty, their grasp on reality is so feeble, that the truth they feel in their bodies is a lie. I wonder how many women are disassociated from their bodies because they don't believe their own history, which is housed in their own flesh.

The truth of our bad experiences doesn't just go away because it's inconvenient to believe it or too gross to contemplate. These feelings live below the surface, biding time until they can be revisited and released, until those exiled parts of ourselves can be made safe and invited back in. This stuffing takes a toll. Being penetrated by the other, whether physically, emotionally, or energetically, cannot be easily undone. When pleasure is involved, even if it stops at simply enjoying the attention, the feeling of eliciting or inviting the attack, or collaborating in some way in the relationship, cannot be easily shaken off.

THE RATES OF SEXUAL TRAUMA

There's the immediate physical trauma of assault, and then the insidious and invisible trauma from the event—including the way our culture programs girls and women to accept responsibility and blame. Traumatic episodes become psychic crimes. The stats, per medical anthropologist Katherine Rowland, are stunning: "Upward of 20 percent of Americans are sexually molested as children. One in five women are subjected to rape or attempted rape in their lifetime, and as many as a third of intimate partners have engaged in violent physical contact, with the numbers rising precipitously on both counts for women of color. One in six women have been stalked at some point in their lives. Nearly half of all murdered women are killed by their current or former partners." Aside from

Indigenous women, who are experiencing a crisis of rape and sexual trafficking (56 percent of Indigenous women have experienced sexual violence, and 90 percent have experienced violence from a non-tribal member),* most contemporary rape is intraracial, meaning white men rape white women, Black men rape Black women, et cetera.

The statistics surrounding Native women aside, no group of men have been painted with a worse brush than Black men, who were cast as rapists of white women to justify lynchings and other atrocities in the wake of the Civil War (in fact, the raping of enslaved women *and* men by "white masters" was rampant for centuries). Yet these are the stereotypes that persist today, though they also blow back in the face of Black women who are deterred from reporting sexual assault by Black men because it's perceived as traitorous. This keeps the stereotype alive that Black men are predators and is yet another pernicious example of how women are expected to sacrifice their bodies and psyches to keep the reputations of others safe. Meanwhile, rape endures as one of the most powerful and horrific tools of oppression. And it lingers as one of the primary collateral damages of war. Rape is not about insatiable lust gone awry; it's about power, dominance, and control.

Rape and sexual assault are about entitlement because men *can*—and typically do—get away with it. Of every 1,000 sexual assaults that even make it to the criminal justice system, approximately 975 perpetrators walk free. We seem to have little interest in holding men accountable: Often, these are men who might be re-

---

* These egregious crimes are happening because of a chasm between tribal and federal law; they're primarily perpetrated by men living in man camps alongside fracking sites that are in, or adjacent to, reservations. The tribes do not have the jurisdiction to prosecute non-Native men, a loophole that is repeatedly exploited to the detriment and devastation of murdered and missing Indigenous women and girls. There is very little interest in these crimes. Case in point: The media frenzy in 2021 around missing-and-murdered twenty-two-year-old Gabby Petito, whose body was recovered in a Wyoming state park, marked a stark contrast to the lack of interest in Indigenous girls and women who met a similar fate. In Wyoming alone, between 2011 and 2020, 710 Indigenous people were reported missing. We didn't hear about any of them.

vered, or who hold status in society, or who just show promise, like Stanford swimmer Brock Turner.* As prosecutor Deborah Tuerkheimer explained to me, the reputation of a powerful man is enough to make the survivor's pain just . . . disappear. There's the assumption that she'll get over it, so why derail some man with plans. This idea is entrenched in patriarchy, and it is wildly disturbing: Women are always deemed less essential, less important than men, even when these men are *abusers*.

This reverence for the ultimate potential of men is also why women are accused of being co-conspirators in their own rapes and sexual assaults. It's the sticky idea that boys and men cannot control themselves. Girls and women are responsible for triggering a compulsion in them to cause harm. We celebrate boys' burgeoning sexuality as part of a normal and natural maturation process and seem to take some cultural delight in believing them to find these urges overwhelming and uncontrollable. When we establish girls as the more responsible party, the babysitters of this rapacious male appetite, we set them up to be blamed. We turn their bodies into the vehicles for their own destruction. We also deny the presence of their own desire, making it inherently deviant.

I was recently forwarded a corporate email that included the following language: "Employees are not allowed to wear suggestive, form-fitting, or low-cut clothing, strapless or halter tops, revealing shirts. . . . Choice of attire should be appropriate for the work environment . . . and not a cause for distraction." While women are not called out, the email is clearly gendered. "Do not cause distraction." What qualifies? It's like being told that having your period

---

* As Soraya Chemaly reports, the assumption is that women are liars: "Most college students surveyed, for example, believe that up to 50 percent of women lie about being raped. Other studies similarly show that police officers with fewer than eight years of experience also believe roughly that percentage of those alleging rape are lying. As recently as 2003, people jokingly referred to Philadelphia's sex crimes unit as 'the lying bitch unit.' This doubt remains true despite studies, conducted across multiple countries, consistently finding that the incidence of false rape claims ranges from just 2 percent to 8 percent, approximately the same as it is for any other crime."

in the ocean will inspire a shark attack—the presence of your body is not safe, and it's your duty to figure out how to make it so. It's a brilliant trick, this foisting of over-responsibility onto girls and women.

This expectation of over-responsibility follows us into courtrooms, in the rare instances when we even bother to seek justice for sexual violence. It's not enough that the perpetrator likely ruined the woman's life; she is then held responsible for ruining his. And as the questioning goes, is her pain really worth it? As Rebecca Traister wrote about the aftermath of peak #MeToo,

> Most women I knew did not *want* the "opportunity" to patrol the borders of patriarchal overreach; we felt torn about both the vague prospect and the observed reality of these men losing their jobs. We thought of their feelings and their families, fretted that the disclosure of their misdeeds might cost them future employment, or even provoke them to harm themselves. But this was something else we were being compelled to notice; the ways in which we were still conditioned to worry for the men, but somehow not to afford the same compassion for women—their families, their feelings, their future prospects—even in a reckoning that was supposed to be about us, not them.

This is the perfect description of "himpathy," a term coined by philosophy professor Kate Manne to describe the ways in which we prioritize the emotions, health, and happiness of men over their female victims. Himpathy happens all the time; it's a reflex. As women, we are so conditioned to be selfless, caretaking, and "other-directed," we fail to recognize this overreach of responsibility. Just as we are not responsible for the actions of raping men, we should not be responsible for the impact of their actions on their own lives. It's perverse that this burden is placed on our shoulders as well.

Therapist Wendy Maltz describes herself as a "patchwork survivor," someone who has "experienced different kinds of sexual abuse at different times in his or her life." In her experience treating patients, this patchworked experience is common—it matches mine, and I would imagine it matches that of most women. In the age of #MeToo revelations, it became evident that sexual molestation, abuse, harassment, and rape have been grossly underreported. The burden of proof in the legal system is high, for one. And then most women recognize nobody will believe them, that it's a matter of he said/she said. Sometimes we try to rationalize what happened as not a crime, even though it felt so wrong. A fifty-something-year-old friend recounted to me recently that she didn't realize she had been raped as a teenager until she was watching a segment on date rape on *Good Morning America* while nursing her firstborn. Because she had known the boys, she hadn't realized it qualified. Her ignorance makes sense. We don't like to talk about events that feel bad. Nobody wants to be accused of wanting to ruin a man's life out of malice or regret for our own bad decisions or behavior. There's never been an upside in reporting. There's no catharsis. Every outcome is terrible. It's re-traumatizing, humiliating, as everyone's "part" is litigated. Was it the "R" word? Was your "no" stated with enough vehemence? How hard did you fight? Were you drinking? What were you wearing? How many sexual partners have you had? Was it enough of a struggle? Did you fear for your life? While we hold stranger rape in our heads as the "prototypical" crime—dark alleys, knives, blackened eyes—it is never as clear-cut as an episode of *Law & Order: Special Victims Unit*. According to the Rape, Abuse & Incest National Network (RAINN), 80 percent of sexually violent crimes against women are perpetrated by people we know and sometimes love.

WHO HAS POWER AND CONTROL?

If rape is the most pointed expression of power and authority, the power structure of the patriarchy rests on the suppression of women: It relies on the patrolling of our purity, the controlling of our procreation, and the threat and success of sexual violence. It's been this way for five millennia and continues to delimit our lives today. This alternately repressed and forced sexuality is the bedrock of our society—and with it comes the belief that men own women's reproductive capacity. Our access to birth control, abortions, even the power to say "no" has become one of the hot-button issues in politics today, entirely limited to the domain of the female body. We continue to debate who "birth control" belongs to and whether it's a woman's right as a human to make decisions about her own body, or whether she continues to be property over which to be adjudicated, even at great risk to her health, employment, and self-sufficiency. By supervising our reproductive powers, men can hold the line. There is no greater lever for keeping women in poverty, in subservience, than to deny them the ability to determine their procreative future.

The irony, of course, is that while the *power* resides with men, the *burden* of birth control—particularly abortions—rests on the shoulders of women. In today's upside-down political climate, and with the overturn of *Roe v. Wade,* there are resurgent laws to prosecute women for ending an unwanted pregnancy and healthcare professionals for assisting them.* Yet men are absolved: there is no conversation about charging these would-be fathers with a crime as co-creators, victims of their own lust, or as co-terminators, eager to free themselves from responsibility and limitation. While women's choices are policed, I've yet to hear the suggestion that men should be forced to pursue vasectomies until they can be responsible for the result of their seed.† We've never contemplated it—

---

* While abortion is now banned in Oklahoma, state legislators also passed a law making it a felony to perform an abortion; convicted doctors will face ten years of prison and a $100,000 fine. Over in Texas, bounty hunting is a perverse reality. Private citizens can collect $10,000 for successfully bringing a lawsuit against someone who helped a woman obtain an abortion. Meanwhile, the maximum fine for sexual assault (including rape) in Texas is $10,000.

† Here's a sick fact: Only thirty-two states allow for the termination of parental rights of rapists if the women they rape become pregnant.

because it's never really been about abortion; it's only ever been about corralling, controlling, delimiting, and policing women.

OUR POROUS BOUNDARIES AROUND INTIMACY AND TOUCH

In her memoir *Girlhood,* Melissa Febos—who spent some of her formative years as a dominatrix, working out her relationship to her early sexuality—writes about going to a cuddle party as an adult with her girlfriend and another friend. She didn't want to cuddle with strangers, but she knew a session focused on intimacy and boundaries might hold some teachable moments. After all, she had always struggled to deny people what they wanted from her body, even if it was just a hug. At the beginning of the party, the organizer outlined the rules. Febos writes that he "acknowledged how difficult it can be to establish clear boundaries around touch. Many of us, he said, did not learn how to say no in our families, or how to differentiate between different kinds of touch. When we got to rule 3, 'You must ask permission and receive a verbal YES before you touch anyone,' he asked us to turn to a nearby person and perform a role-play. One person was to ask, 'Do you want to cuddle?' The other was to answer, 'No.' The first would then respond, 'Thank you for taking care of yourself.'" During the session, multiple men asked Febos if she wanted to hug or spoon. In response, she felt unnerved, writing, "How powerful my instinct was to give them what they wanted, as if I didn't have a choice." More powerfully, she describes their frustration—present in only a flicker on their faces—when she denied them: "Misogyny filters so granularly into action. Those men did not hate me, as a hungry person does not hate a refrigerator. They simply valued their own needs above mine. And I had seen that flash in their eyes when I refused them, as a hungry person might grow frustrated with a refrigerator that does not open." Such is the power to compel women, buried in the minds of men as a subconscious right.

There is much about affection in our culture that's on demand—as children, particularly as girls, we supplied kisses, hugs, and smiles to all who asked. To reject the inquiring relative, parent, or even stranger was a horrible snub. But sometimes a kiss on the cheek does not feel innocuous; it feels like a trespass. The coaching to prioritize the comfort of the other taught us to snowplow over our instincts, again and again. In this formula, our own wants did not matter. We had to accept or provide touch, be pliant, show gratitude for the affection.

MY STORY

The first time I ever had an orgasm in the presence of someone else, I was raped. I've only recently decided I can call it that, after a conversation I had with Lacy Crawford, author of *Notes on a Silencing,* a memoir about being orally raped by two older boys at the boarding school we both attended. I told her what had happened, and she suggested that I name it what it was: an encounter I worked hard to avoid and did not want.

I was a sophomore, or fourth-former, on the cusp of my sixteenth birthday. I had been at the school for only a few months and had made some friends after a lonely fall. I went with these new friends to Boston during a long holiday weekend, when we were unleashed from our school-every-day-except-Sunday schedules and allowed some teenage freedom. Three of us shared a room in the hotel where about sixty other kids from school were staying.

One of the friends I was bunking with, who would become something of a sister by the time we graduated, was with her boyfriend, a wrestler at the school. I'll call them Jane and Jack. Jack's best friend, also a wrestler, had been kicked out of our school before I'd arrived. We met up with this kid, whom I'll call Greg, that afternoon at the hotel pool, and he took a shine to me. Jane and Jack were excited about the prospect of Greg liking me. Greg

creeped me out, I wasn't interested, but I didn't mind the attention—
that is, until he met up with us again at dinner and we went to his
house afterwards. There he cornered me in a dark study and pinned
my arms behind my back in some sort of wrestling hold. I strained
against his single hand to get free—I remember that detail, a symbol of his dominant strength, the way he held me so easily with one
palm as he tried to kiss me. I struggled, he released me, and I re-
joined the group, shaken.

Later that night, after we had left him at his house and were
back at the hotel, I was in the hallway, drinking and mingling with
other kids from school, when I saw him again. My stomach sank.
He was stalking me, and nobody was paying attention. I approached
a senior boy, whom I had befriended in math class, to use as a shield
against Greg, but this senior made a sloppy, albeit friendly, pass at
me. I told Jane I was uncomfortable, but she shrugged it off, drunk
and hazy and not understanding why I was alarmed when she
thought I should be flattered. When I went back to our room, Jane
and Jack were passed out in one bed and Greg was in the other,
awake, waiting for me. I went into the bathroom, but another
friend of ours, someone I barely knew at the time, was asleep in the
bathtub. I sat on the edge of the bed, feet from Greg, and considered my options.

I had always believed I would lose my virginity while roofied in
some college dorm. Maybe it was precognition, or maybe it was
just the culture we grew up in, where sex was described to us in the
same sentence as unwanted pregnancy and HIV/AIDS. I recognize
this sounds perverse, but I think I held firmly to this belief because
I knew from a young age that my body made me unsafe—and that
hypervigilance wouldn't be barrier enough, my defenses would be
overwhelmed. At the time I was a virgin, and I had a limited understanding of what sex even was—only that preserving "my first
time" was important, that a bad situation would be ruinous. Now I
chastise myself for not waking my parents with a phone call and
asking them to buy me my own hotel room, but at the time, scared

and phone-less, it didn't seem like an option. I felt like I should be able to handle myself, young adult that I was—tall, smart, *competent*. I hadn't been roofied. I wasn't drunk. I thought if I fell asleep, I'd wake up in the middle of the night to find him inside me, stealing something precious and inviolable, something I could never get back. As I lay there, listening to his expectant breath at my back, I plotted. I decided if I kissed Greg, maybe he'd be satisfied and leave me alone. And so, I rolled over, toward him. And, like some sort of superhuman tarantula, he pulled my pants off and put his head between my legs. I tried to pull him up by the arms, straining against his wrestler's heft, trying not to make any noise so as to raise the suspicions of everyone in the room, horrified by what was happening. But it was like trying to move a wall. And within maybe sixty seconds, I had an orgasm, wilting into the bed with the shame that my body had betrayed me with its own pleasure. I had brought the assault on myself. My orgasm was enough for Greg: Self-satisfied, he left me alone and fell asleep, arm encircling me. I lay there all night, paralyzed, willing myself to forget. It took me twenty-six years to understand what I felt as the ultimate shame—that I had apparently enjoyed something I *did not want*—was self-protective. Now I know that victims of sexual abuse and trauma often orgasm because of a fear response; then, I assumed I had orgasmed because I had liked what Greg had done to me.

The next morning Jack and Greg had breakfast together; I know because when I saw Jack later that day he cackled and told me Greg had been busy "pulling pubes out of his mouth" over eggs. That night, back on campus, as I walked around the pond to dinner, I passed a senior who I thought was cute. "Hey, Elise, I heard about Boston!" he called, giving me a knowing smile. How ironic that girls are the ones labeled as gossips. While I hoped to bury my shame deep inside, my humiliation had been through the whisper network of boarding-school boys in fewer than twelve hours.

I didn't know what to call what had happened—I had allowed it, I had apparently *enjoyed* it—and so I shuddered it away, put it in a box. But as the years and decades have ticked by, I still feel Greg's presence as a specter. I can see his leering face in my mind's eye, laughing that he's still with me, affecting my life today. In recent years, I've had to face how significant it was. I realize now that the experience is present with me every time my clothes come off: that I am still trying to revoke that orgasm, to take it back, to prove I have control. To choke it out, I tamped down on my sexual energy. In college, four years later, I was drunk and disinhibited and with a boy who loved me—my hypervigilance obliterated enough so my body could do its thing. That was the only time I was able to let go, for a long time. But at least it happened, like a ghost knocking on the attic door, assuring me of its possibility.

By attempting to suppress one emotion, I suppressed them all. Instead of allowing my feelings, I higher-minded or intellectualized them, assumed I could rationalize them into coherence, miraculously make the shame go away, talk myself out of it. Brené Brown calls this instinct stockpiling: We might think our feelings are gone, but every unexpressed emotion is biding its time in our bodies, waiting to come out. When we refuse to listen, to process and metabolize every icky or hard feeling we've shoved down, the experiences don't evaporate. They metastasize. And what our bodies are trying to tell us becomes harder to parse, like a dialect that's lost if not spoken. But revisiting the trauma can liberate. As psychotherapist Galit Atlas explains, "When our minds remember, our bodies are free to forget."

In that hotel room in Boston in high school, when my body had its own agenda and acted without my consent, I decided my body and I were separate. I disowned it, not understanding I couldn't simply numb out the emotions and feelings I found undesirable without numbing out everything else in the process. Like Febos, I'm now on the path of learning to listen, strengthening the connection, plumbing the shame. I'm trying to put down the bully stick, to stop punishing myself for how things could have, should have gone on that cold winter night.

WHERE DOES SEXUAL DESIRE LIVE IN OUR BODIES?

As I've begun to tease out my feelings, I've found some solace in the research of sexologist and psychologist Meredith Chivers, at the Sexuality and Gender Laboratory at Queen's University in Ontario, Canada. Her groundbreaking work examines the way men and women—from straight, to queer, to everything in between—respond to visual and audio sexual stimulation, and how that tracks against what they self-report in arousal. In one study, Chivers showed participants a range of material, from gay sex to straight sex, to exercisers, to masturbators, to humping bonobos.* The men responded in predictable ways, their arousal patterns matching their stated preferences—and neither straight men nor gay men were interested in the primates. Women on the other hand, and *specifically* women who identified as straight, were physically aroused by almost everything, even when those images were the opposite of what they reported turned them on. Lesbians matched their stated preferences. People have had a field day interpreting this data, arguing that heterosexual women are animalistic and into everything, while men are inhibited. The reality, I think, is that straight women don't know what they want because they've been told they shouldn't have any sexual wants at all. Our desire is off the charts simply because we haven't been taught to map it.

We think of sexuality as a physical response from the body. But arousal starts in the mind—the brain is a sex organ too. Ideally, the brain and body are aligned. But just as we don't instruct our hearts to beat or our lungs to breathe, the body will do what it will, which leads to one of the most important takeaways from Chivers's research: Physical arousal does not correlate to subjective and stated desire. A wet vagina is not an invitation for unwanted penetration

---

* Participants reclined in La-Z-Boys with their genitals hooked up to plethysmographs, which measure changes in blood flow.

(and in the same way, a dry vagina doesn't indicate a lack of sexual appetite). Chivers and other scientists believe lubrication during unwanted sex might be protective, to help prevent discomfort and injury. (Men *should* be able to relate to this amid the anguish of erectile dysfunction and inopportune or uninvited erections.)

So what, then, explains the disconnect between a woman's body and her mind? Is it that we're biologically primed for sex as a defense mechanism, that we know to expect unwanted sex and rape? Does the female body apprehend that it's the object, or vessel, and recognize it might necessarily need to oblige for its own survival? Or are heterosexual women so disconnected from our bodies that we short out and run a "do not compute" message when we see anything we interpret as sexual? I think the confusion Chivers observed in heterosexual women exists in part because we are inexpert in understanding, naming, and talking about our pleasure and desire. Our minds—what we state we find arousing—and the response in the body are not always connected, because it's a path not well defined, much less well trodden and entrained. Do lesbians track more precisely because they have needed to assert their desire through a clearer expression of what they want, how they want to be touched, and whom they want to do the touching? Is it because they've sharpened their desire in the face of a culture historically inclined to reject—or fetishize—them? And are so many heterosexual women still stuck in the space of objectification, intent on doing the pleasing with little regard for their own pleasure? What is it to want instead of merely responding to being wanted?

WHAT OUR FANTASIES TELL US

While Chivers's research seeks to understand the Venn diagram of physical arousal and desire, cultural conditioning dictates that women should respond sexually to a man's intense longing: If he wants me, then I come alive. This idea of needing to be desired gets complicated for people who confuse the idea of being wanted with being wanted without consent. It is the difference between ravaging and rape, which share an etymological root: *rapere, raptura*. As Jungian therapist Marion Woodman writes, "Rape suggests being seized and carried off by a masculine enemy through brutal sexual assault; ravishment suggests being seized and carried off by a masculine lover through ecstasy and rapture. Rape has to do with power; ravishment has to do with love." The ideas are close. When someone cannot restrain themselves from your body, when your presence encourages them to cede control, that's a form of power—nested in the safety of mutual desire. Their loss of control is a bid to liberate you to exult in your pleasure too. Rape has everything to do with power too—it's just one-sided and has nothing to do with pleasure or love.

We get twisted, though, when many women's fantasy lives are centered on elements of ravishment: of wanting to be desired sometimes to the point of domination. I believe that this is so prominent because it's culturally condoned: a woman being forced to be sexual to service male desire. Many women experience shame around submission, though, and not only because it conjures whips—it feels perverse. Every good feminist knows not to submit in life; embracing surrender in the bedroom seems contrary to everything we're supposed to want. San Francisco therapist Michael Bader spent much of his career exploring people's sexual fantasies, using their arousal maps to understand how they've been primed to receive love—and how they perceive safety. He asserts that you can't let go, and can't surrender to the chaos of pleasure, when you don't feel safe. While we like to think of sexual arousal as a natural, biological, and physical response to stimulation, actual excitement is more complicated. As he writes, "Excitement is generated by the mind, a mind that endows images and sensations with just the right meaning to create pleasure. When it comes to sexual arousal, psychology makes use of biology, not the other way around." You might "seem ready," or show physical signs of interest, but absent an excited mind, there's nothing real there, as Chivers's work under-lines.

Bader makes the brilliant connection that our fantasies don't necessarily invoke what we *like* or what we *want*—they are mental stimulation, not reality—but do illustrate what's required to feel safe enough to get turned on. In his view, many women who fantasize about being dominated might be culturally programmed with the idea that they are "too much." In a fantasy, if they are being bossed, there is no way they can be accused of overpowering the other. In this vein, women who might classify their fantasies as "rape" are talking about ravishment.* He writes, "By empowering someone else to hurt or degrade them, the[y] reassure themselves that they are not the ones doing the hurting or degrading. The unconscious logic is a kind of perversion of the Golden Rule: *Have others do unto you what you feel guilty about doing unto others.*" If you worry you're overwhelming, it makes sense you'd want reassurance that you can be easily overwhelmed.

It's not surprising that women—operating under the cultural delusion that infects us from birth that sex is bad, dirty, immoral, wrong—frequently fantasize about being forced to be sexual. As Bader explains, "a fantasy in which one is forced to have sex" is a creative way the mind solves "a pathogenic belief that one is not supposed to be sexual. . . . It is telling one's conscience, family, and culture 'It's not my fault.' Men have been using this excuse for cen-turies." Bader has observed other fantasies that live in this family, like the hand under the table at the dinner party while conversation continues: Innocence is maintained, the advance can't be stopped without drawing attention. Enter the world of women's romance novels and erotica, which offer the consummation, two-thirds of the way through, of slow-burning, unacted-upon desire. The reader

---

* Somatic sexologist Jaiya told me she believes that "60 percent of cisgendered women have those fantasies of being taken, of being ravished, of being out of control in that way." She coaches her clients to play out these fantasies so long as it's in a safe container where consent is clearly established.

is engaged in a literary pursuit that's ostensibly about love—and then suddenly everyone is having sex. We can argue women are relational, that there must be a romantic preamble to climax, but these types of books ring as the very definition of what Bader describes: being forced to be sexual, driven to climax by the structure of the book itself.

What's complicated about fantasies is that for women who are already anxious about their sexuality, what the mind finds titillating can compound shame, cornering them into believing they're deviant, or that a fantasy should be cured. Bader's work is empowering because it suggests fantasy is a map to feeling safe within our sexuality, a path to reclaim our lust and sexual agency, to short-circuit our inhibitions—many of which are cultural—in order to get aroused. It may well be the means to regain our lustful birthright and enjoy sex rather than just endure it.

THE IMPORTANCE OF RELEASE

Enjoying sex, encountering the feelings of being fully alive that can accompany it, requires trust, safety, and a willingness to be held as you let go. It is, in many ways, the ultimate act of vulnerability—to open yourself to someone else, relinquish control, and let someone else make you feel good. There is a sacred aspect of sex, deeper than any biological urge to mate—after all, procreation does not require a female orgasm. And it's not just a fun bonus either. The pleasure of women is a vortex, a gate to a deeper experience of surrender and awe. This is the space I visited back in that college dorm, a realm I felt and saw, a place I went. This space has been described as the "maternal matrix," a way to touch the divine and the deepest impulses of life. It is accessible to all of us.

It is ironic, of course, that chastity has historically been held up as the surest path to God—denying the body means you barely live at all. To avoid the body is a disavowal of the beauty of our humanness, the creative matter of life, and arguably the reason we're here: to experience the world through our senses, to be fully in ourselves. Plus, if we've learned anything from mythology and religion, it's that you can't go up until you go down. Jesus descended before he ascended; so did Dante, Odysseus, Aeneas. The Divine Feminine, the Black Goddess, waits for us below, willing us to liberate her from the clamp of patriarchal control. Across history, the Black Goddess represents the full cycle of life—in one expression, she is Kali, the Hindu goddess of time and death, the end of the arc, the seeds of a new beginning. In another, she is Hecate, Artemis, Inanna, Persephone, Nyx, Demeter, and Isis. She has many faces and just as many names; she resides in us all. She guards the underworld and she ushers in new life—marking the entrance to the void, the cave, the womb, and the tomb. These are essential passages, the structure of all of life. It is no mistake that orgasms are called *le petit mort,* "the little death." When we release, we go somewhere—then resurrect anew.

Our bodies are a microcosm of the world; they are natural and political. When we repress and deny this life force, we all lose access not only to our pleasure but to our potency, a power source whose dimensions we don't yet fully understand. This is why women's sexuality fills our culture with fear: fear of the body and its appetites, fear of the loss of control, fear of death. But we are entering a new era, one that will require us to reconnect to this maternal matrix, to be fully here, inhabiting all of our senses and feeling them all. Our bodies are portals; lust is the invitation to enter.

As we map the way we've related to nature and each other over time, we can recognize that hierarchical and imbalanced power inhibits all of us from full expression. Patriarchy pins us down. In the nineties, two feminist, Jungian therapists mapped our patterns of relating across time. When I happened on their chart, its suggestions for the future felt prophetic. Looking at it now, I see how this chart articulates the contours of a new era, one they've labeled androgynous; it suggests that if we can move forward to embrace this paradigm, not only will we supersede gender, but we will come to understand and respect power as an expression of love, rather than of dominance. The promise of this map is that we will learn how to relate to each other as people with bodies, rather than as people with very specific body parts: We will become fully human.

MAJOR PARADIGMS IN HUMAN EVOLUTION

MATRIARCHAL	PATRIARCHAL	ANDROGYNOUS
Instinctual self, tribal, polytheistic	*Ego self, hierarchical, monotheistic*	*Soul/spirit self, ecological, inner marriage (interiorized spirituality)*
Power *from* nature	Power *against* nature	Power *with* nature
CULTURAL EXPRESSION Power as gift	**CULTURAL EXPRESSION** Power as strength	**CULTURAL EXPRESSION** Power as love
PSYCHOLOGICAL STATE Dependence	**PSYCHOLOGICAL STATE** Independence	**PSYCHOLOGICAL STATE** Interdependence
APPROX. TIME SPAN 30,000 years (ago)	**APPROX. TIME SPAN** 4,500 years (ago) to present	**APPROX. TIME SPAN** TBD

The age we are entering is not matriarchal or patriarchal but *balanced,* an age where these essential energies are meted out and honored appropriately. We recognize the advent of these ideas now, particularly as we contemplate the contemporary trans movement: We may be tripping over language, but there is a deep cultural desire to dispense with binaries, to move to a spectrum, somewhere in the middle, without concrete definition, where we might meet a truer version of ourselves. In this world that is predicted, we will eventually transcend the need to dominate nature and will instead work in partnership with it, harnessing potentialities without causing harm. And we will transform the fallacy of independence into the righteousness of interdependence, recognizing and honoring the mutuality of relationship that we have with every other living creature.

This framework feels promising—not only as a bridge to a sustainable and peaceful future but as one that could be more loving too, one where we can embrace and excavate our desire and explore where it can take us. Perhaps we may learn how to initiate our children into sexuality without submitting them to a traumatic start; perhaps we may teach responsibility and joy, so they assume the power for their own experience (and nothing more). This future may be more appropriately lustful—after all, when we repress our desire to live fully, to express ourselves creatively in all ways, sexually and spiritually, that energy must go somewhere. Let it expand our consciousness and refine the path between body and mind instead. May the former serve as the mechanism by which we can experience the world, not from a place of fear and white-knuckled restraint, but in full-body surrender, open to mystery, magic, and pleasure.

Accepting lust as essential, we can reclaim pleasure and harness the full power of our creative potential.

ANGER

Believing Anger to Be Sinful,
We Deny Our Own Needs

WHERE I RECOGNIZE I'M ANGRY

A couple of years ago, I noticed a dull ache in my jaw. It was intense and unrelenting, no matter how much I stretched my mouth open or massaged my cheeks. One afternoon, I called a wise friend of mine, psychologist and astrologer Jennifer Freed. I told her about my throbbing jaw, and she offered: "Jaw pain suggests you want to bite someone and are being held back. You're muzzled."

"But I have nothing to be mad about."

"OK, lady, whatever you say," came her retort. I laughed but wondered if she was right.

Every time I open my mouth for my biannual teeth cleaning, my dentist chastises me for grinding. "Soon you'll break your teeth." I know I need to stop, yet I snap at my nightguard like a hippo while I sleep. Plus, while the plastic appliance might protect my teeth, it offers no reprieve for my well-exercised masseter muscles that give me the face shape of Tom Brady. I catch myself in a grimace all the time, something I started doing as a young child. My jaw goes sideways and I bite down until the veins in my neck pop. It's my concentration face, a face of forcing, more reflexive than my smile. After I noticed my son doing the same, I decided I needed to solve this issue for both of us. He also has a migraine disorder and hyperventilates, which affects his sleep. A trip to an ENT revealed that we are both tongue-tied: the connective tissue under our tongues is tethered too tight, limiting the movement of our jaws. It might be the reason my upper body feels taut and contorted, why my neck is always out.

What a rich metaphor for my aching jaw: It's restrained, by unknown factors. It could be structural or emotional. When I asked a myofunctional therapist if releasing my tongue would relieve my tendency to clench and grind, she cocked her head and offered a noncommittal "Perhaps." After all, when you alter something so central, chaos can ensue. How would my body reorganize itself if it wasn't pulled so tight? Would I still be able to control my tongue once it was unleashed?

We love to diagnose. We love tidy answers. A few years ago, I paid $12 to determine my Enneagram, which is a nine-type personality test. I saw myself clearly in the One—idealistic, perfectionistic, rigid—and filed the pdf away. One morning, as I struggled with writer's block and decided to organize instead of work, I noticed *The Sacred Enneagram,* a book I had bought but never opened. I moved it to my bedside table. And then I loaded a podcast episode of an interview with Chris Heuertz, the book's author—and set out on a stroll. As I huffed up a hill, Heuertz listed the "Passion" of each of the nine personality types, explaining that Type Ones typically have somatized jaw pain because of their latent anger.* Ac-

---

* I know you're taking your Enneagram test right now. The Type / Passions per Enneagram founder Oscar Ichazo are: Type One: The Reformer / Anger; Type Two: The Helper / Pride; Type Three: The Achiever / Vanity; Type Four: The Individualist / Envy; Type Five: The Investigator / Avarice; Type Six: The Loyalist / Fear; Type Seven: The Enthusiast / Gluttony; Type Eight: The Challenger / Lust; Type Nine: The Peacemaker / Sloth. Heuertz does warn, "It's easy to overidentify with our Passion because it often drives so much of what we do. In fact, when people attempt to self-diagnose their

cording to Heuertz, our "fixation" is resentment, because the world is not as we would like it to be. As his voice poured through my headphones, I stopped to rewind, again and again. When I got home and looked for the transcript, I saw the episode had been removed after Heuertz had been accused of abusive behavior— I don't know how I managed to play it.

The story gets stranger. The Enneagram, which has recently become part of pop culture, has a much longer and more interesting history that can be traced across the globe. A Bolivian mystic named Oscar Ichazo gave the Enneagram its current shape and structure, which he taught as part of his Arica School in the sixties and seventies. Ichazo's work is partially based on the *symbol* of the Enneagram, which in Greek translates to "nine diagram"—it's a circle overlaid on a triangle overlaid on a hexad, which looks like an open-bottomed star. The symbol and its mathematical structure date back to Pythagoras and show up in various wisdom traditions including Kabbalah, Islam, and Taoism, and in the philosophy of Socrates, Plato, and the Neoplatonists. Most famously, G. I. Gurdjieff (1866–1949), an Armenian mystic and Sufi, brought the symbol of the Enneagram forward through dancing its nine points and enigmatically stating that it contained all knowledge. Gurdjieff is often erroneously credited with creating the entire psychological personality system, an honor that belongs to Ichazo.

The Enneagram symbol also shows up in early Christianity: Evagrius Ponticus, the same fourth-century desert father of the early Christian tradition who gave structure to the eight passionate thoughts (*logismoi*) that became the Seven Deadly Sins, also articulated an early version of the Enneagram's mathematics. Ichazo used Evagrius's list as the Enneagram's Passion/Fixations, adding "Courage/Fear" to make nine. As Don Richard Riso and Russ Hudson,

---

type, the list of Passions often seems most relatable. By accepting our Passion as an intrinsic part of ourselves (or our innate fatal flaw *when* it becomes an addiction), we find confidence in the Enneagram's ability to describe our character structure."

the founders of the Enneagram Institute, explain, "How the original *nine* forms, in the course of their travels from Greece to Egypt over the course of a century, became reduced to *seven* deadly sins remains a mystery." While the roots are the same, the Enneagram is not religious, offering only scarily accurate psychological insight. It doesn't condemn you to hell, only points you to where you're most likely to go out of balance and what's required to share the strengths of your gifts.

Reading about the Enneagram and its connection to the Seven Deadly Sins, and seeing how my Enneagram type mapped to anger and resentment, threw me. I am angry; I had just failed to recognize its low-grade, low-heat form. I can certainly be unfiltered: I'm known for being direct and *clear* with my thoughts. But I rarely let my words reach a crescendo. I don't remember the last time I yelled. I reside in the land of incessant impatience, irritation, resentment, the slow and soft boil that captures so many frogs unaware. In many ways my tongue does stay tethered. Like the metal helmet on a bottle of champagne, I much prefer to think of myself as having everything under control, including my own feelings. Acknowledging anger feels shameful, unpolished, *indelicate*. I know how to vent—to siphon air off the top so I don't explode—but I've never learned how to name, process, or own the underlying emotional state for what I need to vent in the first place. That feels too scary. A friend once offered that she never cries because she's convinced if she starts, she'll never stop; I worry that once I start screaming, I'll never shut up.

THE STICKY CONTINUUM OF ANGER

Thanks to its endless variations and temperatures, anger goes by many names. And its reputation is complex. Within the Christian tradition and arguably the culture at large, there is little consensus about when anger is justified, even *good,* and when it crosses an imperceptible line. Obviously, tolerance for the emotion depends on *who* is angry. After all, the God of the Old Testament is frequently referred to as wrathful—*wrath* and *anger* are used synonymously in the Bible*—which created a bit of a predicament when it came time to tell all of humanity that anger is a sin. The fathers of Christianity struggled to integrate the paradox and so made the case that God wasn't angry, he was just trying to scare humans into behaving well, into upholding the Ten Commandments, and his anger was justified in punishing those who violated them. Jesus was different, although he *did* flip tables (Mark 11:15–19) and rebuke a leper (Mark 1:40–45), which also created a bit of consternation for theologians. Jesus is most famous, though, for evolving Hammurabi's Code into nonviolence: "You have heard that it was said, 'An eye for an eye and a tooth for a tooth.' But I say to you that you must not resist those who wrong you; but if anyone strikes you on the right cheek, turn the other to him also" (Matthew 5:38–39). This is one of Jesus's legacies: Let it roll off your back.

As a monk, Evagrius Ponticus pursued *apatheia,* a state of singular peace, free from excitement and emotions. He believed that anger in any iteration was a demonic thought, as it distracted the supplicant from prayer. As he writes in *Practices* (*Praktikos*), which consists of one hundred short "chapters" of guidance for other monks,

> The most fierce passion is anger. In fact it is defined as a boiling and stirring up of wrath against one who has given injury—or is thought to have done so. It constantly irritates the soul and above all at the time of prayer it seizes the mind and flashes the pictures of the offensive person before one's eyes. Then there comes a time when it persists longer, is transformed into indignation, stirs up alarming experiences by night. This is succeeded by a general debility of the body, malnutrition with its attendant pallor, and the illusion of being attacked by poisonous wild beasts.

★ "A soft answer turneth away wrath, but grievous words stir up anger" (Proverbs 15:1).

I love that he hits on a spectrum that ranges from indignation to wrath to feeling like you're being attacked by poisonous wild beasts. One biographer believes he's describing depression.

Thomas Aquinas, in his *Summa Theologica,* which summarizes the thinking of many early church fathers, including the desert monks, Pope Gregory I, Aristotle, and the Stoics, expands on anger prodigiously. He defends it as a useful human emotion—one present in Jesus, after all—that's sometimes appropriately exercised for justice when applied correctly and with restraint. However, to quote Calvin University professor Rebecca Konyndyk DeYoung, Aquinas believed its expression can become disordered and sinful in three ways: "We can get angry too easily (for example, when we are quick-tempered); we can get angrier than we should (for instance, when our anger is too vehement or otherwise disproportionate to the offense); and we can stay angry too long (that is, when anger smolders into resentment and grudge holding)." Within these bounds, it's hard to tell where the line is—what exactly is too much, too fast, or too long-lasting? And whose anger counts as valid?

THE PROBLEM WITH ANGRY WOMEN

Anger, wrath, and rage all carry the energy of vengeance, particularly when exercised in public: A wrong must be put right, someone must be punished. There's an expectation not only of validation, but of justice being served. So long as you're a man. Women fare better as passive, crying victims than when we harness our fury—but even then, justice is rarely a given (see chapter 7: Lust). The public perception of anger is that it's only ever righteous and proper for men to be visibly enraged. Therapist Harriet Lerner, who wrote the 1987 classic *The Dance of Anger,* nails this concept in a way that still holds true three decades later: "The direct expression of anger, especially at men, makes us unladylike, unfeminine, unmaternal, sexually unattractive, or, more recently, 'strident.' Even our language condemns such women as 'shrews,' 'witches,' 'bitches,' 'hags,' 'nags,' 'man-haters,' and 'castrators.' They are unloving and unlovable. They are devoid of femininity. . . . It is an interesting sidelight that our language—created and codified by men—does not have *one* unflattering term to describe men who vent their anger at women. Even such epithets as 'bastard' and 'son of a bitch' do not condemn the man but place the blame on a woman—his mother!" When Lerner and I spoke, she paused to stress how perverse this language is—that it paints men as victims of women's wrath, helpless against our anger. Yet how many men do you know who palm pepper spray as they walk to their cars at night, fearful of being attacked by a woman? Instead, when our voices reach the crescendo of rage, we're seen as being *mad,* in the pathological sense. Loud women are unstable, dangerous, dramatic, delusional, barking, insane.

While angry women are deemed "unhinged," it continues to be culturally appropriate for men to get their anger out, expressing aggression all over the place: Think of Brett Kavanaugh, foaming at the mouth like a belligerent frat boy during his Supreme Court hearings, juxtaposed against the imperturbable Christine Blasey Ford. Ford, who had every reason to be enraged, walked a tightrope of composure and emotional constraint. And her testimony was still deemed irrelevant.[*] Or there's the raging and domineering Donald Trump, who visibly stalked Hillary Clinton during the third 2016 presidential debate, all while she was considered irredeemably power-hungry, unlikable, a shrew.[†] Or consider John

---

[*] The etymology of *testimony* is testicles—i.e., to swear on them—which is a lovely reminder of how gendered our legal system continues to be. Meanwhile, the word *seminal* is another frustratingly gendered word, whereas *hysterical,* a descriptor ascribed to upset women throughout time, can be traced back to the womb, which was thought to wander and create mental illness. The definition of *woman* itself is fraught, as its etymology is "wiffmon," or "wife of man."

[†] In business and politics, anger is lauded in men and vilified in women. As Carol Gilligan and Naomi Snider assert in *Why Does Patriarchy Persist?,* "A 2008 study entitled 'Can an Angry Woman Get Ahead?' concluded that men who become angry are rewarded but that angry women are seen, by both men and women, as incompetent and

McEnroe, having his famous temper tantrums and abusive melt-downs on the tennis courts, juxtaposed to Serena Williams in the 2018 US Open final, when she openly fought with umpire Carlos Ramos. He punished her with three violations: The first, a violation for coaching (her coach flashed her a thumbs up from the stands, which she argued was not a "sign"); the next one, a point penalty for racquet abuse; and then, finally, a game penalty, for arguing the merits of the first two violations with the umpire. The penalties may or may not have cost her the match (many fans felt they did). This punishment for anger is a problem beyond being a woeful double standard: Righteous indignation changes the world. It is the spine of social change, the force of progress. When women are restrained from expressing anger, it gets sublimated and repressed. Or we turn it on ourselves and each other. Harriet Lerner laments, "You know, really educated college women say things today, like 'I believe in equality, but I'm not a feminist because I'm not one of those angry women.' "

There has always been an aversion to listening to women express anger in public—specifically when its target is someone in a more powerful position. As Rebecca Traister, author of *Good and Mad,* writes, "We are primed to hear the anger of men as stirring, downright American, as our national lullaby, and primed to hear the sound of women demanding freedom as the screech of nails on our national chalkboard. That's because women's freedom would in fact circumscribe white male dominion." When women raise their voices, ears are at best plugged—at worst, said women are denounced as awful. As British historian Mary Beard explains in

---

unworthy of power in the workplace. . . . This is especially true in the political context. A 2010 Harvard study found that when participants saw female politicians as power-seeking and thus having agency they also saw them as having less communality (i.e., being unsupportive and uncaring), and consequently as subject to moral outrage. This was not true of the participants' perceptions of or reactions to power-seeking male politicians, who were instead seen as exhibiting greater competence and agency. In a patriarchal framework, women's expressions of agency and anger, their fighting for what they want or believe in . . . [are] instead viewed as selfish and thus at odds with maintaining relationships."

Women and Power, "There are only two main exceptions in the classical world to [the] abomination of women's public speaking. First, women are allowed to speak out as victims and as martyrs, usually to preface their own death. . . . The second exception is more familiar. Occasionally women could legitimately rise up to speak—to defend their homes, their children, their husbands or the interests of other women." Beard has received death threats for her work. (On Twitter, one man threatened to cut off her head and rape it.)

It's interesting that women's rage is so threatening when we theoretically have so little power. If we follow the breadcrumbs established by Beard and other historians of our more ancient history, it's easy to see fear of women's anger as fear of the long-repressed goddess. Until all but extinguished by the patriarchy in the Indo-European world, the goddess represented both creation and destruction, the latter making way for new life. Many goddesses are still revered in parts of the globe today. There's the Hindu goddess Kali, celebrated as one of the supreme deities, who is typically portrayed in all black tones* with her tongue out and decapitated skulls strung around her neck. There's the fiery goddess Pele, the creator of the Hawaiian islands, whose spouting lava creates new earth. Where Christianity came to reign, the church transformed many goddess constructs into terrifying witches, a warning to women everywhere about the monstrousness of our power. There's the ferocious Russian Baba Yaga, who both helps and hurts those she meets in the woods (she's an early precursor to many of the figures in fairy tales, like the old woman in "Hansel and Gretel"). Meanwhile, in mythological systems, the goddess—who went by many names—represented the full cycle of life.† Only later did goddesses

---

* According to the anthropologist Marija Gimbutas, the symbolism of black and white also reversed in more recent millennia. As she explains of the pre–Indo-European world, "Black did not mean death or the underworld; it was the color of fertility, the color of damp caves and rich soil, of the womb of the Goddess where life begins. White, on the other hand, was the color of death, of bones."

† As Joseph Campbell explains, "In the Roman Empire, during the golden era of Apuleius in the second century A.D., the Goddess was celebrated as the Goddess of Many

come to represent distinct emotions, like anger. In Greek mythology, Nyx, feared by Zeus himself, was the goddess of night. She had many children, including Lyssa, the spirit of madness and rage, and the Maniae, who appropriately represented mania and insanity. And of course, there were the Furies, a.k.a. the Erinyes, possibly children of Nyx, who took vengeance on men. In the Aeneid, they were called Alecto ("endless anger"), Megaera ("jealous rage"), and Tisiphone ("vengeful destruction'). And let's not forget the Gorgon, Medusa. Anthropologist Marija Gimbutas explains that before Medusa became a monster slain by Perseus (her face, encircled by live snakes, could turn man to stone), she represented one-half of the goddess. The symbolism of the snakes is no accident. While Medusa became a monster—or, as Beard points out, a popular meme for Hillary Clinton during the 2016 election, with Trump posed as Perseus—she was originally so much more. It's telling though, that in the mythmaking, Medusa turned only men to stone, never women.

Angry women are unacceptable in the public sphere, of course, unless they are used as a shield to protect patriarchal men, or any system of power and oppression.* After all, there's a critical exception made for women like Sarah Palin or Phyllis Schlafly or Ann Coulter, where the establishment defends their rage. Traister writes that "Mama Grizzlies," prominent in all points of history, "were permissioned to cast themselves as patriotic moms on steroids, some bizarro-world embodiment of female empowerment, despite the fact (or, more precisely, *because* of the fact) that what they were advocating was a return to traditionalist roles for women and reduced government investment in nonwhite people." One of Schlafly's slo-

---

Names. In Classical myths, she appears as Aphrodite, Artemis, Demeter, Persephone, Athena, Hera, Hecate, the Three Graces, the Nine Muses, the Furies, and so on. In Egypt she appears as Isis, in old Babylon as Ishtar, in Sumer as Inanna; among the western Semites she's Astarte. It's the same goddess, and the first thing to realize is that she is a total goddess and as such has associations over the whole field of the culture system."

* There's a precedent for using an angry woman as a shield, as Athena apparently used Medusa's head for precisely that.

gans was STOP—Stop Taking Our Privileges. She asserted that feminists were assaulting the natural position of wives and mothers, who belonged under the protection of (white) men. It was a move to defend the patriarchy, to assert her allegiance to this system. This battering ram to gather behind is the appeal of patriarchy for many white women, who recognize that it offers them certain protections and status.

OUR UNEXPRESSED NEEDS AND INTERNALIZED PROTEST

Censure for appearing visibly angry has deep roots: There is no realm, private or public, where women and girls get to work with their anger. We've been trained to make other people comfortable. We've been directed toward passivity and its implied dependency and victimhood. We've been instructed to suppress our natural aggression, or we've been told we shouldn't have any at all. Because we cultivate no appropriate channels, this aggression finds its way out sideways. From childhood, we were not raised to acknowledge or understand our "bad" emotions. Nobody modeled proper exploration and expression or coached us in our feelings as we grew. There are repercussions: We struggle to exist in discomfort without rushing to paper it over, to make everything OK. We are so eager for reassurance that we are worthy of love, that we are *good*. And for many of us, *goodness* has required obedience, compliance, softness, "femininity." We are taught that we are nurturers, limited to the domain of caring; we are taught that our first instinct when stressed is "tend and befriend," rather than "fight or flight." It's not possible to say whether our behavior is conditioned into us or truly "natural." This training to focus on other people first is a heavy legacy, implying that it is our mandate to put the emotional needs of everyone else before our own, that prioritizing ourselves is a sign of deviance. Good girls don't fight, good girls don't yell: We're more mature, more emotionally evolved.

I'm not buying it. History, and our own lived experience, certainly tells us that it's more complicated—and that caring for others and meeting our own needs should not be mutually exclusive. This radical revision would simply require reciprocity—a subtle restructuring of both relationship expectations and society itself, where women's care is no longer taken by men to be a patriarchal right or foregone conclusion. The late Marshall Rosenberg, famous for creating and training people in "nonviolent communication," was a master negotiator, dispatched to save crumbling marriages and flailing peace deals. He spent a lot of time working with parties in high-conflict situations, helping each side state their needs. The goal of resolution is not compromise, per Rosenberg, it's satisfaction, which requires feeling heard. Not listened to, but *heard*.

Rosenberg believes that one of the roots of our collective inability to assert ourselves and understand each other comes down to the structure of our language. He writes, "We have inherited a language that served kings and powerful elites in domination societies. The masses, discouraged from developing awareness of their needs, have instead been educated to be docile and subservient to authority. Our culture implies that needs are negative and destructive; the word *needy* applied to a person suggests inadequacy or immaturity. When people express their needs, they are often labeled selfish." An aversion to expressing needs is particularly pronounced in women, who have been at the subservient end of the patriarchy since its inception. And because women are socialized to believe that being caretakers and nurturers is the be-all and end-all of our existence, our moral duty, Rosenberg argues that we don't know how to express them. He writes, "If they ask for what they want, [women] will often do so in a way that both reflects and reinforces that they have no genuine right to their needs and that their needs are unimportant." Sound familiar? Rosenberg puts words like *should* and *have to* in the bucket of deferential, "life-alienating communication," arguing that as soon as we begin to identify how we feel and what we need, we become much harder to control and oppress. How many of us are compelled in our daily lives by what we think we *should* do? By what we *have* to do? In all this caretaking, we backburner our own needs, never lending them any heat, hoping, perhaps, that someone will notice our selflessness and reciprocate by taking care of us. This is often futile: It's impossible not to feel resentful, to take that anger and turn it toward ourselves.

Feelings are tough, and most of us were never taught to express them, much less understand them. As Brené Brown explains, we can typically identify only three emotions: happy, sad, and pissed off. We're generations-strong in feeling disconnected from our internal lives. When we feel anger, we might *think* we know what it's about—someone cut us off in traffic, we were ignored at work, our partner left the milk out overnight—but that's rarely what it's *really* about. As Rosenberg instructs, anger stems from our overlooked needs; instead of determining which needs are going unmet, we immediately begin analyzing and judging. It is difficult to go beyond the initial irritation, to figure out its real root, simply because we lack the tools to unpack and metabolize what's underneath; it's more comfortable for us to shift our focus to "out there"—to the systems, the people, the co-workers, the partners, the friends who are making these bad feelings and thoughts happen. Our anger terrifies us. It's easier to blame others.

I once attended a four-day meditation retreat with a monk from the Bon Tibetan tradition. One afternoon, we sat huddled in the hotel gym as he lectured us about anger, which he called "the most damaging of all the emotions." In his tradition, there are two types—one that is fiery and hot and red, and one that is frozen and icy. The former, the fastest to damage ourselves and our relationships, happens in five stages: (1) impatience, (2) irritation, (3) tantrum, (4) anger, and (5) rage, which left unchecked destroys all it touches: "It takes one hundred years to grow a forest, but a fire can burn it down in two hours." My anger tastes like 1 and 2—I am definitely impatient, often irritable. I vent to my husband, I vent to my friends, but that is not a salve. Vietnamese monk Thích Nhât

Hanh suggests that venting only inflames anger. He writes, "You may think that anger is no longer there, but that's not true; you are simply too tired to be angry." We think we're getting it out of our systems, but instead we are just breaking it down so that, like a muscle, it can build back stronger, still unresolved.

In the movie *The Break-Up*, stars Jennifer Aniston (Brooke) and Vince Vaughn (Gary) have a memorable fight, where Brooke walks into the living room as Gary plays video games. They've just hosted a dinner party, and she tells him she's going to do the dishes. He responds, "Cool."

"It would be nice if you helped me," she says. He looks at her and responds, "No problem, a little bit later," and then tells her he's exhausted and needs to let his food digest. She tells him that she doesn't like waking up to the dirty dishes, that she worked all day, put on a dinner party, and would like him to help her with the dishes. He throws his controller on the floor in a tantrum and gets up to help.

She responds, "No, you know, that's not what I want."

"You just said that you want me to help you do the dishes," he responds.

"I want you *to want* to do the dishes."

I'm guessing all women can relate to Brooke: We want our needs to be anticipated, even if unspoken, and our boundaries to be respected, even when not visible. When this frustration erupts into outright anger, it's too late. As the movie title suggests, they break up, the culmination of long-standing, open frustration from Brooke's unmet needs—and the fact that Gary never presumes that she has any.

OUR FEAR OF RELATIONSHIP LOSS

When needs go unmet, relationships enter conflict, which is normal and healthy when it's productive—but as anyone who has been married or in partnership for a long time can attest, you often find that you're fighting about the same issues, ad nauseam. Or conflict is avoided, leaving you to bathe daily in resentment, unsure how to move frustration into action or resolution—and this can happen until you've poisoned your relationship from within. According to legendary marriage therapists Drs. John and Julie Gottman, in their research they found that 69 percent of conflicts between couples will *never be resolved,* typically because there are significant differences in personality or lifestyle needs. So maybe you, with your desire for cleanliness and order, are matched by a partner who refuses to make the bed—and maybe the deeper trigger for your partner, the reason they are so fixed on not meeting your standards of cleanliness, is that they grew up in a house where the furniture was wrapped in plastic and they weren't allowed to touch anything. Who knows. The Gottmans' point is that this is a conflict that won't be solved. John Gottman, the founder of the "Love Lab" at the University of Washington with fellow researcher Sybil Carrère, observed couples and was able to predict—with 94 percent accuracy—who was destined for divorce, primarily through evidence of "the Four Horsemen of the Apocalypse," namely (1) criticism, (2) defensiveness, (3) contempt, and (4) stonewalling. They found that women overindex on criticism, whereas men are more inclined to stonewall (cross their arms, emotionally withdraw, and resist eye contact). Meanwhile, women raise issues 80 percent of the time. Many of us are frustrated and unhappy, yet we're unclear how to instigate change.

My husband Rob and I spent a rainy weekend in Seattle with the Gottmans doing a relationship workshop alongside hundreds of other couples. Over the course of two days, we went on quite a ride: John and Julie—who have been married for decades— role-played scenarios on a stage, and then we scattered across the auditorium to pods of folding chairs to work through the activities on our own. (Because it was a huge space, and we were all talking simultaneously, we had what is called "acoustic privacy.") We spent the first day with the Gottmans building up our relationships: shared dreams, priorities, appreciation sessions, fondest memories, plans for increasing time spent and intimacy when we returned to our regularly scheduled lives. When the Gottmans dismissed us at the end of the day, many couples held hands, excited for a date night. And then day 2 rolled around, when the Gottmans sent us into war. This is easy to do. Ask a couple to pick the scab off a typical, intransigent argument and watch faces flush red fast. There were Gottman-trained facilitators roaming around, responding to "ASSISTANCE PLEASE" placards, but most people went it alone, and it was fascinating. Arms crossed, faces turned away, and then there were those who leaned forward and yelled (only men, by my count) while the person in front of them (typically a woman) crumpled. We saw tears, we saw silence, we saw one scary man who appeared close to violence.

While I was attending to write about the event, with Rob as an unwilling co-pilot (though he didn't want to go, he turned into a Gottman superfan and exited through the gift shop, buying one of everything), we also did the exercises. Following the prompts, I realized that one of our oldest arguments—Rob's obsession with investing in state-of-the-art gear for himself and my insistence that I continue to use ski boots that are twenty-seven years old despite really wanting new ski boots—is about the shame I have from childhood about wanting new things, that idea of greediness. To translate it into Rosenberg's views on unexpressed needs, I needed to give myself permission and accept Rob's support; his ease at rewarding himself with new snowboard boots felt like an affront. Not a particularly high-stakes issue to fight about, admittedly, but there we were: The conversation felt like progress, as our usual M.O. as a couple is to bicker a little bit and then wait for a huge, twice-yearly blowup, after which we don't speak directly to each other for at least a few days, communicating through our children. Healthy! But being in that auditorium full of people who wanted to work on their relationships and were struggling to do so was a reminder of how we all struggle when we're upset—and how easy it is to put each other on the defensive.

It makes sense to me that we're bad at conflict. Fighting is shameful—*particularly* for women, where there are no cultural accolades for expression, just easy deprecations of us as scolds, nags, old ladies, and bitches. Most of our parents fought behind closed doors, often within earshot but out of sight, which made the whole spectacle particularly scary. (When I interviewed psychologist Adam Grant, he offered that one of the best moves we can make as parents is to ensure that our children *watch* us resolve conflict—a revelation that felt so counter to my desire for a "nothing-to-see-here" existence.) I didn't grow up understanding that conflict is both healthy and necessary for functioning relationships.

The worst-case scenario for many women, the reason we're so loath to put on the boxing gloves, is relationship loss. According to Harriet Lerner, our biggest fear around self-expression and setting boundaries is that doing those things will mean we'll get dumped. We are terrified to hold our ground—particularly women who find themselves in a more patriarchal relationship. After all, my husband is a lamb, I'm the primary breadwinner, which makes him happy, and he has progressive values—yet it's still hard for me to voice what I want. So I don't, hoping he'll order me to. Lerner explains that we all tend to hold on to the futile hope that our partners, parents, or friends will be supportive when we assert our own needs. "I'm so proud of you for refusing to do this thing for me, for not letting me have my way. Good job!" This is never going to happen. Instead, we must reckon with holding a boundary, acknowledging that refusing compliance to someone else's desires means we can't control how the other person will react. Being assertive is almost opposite to how many women are programmed to function in relationships, which is typically more as master manipulators. Many of us learn young how to maneuver to get what we want, while making it someone else's idea. This skill set is one of the functions of "traditional femininity." Per Terry Real, another couples therapist who primarily focuses on how the patriarchy injures men, women are often inclined to "offend from the victim position." As he explained to me, there is no movie scene he hates more than one in *My Big Fat Greek Wedding* when the mother effectively says: *The man is the head of the household, but the woman is the neck. She can turn the head anywhere she wants.* "Everybody thinks that's really adorable," he said, "but I was ready to throw up. It's a celebration of manipulation."

Harriet Lerner tells the story about a woman named Barbara whose husband stopped her from attending one of Lerner's anger and boundary-setting workshops. When Barbara called Lerner for a refund, she told her that her husband thought it was a waste of money, even though he acknowledged Barbara had an anger issue. Barbara argued with him about Lerner's qualifications, sidestepping the real issue, which was about who controlled the finances and who had freedom to do what they wanted. As Lerner explained to me, "It's very scary because it may be easy to make one change, but it's really hard to make only one. So if Barbara takes a new position on the workshop, surely there are a lot of other issues in the marriage that are there. And if she does take a position, she will be more likely to take others, and she will be in the process of change and growth. And will he change along with her?" Fear of losing our relationships is the nut of it for women: If we push, self-define, and assert ourselves overtly, will we still belong? Will someone stick with us if we prioritize our own needs and desires first? It's terrifying to contemplate. And for many, it's easier to hold those unexpressed needs inside, letting them ferment into internalized anger rather than outward dissent.

This internalized anger, or protest, often manifests as depression. One researcher surveyed sixty women who felt unheard in their relationship and who felt pressured by societal norms to be as selfless as possible, to put aside their own needs in service of their partners and children. The result was quiet anguish. The researcher describes one thirty-four-year-old married woman named Jenny who had two young children. Jenny talked about the anger she felt about effacing herself for the health of her family, and the despair she felt about impossible cultural standards. But even so, she felt she couldn't renegotiate the roles of her marriage, simply because she didn't know if her marriage, and thus her family, would survive. She would rather swallow her anger and let it devour her as depression. For too many women, anger feels both unsavory and unsafe.

A few months ago, I emailed family medicine doctor and addiction specialist Gabor Maté to check in about his newest book, *The Myth of Normal.* We have become friendly over the years, and he has offered advice to me and Rob about our own health.

"How are you?" he asked.

"Rob is doing pretty well," I responded, before carrying on about my husband.

After inquiring if I would be open to a comment, Maté wrote: "I had asked how *you* were doing. You responded, *He's doing pretty well.* Nothing about you. . . . This is not a criticism, but another marker of the patriarchal culture and, at the same time, a source of ill health for women. . . . The programming runs very deep."* This "ill health" that Maté mentions is the rampant autoimmune disease that overwhelmingly affects women, which he has treated and written about for decades: He continually points to women with "superautonomous self-sufficiency," or an unwillingness to ask anything of anyone else, as well as "niceness" and its correlation with cancer, ALS, and autoimmune diseases like rheumatoid arthritis. This "niceness" can be understood as an avoidance of conflict and suppression of anger. He cites the "type C personality," a term coined by psychologist Lydia Temoshok in 1987. She interviewed 150 people with melanoma and found them all to be *pleasers,* with "type C personality" traits like being "cooperative and appeasing, unassertive, patient, unexpressive of negative emotions (particularly

---

* In that single afternoon-long email exchange, I deflected his inquiries into my emotional state *two more times.*

anger) and compliant with external authorities." In short, unprocessed and sublimated anger is killing us.

HOW ANGER SHOWS UP AS SOCIAL AGGRESSION IN GIRLS

Our cultural ineptitude around anger means we fail to teach our children how to appropriately express it too. While we recognize aggression in its physical and verbal forms, there's a third type, social aggression, otherwise known as gossip, alliance building, silent treatment, and exclusion. We socialize boys to the first two types— "Boys will be boys." We socialize girls to the third, the least confrontational. While we teach girls to be nice, praise-seeking *good girls,* as anyone who has encountered the barbed edges of female friendships—in grade school and occasionally as adults—can testify, repercussions from this training can be long-lasting and devastating. Women can behave in ways that are cruel. Just because social aggression might be more passive doesn't make it less hurtful than getting punched in the face.

To be clear, of the three types, no form of aggression is great. But schools and homes are better prepared to handle physical aggression. For one, it's visible. When girls engage in social aggression it is often imperceptible to the adults in the room. Throw onto this bonfire the unrelenting desire many parents have that their kids be well-liked and popular, and you have a potential disaster for any child who finds her friends have turned on her. Rachel Simmons's 2001 classic, *Odd Girl Out,* resonates with what I experienced in my own childhood, with what I've observed in the daughters of friends, and even with what I've encountered as an adult. As Simmons writes, "Our culture refuses girls access to open conflict, and it forces their aggression into nonphysical, indirect, and covert forms. Girls use backbiting, exclusion, rumors, name-calling, and manipulation to inflict psychological pain on victimized targets."

There's plenty of research to measure the effects of being left out. In "Cyberball" studies, there are two researchers in the waiting room, unbeknownst to the participant. The researchers start tossing a ball between all three people and then, without comment, they leave the participant out, who looks invariably stricken and stressed and starts searching the room or their bag for something to do for distraction. As journalist Amanda Ripley writes in *High Conflict,* "More than five thousand people have now participated in these Cyberball studies, across at least sixty-two countries. Some of these people had their brains scanned while they played. The scans show heightened brain activity in the same areas triggered by physical pain." It hurts palpably to be left out.

Simmons's theory is that girls suppress their natural aggression until they become overwhelmingly pissed at whichever girl happens to be in their crosshairs, having stored up all sorts of slights, irritations, and annoyances. The other girl becomes a place to offload the emotion, the trash bag, so to speak. Because it feels "bad" to unleash directly on someone, though, bringing someone to their knees becomes a covert operation. Other girls are enlisted to share the burden and offer support. The consequence for the loser is devastating. She ends up isolated from others, giving her exactly what she fears conflict begets: exclusion. The result is trauma—both lowercase and uppercase. It also ensures a lifelong reluctance to engage in direct conversations, because we don't know how and the stakes feel too high.

OUTSIDER STATUS AND ANGER IN CHILDREN

Research suggests that Black girls are more comfortable with conflict, that the insidiousness of "nice girl" programming targets those who are most likely to be closest to power. As Simmons explains,

The now famous American Association of University Women's 1990 report on girls found that Black girls scored highest on self-

esteem measures through adolescence. In interviews . . . psychologist Niobe Way discovered [that] girls . . . who came from
predominantly working-class African American families described
relationships [that were] empowered, not dissolved, by conflict.
These girls are exceptional. The heart of their resistance appears
to be an ease with truth telling, a willingness to know and voice
their negative emotions. When girls make a choice to value their
emotions, they value themselves. They tell the truth because their
survival may depend on raising their voices in a hostile culture.

Girls of a lower socioeconomic status also don't struggle as much
with expressing anger physically and verbally, though Simmons and
other researchers stress that there is no single experience or story
for any "type" of girl, particularly because so much research focuses
on white, middle-class ones. Plus, a comfort with conflict doesn't
always require emotional granularity, or an intimate understanding
of what you're feeling.

More ease with anger doesn't mean women of color are immune from patriarchal programming either. On a recent visit to my
optometrist, a subtly mohawked, forty-something Cuban lesbian
raised in a lower-class family on the East Coast, she told me, while
we waited for my eyes to dilate, about the wedding of her best
friend that she had just attended. My optometrist's ex-wife, also in
attendance, stalked and trolled her throughout the weekend, even
though she had communicated to her in advance that she would be
bringing her new girlfriend and that she wanted space and zero
conversation.

"I made it clear that I wanted nothing to do with her, but she
kept approaching again, and again," she said, visibly upset. "I failed
to protect my girl. It was awful." When I asked her why she hadn't
taken her ex-wife on, particularly if her current girlfriend was
upset, she told me she struggled with boundaries and didn't want
to make a scene. "It's all that good girl programming. I didn't want

to get into a big fight. But I ended up letting my girl down, and I'm so upset with myself, and frustrated, and I let my ex ruin my time at my best friend's wedding."

One of my close friends, Elaine, whose parents are Taiwanese-Indonesian immigrants, describes her mother's familiarity with anger: "My mom has a terrible temper, she is not afraid to lash out." Her mother was poor as a child, though not as an adult; Elaine grew up in a wealthy white community. "There might be some model minority, Asian stereotyping in there, but I don't know if it was about race," Elaine told me. "The angry spots in my family were taken by my mom and my brother. I had some moments of being a mean girl around the third grade that still give me chills." To this day, Elaine is more inclined to go for the funny snide re-mark than to raise her voice. I've never seen her get mad. Like me, she became a magazine editor: happy to stand back, observe, and then write her judgments down without fear of immediate reprisal. "I deal with my anger now on my Peloton."

Another close friend of mine, Regina, who moved to Texas from Guadalajara when she was ten, mentioned that she is fre-quently stereotyped as a fiery Latina. "There is a lot of resentment of that stereotype in the community because it's misunderstood—as Latinos, we do everything with more emotion and are comfortable with expression. We are huggers, kissers, we cook with heat. . . . However, it is still a patriarchal culture, and there is a line that women are not supposed to cross. We are supposed to be passionate but still deferential. It's made it difficult for me to express my anger without feeling like I am playing into a stereotype—I often feel like I'm caught." She went on to note that she doesn't know if her white friends like me are angrier, but we seem more disinclined to express ourselves. "I find myself constantly saying, 'But aren't you pissed? Why aren't you more pissed off? Do you have Stockholm syndrome?'" While it's never great to generalize, it is easy to see how our childhood programming prepares us for conflict in the wider world—or not. Regina won debates as a kid and became a high-powered attorney—but still struggles to exist within the confines of being an obedient daughter.

WHEN WHITE WOMEN SIDESTEP OUR RAGE

While unexpressed anger in the private sphere delimits our lives, unexpressed anger in the public sphere depreciates our rights and our very sovereignty. Women of color—who hold the least amount of political power in our patriarchy—understand what's at stake and bear most of the weight of equity. While white women understand this intellectually, we've been woeful allies in the past, unwilling to fully step into the fray.

After all, white women can pick—and very notably *have* picked—only the most opportune moments to engage with anger in public. Women of color don't have that luxury: For many, addressing an oppressive system where misogyny is compounded by racism is a daily practice. As professor Brittney Cooper writes in her masterpiece, *Eloquent Rage,*

> Black women have the right to be mad as hell. We have been dreaming of freedom and carving out spaces for liberation since we arrived on these shores. There is no other group, save Indigenous women, that knows and understands more fully the soul of the American body politic than Black women, whose reproductive and social labor have made the world what it is. This is not mere propaganda. Black women know what it means to love ourselves in a world that hates us. We know what it means to do a whole lot with very little, to "make a dollar out of fifteen cents," as it were. We know what it means to snatch dignity from the jaws of power and come out standing. We know what it means to face horrific violence and trauma from both our communities and our nation-state and carry on anyway.

Double oppression—the intersection of gender and race—and triple oppression for those who are also of a lower economic class are focusing lenses. White, middle-class women stand adjacent to power; women of color are typically the farthest from its protective embrace.

I believe white women—seemingly confined by the "civilizing" prison of goodness—feel stuck between their identities as "white" and "woman," with nowhere to dump their distress. While terrible stereotypes abound about angry Black women (cue the consistent media coverage of Michelle Obama), Black women's overwhelming anger is a fallacy. A frequently cited Esquire/NBC News survey from 2015—*before* Trump, COVID, George Floyd, Uvalde, the overturning of *Roe v. Wade*—found white women to be the angriest. The generalized reasons cited for their anger range from taxes, to school shootings, to Bill Cosby. In a follow-up by *Elle* in 2017, the results were the same. Perhaps it's because we lack the tools to unpack, metabolize, and understand it—but more likely, it's because we feel we have more to lose by doing anything more with our anger than venting to a survey administrator, or our friends. It's so much easier to maintain the status quo. This is a bad choice, a false one: By continuing to prioritize and empower a system that depends on the secondary status of women, by prioritizing our whiteness over our gender, we perpetuate our own submission. Women of color are much more clear-eyed about the ways the patriarchy holds white women in its thrall, in part by the continued promise of power.

It's not by chance that Black women are engaged in community organizing and activism, that they delivered our democracy from fascism in 2020. As outsiders, they have a healthier relationship to anger; they understand how to transmute it into action in highly productive ways. Researchers at Clayton State University found this to be true. As professor Kristin Neff explains in *Fierce Self-Compassion:* "Black women were found to report lower levels of reactive anger in situations in which they were criticized, disrespected, or negatively evaluated compared to others. These findings were interpreted to demonstrate the maturity that develops from having to deal with racism and sexism on a daily basis; Black women are able to recognize the protective function of anger but are also more able to regulate it." While it's easy to respond to these studies by applauding the resilience and long fuses of Black women, needing to emotionally armor oneself against perpetual racism for survival is a symptom of a very sick society. And it's making white women ill too, even as we fail to identify our collective flu: We stuff our anger down, unsure of where to start, wary of turning over applecarts.

METABOLIZING OUR ANGER—AND MOVING PAST AFFIRMATION

Our resentment, frustration, and anger live in us. When our partners, our parents, our bosses, the system itself, refuse to absorb our wrath, to hear us, we don't know where to put these bad feelings—and they must go somewhere. We shift into blaming and shaming. We become angry with ourselves and each other. And then, when we engage in the public sphere with our unrealized rage—the result of long-unmet needs and resentment—we get into trouble.

We have to start at home, with ourselves—and this is difficult. Weathering conflict and confrontation in the private sphere is scary, as Harriet Lerner confirms, because it might be the first time we've asserted needs and established boundaries when we've always been told that doing so is selfish. We have every right to believe that this bid for reciprocity might make us less lovable, or less "useful," to our partners—that they might, in fact, revolt or retaliate, and that new lines might need to be drawn. It is here that we find a Venn diagram of overlapping private and public constraints: Many women are practically bound to the patriarchy, through marriage, employment, and family. Asserting any autonomy and self-definition can feel like placing oneself under existential threat. As Rebecca Traister writes, "Women's challenge to male authority or power abuse can send a family into disarray, end a marriage, provoke a firing, either of a woman *or* of a man on whom other women—colleagues and family members—rely economically. Fear[s] of these repercussions (alongside a long-ingrained and realistic fear of simple futility) are very often fierce enough to inoculate women against expressing, and perhaps in many cases even feeling, the outrage at men that they might otherwise make known." Whether consciously or not, many women are stuck. This is no small thing—but anger turned inward is no salve either.

We don't want to give up our proximity to power, yet we want credit for rejecting it. We are caught in the middle, trying to have it all ways, trying to not ruffle feathers, to play nice, to be fair. We want to be thought of as one of the "good ones," always on the right side of history. We recognize that if we begin to assert ourselves, to join up with fellow women, there's risk. But by not engaging, we rightfully incur censure. The problem is that we lack practice stepping into the action, and our ineptitude makes us clumsy; we get in the way.

We also get frustrated and resentful, because we recognize our own oppression—and want to be validated for what we've endured. We understand how our training to focus on others first has held us back from meeting our own needs. When white women engage in social justice with women of color, we wrongly believe we should meet a sympathetic audience who will hear and empathize with our complaints. And often, when we are told that it's not actually our time to talk, we respond with further—this time misplaced— outrage. Even a hint of that feedback is enough to send many of us into a tailspin. We want to be heard—not *to hear* that we've also been weapons of oppression. That fact feels intolerable—and it abrades our desire to be seen as good. We alternately internalize and offload this shame.

White women, in particular, self-flagellate, prostrate ourselves, and resign from jobs at any suggestion of wrongness or badness. We turn our venom on each other and lick wounds, rather than confront our feelings, take empathic accountability, or figure out the most effective path forward. In our frustration and fear, we struggle to own our participation in past behavior or even to acknowledge that change is part of the process. We aim for perfection, shuddering at the moments when we've said the wrong thing, missed an opportunity, put our foot in our mouth. When this happens, many women (especially white women) get scared—and we stop engaging. We struggle to move forward because we spend too much time defending our "goodness," stuck in the binary that if you're not impeccable in your behavior—across the arc of time—then you must be bad. And badness, of course, means you're undeserving of love; you'll be cast out of your community, canceled by the culture. This is happening—canceling, silencing—in part because we are allowing it. We are not going to be perfect. There are no hurdles to clear, no lists to check off. It's a process that requires a willingness to engage, learn, evolve, and repeat. We can't skip steps to perfection or doneness. Fear keeps us out of these conversations, prevents us from sharing thoughts or ideas, stops us from asking questions or showing up. Perhaps, to quote professor Dolly Chugh, author of *The Person You Mean to Be,* instead of gunning to be perfect in our goodness, we should aim for "good enough."

White women are wrapped up in so much self-consciousness it's counterproductive, inhibiting our ability to be effective allies—or even allies at all. Rather than quietly doing the work—educating ourselves, changing our hiring practices, writing to Congress, speaking out when we witness microaggressions, showing up at rallies and protests, taking on Uncle Joe at Thanksgiving, getting behind community organizers, registering people to vote and driving them to the polls—we spend our energy on defensive moves, securing safety from criticism through virtue signaling on Instagram and car bumpers. This desire to always do and say the "right" thing with no real action to back it up is what earns the title of a performance. Activism is not Broadway. There's no script, rehearsal, standing ovations. I love a good meme, don't get me wrong. Bumper stickers and hashtags are all fine too. But only so long as we *do something* and push past the need for constant validation. I understand this is hard: We are so well trained to seek approval as little girls. As Chugh explains, "Most of us have . . . a central 'moral identity.' Moral identity is a measure of whether I care about being a good person, *not* whether I am a good person. . . . Most of us want to feel like good people. This is an identity we claim and want granted." This is why our craving for affirmation is so stark and insistent—the identity becomes the only thing that matters, not whether our purposes are achieved. We want to be celebrated for our efforts. We want our affirmation cookies, reassurance that we are good and, as a result, safe. We lack durability in the face of conflict. We must reparent ourselves for difficult conversations and learn the skills now that we were not taught as kids.

THE PATH TO EMOTIONAL LIBERATION

We have work to do before we can assert ourselves in intimate relationships, in the workforce, and then, ultimately, as effective allies, invoking the changes that all women need. Part of evolution is allowing our humanity to emerge without rushing to stuff it down. We need to resist letting stories about who we're supposed to be— good, pliant, obliging—define us. We must do the work of defining ourselves first. For those of us who feel buried under layers of cultural expectations and programming, anger can be a guiding light, a means of showing us what and where our boundaries are. Per Marshall Rosenberg's theory of "nonviolent communication," anger serves as an internal alarm, indicating that something is wrong. We must learn to hear and address the warning. And on the flip side, when people direct their anger and pain toward us, we must learn how to respond appropriately and effectively. Per Rosenberg, when someone comes at us with anger, we can blame ourselves or other people, or we can sense into what we're feeling and needing and sense into the unstated feelings and needs of the other person and what they're trying to say. Many of us are stuck in blame, spinning out in a futile search for retribution, when peace and resolution are possible only through understanding and addressing needs.

Rosenberg believes that we cannot express ourselves and listen to others until we become conscious of what we need. Instead of "I am angry because they . . . ," he urges us to flip the script and say: "I am angry *because I am needing. . . .*" This is not easy. As women, we have been trained to not overtly *need* anything—it is one thing to acknowledge needs exist and another to assert them confidently. But absent this work, we are drowning in our own anger and resentment, futilely waiting for someone, anyone, to do this work on our behalf, to anticipate what we want and eagerly address it so we don't have to say anything at all.

Until we become flexible, resilient, and more sure-footed, we will not be equipped for the healthy conflict required for effective allyship. While we must hurry, since the battle for gender equality in the public sphere is essential, we cannot skip steps in orienting ourselves in the conversation and examining our own plumbing. We must become more durable as we engage with others, particularly when the scent of conflict is in the air. Too often, when we say or do something wrong, we rush to defend ourselves rather than pausing, listening, reflecting back what was said, empathically understanding the other person's pain. As we move to understand each other's uncomfortable realities, we must resist the urge to analyze, fix, or minimize. I get it. It's scary as hell when things get heated, when you feel eyes turn to assess your moral character, when you feel compelled to respond immediately and to defend yourself. It's terrible to feel judged. I've observed friends, coworkers, and strangers struggle to have hard conversations. I do as well. Criticism, and sometimes even feedback, can feel like a wholesale rejection. We fear that we must be bad, that an imperfect step means we'll lose everything. I understand why our ineptitude is insufferable for others, why it's followed by impatience and then chastisement.

It is my hope that the coming years clear the way for white women like myself to be sharper with our dissatisfaction, more clear about what a unified future looks like, and less tripped up in whether we are impeccable in our activism. Throwing off this idea of perfection will require grace for ourselves and each other, because we will mess up, but it feels imperative for this next phase of our collective advancement. As Brittney Cooper writes in *Eloquent Rage,* "I have too much feminist shit to do to spend my time hating white women. Any time a white woman says something wrong in the public sphere these days, there is an army of Black feminist writers at the ready with think pieces that can snatch her wig and have her picking her face up off the floor months later. Going after white women online will get you lots of clicks and likes. But you'll feel exhausted at the end and, often, white women's attitudes won't have changed one iota." Black women don't have time for us, and they shouldn't—at least not until our anger is transmuted into something useful and spent trying to overthrow the unequal systems that oppress us all. Our best shot here is to show up and do the work. While history is littered with examples of white women who promised to lift all women as long as they themselves could get ahead, we must shake off the lie that women in power in the same patriarchal system won't be warped by toxic masculinity too: We must prioritize the needs of those who are most marginalized, as a bottom-up movement and not top down. This can't be about white women protecting their status—and then reaching out a hand. It will require our exile from the system itself, a fresh vantage point, a chance to build back anew. We will need to stop clutching at this structure and recognize that our fear keeps us bound, not safe, and that what we all *need* is equity within a society that is balanced and humane.

We must create a movement that ensures all women thrive. In our earliest days, women were engaged in a sisterhood; we must find our way back to this, recognize the ways in which we belong to each other. Unvarnished rage doesn't work, we know this. We need to start by tending to our own pain and anger, using that as a guide for wider change—because we cannot fix what's *out there* until we metabolize our own deeply buried *internal* frustration and resentment. We have much to learn from Black women and activists about how healthy anger functions. If you look at those who moved the needle—Martin Luther King Jr., Gloria Steinem, Gandhi, Rosa Parks, Bryan Stevenson, Greta Thunberg—you'll note that they struggled at times with overwhelming anger, hurt, and grief. But they managed anger well: Their action came not from the seeping wound, but from a place of integration, from the scar. They operated, or still operate, from grace—firm, heated grace—but not unbound wrath. Yes, we're upset about the environment, the state of policing, the overturn of *Roe v. Wade,* a dearth of gun control laws, and lack of financial equity, but progress does not require being permanently pissed. Action is more powerful when it comes from a place of love. We'd recognize that if we plumbed our emotions more—they're more useful and usable once transformed. Anger points us to what we care about deeply—our own dignity and autonomy; it clarifies what matters and the cost of suppressing our own needs. Anger well used, anger understood, becomes righteous indignation. This indignation transforms irritation into just action. It fuels the grace from which we can serve the world.

Several years ago, I interviewed Byron Katie about her method, which she calls "The Work." She coaches people to approach the idea that they've been wronged by creating statements and asking repeatedly, "Is that true?" Her point is not as simple as "There are two sides to every story"—it's that we continue to stay engaged with our tormentors, ritually replaying something that was upsetting, thereby victimizing ourselves in our refusal to let go. As she writes in *Loving What Is:* "They all began by realizing a truth so basic that it is usually invisible: the fact that (in the words of the

Greek philosopher Epictetus) 'we are disturbed not by what happens to us, but by our thoughts about what happens.'" When you do "The Work," you start to unhook yourself from whatever is upsetting you, whether it's extreme (an abusive parent or spouse) or common (a partner or roommate who doesn't put dishes in the dishwasher). In Katie's world, you can go through life feeling aggrieved, or you can take responsibility for what's causing you frustration, resentment, anger, and ultimately pain. You can clean up your own emotions. As she writes about her own kids, "Day after day, they left their socks on the floor, after all my years of preaching and nagging and punishing them. I saw that I was the one who should pick up the socks if I wanted them picked up. My children were perfectly happy with their socks on the floor. Who had the problem? It was me. It was my thoughts about the socks on the floor that had made my life difficult, not the socks themselves. And who had the solution? Again, me. I realized that I could be right, or I could be free." She's talking about socks, yes—but *she could be right, or she could be free.* How many of us get corralled into grievances, expending all our emotion on "should have, would have, could have" retorts and "someday, I'll be vindicated" fantasies? How many of us are spending our good anger on what everyone else is doing wrong—the blaming and shaming—rather than figuring out how to bring peace and change, first to ourselves, then to the world?

DIAGNOSING AND UNDERSTANDING MY OWN ANGER

A couple of years ago, I stood on a Utah mountaintop with a group of friends. We were on a retreat, and on one of the final late-fall days we took several chilly chairlifts to the top of a mountain to release rehabilitated birds into the wild, including a golden eagle named Sautee. Hit by a car, Sautee had spent years recovering in a small room, building strength for this moment. We huddled together in excitement as her caretakers opened the cage door to freedom; in response, Sautee clung to the cage's metal side, beating her wings against her keeper's attempts to pull her out. Each of her talons had to be disengaged with pliers until she could be placed on the gloved arm of her caretaker, calmed, and walked to the mountain's edge. A Ute medicine man offered a blessing and tied a feather to her tail so she could carry it to his ancestors above. He removed her leather hood and murmured to her. She surveyed the ocher swath of aspens below and turned her head to take in her quietly crying caretaker. On our collective count of three, Sautee's caretaker tossed her gently into the air. Wings unfurled, she spiraled above us for many minutes before disappearing into a radial rainbow. There was no way Sautee was returning to her cage.

Watching Sautee resist liberation was a powerful testament to how scary it can be to have agency and freedom, to be responsible for yourself. We often fight like hell to stay confined to a small, familiar cell, even as we simultaneously beat our wings against its restrictions. I would know: Two weeks before this trip with friends, I found myself pushed out of a nest I had spent years building, newly unmoored, suddenly free. I hadn't planned to be on this mountaintop, I had planned to be doing my job. In that moment on the mountain, as I watched Sautee circle higher and higher, relearning to fly, I realized that, like her, I had been aching to leave. And like her, I hadn't known it. I had clung to my own cage, refusing to honor my desire to let go.

Months later, when I finally acknowledged that the clench of my jaw might be from anger, I had to begrudgingly admit it was about no longer having my job. Because I was intent on "higher-minding" the experience, when I was first exited, I rushed to assure everyone, even myself, that I was OK. I wasn't letting my feelings come up. I was *fine* even as my body told me I was not. The more I tried to let my emotions float to the surface so I could diagnose them and file them away, the more elusive they became—I didn't know *what they were*. If I'm honest, I didn't want to know, because that would require admitting I was pissed. On some level I was at peace: I felt relief, I was free to do something else—like Sautee. But I couldn't rush to the place of acceptance; I needed to process it first. My emotions lagged behind my rational mind. I struggled to match the two.

When I was asked if I wanted to talk later, I demurred for months, knowing I would rush to make our relationship easy and comfortable rather than honoring my own pain: I didn't trust myself not to abandon myself. Plus, I wanted to be over it, to be in peace as *fast as possible,* because accepting that I wasn't OK would require acknowledging that I felt hurt.* I didn't want to feel like I had no agency, which felt disempowering, reductive, inaccurate.

My jaw pain forced me to listen to my body. And what I realized was that I could allow the anger to come up without offloading it on anyone else. There was nobody to blame. I was frustrated with myself. And it wasn't about the end of my tenure. It was the opposite: I was frustrated I had waited to be pushed instead of taking the leap myself. I knew I was being called to move on, that I was curious about what was next—I should have been courageous rather than making this someone else's responsibility. More pointedly, I was angry because I had crossed my personal boundaries with my professional existence. Or really, I hadn't set any boundaries at all. I was angry I had spent a vast majority of my waking hours thinking about and attending to work rather than my kids, my marriage, my friends, and that I had deluded myself into believing this level of sacrifice was required or worth it. I was also angry with myself for spending all my energy building something that *felt* personal but at the end of the day was not mine. The most painful part was that I had wrapped up my value with my job—my success

---

* In an early draft of this book, I wrote here that I had been hurt, using a passive voice. According to Rosenberg, this language is typical yet inaccurate and limits us from taking accountability for our feelings. Effectively, I was assigning my feelings to someone else's action. As he coaches, achieving "emotional liberation" means we recognize we are not responsible for other people's feelings and we don't make them responsible for how we feel either.

there was a testament to my *goodness*. I had thought that I was irreplaceable, that my fealty had earned me endless loyalty, a perpetual place, even as needs on both sides shifted. I had worked so hard, given so much. I thought my excellence and effort and workaholism would safeguard my security.

These were healthy revelations. But I needed to take a shovel and keep digging to find the real roots of my anger, that deeper unstated *need*. I let my anger rise to show me where I had betrayed myself. And, of course, it had started young: I had learned—through my parents and the culture at large—the fallacy that love is conditional. I had trained myself to believe that I didn't deserve love unless I was doing for others, that my worth was tied to my output, my ability to service people's needs, that focusing on what I wanted was selfish, an instinct that should be suppressed. The little girl in me, whose needs for space, stillness, love without stipulations had not been appropriately honored or addressed: She was *pissed*.

My therapist says that anger can sometimes be a mirage—it is often a secondary or reactionary emotion to sadness, fear, and shame. This advice is helpful, if hard, since it's easier to be mad. Anger is satisfying when it offers vindication, when you get to feel it toward someone else. But rushing to blame, as we know, is a cop-out. It's a type of violence that solves nothing. True to every therapist's word, the emotion that emerged once I reached bedrock was grief—a lot of grief—some with visible roots, some so old it was disconnected from any original event. I was very sad.*

A healer explained to me that anger is one of our most insistent animating energies: "It's what impels the seedling to break free from the husk and push toward the light. It's the energy that says, 'Don't tread on me.'" When harnessed, it can be beautiful. Using our anger healthfully is different from venting or blowing off

---

* *Anger's* etymology underlines this connection: It comes from Old Norse, *angr*, "grief," and *angra*, "vex."

steam—we can move it into action instead of more pain. Doing this skillfully requires practice. But we need the skills so that we can channel our feelings appropriately. We have a choice: Our anger can push us into discord, disharmony, hate, cycles of blaming and shaming and judgment. Or our anger can provoke change and establish new ways of being in the world through grace and peace. The latter is a hard path to walk, but essential if we want to move ourselves and society forward without creating more burdens—for ourselves, for our children, and for each other.

REAPING WHAT WE SOW

In the Bible, Jesus recounts the hypocrisy inherent in shaming someone for something that might hold true for yourself. "Do not judge and you will not be judged. For, just as you judge others, you will yourselves be judged, and the standard that you use will be used for you. Why do you look at the speck of sawdust in your friend's eye, while you pay no attention at all to the plank in your own? Hypocrite! Take out the plank from your own eye first, and then you will see clearly how to take out the speck from your friend's" (Matthew 7:1–5). In this teaching, he seems to be suggesting accountability: If you throw boulders into your neighbor's yard, be prepared to take those boulders back. Rather than pushing social justice issues and environmental devastation onto future generations to solve, we must "re-solve" them now. Hot potato–ing accountability isn't tenable. We must learn how to tend our own gardens, to plant seeds of peace rather than seeds of shame and blame. We must take responsibility for our emotions and stop flinging them at each other. We must learn how to express ourselves clearly and calmly—even in conflict. Leaning into honesty requires facing our fears of relational loss. It requires relinquishing the desire to please. It requires advocating for our own interests and needs, without apology.

We need to allow our anger as part of a cycle of required emotions. Sometimes our equanimity will be disrupted by life. Like the planet that surrounds us, we are changing. Nature also has her seasons and her rituals. As scary as forest fires can be, they are a necessary part of our ecology—they bring a purifying energy that clears out the dead brush, makes way for new growth, and establishes new perimeters. Our primordial mother, the goddess at our feet, Gaia, shows us movement is essential. When we stop fires from burning, when we don't allow the pressure to release, we feel the consequences of this unspent rage on a greater scale. When we deny the need for release, it's reflected in our bodies. When we overload our jaws, hips, and lower backs with pent-up feelings, we tempt eruption. Instead, we can unpack and examine our red-hot emotions until we understand their source. Then, knowing their true origins, we can begin the work of repair and transformation.

I recently chatted with Susan Olesek, who runs the Enneagram Prison Project. Though she teaches the Enneagram in jails, she also works with plenty of people outside of the penal system, asserting that we all live behind bars in our own minds. Like me, Susan is a Type One, and like me, it took her a long time to process her shame about her anger. As we talked, I lamented my rigidity, idealism, and perfectionistic tendencies, my frustration that we don't live up to our collective values and that I don't know what to do with my anger.

"I learned this from one of my teachers, Russ Hudson, who wrote *The Wisdom of the Enneagram,*" she told me. "Russ said, 'You know, you can say a lot about Ones. You can say Type Ones are judgmental, and perfectionistic,'—and all those qualities you listed, Elise—'but you can never say about a One that they don't care.' And when he said that, everything that was ready to fight in me just relaxed." Susan went on to offer that anger is an essential intelligence and that our collective practice—not just for Type Ones—is to understand when anger is running us rather than informing us. When it informs us, it is a drive shaft of compassion and *care;* when mined for its lessons, metabolized and transmuted, it is the energy that changes the world. When properly expressed, it cleanses, leaving the foundation for new growth and fresh starts, a revitalized postpatriarchal landscape. There may we sow a truer, fairer future, one that can be reaped for all. Harnessing the power of women's anger is essential for the process; the same is not true for the anger of men. As we'll now explore, those who are captured in the maw of toxic masculinity must look beneath their destructive anger and plumb the sorrow in their souls instead. Our collective future depends on it.

Accepting anger as essential, we can better recognize our individual and collective needs, and forge a more equitable future.

SADNESS

Believing Sadness to Be Sinful, We Deny Our Own Feelings

RECLAIMING SADNESS

The Seven Deadly Sins were once eight thoughts. For no easily discernible reason, sadness was excommunicated, replaced by sloth, while vanity was subsumed by pride. The absence of sadness, though theoretically one less thing to police ourselves about, offers an unexpected and terrible legacy: I believe that the disavowal of sadness holds society by the throat. Of all the sins, sadness feels like it should be the most important, the crown—after all, to allow for sadness requires opening ourselves to all of life. Absent its undertow, one could argue that we are only partially alive, trying to cherry-pick the parts of existence that appeal. Denying sadness hurts women, but the consequence of sadness's exclusion is particularly dire when it comes to men, both in the experiencing of their own lives and in collateral damage that affects our entire culture. When men refuse to metabolize this emotion, we must consume it for them.

Today, we can only speculate about why sadness was officially clipped from the list. Perhaps it fell away because sadness makes people docile, quiet, unthreatening—there's no need to restrict anyone beyond sadness's inherently limiting capacity. My guess, though, is that sadness was determined to be more of a fixation or foible for the desert monks who first defined these problematic thoughts than it was for everyday people: Evagrius described the demonic idea of sadness as homesickness, a longing for something you've lost. After all, his fellow brothers had chosen to abandon their loved ones and take to a cell. As he explains, "Certain thoughts first drive the soul to the memory of home and parents, or else to that of one's former life. Now when these thoughts find that the soul offers no resistance but rather follows after them and pours itself out in pleasures that are still only mental in nature, they then seize her and drench her in sadness." Evagrius, ever in search of his *apatheia,* or unfailing communion with God through prayer, describes how sorrow pulls monks out of the present moment to dwell on something that is no longer theirs to claim. Pointedly, he describes sadness's effect on a *feminine* soul. This is the crux of it: It seems to me that sadness is the "sin" that's most destructive to men precisely because it's perceived as womanly, as weak. Because it slipped from the rules about morality, women are better at recognizing and then allowing it. Men, on the other hand, reject this emotion, or they repress it and let it cripple and destroy them.

Evagrius and his fellow brethren modeled a life of detachment—extreme asceticism. They let go of their worldly goods and, most pressingly, their emotional attachments, asserting that the only relationship they needed was with God. This is extreme and antithetical to what it means to be human: We are only now beginning to understand that our interdependence—the strength of our connections to each other and the wider community—is perhaps the most critical linchpin of our survival *and* sanity.* But here's the thing

---

* As Dr. Jeffrey Rediger reports in his stunning book *Cured,* loneliness is killing us. As he explains: "A recent review of twenty-eight studies, involving over 180,000 adult subjects, showed in stark relief how deadly it can be if you're cut off from social connection. After examining the data, the review panel found that loneliness, social isolation, or both are associated with a 29 percent increased risk of heart attack and a 32 percent greater risk of stroke—a huge increase. People who reported fewer social connections also showed

about attachments: They underline the exquisiteness of our vulnerability. To love requires that you will lose. But it is our one human
imperative to wager it all, constantly. We must accept the prospect
of grief and anguish in exchange for love. Too many of us attempt
to keep both at bay, insisting that by avoiding the messiness of attachment we can control life and protect ourselves from loss.

THE FEAR OF LOSS

We all have many reasons to be sad. Sometimes the cause is brief,
fleeting, a flicker of disappointment and dismay. Sometimes it's the
biochemical stew of chronic depression—a complex and intransigent disease that also has environmental and social factors. And
sometimes our sadness is pegged to loss, both nagging and acute:
loss of opportunity, loss of job, loss of health, loss of our planet, loss
of functioning government, loss of relationship, and, most pressingly, loss of life. Sadness is the most existential of all emotions—it
is the death of connection—and its only cure is grief.

Perhaps it's because we've had so little control over our lives, but
women seem to have a much better understanding of this universal
truth: You can't fight sadness. Yes, women are capable of oppressive
despair—it just doesn't come for us with the double-barrel of
shame. Sadness is difficult. Sadness can stay awhile, be unyielding
and impenetrable, suffocating. It's a disorienting abyss, with no
clear boundaries for when you'll be through it, or if you ever will.
Sadness is also typically followed by a cattle prod from a world that
wishes you would just get over it already. But that's not how sadness
works. It yields to no commands or timetables; it has its way with

---

disrupted sleep patterns, altered immune systems, higher inflammation, and greatly increased levels of stress hormones. And consider the sociological landscape here—in the
United States, one-third of those over age sixty-five live alone, as do more than *half* of
the 1.6 million people who live in Manhattan. In the UK, sociologists saw a marked increase in the number of people living alone over the course of a decade; between 2001
and 2011, it went up by 600,000 people, over 10 percent of the population."

you. Submission and surrender are required. Getting on your knees is paramount to being able to get up again, an essential component of resurrection—to die to little things like hope, dreams, relationships, and jobs, again and again, to feel the loss, to understand that it meant something to you, it mattered. From what I've observed, those who can accept the inevitable hits of life—these bursts of loss and pain—and crumble for a time are the ones who become more durable and flexible. Denying this reality fells people like an ax to a tree.

We live in a culture that exhorts us to be happy and suggests that consistent and constant happiness is attainable and natural through optimistic thinking and positivity. Just *smile*. The pressure to be up *all the time* makes the down periods feel like missteps, as if we're doing it wrong, which only exacerbates the idea that life is something to control. While many of us will avoid the quicksand of unrelenting depression (more on that later) and just have moments, days, or weeks when we feel blue, grief is unavoidable. It's the payment come due for love and attachment. It's a gauntlet we must walk, to be separated from those we love, sometimes permanently. And we're terrible at it.

THE DENIAL OF DEATH

Our culture pretends to be immune to loss. We deny the cycle of life. But nobody has yet outsmarted death. In her feminist classic *The Crone,* Barbara Walker argues that the third, ultimate part of the female archetype—the trinity of the Virgin (Creator), Mother (Preserver), and Crone (Destroyer)—is rejected because she represents the waning of vitality, the immediacy of the end. This trio—sex, birth, death—represents the full cycle, an immutable reality. But in banishing the Crone, we bid ourselves to look and feel forever young, immortal. Walker explains, "That sad knowledge [of our own ultimate destruction] is acutely perceived by humans alone among all the animals on earth, and may be called the true curse under which we live—part of the price we pay for intelligence. We are forced to recognize the impermanence of our existence, regardless of our personal wishes."

One of the fascinating phenomena in the first few months of the coronavirus pandemic was to watch people everywhere seized with the sudden revelation that *they could die.* Toilet paper was hoarded, canned goods were stocked, PPE was seized, all as a bulwark against this potential. I suspect it was the first time many people had allowed this reality to pierce their consciousness; in response, it held them by the neck, in paroxysms of fear. I was not scared. Perhaps it was because I'd been forced into intimacy with death, experiencing what Joseph Campbell describes: "The conquest of the fear of death is the recovery of life's joy." Acknowledging the door that must be walked through releases the anxiety of this passage. It doesn't mean that accepting the end precludes sadness. But sadness is a gift—while it can feel oppressive enough to pin you to the bottom of the ocean, when it's survived and endured it is proof of flexibility and resilience. This allowance is the conquest of fear Campbell writes about. It's also a liberation from a bond to perfection, from the futility of control.

As a culture, we have done our best to sanitize death from our existence. We modulate our environments to protect us from the waxing and waning of days and months, we eat out-of-season produce and try to erase the march of birthdays and gravity from our bodies and faces. I cry out with dismay when one of my cats murders a lizard in our yard and drops it at my feet, yet I eat fish, poultry, and meat, participating in an economy of killing and death without giving it much thought. Whether or not that's our birthright at the top of the food chain, the conveniences of modernity spare us from thinking through this truth. We refuse to contemplate where our plastic-wrapped chicken at the grocery store comes from, we turn our faces from roadkill, we have no clue where our sewage goes or our trash ends up. What dies creates space for new birth, and decomposition feeds renewal. But we've tried to take ourselves out of the cycle.

Death may be life's biggest question: What happens when we die? Do we dissolve into the darkness of the living earth, or does our spirit, or soul, untether and return to some sort of source point just on the other side of the perceptible veil? Is it both—matter back to matter (or *mater,* mother) while our spirits disintegrate into an energetic whole? Or, if you believe this sort of thing, are we judged for our sins and marshaled off to either the pearly gates of heaven or the furnace of hell? We find it terrible and terrifying to contemplate what happens, yet each of us will take a final breath.

PETER

While I had mourned the death of two grandparents—as a child, mourning meant watching my parents be sad—I had two close brushes with loss that convinced me I was safe from bad things happening for a bit. My mom almost died from a partially ruptured brain aneurysm when I was in high school; and in my early thirties, a mentally ill man in New York City's Riverside Park stabbed five people with gardening shears, including my brother Ben. Ben lost his spleen, parts of some other vital organs, and a Patagonia vest but was otherwise preserved. As I sat in his hospital room with his husband, Peter, who moonlighted as my best friend and other "real" brother (Ben and Peter met their first week of college, when I was sixteen), we marveled at the close call and the karmic debt that had presumably been paid. And then the universe laughed, because three and a half years later, Peter went to sleep and never woke up. While he had a diagnosed and treated arrhythmia, he died from a rare and undiagnosed heart condition called Loeffler's endocarditis.

When a phone's ring pierces the air before the sun is up, the news is rarely good. My parents, choking on despair, called to tell me that Ben was at the hospital, where they were still attempting to revive Peter, but that they believed he was gone. I flew to my brother before my children awoke, with two white T-shirts rattling around in an otherwise empty duffel. How do you pack for what feels like the end of the world? I was terrified to call Ben. I didn't know what to say to someone whose partner of twenty-one years had just improbably died, three months shy of his fortieth birthday. I also didn't want the confirmation it was real. Maybe it was a mistake: Peter would reanimate and shudder alive. Instead, as I traveled, I called a few of our friends, setting the phone tree in motion for the cavalcade of grief. When I physically reached Ben later that morning, I was relieved to find him still speaking. He hadn't folded into himself, which would have been my instinct. He told me one of the emergency room nurses had offered essential advice in the early-morning hours: "You have to just keep talking." He continued to put words to what he was feeling even if it was only to express shock that somehow, despite what had happened, he was still breathing, finding the will to survive. In the following weeks with him, I assumed the mantle of the overfunctioner, orchestrating a funeral for 1,500 and unwinding the technicalities of Peter's life. I did not want my brother to be left to terminate an AT&T account, a gym membership, a long-planned trip to Berlin. It was easier to numb my own grief by cleaning out Peter's office and their hall closet. I tired from explaining that my brother-in-law had died, and yes, I was very affected: "He was also my best friend, really my real brother, the one I spoke to every day." I was also trying to stay attuned to Ben—who admittedly had left many of the "older brothering" activities to the more emotionally capable Peter. I was eager to rebuild intimacy with Ben and to make sure he was OK enough, all without making myself burdensome.

Ben taught me a lot about the nature of grief, most notably how to ride its oscillations. He showed me that it was OK to make jokes and laugh, that we could continue to talk about Peter all the time without being captive to the past. Peter died, but our love for him did not. He showed me what it looks like to keep going with loss as a permanent state. While we've been taught by Elisabeth Kübler-Ross that grief has stages—denial, anger, bargaining, depression, acceptance—there's no science to support this theory. In fact, Kübler-Ross expressed much dismay later in her life that her work had become a linear framework to "tuck messy emotions into neat packages," something to get through so you can be done with all that sad stuff. Grief is never so tidy.

On top of that, grief is something for which we have little cultural tolerance. We want people to show action, to "move on," to medicate, treat, or work through it—to put it away, not to wallow or get stuck. The underlying message seems to be that it's best to prioritize the comfort of those who would rather not bear witness to your pain—people who don't want to contemplate how someone can be there one day and gone the next, or even that emotions are hard, requiring feeling and processing. Americans have an expiration date on both racial wrongs and grief: At a certain point, you're expected to get over it.

Because of this intolerance, Kübler-Ross's stages do have a lot to recommend them: They indicate that progress is possible, or that grief can be dealt with and checked off the to-do list. Have you moved from denial, to anger, to bargaining? Check, check, check. Are you feeling depressed? That's great, because soon you'll move into acceptance. To be fair, her stages do seem to adhere to the process of *dying*—and perhaps they're an accurate representation of grief for some. But her process was not my experience. Instead, grief for me continues to come as waves—out of nowhere, I'll find myself plowed over with sadness. At other times, I startle, shocked at what feels like a still-fresh realization that Peter is dead and I'll never speak to him again.

Or speak to him in the same way. A few months after his death, I met Laura Lynne Jackson, one of the greatest living mediums. Earlier that year, when Peter was still alive and presumably well, I had decided to write a series of stories about dealing with the practicalities of death. I've come to believe that the impulse to explore death was my soul's attempt to prepare me, because I started pulling books off my shelves that addressed all its facets, including Jackson's *The Light Between Us*. I had never before cared to explore mediumship or even psychic phenomena, but I took home her book, which teases out the ways in which the souls of our deceased loved ones remain all around us, and I devoured it. That was just days before Peter died. In the hours after he passed away, I was armed with the idea that maybe he was still present, in an imperceptible way; maybe he could still see and hear me.

Months after Peter died, Laura was on the other end of the phone line. I was physically ill from grief—I'd contracted two back-to-back ten-day viruses, the latest of which had given me a high fever and viral pink eye—and I had no expectation of getting a reading, since I had scheduled only an interview. But halfway into our call, she told me someone wanted to come barreling through. I've since spoken to many mediums—some of obvious skill, some terrible—but Laura is special. Not only does she communicate ungoogleable facts, but she also relays stories and inside jokes, small quips only you and your dead person would understand. You can feel the presence of the person who has passed in her voice, in the impression of her energy, in the way the messages come. That day, when joy felt far away, Peter made me laugh again. He made fun of me, Ben, my mom, Rob, in all the ways he had done when he was alive. Laura reoriented me to the idea that I could still have a relationship with him—it would just be different. Peter stressed we would still talk, even absent his arms and voice box and access to a medium, who is essentially a translator. He told me that he would find ways to get me messages and signs, that he would help and support me from the other side. I recognize that admitting I talk to dead people will cue an eyeroll in many; skepticism, cynicism, and even nihilism in our culture are more intellectually respectable than acknowledging that you think that there's something more, that our existence is larger than what we can currently perceive or measure. To me, there is nothing *sadder* than a materialist point of view:

the almost fanatical belief some have that what we do with our lives doesn't matter, that there's no greater mystery to reveal. For this tribe, any sort of intuition or extrasensory perception is often rejected as pablum or delusion. I've never found it surprising that most of the great mediums and intuitives are women, able and willing to access information that doesn't abide by the structure we culturally validate.

CHOOSING FAITH OVER CONTROL

This is a weird thing to say, but Peter's death and my relationship with him since have been priceless gifts. Yes, I would barter almost anything for one more chat over wine and takeout, but his departure gave me a much bigger spiritual context. It has forced me into conversation with the universe. If I want to talk to him, I must *go there*. His death opened a door I walked through. His short life also showed me what it is to have a life of meaning, however truncated it may be. As my brother said in his eulogy, Peter believed if your generosity wasn't making you a little uncomfortable, you weren't giving enough. I talk to Peter all the time—in the car, in the shower, when I'm stuck and need a nudge or an intervention, when I'm desperate for a parking spot. Sometimes he visits me in my dreams, his presence so palpable I know it's not just wishful thinking. He looks as he did in college, and we communicate through telepathy, or not at all. Knowing we're still connected did not end my grief—there is no point in sidestepping or bypassing the sadness, I'm crying as I type this—but having him on the other side tethered me to something much larger. It gave me a certain type of faith that there is an unseen and expanded order to the universe that is not for me to understand. Not that the universe is "fair," or that nature is "moral," or that "everything happens for a reason." Those types of beliefs have nothing to do with faith; faith revolves around an attachment to something much bigger than my own existence, something that is not my work to rationalize. I love the philosopher Alan Watts's definition of the two. He writes:

> We must here make a clear distinction between belief and faith, because, in general practice, belief has come to mean a state of mind which is almost the opposite of faith. Belief, as I use the word here, is the insistence that the truth is what one would "lief" or wish it to be. The believer will open his mind to the truth on condition that it fits in with his preconceived ideas and wishes. Faith, on the other hand, is an unreserved opening of the mind to the truth, whatever it may turn out to be. Faith has no preconceptions; it is a plunge into the unknown. Belief clings, but faith lets go.

There is a surrender in faith that offers relief from the oppressive idea that we should have it all figured out, that there is no magic at play in the universe, only knowable facts.

In the weeks before the pandemic, I flew to North Carolina to interview Kate Bowler, a Duke divinity school professor who has lived for an improbably long time with stage 4 cancer. She contemplates death every day, living in a space few of us will visit, where she is simultaneously celebrating and mourning each finite day. In her book *Everything Happens for a Reason: And Other Lies I've Loved,* she describes the irresistible lure of the prosperity gospel, which coincidently she had studied and written about for years before her diagnosis. She talks about how it coddles us with its promise of Newtonian rules of cause and effect: that God will reward us with wealth and health for good deeds and donations to megachurches. For Bowler, and others, it's hard to attribute her diagnosis to randomness because then we must acknowledge we have little control. "At 2 P.M. I would tell you, it's not me. I'm a really sophisticated person. I understand that cancer just appears, but if you ask me at 2 A.M., I'll be like, 'Wait, what did I do? How can I get out of this?' . . . You are desperate to find causality even when there is none." Causality offers a simple equation; basic math brings so much comfort. It's belief, rather than faith.

It's impossible to overstate this desire for simplicity, which is as ancient as humanity. If we can work out the logic of the universe, of nature and God, then we can avoid its tolls. We can do the right thing and live long and prosper. We can protect those we love from pain. Elaine Pagels, a famous religious history professor at Princeton known for her work with the Gnostic Gospels, published a beautiful memoir about her first marriage. She and her husband, Heinz, buried their six-year-old son, Mark, diagnosed with a rare lung disease, and then Heinz fell to his death in an accident fifteen months later. Pagels writes about being in the hospital with Mark as a baby, after he'd had a lifesaving surgery. He tried to move his body—tethered by needles and tubes—toward her voice, and a nurse reprimanded her for disturbing him. She writes, "In that terrible moment, I felt as if the nurse was right: I was guilty of causing Mark's fragile, nearly desperate, condition. Only much later did I realize the truth: *I'd rather feel guilty than helpless.* For guilt, however painful, often masks a deeper agony, even more unbearable. Standing there, seeing Mark in intensive care, a huge scar on his thin chest where the physicians had cut it open, broken his breastbone, and stopped his heart to repair it, we were utterly helpless—helpless to do anything at all about what mattered more than our own lives." She explains how these types of beliefs have a stranglehold on us regardless of religious denomination—the word *illness* itself comes from "evilness." As she then explains, "If guilt is the price we pay for the illusion that we have some control over nature, many of us are willing to pay it. I was. To begin to release the weight of guilt, I had to let go of whatever illusion of control it pretended to offer, and acknowledge that pain and death are as natural as birth, woven in separately into our human nature." What a profound sentiment, this idea that guilt is an expression of power and control. It suggests there is something we could do—if we just knew what it was!— rather than recognizing our only option is to let it be, to allow. I wonder if a desire for control, the belief that control is possible, is why so many of us—men in particular—do not permit our own sadness to emerge.

ALLOWING GRIEF TO COME

According to resilience and bereavement expert and psychologist George Bonanno, allowing all emotions to emerge is essential for recovery from grief. Bonanno conducted research with psychology professor Dacher Keltner, and they "found that the more widows and widowers laughed and smiled during the early months after their spouse's death, the better their mental health was over the first two years of bereavement." This research holds for any type of grief, even if it's "ambiguous loss," the types of unresolved issues that are not well acknowledged by society, like miscarriage, divorce, dementia, abandonment, infertility, long-term singledom, or illness. Bonanno and Keltner believe there are many reasons why grievers fare better when they allow themselves to smile, most notably because it offers a reprieve from the tumult of sadness, a moment to breathe. They also hold that these moments of joy make the mourner more bearable for others to support. Nobody better represents the full emotional span of grief than young widow Nora McInerny, co-founder of "the Hot Young Widows Club." She delivered a wonderful TED Talk—"We don't 'move on' from grief—we move forward with it"—that has racked up millions of views. Nora was a grief shepherd for Ben, introducing him to the strange and sometimes dark corners of his new world: the ambivalence that comes from conflicting emotions, what it's like to love multiple people simultaneously, and the painful recognition that the life you need to rebuild will be constructed upon the foundation of what you lost.

What Nora has done for our national conversation about grief is considerable: She is one of our only public examples of what it looks like *not* to "get over it" but to survive grief by moving forward and living a life that's a testament to the person who died. Within the span of six weeks, Nora miscarried her second child and then buried her dad and her first husband, Aaron, who both died from cancer (her dad was sixty-four, Aaron was thirty-five). Nora is remarried now and has a blended family of four kids, including a baby she had with her second husband, Matthew. She talks daily with those who have looked down the barrel of grief and emerged somehow stronger for it. These people are typically surprised by their misfortune, too young to give up and step away from life. Staying engaged requires grappling with a complexity of feelings—sadness and joy, anger and acceptance, facing a larger world that didn't stop when your own small one came crashing down. As Nora explains, "There was a version of me that thought loving another person would somehow diminish the love I still felt for Aaron. A version of me that thought that if I was happy, I must not be sad anymore, and if I wasn't sad anymore, then I guess I didn't love Aaron as much as I said I did." As Nora learned, she had to start leaning into *and*, rather than *but*.

We need this cultural conversation, because painful transitions happen all around us—the end of a relationship, the loss of a job, the inability to find a partner or carry a child—and we have had little tolerance for the drag of others going through these things, or even for acknowledging that their pain is worthy enough to be considered, that it makes sense that it's huge enough to topple them. We need to develop reverence for the process of being sad, for allowing the bottom to drop out, for recognizing that every mountain has its corresponding valley. This process of grief seems *particularly* difficult for those men who attempt to white-knuckle through their pain, to grin and bear it in the comparative suffering Olympics. While we think of grief as something that corresponds only to death, we experience small ego deaths all the time. Allowing sadness—feelings of disappointment, rejection, loss—is essential.

There's a famous parable in Buddhism about a wealthy woman

named Kisa Gotami. After her only child dies, she goes to various homes asking to buy magical medicine to bring her one-year-old back to life. Someone advises her to seek out the Buddha, who tells her to secure four or five mustard seeds from any family in which there has never been a death. She goes from house to house to no avail, ultimately realizing death and suffering come to everyone; her wealth is no protection. There is no reprieve; instead of rejecting this reality, it would benefit us all to contemplate its nature. We need to increase our tolerance for discomfort and hard emotions, to hold space for those who are mourning and struggling, to watch, allow, and learn. It's easy to show up for a funeral, to send a note of condolence (though you'll be surprised by those who struggle to do even that), but it becomes apparent how difficult it is for people to continue to show up when the acuteness of the event passes, when people stop calling—and stop *asking*—only months after the fact.

On the first anniversary of Peter's death, in a weird fit of synchrony, I took another early-morning flight, this time to interview Lucy Kalanithi, the widow of Paul Kalanithi, author of *When Breath Becomes Air*. She told me that her greatest fear is that people will stop talking about Paul, stop telling their daughter stories about him, stop adding to their now-finite pool of memories. Those who grieve live in a liminal space—we need to learn how to join them there, without fear. For denying the existence of death doesn't work; it simply divorces us from the other, equally essential side of life—the joy that is our birthright, our reprieve from suffering, its balance and counterpolarity.

HOW WE LEARN TO FEEL—OR NOT

When I survey our beautiful and damaged world, I can't find many women to blame for its destruction. And in writing this book, I've been loath to give women more "to do," even when the punch card of activity I'm suggesting requires unwinding programming so that women *do less*, so they can *be more*. In past decades, women have frequently been encouraged to behave more like men: to grab and wield power, to rule. The suggestion is that we can take power and sanitize it with our gender, make it softer and more gentle, somehow less patriarchal. Though this instinct toward balance is problematic, I understand why it makes sense—our innate Divine Masculinity deserves its space. But the more urgent need is the reverse. We need men to embrace their Divine Feminine, to reconnect to compassion and care, to yield, and to move from the traits of toxic masculinity to a version that's balanced. Doing this requires men to lay down a quest for control, power, and dominance and to allow their feelings to come up—all of them. This feels particularly critical when women are being asked to balance society by stepping into power; masculine power as it's performed now, particularly at work, is not the right model.

A female friend who leads a large business told me how ambivalent she feels about her sadness at the office—even though she leads a team that is predominantly women. Predictably, tears are easier for her than anger—when she cries in frustration she recognizes it's actually because she's full of rage—but those tears are *always* private.

"When one of our co-workers died and the whole team was devastated, I kept apologizing to them for crying as I addressed them—I couldn't help myself from saying sorry, even though grief was in many ways the only appropriate response. It still felt wrong to cry as a leader, like I should be stronger and in control of myself." She then went on to tell me how she had recently picked up some papers at the copy machine and found a printout for a new employee. "It was so sweet," she said. "It was a guide to all the best neighborhood spots for coffee and lunch, along with protocols for meetings and monthly deadlines. And then my heart fell because it included the best spots to go to cry." To abide in business, women are behaving like men—choosing power and control over humanness and fallibility and the full expression of feeling. The conse-quences are far-reaching.

Nobody gets out unscathed. Yet confronting death, or rejec-tion, or disappointment, or loss still makes us feel weak; feeling powerless is hard for men in a society that asserts they should be dominant, on top of it, in control, never succumbing to the chaos of fear or the abyss of the emotion states. Our men must be ever-strong, valiant protectors, heroic. In *The Dance of Anger*, therapist Harriet Lerner explains that in any couple, we are inclined to over-function or underfunction to bring a relationship into balance so *someone* is metabolizing the feelings. This off-loading can happen between parents and children, between partners, or even at work. While she believes that men today are a bit more emotionally com-petent than they were when she wrote her book in the 1980s, she sees that many of them still outsource their feelings to the women in their lives, who are expected to overfunction in the relational capacity. In a heterosexual marriage, women typically do the job of processing their own feelings, as well as a second shift processing the feelings of their husbands, so their husbands do not have to explore their own emotions. Lerner writes, "In the majority of couples, men sit on the bottom of the seesaw when it comes to emotional competence. We all know about the man who can tie good knots on packages and fix things that break, yet fails to notice that his wife is depressed. He may have little emotional relatedness to his own family and lack even one close friend with whom hon-est self-disclosure takes place. This is the 'masculinity' that our so-ciety breeds—the male who feels at home in the world of things and abstract ideas but who has little empathetic connection to oth-ers, little attunement to his own internal world, and little willing-ness or capacity to 'hang in' when a relationship becomes conflicted and stressful." The muscles of connection and intimacy atrophy—or fail to develop in the first place.

The science suggests that *atrophy* and *underdevelopment* are the right words, as boys are *more sensitive, needy, attached* than their sisters, not less. As therapist Terry Real explains, "Little boys and little girls start off with similar psychological profiles. They are equally emotional, expressive, and dependent, equally desirous of physical affection. At the youngest ages, both boys and girls are more like a stereotypical girl. If any differences exist, little boys are, in fact, slightly more sensitive and expressive. They cry more easily, seem more easily frustrated, appear more upset when a caregiver leaves the room. Until the age of four or five, both boys and girls rest comfortably in what one researcher has called 'the expressive-affiliative mode.' Soon thereafter, studies indicate that girls are permitted to remain in that mode while boys are subtly—or forcibly—pushed out of it." We shame our boys for their sweetness, their softness; we firm them up to take on the challenges of life. We cut them off so they can function in our patriarchal culture.

It's understandable that men armor up around emotional expression. I've even watched my most sensitive, feminist friends turn away from husbands and boyfriends who are struggling. It's scary and unsettling, and can seem unseemly and unattractive for someone who is supposed to be strong to cry or break down. If men acknowledge they've suffered harm, then they're weak, more like a woman. As professor bell hooks explains in *The Will to Change,* "By supporting patriarchal culture that socializes men to deny feelings, we doom them to live in states of emotional numbness. We construct a culture where male pain can have no voice, where male hurt cannot be named or healed. . . . When the feminist movement led to men's liberation, including male exploration of 'feelings,' some women mocked male emotional expression with the same disgust and contempt as sexist men. Despite all the expressed feminist longing for men of feeling, when men worked to get in touch with feelings, no one really wanted to reward them." In many ways it's more comfortable to rail against an enemy who seems perfectly stoic, immovable; to be expected to sympathize with those who oppress us seems like an affront. How dare men ask for our sympathy when they've already extracted so much? Weakness seems like a joke when we've always been told that they are stronger, that this strength means women must be small, dependent, and constrained. *We're supposed to lean on them;* isn't that the point of the Faustian bargain of the patriarchy?

It's only recently that showing vulnerability—in the vein of the Dax Shepards of the world—has become a little bit sexy, valorized as a new facet of modern masculinity. At times, it can seem a bit like a performance, as even Dax is attached to the trappings of his machismo, equipped with Alcoholics Anonymous war stories, an extreme pain threshold, libertarianism, overalls, and high-horsepower cars. But at least he publicly discusses his pain, his moments of weakness, and his hitting rock bottom. It's a start, because we all need tools, particularly parents, who are trying to bring up future generations in a different way, allowing for feelings to find proper expression before regulation.

RATES OF DEPRESSION IN WOMEN AND MEN

If you look at national statistics, it appears that sadness is a problem for women, that women are far more depressed than men. According to data from the National Institute of Mental Health, the prevalence of major depression in women was 10.5 percent in 2020, versus 6.2 percent for men.* But this statistic offers a limited perspective. Women are more equipped for our sadness, though that doesn't make us *more* sad. In *I Don't Want to Talk About It,* perhaps the landmark book on male depression, therapist Terry Real asserts that the men in his practice are no less affected by depression; it just manifests differently. He argues that many men are struggling with undiagnosed "covert" depression, which is often paired with an addictive defense. After adding up all the mental illness stats—affective

---

* According to the same statistic repository, major depression is highest among those who report being multiracial (15.9 percent).

disorders, anxiety disorders, substance abuse disorders, and personality disorders—he found the totals evened out. While women officially overindexed on depression, men made up significant ground in substance abuse and personality disorders. This makes sense, as men are four times as likely to die of suicide and other deaths of despair.

Something feels wrong with the emotional health of men—look no further than the havoc they wreak on society. It is overwhelmingly men who rape, kill, and abuse—it's men and boys who pick up semiautomatic guns and mow people down. The Bushmaster XM-15 E2S Shorty AK—advertised with the slogan "Consider your man card reissued"—is the gun a twenty-year-old used to slaughter twenty-six people, primarily first graders, at Sandy Hook Elementary School in 2012. A decade later, an eighteen-year-old mowed down twenty-one people in Uvalde with an AR-15 from Daniel Defense, a company that relies on machismo statements in its Instagram marketing like "Nobody has the right to tell me how to defend [my family]" and "Defending your nation, defending your home." We are in a crisis of toxic masculinity, and we must address what's happening to drive boys and men to murder *children*. It's clear that men have a problem, and it puts us all at risk.

According to Real, there are good reasons men don't acknowledge what's happening inside of them. For one, there's no cultural template for supporting depressed men. He cites the research of Constance Hammen and Stefanie Peters, who ran a study of college roommates across genders. They found that when women tell roommates they're depressed, they're met with nurturance and compassion; men, meanwhile, are met with social isolation and unkindness. We are not well equipped for supporting boys and men who feel otherwise when the social expectation is that they be stoic and strong. A second reason Real cites is the ways in which we acculturate our boys. As he explains, "Men do not have readily at hand the same level of insight into their emotional lives as women, because our culture works hard to dislocate them from those aspects of themselves. Men are less used to voicing emotional issues, because we teach them that it's unmanly to do so. Even a cursory look at gender socialization in our culture indicates that a man would be far more likely to act out distress than to talk about it, while a woman would have the skills, the community, and the ease to discuss her problems." This is adding insult to injury. We discourage our boys from developing the capacity to metabolize their emotions and then stereotype them as being less equipped.

We must cultivate emotional granularity. It may seem obvious, but it's worth stating, particularly in a culture that's *just* coming around to the idea that, even in business, emotional quotient (EQ) might be as important as—if not potentially more important than— intelligence quotient (IQ), which has been the standard for more than one hundred years. The idea of emotional intelligence is only thirty years old. As psychologist Marc Brackett explains, "Scientists don't like emotions because, unlike intelligence, they can't be measured with standardized tests. IQ relies primarily on 'cold' cognitive processes such as remembering a strand of digits or historical facts, while emotional intelligence relies on 'hot' social-emotional- cognitive processes that are often highly charged, relationship driven, and focused on evaluating, predicting, and coping with feelings and behaviors—our own and other people's." Unlike IQ, there's no standard test—though it's also easy to argue IQ is not an appropriate test of innate, immutable intelligence, as indicated by the fact that the United States increased IQ by fifteen points when iodine was added to salt, correcting a pervasive nutritional deficiency at the time.* We've organized our society and the perception of intelligence around a system that prioritizes only half of what it

---

* Harriet Washington's incredible book *A Terrible Thing to Waste* explores the ways environmental racism delineates and limits the lives of marginalized communities, and the terrible ouroboros of standardized tests, which suggest that communities of color have lower IQs. As she writes, "Lead exposure has cost us a total of 23 million lost IQ points nationwide every year—even more than the 13 million IQ points lost to pesticide exposure as documented by a European Union study." Lead exposure is rampant in marginalized communities, Flint, Michigan, being the most recent example.

is to be human. And then we've trained the ambitions of men on the sole pursuit of that element.

Nancy Eisenberg of Arizona State University is one of the foremost researchers on prosocial behavior, empathy, and the development of morals. Many of her decades-long findings underline the disparity between how boys and girls are taught to process emotions by their parents: Mothers spend a lot more time talking to their daughters about feelings (including their own) than they do to their sons, and dads use harsher language with boys and discourage them from being vulnerable. They even found that moms are more expressive with baby girls than baby boys and talk to daughters about sadness and sons about anger. Parents, despite their professed and apparent sensitivities, still hold the prevailing cultural belief and bias that emotions and relational wisdom should be cultivated primarily in girls, that the language of feelings will serve boys badly or is not something they need.

Terry Real believes that we've collectively subscribed to a myth that boys must be *turned into* men, that they can't achieve manhood without initiation into the cult of masculinity. He observes this doesn't happen for girls; he writes, "Masculine identity is perceived as precious and perilous, though not a shred of evidence has emerged to indicate the existence of this supposed precarious internal structure, masculine identity. Studies indicate that both boys and girls have a clear sense of which sex they are from about the age of two." The belief that maleness must be "achieved" persists, though, and I have to wonder if it's because masculinity as our society perceives it is a mask anyway, a coerced act of disconnection, as if to be a man requires playing one on TV.

The disconnection begins when we pull boys out of their mothers' arms, when we shame them for seeking comfort, hugs, a safe port for their emotions. It happens when we give in to this idea that a woman will ruin or spoil her young child's chances for ascendancy to the masculine by keeping him mired in the feminine. In the not-distant past, mothers were blamed for turning their sons gay by tethering them to their apron strings, entrapping them in their laps. Real expounds: "The idea that boys must rupture an effeminizing connection to mother is one of the oldest, least questioned, and most deeply rooted myths of patriarchy. Freud himself sounded the clarion call close to a century ago, when he wrote: '[The boy's] relationship to the mother is the first and most intense. Therefore, it must be destroyed.'" By ripping them away, we are committing some form of soul murder, teaching boys to despise the part of themselves that is soft, warm, and tender. And pushing our boys away is heartbreaking for mothers too, though according to bell hooks, it's one of the patriarchy's first demands. In *The Will to Change* she writes, "Mothers who ally themselves with patriarchy cannot love their sons rightly, for there will always come a moment when patriarchy will ask them to sacrifice their sons. Usually this moment comes in adolescence, when many caring and affectionate mothers stop giving their sons emotional nurturance for fear it will emasculate them. Unable to cope with the loss of emotional connection, boys internalize the pain and mask it with indifference or rage." It's a form of abandonment, an insidious and subtle trauma our culture rarely acknowledges.

THE TRAUMA OF TOXIC MASCULINITY

As a culture, we are only now becoming capital "T" trauma literate: It is only in recent decades that we began to contemplate and study the long-tail, intergenerational repercussions from the rapes and sexual assaults that women frequently endure, the impact of child abuse, the consequences of sending soldiers out to kill strangers with the expectation that they will be able to reassimilate into society with no ill effects. While conflict is ancient, we've blindly assumed that violence reflects the immutable nature of men, their destiny. This is culture, though: We train men to kill, valorize warfare and aggression, and then dissociate them from reality by showing them bad guys who die thousands, if not hundreds of thousands, of times on screens big and small, animated and CGI.* Children are desensitized to what death means until we shatter them in combat or shame them for not wanting to participate in these "heroic" rituals. How easily we forget that the Nazi government gave soldiers methamphetamines to spur them on: We need to drug men to murder each other so easily.

Big, capital "T" trauma—overt and unmistakable abuse and violence—must be addressed. It's a hurricane in the souls of those who attempt to bury it in their bodies. But we also shouldn't understate the importance of lowercase "t" trauma, the kind that is subtly insidious yet also painful and limiting. These are the kinds of assaults that are sometimes harder to bear because there's no inciting event that qualifies on the list of societal no-no's, no distinct memory around which to gather. This trauma is neglect, emotional disconnection, and abandonment, and it's far more common than its "active trauma" brother. Trauma is what happens to you, certainly, but it's also what you never receive. As Real explains, "I think not touching a child for decades at a time is a form of injury. I think withholding any expression of love until a young boy is a grown man is a form of emotional violence. And I believe that the violence men level against themselves and others is bred from just such circumstances." This disconnection is the trauma of feeling unseen, unlovable, unsafe as yourself—it's the trauma of being forced to leave your identity to don the armor of society's dictates.

As the mother of two young boys, I think about Real's insights daily: What does it look like to hold space and to see your children without distorting their perception of themselves? What should I bear for them, versus pushing them to find the edges of their own capacity to process feelings? Too many of us function as the prefrontal cortex for our children, letting our kids outsource their self-

---

* Is it not strange that we show so much death, yet the prospect of watching a birth is so gruesome, most men can't even watch their own children emerge?

regulation to us, because it's so hard to watch them struggle, even when struggling, as we know, is how we learn and grow. So we overfunction for our children, processing those hard feelings for them to spare them from despair. My older son, Max, is sensitive—he is a walking, trembling feeling, so easy to unmoor. His emotions—and the freneticism of his younger brother—overwhelm him multiple times a day. There are a lot of tears, which tumble easily, copiously. I've noted how much easier it is for me to be with Max when he is in distress than it is for Rob. The irritation and discomfort rise quickly in Rob, the urge to tell Max to get it to-gether (but fortunately, never to "be a man"). Understandably, Rob wants Max to "toughen up" before his friends, and the wider cul-ture, insist on it for him. I suspect Rob feels triggered by Max's sensitivity because he sees himself in our son and feels compelled to protect him as best he knows how. My guess is Rob was a sensitive boy with a hypermasculine dad who was quick to anger. It's hard to know for sure, though, because Rob's dad died many years ago, and Rob has approximately zero memories of his childhood. They are in a black box somewhere and Rob is scared to look, uncertain how to pull the dam out of the river and let his feelings come with-out getting overwhelmed and swamped by hard emotions.

The disconnection from feelings is devastating for all people. While women might tamp them down to function in what other-wise might be dysfunctional relationships or a dysfunctional society, at least we're allowed to cry. Many men are stuck. In Terry Real's worldview—predicated on his expansive work with men in one-on-one, marital, familial, and group workshops—men are being destroyed by internalized disconnection, and these "wounded boys" in turn become "wounding men" who inflict their unacknowl-edged distress on their family and the culture at large. This depres-sion becomes a family pattern passed down, wreaking havoc on future generations. In Real's model, the trauma is wrapped in an addictive defense—drugs, alcohol, infidelity, workaholism—and plastered over with covert depression. The pin must be pulled so

that the covert depression becomes overt. At that point, the wasteland back to life can be crossed. As Real explores, the cure for sadness is grief, the act of acknowledging and expressing your feelings
of loss and despair. As the saying goes, you can't heal what you can't
feel. The feelings must be allowed to come up.

While men theoretically benefit from the advantages of patriarchy, they suffer under its yoke as well. The power that comes from
the advantages is significant, and much ink has been devoted to the
inherent injustice of unequal starting blocks. But winning at the
expense of others also extracts a toll. Asserting power over others
creates significant psychic burdens—in the moment, and for future
generations to address. If we want to free ourselves from this system, the liberation of men can't be an afterthought. Nor is it worth
criticizing all of them for participating in a structure of which
they've barely been conscious. None of us have known any other
way. As more of us wake up to norms that drive society, we can
begin to shift them.

It doesn't feel good to be the oppressor, even if you've never
been conscious of your exalted status or weaponized it in a way that
causes harm. It doesn't feel good to imagine that the résumé of
your life—what you've achieved, what you've amassed, the moun-
taintops you've reached—could be ill-gotten, that you had an outsized advantage, that it was never a fair fight. As economist Max
Weber explained in 1915, "The fortunate man is seldom satisfied
with the fact of being fortunate. Beyond this, he needs to know
that he has a right to his good fortune. He wants to be convinced
that he deserves it and above all, that he deserves it in comparison
with others. Good fortune thus wants to be legitimate fortune." As
we continue to wrestle with the realities of our patriarchy—in
America at least—our "fortune" is a painful consideration, if not an
affront. Did I not come by my life honestly? Who has been collateral damage to my success without my intention? And how do I
make this right? These are uncomfortable questions to answer, each
one its own complicated eddy. They bring with them a wash of

sadness that we are ill-equipped to address. We have been made complicit in a culture that we did not choose, in the same way that we didn't choose the factors of our birth—the tone of our skin, our gender, our sexuality, our place of birth, our class. The divisiveness, denial, rejection, and rage that we're seeing in our culture right now seems to be a reflexive response to our guilt with no name. We don't know where to put it.

Perhaps it's strange to end a book that's about the emotional experiences of women by including those of men, but sidestepping our femininity to become "more like men" as the antidote to our problematic culture is a dangerous promise. While men hold a per-haps enviable amount of power in this patriarchy, they are less equipped than women to lead us out of its strictures. They have more to lose—but ironically, they also have so much to gain. Sad-ness is a gateway to feeling and to life—it must be reclaimed from the idea that it is weak or "womanly." Only when sadness is em-bodied can men access their tenderness, a fuller experience of love, a more complete expression of themselves. The health of our cul-ture requires this submission. I have faith that men will be more than willing allies if we can show them the path to peaceful sur-render, if we can teach them that mutual support is essential for our collective future. It is human to sometimes be sad. Women under-stand and allow this, and we must now bring sadness to all spheres. We must give sadness its rightful throne and accept its lessons. There is much to mourn, the grief must come: Women can lead us through this wasteland, to where a more balanced era awaits.

Accepting sadness as essential, we can embrace our full humanity and reengage with the cycle of life.

CONCLUSION: REALIGNMENT

The Return to Ourselves

In early 2020, I spoke to Carissa Schumacher, a woman who channels the dead (including Jesus). In these intervening years, her wisdom has touched me so deeply that she's become a friend and spiritual mentor, but this first conversation with her shook me. In it, she explained: "If you don't make space, we'll make it for you." The "we" she was referencing here was the Divine. I laughed uncomfortably. Sure, I was wearing myself down, hopping from flight to flight, trying to be a present parent and partner, firefighting life, generally failing as a friend. But I saw no alternative: What exactly was I supposed to put down? Maybe, I asked her, a daily meditation practice or more hiking would help? "No," Carissa responded. "Space. Stillness." Indeed, a few months later, space came: COVID, and then, for me, the end of my full-time job. In this pause, I realized how thoroughly I had been eroding under the grind of busyness. I needed to make room to maneuver, to pivot, to contemplate where I was—and how to then go a different way.

The pandemic was undoubtedly awful. Many, many people were ill, and many, many people watched loved ones die or, worse, couldn't be there as loved ones took their last breaths. Children went without school and breadwinners lost their livelihoods. And yet everyone I've spoken with has acknowledged that the pandemic was a paradox, containing many meaningful lessons. Even those who lost a lot have told me that the time-out felt essential; they explain how unsustainable and unfulfilling their days had been, how they realized they had been forsaking themselves, *waiting*, really, for the time and opportunity to . . . live. Many of my friends now refuse to engage with the world in the 2019 way, and they are thriving in their scaled-back, less compulsively busy realities. The disruption of everything offered us an opportunity to replumb: ourselves, our families, the wider culture. For me, this introspection included a deep excavation of the stories we tell about who we are, the ways we've been conditioned to behave, and how we conform ourselves to meet society's standards. The pandemic was a collective opportunity to reject old paradigms and craft new ones.

With space, stillness, and sacred pause, I began to recognize how cultural distortions were showing up in my own life and my own body. I found the room to see the crevasse between who I really was and how I had been *performing* myself in the outside world. I thought a lot about that breathless, overwhelmed girl inside me, suffocating from the strictures of a society that insisted I prove my good-enough-ness ritually. This book became the container in which I processed all the ways I'd been programmed by the cultural codes of virtue, by the ways I'd been convinced that if I was perfect in my behavior, I'd be lovable, safe, and accepted. As I realized how deeply these codes of "goodness" were woven into our social fabric, and how indelible and invisible they were, I began to see how we each acted them out. It was only from this new perspective that I realized the freedom and spaciousness I craved would never come from an exterior authority: I had to find this within myself. To reclaim my selfhood, I needed to grant *myself* permission to credit and celebrate myself (and explore my pride), pleasure myself (and allow my lust), feed and secure myself (and permit my gluttony and greed), assert my needs (and listen to my anger), relax and rest (and indulge sloth), and determine exactly what I wanted and then go after it (and make use of my envy). And as a wife to a man, and a mother to two boys, I needed to become insistent that they stay connected to their feelings, particularly the hard ones (sadness) in a culture that pushed them to dissociate.

This work is not easy. The Seven Deadly Sins as they're understood today are lodged deep in our collective psyche. Women must contend with the ways that each "sin" limits our lives. And then we must reject the system that uses these sins as a tool of oppression; we must build something truer in its stead.

WRITING THIS BOOK CHANGED me. Grappling with each of these sins has forced me closer to myself. I now see pride, lust, gluttony, greed, anger, sloth, envy, and even sadness not as sinful but as neutral cues. It's society that has turned these innate human impulses into the makings of morality. We must reject the cudgel-like way they've been wielded culturally and reclaim them for their true purpose: They are an internal guide. The sins are touchstones for *where* we tend to warp ourselves—both in overindulgence and asceticism. They're simply signals, GPS points, from the human soul. When understood as guideposts, not cliffs of damnation, they are an invitation to look and come closer to who we are, what we need, what we want, and how we can discover our purpose.

It's always been striking to me that the codification of the sins emerged out of the Egyptian desert and not from the Bible—that what is presented, culturally, as religious law really has no formal provenance. But I've come to believe that these sins predate Evagrius Ponticus: Evagrius collated them from already existing sources, sources that then disappeared. When he lived and wrote, there were many gospels in circulation; the New Testament and its "orthodoxy" had just come out of Rome. And it just so happens that the sins *did* appear in a gospel circulating at the time—a gospel deemed too heretical for the New Testament. The sins were woven into the Gospel of Mary.

In the New Testament, Luke (8:2) and Mark (16:9) describe Mary Magdalene as the one from whom Jesus exorcised seven "demons."* Pope Gregory I later cast these seven "demons" as the Seven Deadly Sins and simultaneously called Mary a prostitute. While Gregory's denunciation of Mary was a gross misinterpretation, these elements are connected, and Mary Magdalene is the key. Mary Magdalene represents all women—the way we've been stripped of our authentic worthiness, left to plead for redemption. She was the rightful first apostle, Jesus's best student, who was then dethroned and debased by all of Christianity, abandoned to a sordid legacy as the penitent prostitute and the carrier of the seven sins, representing impure thoughts transformed into unholy desires. *And yet* the truth of who she actually was remains in plain sight. Reclaiming her legacy, her teachings, and what she represents can help point the way back to ourselves. Her gospel, the Gospel of Mary, one of the Gnostic texts the Council of Nicaea marked as heretical when they made their list of "orthodox" canons in the fourth century, is a *radical* revisioning of Christianity: In it, Mary insists that we are born innately good, *not* full of sin, and that the road to becoming a *real human being* requires that we not evade who we are but come to own it. The sins that Mary encountered in her life and the "powers"† Jesus faced in his ascension back to God—as described in her gospel—are the same. These human qualities—what later came to be understood as the Seven Deadly Sins—are a road map to what we must *reconcile*. They were never meant to be abnegated, destroyed, or denied.

The Gospel of Mary is a master class in self-knowledge and faith; it recognizes and teaches that we each *already have* both the answers and a direct connection to the Divine. Staying close to our

---

* Again, I think the Greek definition of *demon* from that time period—that it is a persistent *thought* and not a modern idea of a devil—is probably a more appropriate translation. The etymology of *exorcise* is "oath" + "out."

† Some theologians translate these "powers" as "energies," "climates," or "authorities."

goodness, which is who we are in our essence, is our sole mandate. Mary's gospel instructs that God, defined in her gospel as "the Good," is not "out there" but instead inside all of us. Christ proclaims: "Bear my peace within yourselves! Beware that no one lead you astray saying, 'Look over here!' Or 'Look over there!' For the Child of Humanity is within you! Follow it! Those who seek it will find it. Go then and proclaim the good news of the realm. Do not lay down any rules beyond what I determined for you, nor give a law like the lawgiver, lest you be confined by it" (Mary 4:1–11). What Christ is saying here is that we must own our sovereignty and not look to any exterior authority for a road map to tell us how to behave (or not), or what to do (or not)—we must look *inside* for the directions, and we already have everything we need. The "ascension," which we'll all undertake, isn't a joyride *up* to heaven but an internal journey *back* to our true selves.

Mary talks about the experience of the divine as a seeing and knowing from the heart, rather than the mind—something sacred and incorruptible within ourselves. Divinity is not something granted; God, the Divine, Allah, Nature, Gaia, whatever you want to call this universal loving energy, is baked right into our souls. This is a radical idea, because today (and, really, starting with the codification of Christianity in the fourth century), what we *currently* perceive as "goodness" is just an adherence to external constraints: It is learned behavior. We have become so enslaved to ideas about how we *should* behave that we are tuning ourselves to the wrong radio station, pulling ourselves away from who we are. Ironically, our attempts to be "good" sever us from "the Good."

In the Gospel of Mary, Mary credits Christ as saying (emphasis mine): "*There is no sin,* but it is you who make sin when you do the things that are like the nature of adultery,* which is called 'sin.' That is why the Good came into your midst, coming to the good

---

* The word *adultery* here does not mean cheating on your partner; according to Episcopalian priest Cynthia Bourgeault, "In this particular metaphysical system, 'adulterous' has the primary meaning of being out of alignment."

which belongs to every nature, in order to restore it to its root" (Mary 3:3–6). This is a shocking refutation of what we hear from pulpits all over the world, a refrain that's been drumbeat into all of us regardless of how we were raised: *Jesus died for our sins.* (For the record, Jesus never said he died for our sins;* it was an interpretation ascribed to him by his followers, like Paul, which then became canon.) In Mary's gospel, Jesus is saying that sin is an invention of man, not an indictment from God—it's what happens when we deviate from who we are at our root, our point of origin.

And the sins, or, as Christ describes them in Mary's gospel, "powers," are necessary points of resistance on the path—they confront us, not so we can skirt or master them, but so we can come into balance with them. They are powerful teaching tools, whetstones for our souls, prodding us to understand who we are. In her gospel, Mary recounts Christ's journey. While the first of the "powers" he meets is apparently listed on pages missing from the manuscript discovered in Egypt, the second power is Desire, the third power is Ignorance, and the fourth power, Wrath, takes seven forms: "The first form is Darkness; the second Desire; the third Ignorance; the fourth Eagerness for Death; the fifth is the Realm of Flesh; the sixth is the Foolish Wisdom of the Flesh; the seventh is Wrathful Wisdom" (Mary 9:18–26). Theologian Jean-Yves Leloup explores Christ's journey and these "climates" in fascinating depth, explaining that it is in the "Fourth Climate," where Christ encounters the seven manifestations of Wrath, that the soul becomes alienated and *possessed.* I've also discussed this list at length with Carissa over the years and resolved that while these might not look as tidy as the Seven Deadly Sins, these "seven forms" are highly secular, relatable, and useful. It seems as if in the game of Telephone

---

* As French theologian Jean-Yves Leloup underlines in *The Gospel of Mary Magdalene,* the idea of "sin" itself has never been thoroughly understood. "Both in Yeshua's time and after, there were those who held that human nature itself is tainted with original sin, that matter, the world, and the body are traps from which deliverance is needed." This idea runs counter to what Jesus says in the Gospel of Mary: Humans are the ones who created sin, and we are not born needing to be redeemed.

over millennia, they were simply reduced, made one-dimensional, and branded as morality. They are, to paraphrase:

FORM 1: DARKNESS This represents when we feel separated from the Divine, nature, and each other; it encompasses insecurity and comparing self to others.	REDUCED AND SIMPLIFIED BY EVAGRIUS TO "ENVY"
FORM 2: DESIRE Leloup defines this as "craving," a slightly more insidious form of longing. This is the need to "get yours" and take more than what's necessary or appropriate, to the detriment of others; it also includes the insatiable desire for power and the impulse for dominance.	REDUCED AND SIMPLIFIED BY EVAGRIUS TO "GREED"
FORM 3: IGNORANCE This isn't about a lack of education. It's about a willful desire not to know: complaining, whining, avoidance, and refusing to accept the truth.	REDUCED AND SIMPLIFIED BY EVAGRIUS TO "SLOTH"
FORM 4: EAGERNESS FOR DEATH This encompasses an obsession with the body and its mortality, an extreme attachment to physical matter. In today's culture, this shows up as a preoccupation with personal longevity (hello, biohackers!) and a paranoid obsession with survival and safety.	REDUCED AND SIMPLIFIED BY EVAGRIUS TO "GLUTTONY"
FORM 5: REALM OF FLESH This involves an obsessive desire for relationships, sex, and attention, along with a preoccupation with external image—it also includes wanting things to be other than what they are.	REDUCED AND SIMPLIFIED BY EVAGRIUS TO "LUST"

FORM 6: FOOLISH WISDOM OF THE FLESH This is the condescension and certainty, often couched in altruism, that comes from thinking we know what's right for other people—it's when we try to control the decisions and lives of others or insist on "saving" others instead of dealing with ourselves.	**REDUCED AND SIMPLIFIED BY EVAGRIUS TO "PRIDE"**
FORM 7: WRATHFUL WISDOM We see this in mob mentality and a frenzied pursuit of an imperfect, human idea of justice—this results in persecutions and crucifixions.	**REDUCED AND SIMPLIFIED BY EVAGRIUS TO "ANGER"**

Because Mary's gospel was deemed heretical and marked for destruction, we were left with Evagrius's simplification and an external edict, rather than the opportunity to puzzle over these more complex and subtle ideas within their original context. When paired with an understanding of or belief in our innate worthiness, these seven forms describe an internal journey, and the continual alignment and balancing required. Looking at these expanded ideas, we can find both ourselves and many of today's most critical issues. These all feel like realms where we collectively lose our way—far more than our immature understanding of the sins today. For example, rather than thinking of sloth as an admonishment against rest, "Ignorance" suggests that the sin here is actually an avoidance of the truth or an insistence on not wanting to understand. Or my favorite, "Foolish Wisdom," cautions us not to focus on fixing other people when we have plenty to refine within ourselves; this feels so much more powerful than a chastisement to never take pride in our accomplishments. What might the world look like if its most popular religion abided by Mary's gospel? And how might the lives of women be better for it? It's time that we unyoke from the precepts of our culture's translation of the Seven Deadly Sins, that we climb out of that sticky web so we can see ourselves for exactly who we are: perfectly human, already divine, on the road back to wholeness.

A PROFOUND VULNERABILITY IS required to strip off the illusions, to be what you already are, not what you think you should be. Many of us, myself included, have spent our lives *doing:* We've been busy finding jobs, mentors, partners, and friends to lean on, to serve, or to placate so we don't have to understand what it would look like to be supported by ourselves. Letting go of old structures and ideas and choosing reliance on our sovereignty, on *self-possession*, is hard. It requires a tremendous amount of faith to rely on this inner knowing, to distill what's right for us and what's wrong. Only when we unhook from exterior edicts and tune in to an internal compass can we find the truer way. This is the path we each must walk: We must strip off the layers of cultural programming so that we can, at last, see and listen to ourselves, just as we are. From that place of clarity and truth and *goodness* we can heal, realign, and evolve.

Walking a straighter path requires balance, a word that's so culturally loaded. Mention balance to any woman—particularly a mother—and you'll see a shiver of protest shudder up her spine (our minds immediately rush to the elusive work/life trade-off). Our understanding of balance is reductive: It's conceived as an equation, a canceling out, a leveling off, a tit for tat, a weighted scale. But we must begin to think of it differently. Instead of making balance a static exchange, it must become an active *state of being*. It's not about achieving balance; it's about being balanced.

I recently interviewed Anna Lembke, MD, an addiction specialist who believes we're all strung out on a continuum of unhealthy relationships to various substances and things. She believes this struggle is unavoidable and inevitable in a society overly engineered for pleasure and immediate gratification. She told me about science's relatively new discovery of the pleasure/pain balance. Homeostasis is our biological imperative: The body naturally restores equilibrium, whether it's healing from a wound or disease or managing temperature or fluids. The brain, it seems, craves balance as well. Remarkably, the part of the brain that processes pleasure also processes pain. When we use substances that make us feel good—sugar, booze, drugs, video games, sex, shopping—we experience a high, but only temporarily. The pleasure they deliver isn't a permanent state. Immediately after engaging with these substances, the body wants to go back to center. "It does that by tipping the balance an equal and opposite amount to the side of pain," Lembke explained. "That's the moment of kind of falling away, when the movie ends, or the book ends, or the video game is over, or you have a come down from alcohol. . . . That's the moment of wanting to stretch out that good feeling and not being able to. It's the balance tilted to the side of pain. Now, if we wait long enough, those gremlins hop off and balance is again restored." When we hit pleasure buttons too hard and too fast, though, we get stuck in addictive cycles, chasing a feeling of relief that becomes increasingly elusive.

I see how this idea is playing out in our culture. We have become addicted to power, dominance, and resource hoarding—stuck in a pleasure center that, paradoxically, only brings pain. Our unrestrained consumption will drive the world to the eventuality of our own extinction. Our lack of equity, particularly the dominance of powerful white men, continues to be embedded shrapnel that keeps us in cycles of pain. We recognize that we need to unhitch from and then retool our problematic systems and structures, yet we're scared of what we'll lose in the process. We're fearful that the countermeasure, a return to the middle, to balance, might hurt. After all, many of us will need to give something up. Some parts of us need to die. We must go through withdrawal and recognize that the power structure we're addicted to is toxic for everyone. We must find a different way to build strength in new models of being.

We know from engaging in physical activity how much easier it is to rely on our major muscles, the ones we've built up with over-use. Why tap your hamstrings when your quads are so strong? Over time, this reliance becomes unsustainable and self-destructive. In this next stage of our evolution—a stage where we must evolve rapidly to catch up with the progress we've made technologically—we cannot move through the world as we have. We must develop new ways, new flexibility, a more stable approach. It's what our bodies crave, how we're wired. And to do this, we must attend to ourselves: We must walk the inner path of alignment before we can rebalance the world.

We must take responsibility for ourselves. We need to give up the idea that we can consume without needing to look at our waste, that what we take has no cost—to other people or the planet. We need to take responsibility for our own energy and the way it spreads in the world. We must find the boldness to let this collective unsustainability end, so something truer can emerge in its place, built on sharing, equity, nurturance, co-creation, and community. As we let go, we can begin to return to our place as part of nature, not outside of it. Then we might remember what it's like to allow the cycle, the ebb and flow, the process of equilibrium to continu-ally reset itself. To get to balance, we can't start with the world out there. Transforming society will require each of us to start in our own homes, with ourselves.

As part of this, we must resacralize the feminine and recognize that the death of the goddess, the demotion of Mary Magdalene, and the subjugation of Mother Earth are doing us no favors. This requires no religious belief, only a faith that we cannot rebalance the world until we reconcile the "Masculine" and its pursuit of truth, order, and direction with the "Feminine" and its tendencies toward creativity, nurturance, and care. Each of these energies is

critical, *in each of us, regardless of our stated gender, in all spheres of life.*
We don't take off our work clothes to put on our parenting clothes:
We must bring our playful, generative, and warm energy to work,
and our directing and organizing energy home. It's from there that
we take flight. Recall the Cherokee prophecy of the unbalanced
bird—as both wings fully unfurl and the bird achieves balance between the masculine and the feminine, a third emanating force
emerges, a force that allows the bird to stop circling and take off.
From wholeness comes freedom.

We must reject the early patriarchal idea—an idea that still
endures—that the feminine must be controlled and choked out and
that the rights of all women must be limited to ensure the dominion of (white) men. In turn, men must let their feminine emerge
and dull the edges of their masculine. If we can unburden ourselves
from an external authority and its prosaic concept of a goodness
that enforces suppression and obedience, we can find the goodness
of our god-self inside. This doesn't require faith in Jesus, Yeshua,
Buddha, Yahweh, God, Allah, or any concept of external divinity—
it requires only faith in our own deep inner knowing. We must
burn the morality map that keeps us from true self-definition. We
must give ourselves and each other space to voice our desires, birth
our purpose, express the fullness of our passion. We must also examine why we are so vehemently judgmental about other people's
choices and beliefs when they cause no harm to others. We must
allow that we are each shadow and light; our complexity is what
makes us human.

May we hold these polarities without tending to either extreme,
ready to bring forth our gifts and offer them to the world. May we
learn to look to each other in communion, rather than competition. May we judge ourselves lightly, and each other not at all. May
we do the work of feeling ourselves, so that we can heal ourselves,
rather than acting out of our wounds in a way that wounds others.
May we begin to relax into the full cycle of life, to claim responsibility for all our actions and desires. May we surrender to the plea-

sure of the exhale as the antidote to the clutch of the inhale. May we learn to embrace loss and death so we can seize life. May we allow ourselves to acknowledge sadness and grief—personally *and* collectively—so we can give full throat to joy. We are not yet lost. We just need to find ourselves again and, wings unfurled, fly home.

ACKNOWLEDGMENTS

Dr. Gerda Lerner wrote in *The Creation of Feminine Consciousness* that historians know of fewer than three hundred learned women in Western Europe from before 1700. Cloistered, denied educations, and kept from one another, women have only been in conversation with each other for a few centuries—and in some parts of the world, not at all. I am immensely grateful to be alive at this moment: to stand on the shoulders of so many women, to speak with them across time, and to be able to braid and distill their work into new forms. I hope readers buy this book solely for its bibliography and its endnotes: My life has been made so much richer by those who came before me, whose scholarship informed my own.

Whit Frick: My greatest concern was that an early draft would be accepted as "good enough," and swept into production. I should not have worried. Thank you for your tireless attention to every draft and for pushing me to clarify every single sentence. Your brilliance made this book immeasurably stronger. Your essence is baked into its pages.

Jenn Joel: Thank you for taking me under your wing when I was not yet worthy of your attention, and for pushing me, for all these years, to write something under my own name. You believed I had a book in me long before I believed this about myself. You may be my agent, but you gave me agency: I am so grateful for your stewardship, your advice, your friendship, and your mighty brain and pen.

Rose Fox: I'm thrilled I'll be able to say I knew you when— thank you for your fearless edits. Andy Ward and Avideh Bashirrad: Thank you for shepherding this book into the world and cracking open my next chapter. Elisabeth Magnus: Thank you for your astute and careful clarifications, teaching me the proper definition of *extol,* and saving me from myself at times. Debbie Aroff, Brianne Sperber, Maria Braeckel, and Michelle Jasmine: Thank you for establishing the vision for this book in the wild—and then advocating for it fiercely. Thank you to Donna Cheng and Jo Anne Metsch for the book's look and feel, Matthew Martin for a veil of protection, and Robert Siek and Benjamin Dreyer for signing off on every detail. Valero Doval: May the contents of the book live up to your stunning cover art.

Carissa Schumacher and Jen Walsh: I'm endlessly grateful that D.S.T. brought us all together when we needed each other the most. Carissa, you've taught me so much, expanded my mind, and reminded me not only *that* I know but of *what* I know. Jen: Thank you for helping me live according to the potential of my highest self, and never letting me slide down the mountain.

Life would have been a lonely walk without my chosen family— both friends from childhood, along with friends for the future: Chloe and Sophie Redmond, Brette Bornstein, Nathan and Mark Ellingson, Leigha Wilbur, Sarah Connolly, Sam Jones, Lily Atherton, Amanda Meigher, Katie Holt, Ali Quade, Ethan Leidinger, Hud Morgan, Angus Burgin, Will O'Boyle, Andy Gustin, Alex Tilney, Rachel Blitzer, Chandler Evans, Emily Hsieh, Robin Edlow, Jen Weinberg, Albertina Rizzo, Lori Bergamotto, Gigi Guerra, Kim France, Kristina Dechter, Kris Chen, Matt Patterson, Sarina Sanandaji, Mia Santos, Julia Boorstin, David Weinrot, Julie

Jen, Kate Wolfson, Diana Ryu, Brittany Weinstein, Kiki Koro-
shetz, Erica Moore, Juan Paul Ramirez, Kim Kreuzberger, Ali
Wyatt, Wendy Lauria, Blair Lawson, Lauren Roxburgh, Alexandra
Grant, Kasey Crown, Lauren Kucerak, Nick Felton, Matt Gryz-
winski, Erika Thormahlen, Andrea Arria-Devoe, Crystal Meers,
Sophia Amoruso, Priscilla Gilman, Will Schwalbe, Kim Jacobs,
Claire Martin, Chrissy Levinson, Jasmina Aganovic, Mandana Day-
ani, Hildy Kuryk, Geraldine Martin Coppola, Michelle An, Annie
Koo, Vanessa Chow, Gina Sherman, Poppy Montgomery, Andrew
Hotz, Kevin Friedman, Jamie Kantrowitz, Nat Doerr, Shauna Mi-
noprio, Andrew Fried, Ashley Hoppin, Connie and Andy Erick-
son, Ben Bennett, Tyler Dawson, Meggan Watterson, Nigma Talib,
Melissa Urban, Nora McInerny, Zoe Winkler, Taryn Toomey,
Brooke Baldwin, Kristin Hahn, Ellen Vora, Sarah Harden, Gene-
vieve Roth, Ben Bennett, Taylor and Jared Stein, Mikal Eckstrom,
Robin Berman, Laura Carlin, and B. J. Miller. Thank you all for
being mirrors, confidantes, co-creators, teachers, and mentors.
Richard Christiansen and Scott Sternberg, I know Peter sent you
both to me, not as a consolation prize but as a continuation of how
he walked the earth. Throughout this process, I've leaned hard on
the energetic hugs and wise counsel of Nattan Hollander, Jennifer
Freed, Anne Emerson, Laura Lynne Jackson, Carla Vidor, Carla S.,
Raymond Silkman, Kathryn Gill, and Jakki Leonardini.

Rumaan Alam, Liz Flahive, Jeet Sohal, and Regina Merson:
Thank you for bearing through early drafts, which I know weren't
the most pleasant reads. I asked because you all know me intimately
and never spare me from the truth. And Taylor Hamra: Thank you
for dragging me through my resistance in the messy middle and
putting me back on my feet. To Jofie Adler-Ferrari, Marysue Rucci,
and Megan Lynch for your early faith in me and in this idea, and to
Gabor Maté, Lisa Taddeo, Lori Gottlieb, Terry Real, and Holly
Whitaker for letting me borrow your confidence in what I made.

I'm thankful for my time at goop, for the kindness, humor, and
brilliance of my remarkable colleagues, and the opportunity to in-

terview so many cultural luminaries, whose wisdom is all over these pages.

My immense gratitude to librarians, booksellers, and professors and teachers who have lit my brain on fire and shepherded me through the halls of knowledge. I am particularly indebted to Bente Winston.

I am thankful to those who have taught me that I don't have to do this alone and have buttressed me with protection and support, with particular gratitude for Vicky Hernandez Rodas, Orin Snyder, Danielle Moss, Jeffrey Schneider, and Seth Adam.

I believe we choose our parents—and I chose well. Thank you, mom and dad, for not only allowing me to use you as examples in this book but for showing me how to live in unyielding integrity and radical honesty. You gave me an incredible education, unbridled access to nature, and a vast library—along with permission to pursue my curiosity and plenty of room to find my own path.

Ben: I'm so proud that you're my brother, not only for your wicked sense of humor but for your dazzling intellect and deep kindness. I've learned so much from watching you navigate the world and have pushed myself to keep up with your mind: You taught me how to study the world critically without judging it. This book is so much better for that, along with all your feedback couched in Downy-soft grenades: "I love you and so I'm telling you . . ."

Rob: You are my heart. Thank you for always giving me room while holding me tight. We may be legally bound, but I'd still always choose you, every single day.

Max and Sam: Love is an inadequate descriptor for how I feel about you. Accounts of your kindness, curiosity, and empathy are my proudest moments. Max: Watching you try to fit your expansive consciousness and intelligence into your little body has been a great teacher; I can't wait to see you extend yourself to the world someday. Sam: Everything about you is art; don't hold back—we all need you just as you are. Nothing I create will ever rival either of you.

SELECTED BIBLIOGRAPHY

Atlas, Galit. *Emotional Inheritance: A Therapist, Her Patients, and the Legacy of Trauma.* New York: Little, Brown Spark, 2022.

Augustine. *Confessions.* Translated by R. S. Pine-Coffin. New York: Penguin, 1961.

Bader, Michael. *Arousal: The Secret Logic of Sexual Fantasies.* New York: Thomas Dunne Books, 2002.

Barr, Beth Allison. *The Making of Biblical Womanhood: How the Subjugation of Women Became Gospel Truth.* Grand Rapids, Mich.: Brazos Press, 2021.

Barstow, Anne. *Witchcraze: A New History of the European Witch Hunts.* New York: HarperOne, 1995.

Beard, Mary. *Women and Power: A Manifesto.* New York: Liveright, 2017.

Blumberg, Bruce. *The Obesogen Effect: Why We Eat Less and Exercise More but Still Struggle to Lose Weight.* New York: Grand Central Life and Style, 2018.

Bonanno, George. *The Other Side of Sadness.* New York: Basic Books, 2019.

Boorstin, Julia. *When Women Lead: What They Achieve, Why They Succeed, and How We Can Learn from Them.* New York: Avid Reader Press, 2022.

Boss, Pauline. *Ambiguous Loss: Learning to Live with Unresolved Grief.* Cambridge, Mass.: Harvard University Press, 1999.

———. *The Myth of Closure: Ambiguous Loss in a Time of Pandemic and Change.* New York: Norton, 2021.

Bourgeault, Cynthia. *The Meaning of Mary Magdalene: Discovering the Woman at the Heart of Christianity.* Boulder, Colo.: Shambhala, 2010.

Boushey, Heather. *Finding Time: The Economics of Work-Life Conflict.* Cambridge, Mass.: Harvard University Press, 2016.

Brackett, Marc. *Permission to Feel: Unblocking the Power of Emotions to Help Our Kids, Ourselves, and Our Society Thrive.* New York: Celadon, 2019.

Brown, Brené. *Atlas of the Heart: Mapping Meaningful Connection and the Language of Human Experience.* New York: Random House, 2021.

————. *Dare to Lead: Brave Work, Tough Conversations, Whole Hearts.* New York: Random House, 2018.

Burkeman, Oliver. *Four Thousand Weeks: Time Management for Mortals.* New York: Farrar, Straus and Giroux, 2021.

Calhoun, Ada. *Why We Can't Sleep: Women's New Midlife Crisis.* New York: Grove, 2020.

Campbell, Joseph. *Goddesses: Mysteries of the Feminine Divine.* Novato, Calif.: New World Library, 2013.

————. *The Hero's Journey: Joseph Campbell on His Life and Work.* Novato, Calif.: New World Library, 2003.

————. *The Power of Myth.* With Bill Moyers. New York: Anchor Books, 1991.

Chemaly, Soraya. *Rage Becomes Her: The Power of Women's Anger.* New York: Atria, 2018.

Chernin, Kim. *The Hungry Self: Women, Eating and Identity.* New York: Times Books, 1985.

————. *Reinventing Eve: A Modern Woman in Search of Herself.* New York: Perennial, 1987.

Chugh, Dolly. *The Person You Mean to Be: How Good People Fight Bias.* New York: Harper Business, 2018.

Cooper, Brittney. *Eloquent Rage: A Black Feminist Discovers Her Superpower.* New York: Picador, 2018.

Cottom, Tressie McMillan. *Thick: And Other Essays.* New York: New Press, 2019.

Darby, Seyward. *Sisters in Hate: American Women on the Front Lines of White Nationalism.* New York: Little, Brown, 2020.

Davis, Angela. *Women, Race and Class.* New York: Vintage, 1983.

Deer, Sarah. *The Beginning and End of Rape: Confronting Sexual Violence in Native America.* Minneapolis: University of Minnesota Press, 2015.

DeYoung, Rebecca Konyndyk. *Glittering Vices: A New Look at the Seven Deadly Sins and Their Remedies.* Rev. ed. Grand Rapids, Mich.: Brazos Press, 2020.

DiPrete, Thomas A., and Claudia Buchmann. *The Rise of Women: The Growing Gender Gap in Education and What It Means for American Schools.* New York: Russell Sage Foundation, 2013.

Doyle, Glennon. *Untamed.* New York: Dial Press, 2020.

Doyle, Sady. *Trainwreck: The Women We Love to Hate, Mock, and Fear . . . and Why.* Brooklyn, N.Y.: Melville House, 2016.

Ehrman, Bart. *Jesus, Interrupted: Revealing the Hidden Contradictions in the Bible (and Why We Don't Know About Them).* New York: HarperOne, 2009.

————. *Misquoting Jesus: The Story Behind Who Changed the Bible and Why.* New York: HarperOne, 2005.

Eisler, Riane. *The Chalice and the Blade: Our History, Our Future.* 1987. Reprint, New York: HarperOne, 1995.

————. *Sacred Pleasure: Sex, Myth, and the Politics of the Body—New Paths to Power and Love.* New York: HarperOne, 1995.

Epstein, Mark. *Advice Not Given: A Guide to Getting over Yourself.* New York: Penguin, 2018.

————. *Open to Desire: The Truth About What the Buddha Taught.* New York: Gotham, 2005.

Evagrius Ponticus. *The Praktikos and Chapters on Prayer.* Translated with an introduction by John Eudes Bamberger. Trappist, Ky.: Cistercian Publications, 1972.

―――. *Talking Back (Antirrhêtikos): A Monastic Handbook for Combating Demons.* Translated with an introduction by David Brakke. Collegeville, Minn.: Liturgical Press, 2009.

Fagan, Kate. *All the Colors Came Out: A Father, a Daughter, and a Lifetime of Lessons.* New York: Little, Brown, 2021.

Febos, Melissa. *Girlhood.* New York: Bloomsbury, 2021.

Federici, Silvia. *Witches, Witch-Hunting, and Women.* Oakland, Calif.: PM Press, 2018.

Finkel, Eli. *The All-or-Nothing Marriage: How the Best Marriages Work.* New York: Dutton, 2018.

Garbes, Angela. *Essential Labor: Mothering as Social Change.* New York: Harper Wave, 2022.

Gay, Roxane. *Bad Feminist: Essays.* New York: Harper Perennial, 2014.

―――. *Hunger: A Memoir of (My) Body.* New York: Harper Perennial, 2017.

Gilligan, Carol. *In a Different Voice: Psychological Theory and Women's Development.* 1982. Reprint, Cambridge, Mass.: Harvard University Press, 1993.

―――, and Naomi Snider. *Why Does Patriarchy Persist?* Medford, Mass.: Polity Press, 2018.

Gimbutas, Marija. *The Language of the Goddess: Unearthing the Hidden Symbols of Western Civilization.* New York: Harper and Row, 1989.

Gordon, Aubrey. *What We Don't Talk About When We Talk About Fat.* Boston: Beacon Press, 2020.

Gordon, James. *Transforming Trauma: The Path to Hope and Healing.* New York: HarperOne, 2021.

Gottman, John. *The Seven Principles for Making Marriage Work.* New York: Harmony, 2015.

Graeber, David, and David Wengrow. *The Dawn of Everything: A New History of Humanity.* New York: Farrar, Straus and Giroux, 2021.

Headlee, Celeste. *Do Nothing: How to Break Away from Overworking, Overdoing, and Underliving.* New York: Harmony, 2020.

―――. *Speaking of Race: Why Everybody Needs to Talk About Racism—and How to Do It.* New York: Harper Wave, 2021.

Heuertz, Christopher. *The Sacred Enneagram: Finding Your Unique Path to Spiritual Growth.* Grand Rapids, Mich.: Zondervan, 2017.

Hill, Anita. *Believing: Our Thirty-Year Journey to End Gender Violence.* New York: Viking, 2021.

Hong, Cathy Park. *Minor Feelings: An Asian American Reckoning.* New York: One World, 2020.

hooks, bell. *All About Love: New Visions.* New York: William Morrow, 2001.

―――. *The Will to Change: Men, Masculinity, and Love.* New York: Washington Square Press, 2004.

Hrdy, Sarah Blaffer. *Mothers and Others: The Evolutionary Origins of Mutual Understanding.* Cambridge, Mass.: Harvard University Press, 2009.

Huston, Therese. *How Women Decide: What's True, What's Not, and What Strategies Spark the Best Choices.* New York: Houghton Mifflin, 2016.

Jackson, Laura Lynne. *The Light Between Us: Stories from Heaven. Lessons for Living.* New York: Dial Press, 2016.

———. *Signs: The Secret Language of the Universe.* New York: Dial Press, 2019.

Katie, Byron. *Loving What Is: Four Questions That Can Change Your Life.* New York: Harmony, 2002.

Kay, Katty, and Claire Shipman. *The Confidence Code: The Science and Art of Self-Assurance—What Women Should Know.* New York: Harper Business, 2014.

Kerner, Ian. *So Tell Me About the Last Time You Had Sex: Laying Bare and Learning to Repair Our Love Lives.* New York: Grand Central, 2021. .

Kimmerer, Robin Wall. *Braiding Sweetgrass: Indigenous Wisdom, Scientific Knowledge, and the Teachings of Plants.* Minneapolis, Minn.: Milkweed, 2013.

King, Karen L. *The Gospel of Mary of Magdala: Jesus and the First Woman Apostle.* Santa Rosa, Calif.: Polebridge Press, 2003.

Kushner, Harold. *When Bad Things Happen to Good People.* New York: Anchor, 1981.

Lamott, Anne. *Bird by Bird: Some Instructions on Writing and Life.* New York: Anchor, 1994.

Leloup, Jean-Yves, trans. (from the Coptic). *The Gospel of Mary Magdalene.* Preface by David Tresemer and Laura-Lee Cannon. Commentary by Jean-Yves Leloup. English translation and notes by Joseph Rowe. Rochester, Vt.: Inner Traditions, 2002.

Lembke, Anna. *Dopamine Nation: Finding Balance in the Age of Indulgence.* New York: Dutton, 2021.

Lerner, Gerda. *The Creation of Feminist Consciousness: From the Middle Ages to Eighteen-seventy.* New York: Oxford University Press, 1993.

———. *The Creation of Patriarchy.* New York: Oxford University Press, 1986.

Lerner, Harriet. *The Dance of Anger: A Woman's Guide to Changing the Patterns of Intimate Relations.* New York: William Morrow, 2014.

Lesser, Elizabeth. *Broken Open: How Difficult Times Can Help Us Grow.* New York: Ballantine, 2004.

Lewis, C. S. *A Grief Observed.* New York: HarperOne, 1996.

Lieberman, Daniel. *Exercised: Why Something We Never Evolved to Do Is Healthy and Rewarding.* New York: Pantheon, 2020.

Long, Jeffrey. *Evidence of the Afterlife: The Science of Near-Death Experiences.* New York: HarperOne, 2010.

Lorde, Audre. *Sister Outsider.* New York: Penguin Classics, 2020.

Malkin, Craig. *Rethinking Narcissism: The Bad—and Surprising Good—About Feeling Special.* New York: Harper Wave, 2015.

Maltz, Wendy. *The Sexual Healing Journey: A Guide for Survivors of Sexual Abuse.* New York: William Morrow, 2012.

Manne, Kate. *Down Girl: The Logic of Misogyny.* New York: Oxford University Press, 2018.

———. *Entitled: How Male Privilege Hurts Women.* New York: Crown, 2020.

Maté, Gabor. *The Myth of Normal: Trauma, Illness, and Healing in a Toxic Culture.* With Daniel Maté. New York: Avery, 2022.

———. *Scattered Minds: The Origins and Healing of Attention Deficit Disorder.* Toronto, Ont.: Vintage Canada, 1999.

McGhee, Heather. *The Sum of Us: What Racism Costs Everyone and How We Can Prosper Together.* New York: One World, 2021.

McInerny, Nora. *It's Okay to Laugh: Crying Is Cool Too*. New York: Dey Street, 2016.
———. *No Happy Endings*. New York: Dey Street, 2019.
Meltzer, Marisa. *This Is Big: How the Founder of Weight Watchers Changed the World—and Me*. New York: Little, Brown, 2020.
Mitchell, Stephen. *Can Love Last? The Fate of Romance over Time*. New York: W. W. Norton, 2002.
Montagu, Ashley. *The Natural Superiority of Women*. Lanham, Md.: Altamira, 1999.
Mullainathan, Sendhil, and Eldar Shafir. *Scarcity: The New Science of Having Less and How It Defines Our Lives*. New York: Picador, 2013.
Murthy, Vivek. *Together: The Healing Power of Human Connection in a Sometimes Lonely World*. New York: Harper Wave, 2020.
Nagoski, Emily, and Amelia Nagoski. *Burnout: The Secret to Unlocking the Stress Cycle*. New York: Ballantine, 2019.
Neff, Kristin. *Fierce Self-Compassion*. New York: Harper Wave, 2021.
———. *Self-Compassion: The Proven Power of Being Kind to Yourself*. New York: William Morrow, 2011.
Newman, Joe. *Raising Lions*. Seattle, Wash.: CreateSpace Independent Publishing Platform, 2010.
Nhât Hanh, Thích. *Anger: Wisdom for Cooling the Flames*. New York: Riverhead, 2001.
Nordell, Jessica. *The End of Bias: A Beginning*. New York: Metropolitan Books, 2021.
Odell, Jenny. *How to Do Nothing: Resisting the Attention Economy*. Brooklyn, N.Y.: Melville House, 2019.
Orenstein, Peggy. *Girls and Sex: Navigating the Complicated New Landscape*. New York: Harper, 2016.
Pagels, Elaine. *The Gnostic Gospels*. 1979. Reprint, New York: Vintage, 1989.
———. *Why Religion? A Personal Story*. New York: Ecco, 2018.
Perel, Esther. *Mating in Captivity: Unlocking Erotic Intelligence*. New York: Harper Collins, 2006.
Pillay, Srini. *Tinker Dabble Doodle Try: Unlock the Power of the Unfocused Mind*. New York: Ballantine, 2017.
Price, Devon. *Laziness Does Not Exist*. New York: Atria, 2021.
Real, Terrence. *I Don't Want to Talk About It: Overcoming the Secret Legacy of Male Depression*. New York: Scribner, 1997.
———. *Us: Getting Past You and Me to Build a More Loving Relationship*. New York: goop Press, 2022.
Rediger, Jeffrey. *Cured: The Life-Changing Science of Spontaneous Healing*. New York: Flatiron, 2020.
Ripley, Amanda. *High Conflict: Why We Get Trapped and How We Get Out*. New York: Simon & Schuster, 2021.
Riso, Don Richard, and Russ Hudson. *The Wisdom of the Enneagram: The Complete Guide to Psychological and Spiritual Growth for the Nine Personality Types*. New York: Bantam, 1999.
Rosenberg, Marshall. *Nonviolent Communication: A Language of Life*. Encinitas, Calif.: Puddlejumper, 2015.
Roth, Geneen. *Women Food and God: An Unexpected Path to Almost Everything*. New York: Scribner, 2010.
Rowland, Katherine. *The Pleasure Gap: American Women and the Unfinished Sexual Revolution*. New York: Seal Press, 2020.

Saini, Angela. *Inferior: How Science Got Women Wrong—and the New Research That's Rewriting the Story.* Boston: Beacon Press, 2017.

————. *The Patriarchs: The Origins of Inequality.* Boston: Beacon Press, 2023.

Schuller, Kyla. *The Trouble with White Women: A Counterhistory of Feminism.* New York: Bold Type Books, 2021.

Schulte, Brigid. *Overwhelmed: How to Work, Play, and Love When Nobody Has the Time.* New York: Farrar, Straus and Giroux, 2014.

Shlain, Leonard. *The Alphabet Versus the Goddess: The Conflict Between Word and Image.* New York: Penguin Compass, 1998.

Simmons, Rachel. *Odd Girl Out: The Hidden Culture of Aggression in Girls.* New York: Mariner, 2002.

Slaughter, Anne-Marie. *Unfinished Business: Women Men Work Family.* New York: Random House, 2015.

Smith, Tiffany Watt. *Schadenfreude: The Joy of Another's Misfortune.* New York: Little, Brown Spark, 2018.

Solnit, Rebecca. *Men Explain Things to Me.* Chicago: Haymarket, 2014.

Taheripour, Mori. *Bring Yourself: How to Harness the Power of Connection to Negotiate Fearlessly.* New York: Avery, 2020.

Tatar, Maria. *The Heroine with 1,001 Faces.* New York: Liveright, 2021.

Taussig, Hal, ed. *A New New Testament: A Bible for the 21st Century Combining Traditional and Newly Discovered Texts.* 2013. Reprint, New York: Mariner, 2015.

Tolentino, Jia. *Trick Mirror: Reflections on Self-Delusion.* New York: Random House, 2019.

Tolman, Deborah. *Dilemmas of Desire: Teenage Girls Talk About Sexuality.* Cambridge, Mass.: Harvard University Press, 2002.

Traister, Rebecca. *Good and Mad: The Revolutionary Power of Women's Anger.* New York: Simon & Schuster, 2018.

Tuerkheimer, Deborah. *Credible: Why We Doubt Accusers and Protect Abusers.* New York: Harper Wave, 2021.

Twist, Lynne. *The Soul of Money: Transforming Your Relationship with Money and Life.* New York: W. W. Norton, 2003.

Valerio, Adriana. *Mary Magdalene: Women, the Church, and the Great Deception.* Translated by Wendy Wheatley. New York: Europa Editions, 2020.

van Schaik, Carel, and Kai Michel. *The Good Book of Human Nature: An Evolutionary Reading of the Bible.* New York: Basic Books, 2016.

Walker, Barbara. *The Crone: Woman of Age, Wisdom, and Power.* New York: HarperOne, 1985.

Washington, Harriet. *A Terrible Thing to Waste: Environmental Racism and Its Assault on the American Mind.* New York: Little, Brown Spark, 2019.

Watterson, Meggan. *Mary Magdalene Revealed: The First Apostle, Her Feminist Gospel and the Christianity We Haven't Tried Yet.* Carlsbad, Calif.: Hay House, 2019.

Watts, Alan. *The Wisdom of Insecurity: A Message for an Age of Anxiety.* New York: Vintage, 2011.

Weber, Max. *The Protestant Ethic and the "Spirit" of Capitalism and Other Writings.* Translated and edited by Peter Baehr and Gordon C. Wells. New York: Penguin Classics, 2002. Weber's original work was published in 1905.

West, Lindy. *The Witches Are Coming.* New York: Hachette, 2019.

Wilkerson, Isabel. *Caste: The Origins of Our Discontents.* New York: Random House, 2020.

Williamson, Marianne. *A Return to Love: Reflections on the Principles of a Course in Miracles.* New York: HarperOne, 1992.

Wilson, E. O. *Sociobiology.* Cambridge, Mass.: Harvard University Press, 1975.

Woodman, Marion. *Addiction to Perfection: The Still Unravished Bride.* Toronto, Ont.: Inner City Books, 1982.

————. *Conscious Femininity.* Toronto, Ont.: Inner City Books, 1993.

————. *The Pregnant Virgin: A Process of Psychological Transformation.* Toronto, Ont.: Inner City Books, 1985.

————, and Elinor Dickson. *Dancing in the Flames: The Dark Goddess in Transformation of Consciousness.* Boulder, Colo.: Shambhala, 1996

Yeshua. *The Freedom Transmissions.* As channeled by Carissa Schumacher. New York: HarperOne, 2021.

NOTES

Introduction: Genesis

xv   **"taught many wrong and unsound things"** Ashley Montagu, *The Natural Superiority of Women* (Lanham, Md.: Altamira, 1999), 75–76.

xxv **"god-like technology"** E. O. Wilson, in James D. Watson and Edward O. Wilson, "Looking Back Looking Forward: A Conversation," moderated by Robert Krulwich, Harvard Museum of Natural History, Cambridge, Mass., September 9, 2009, https://hmnh.harvard.edu/file/284861.

xxv **"progress without evolution"** Yeshua, Yeshua transmission in Utah, as channeled by Carissa Schumacher, October 2020.

xxvi **"Or are you self-determined?"** Loretta Ross, "Calling in the Call-Out Culture," interview by Elise Loehnen, *Pulling the Thread Podcast,* September 23, 2021.

Chapter 1: A Brief History of the Patriarchy

3   **"discover something new about it"** David Graeber and David Wengrow, *The Dawn of Everything: A New History of Humanity* (New York: Farrar, Straus and Giroux, 2021), 21.

4   **birth is a miracle** Understandably much has been made of the wealth of "Venus" figurines that have been discovered from Neolithic sites. While we'll never know exactly what they are—dolls, birthing talismans, goddesses—there is markedly no male correlate. It's also worth noting that these figurines fed Victorian-era theories that Neolithic people were entirely matriarchal, which is not true (DNA evidence from the period suggests men ate better than women, for one). But it doesn't mean that these figurines are not telling. As Graeber and Wengrow explain, "Today, most archaeologists consider it deeply unsound to interpret prehistoric images of corpulent women as 'fertility god-

desses.' The very idea that they should be is the result of long-outmoded Victorian fantasies about 'primitive matriarchy.' In the nineteenth century, it's true, matriarchy was considered the default mode of political organization for Neolithic societies (as opposed to the oppressive patriarchy of the ensuing Bronze Age). As a result, almost every image of a fertile-looking woman was interpreted as a goddess. Nowadays, archaeologists are more likely to point out that many figurines could just as easily have been the local equivalents of Barbie dolls (the kind of Barbie dolls one might have in a society with very different standards of female beauty); or that different figurines might have served entirely different purposes (no doubt correct); or to dismiss the entire debate by insisting we simply have no idea why people created so many female images and never will, so any interpretations on offer are more likely to be projections of our own assumptions about women, gender or fertility, than anything that would have made sense to an inhabitant of Neolithic Anatolia." Graeber and Wengrow, *Dawn of Everything,* 213. Mythologist Joseph Campbell explains that these figurines give us many clues in their nakedness. He explains, "Her body is her magic: It both invokes the male and is the vessel of all human life. Woman's magic is thus primary, and of nature. The male, in contrast, is always represented in a role of some kind, performing a function, doing something." He also describes the woman in prehistoric art as positioned as the "transformer," in between a child and a man. Joseph Campbell, *Goddesses: Mysteries of the Feminine Divine* (Novato, Calif.: New World Library, 2013), xiv.

4   **early tribes were matriarchies** There is evidence of some matriarchies throughout history, as well as strong female leaders (including various queens of England): In Thebes, princesses reigned from 754 to 525 B.C., and there was primarily female leadership among Haudenosaunee (the Iroquois), the Hopi, the Zulu, the Minangkabau of Sumatra, and the Moche in Peru, among others. Here are Graeber and Wengrow on Minoan Crete and its powerful and perplexing history: "By far the most frequent depictions of authority figures in Minoan art show adult women in boldly patterned skirts that extend over their shoulders but are open at the chest. Women are regularly depicted at a larger scale than men, a sign of political superiority in the visual traditions of all neighboring lands. They hold symbols of command, like the staff-wielding 'Mother of Mountains' who appears on seal impressions from a major shrine at Knossos; they perform fertility rites before horned altars, sit on thrones, meet together in assemblies with no male presiding and appear flanked by supernatural creatures and dangerous animals. Most male depictions, on the other hand, are either of scantily clad or naked athletes (no women are depicted naked in Minoan art); or show men bringing tribute and adopting poses of subservience before female dignitaries. . . . Pretty much all the available evidence from Minoan Crete suggests a system of female political rule—effectively a theocracy of some sort, governed by a college of priestesses. We might ask: why are contemporary researchers so resistant to this conclusion? One can't blame everything on the fact that proponents of 'primitive matriarchy' made exaggerated claims back in 1902. Yes, scholars tend to say that cities ruled by colleges of priestesses are unprecedented in the ethnographic or historical record. But by the same logic, one could equally point out that there is no parallel for a kingdom run by men, in which all the visual representations are

depictions of women. Something different was clearly happening on Crete."
Graeber and Wengrow, *Dawn of Everything*, 219–20, 380–81, 387, 435, 438.

4   **perceived as superior to men** In a section entitled "In Which We Enter
Something of an Academic No-Go Zone, and Discuss the Possibility of Neolithic Matriarchies," Graeber and Wengrow establish the prevailing misogyny
in academia around this period. "It's not just the idea of 'primitive matriarchy'
that's become such a bugaboo today: even to suggest that women had unusually prominent positions in early farming communities is to invite academic
censure. Perhaps it's not entirely surprising. In the same way that social rebels,
since the 1960s, tended to idealize hunter-gatherer bands, earlier generations
of poets, anarchists and bohemians had tended to idealize the Neolithic as an
imaginary, beneficent theocracy ruled over by priestesses of the Great Goddess, the all-powerful distant ancestor of Inanna, Ishtar, Astarte and Demeter
herself—that is, until such societies were overwhelmed by violent, patriarchal
Indo-European-speaking horsemen descending from the steppes, or, in the
case of the Middle East, Semitic-speaking nomads from the deserts. How people saw this imagined confrontation became the source of a major political
divide in the late nineteenth and early twentieth centuries. . . . With such intense politicization of what were obviously fanciful readings of prehistory, it's
hardly surprising that the topic of 'primitive matriarchy' became something of
an embarrassment—the intellectual equivalent of a no-go zone—for subse-
quent generations. But it's hard to avoid the impression something else is going
on here. The degree of erasure has been extraordinary, and far more than is
warranted by mere suspicion of an overstated or outdated theory. Among academics today, belief in primitive matriarchy is treated as a kind of intellectual
offense, almost on a par with 'scientific racism,' and its exponents have been
written out of history: [Matilda Joslyn] Gage from the history of feminism,
[Otto] Gross from that of psychology (despite inventing such concepts as intro-
version and extroversion, and having worked closely with everyone from Franz
Kafka and the Berlin Dadaists to Max Weber)." Graeber and Wengrow, *Dawn
of Everything*, 214–15.

4   **predicated on continual oppression** Riane Eisler, *The Chalice and the Blade:
Our History, Our Future* (1987; repr., New York: HarperOne, 1995), xxi. Graeber and Wengrow cite evidence of ancient megasites like Stonehenge and
Göbekli Tepe as being spots for momentary celebrations, with hierarchy, before peoples would return to nomadic lifestyles for the rest of the year. "Almost
all the Ice Age sites with extraordinary burials and monumental architecture
were created by societies that live a little like Levi-Strauss's Nambikwara, dis-
persing into foraging bands at one time of year, gathering together in concentrated settlements at another. True, they didn't gather to plant crops. Rather,
the large Upper Paleolithic sites are linked to migrations and seasonal hunting
of game herds—woolly mammoth, steppe bison or reindeer—as well as cycli-
cal fish-runs and nut harvests." Graeber and Wengrow, *Dawn of Everything*, 104.

4   **generated, and processed, by women** Ashley Montagu, *The Natural Superiority of Women* (Lanham, Md.: Altamira, 1999), 69.

4   **equal amount of time inside** Science journalist Angela Saini interviewed
Stanford University archaeologist Ian Hodder, who led the Çatalhöyük Research Project until 2018. He explained to her that it was "an aggressively

egalitarian community." She writes, "'Most sites that archaeologists dig, you find that men and women, because they have different lives, they have different food and they end up with different diets,' [Hodder] says. 'But at Çatalhöyük you don't see that at all. They have identical diets.'" Other biological measurements from human remains show the same lack of difference. For instance, Hodder's team found that both men and women had soot on their ribs, most probably from indoor ovens and a lack of ventilation in their small boxlike houses. This indicated that men didn't spend more time indoors than women did. What's more, although the men were taller than the women on average, the size difference between them was slight. Angela Saini, *The Patriarchs: The Origins of Inequality* (Boston: Beacon Press, 2023), 76.

5   **were the bodies of women** Annalee Newitz, "What New Science Techniques Tell Us About Ancient Women Warriors," *New York Times,* January 1, 2021, https://www.nytimes.com/2021/01/01/opinion/women-hunter-leader .html.

5   **handprints were primarily female** Virginia Hughes, "Were the First Artists Mostly Women?," *National Geographic,* October 9, 2013, https://www.national geographic.com/adventure/article/131008-women-handprints-oldest-neolithic -cave-art.

5   **rivers throughout Eurasia** "At the beginning of the Holocene, the world's great rivers were mostly still wild and unpredictable. Then, around 7,000 years ago, flood regimes started changing, giving way to more settled routines. This is what created wide and highly fertile floodplains along the Yellow River, the Indus, the Tigris and other rivers that we associate with the first urban civilizations." Graeber and Wengrow also explain how soil formation north of the Black Sea led to large-scale Neolithic building in modern-day Ukraine, which was subsequently destroyed. Graeber and Wengrow, *Dawn of Everything,* 285, 290.

5   **third millennium B.C.** I love Graeber and Wengrow's exploration and defense of Gimbutas. As they write of the misogyny, "Many archaeologists and historians concluded that Gimbutas was muddying the waters between scientific research and pop literature. Before long, she was being accused of just about everything the academy could think to throw at her: from cherry-picking evidence to failing to keep up with the methodological advances; accusations of reverse sexism; or that she was indulging in 'myth-making.' She was even subject to the supreme insult of public psychoanalysis, as leading academic journals published articles suggesting her theories about the displacement of Old Europe were basically phantasmagorical projections of her own tumultuous life experience, Gimbutas having fled her mother country, Lithuania, at the close of the Second World War in the wake of foreign invasions. Mercifully, perhaps, Gimbutas herself, who died in 1994, was not around to see most of this. But that also meant she was never able to respond. Some, maybe most, of these criticisms had truth in them—though similar criticisms could no doubt be made of pretty much any archaeologist who makes a sweeping historical argument. Gimbutas's arguments involved myth-making of a sort, which in part explains this wholesale takedown of her work by the academic community. But when male scholars engage in similar myth-making—and, as we have seen, they frequently do—they not only go unchallenged but often

win prestigious literary prizes and have honorary lectures created in their name. Arguably Gimbutas was seen as meddling in, and quite consciously subverting, a genre of grand narrative that had been (and still is) entirely dominated by male writers such as ourselves. Yet her reward was not a literary prize, or even a place among the revered ancestors of archaeology; it was near-universal posthumous vilification, or, even worse, becoming an object of dismissive contempt." Graeber and Wengrow, *Dawn of Everything*, 217–18.

5   **overwhelmingly male Indo-Europeans** Per Angela Saini, "In 2017, researchers at Stanford University and Uppsala University published a paper looking at the DNA of prehistoric people who had lived in Europe. They suggested that there was something unusual about the migration patterns of those who entered the region from the steppes and spread during the late Neolithic and early Bronze Age. 'We estimate a dramatic male bias,' the authors wrote. They believed there may have been between five to fourteen males migrating for every one female who moved with them. In other words, most of the people who made this journey appeared to have been boys and men." Saini, *The Patriarchs*, 91. In addition, Saini points to evidence from military historian Pamela Toler that the women who did descend from the steppes, though in the minority, were also fighters. "Some of the earliest archaeological evidence of female warriors comes from a burial mound, thought to be roughly three thousand years old, of three armed women near Tbilisi in Georgia, writes Toler. One died with an arrow in her skull." Saini, *The Patriarchs*, 89.

5   **desert in the South** Joseph Campbell relies on Marija Gimbutas and her work, which explores the influx of peoples from the north, though he also draws on the idea of Akkadians and other Semitic tribes emerging from the south. Both groups rejected the goddess. Campbell, *Goddesses*, 57.

5   **elevated some and oppressed others** Marija Gimbutas, "The First Wave of Eurasian Steppe Pastoralists into Copper Age Europe," *Journal of Indo-European Studies*, no. 5 (Winter 1977): 297.

5   **dominate, control, and order** One fascinating example of this is Uruk (modern-day Iraq). As Graeber and Wengrow explain, "By the late fourth millennium BC it had a high acropolis, much of which was taken up by the raised public district called Eanna, 'House of Heaven,' dedicated to the Goddess Inanna. . . . Much of this remains speculative, but what's clear is that in later periods things change. Around 3200 BC the original public buildings of the Eanna sanctuary were razed and covered with debris, and its sacred landscape redesigned around a series of gated courts and ziggurats. By 2900 BC we have evidence for local kings of rival city-states battling it out for supremacy over Uruk, in response to which a five-and-a-half-mile fortification wall (whose building was later attributed to Gilgamesh) went up around the city's perimeter." Graeber and Wengrow, *Dawn of Everything*, 305–6.

6   **engine for many cultures** "The crucial invention, over and above that of brutalizing another human being and forcing him or her to labor against their will, is the possibility of designating the group to be dominated as entirely different from the group exerting dominance. Naturally, such a difference is most obvious when those to be enslaved are members of a foreign tribe, literally 'others.' Yet in order to extend the concept and make the enslaved into *slaves,* somehow *other* than human, men must have known that such a designation

would indeed work. We know that mental constructs usually derive from some model in reality and consist of a new ordering of past experience. That experience, which was available to men prior to the invention of slavery, was the subordination of women of their own group. The oppression of women antedates slavery and makes it possible." Gerda Lerner, *The Creation of Patriarchy* (New York: Oxford University Press, 1986), 77–78.

6   **Women simply went first** There is evidence that this type of capturing predates patriarchy: there's evidence of mass graves throughout the world where the bodies of young women are missing from the brutalized massacred, suggesting they were taken and not destroyed with the others. In Mesolithic Brittany, "Human remains . . . show anomalous levels of terrestrial protein in the diet of many young females, contrasting with the general prevalence of marine foods among the rest of the population. It seems that women of inland origin (who until then had been eating largely meat, not fish) were joining coastal groups. What does this tell us? It may indicate that women had been captured and transported in raids, conceivably including raids by foragers on farming communities. This can only be speculative." Graeber and Wengrow, *Dawn of Everything*, 261, 263.

7   **perhaps as primary** "In other instances, the Great Goddess herself became transformed. In the earlier period her attributes had been all-encompassing— her sexuality connected with birth, death, and rebirth; her power both for good and evil, for life and death; her aspects those of mother warrior, protector, and interceder with the dominant male god. In the later periods her various qualities were split off and embodied in separate goddesses. Her warrior aspect diminished, probably relegated to the male god, and her qualities as a healer were more and more stressed. This does appear to reflect a change in concepts of gender in the societies in which she was worshipped. Her erotic aspect was emphasized in the Greek goddess Aphrodite and in the Roman goddess Venus. Her quality as healer and protector of women in childbirth became embodied in the goddess Mylitta in Assyria and in Artemis, Eleithya, and Hera in Greece. The cult of Asherah in Canaan, which coexisted for centuries with the cult of Yahweh and which is frequently condemned in the Old Testament, may have been due to the association of the goddess with protection in childbirth. . . . We may be justified in regarding the extraordinary persistence of fertility and goddess cults as an expression of female resistance to the predominance of male god figures. There is as yet no hard evidence to prove this speculation, but it is difficult to explain the persistence of these female cults in any other way." G. Lerner, *Creation of Patriarchy*, 159.

7   **demoted to concubine or slave** "When we consider that as late as the 11th century men of European nobility still engaged in concubinage, the competition was real and tended to divide noble women one against the other. Not only concubinage but also male adultery with lower-class women posed a threat to the economic security of wives." Gerda Lerner, *The Creation of Feminist Consciousness: From the Middle Ages to Eighteen-seventy* (New York: Oxford University Press, 1993), 119.

7   **survived and reemerged** Campbell, *Goddesses*, 135.

7   **something to battle and subjugate** Joseph Campbell credits Henri Frankfort

and his book on archaic thinking, *Before Philosophy,* for this idea. Campbell, *Goddesses,* 15.

7   **his own *daughter* was to die** Two of the most prominent rulers of this era—Sargon (ca. 2334–2279 B.C.) and Hammurabi (1792–1750 B.C.)—are thought to be the bases of key biblical leaders (Moses and Nimrod, respectively). Hammurabi's Code is profoundly misogynistic, and the Middle Assyrian Law Codes (ca. 1175 B.C.) are no kinder. Campbell, *Goddesses,* 85. As Gerda Lerner elaborates: "Women's sexual subordination was institutionalized in the earliest law codes and enforced by the full power of the state. Women's cooperation in the system was secured by various means: force, economic dependence on the male head of the family, class privileges bestowed upon conforming and dependent women of the upper classes, and artificially created division of women into respectable and not-respectable women." G. Lerner, *Creation of Patriarchy,* 9.

7   **laws and rituals were written down** Joseph Campbell articulates the sad reality of the calcification of a belief structure when it is codified in this way. As he writes, "The deity does not continue to grow, expand, or take into account new cultural forces and new realizations in the sciences, and the result is this make-believe conflict we have in our culture between science and religion. One of the functions of mythology is to present an image of the cosmos in such a way that it becomes the carrier of this mystical realization, so that wherever you look it's as though you are looking at an icon, a holy picture, and the walls of space and time open out into the deep dimension of mystery, which is a dimension within ourselves, as well as out there." He adds that in Greek and Indian traditions there is no authority that can determine orthodoxy, which allows a different experience of these mythologies. Campbell, *Goddesses,* 107.

7   **existing myths and belief systems** As Gerda Lerner writes, "It is by now taken for granted that earlier Sumero-Babylonian, Canaanite, and Egyptian cultural materials were adapted and transformed by the writers and redactors of the Bible and that contemporary practices, laws, and customs of neighboring peoples were reflected in its narrative." G. Lerner, *Creation of Patriarchy,* 161.

8   **Judaism's official patriarchs** Abraham (1996–1821 B.C., which, yes, suggests he lived to 175) is the father of monotheism—of Judaism, Christianity, and Islam. He was born in Ur, the capital of Mesopotamia, and legend has it that his father was an idol-maker and that Abraham smashed all the idols in his shop save one, demonstrating his devotion to one God. Supposedly, Abraham throughout his life made several covenants with God, who told him his people would inherit the land after four hundred years of slavery. He moved all over the place with his wife, Sarah—Canaan, Egypt—but in a nutshell, he fathered his first child, Ishmael, with Sarah's handmaiden Hagar (Sarah was barren, so she offered Hagar up as an alternative piece of patriarchal "property"), and then Sarah became pregnant with his second son, Isaac, when she was ninety years old. Both Hebrew traditions and Muslim traditions claim Abraham: In the world of the former, Isaac is Abraham's rightful heir (followed by his son, Israel, a.k.a. Jacob); for the latter, it's Ishmael. Jacob, Isaac, and Abraham are officially labeled as "the Patriarchs" of "the Patriarchal Age" (2000 B.C.).

8   **delivered the Ten Commandments** The Old Testament is laced with laws,

613 *mitvohs* to be exact, which run from the well known (do not oppress the weak) to the mundane (do not tattoo your skin) to the esoteric (do not have fringes on the corners of your garments).

8 **(Exodus 20:17)** King James Version.

8 **no eviction from paradise** Joseph Campbell explains, "The power of life causes the snake to shed its skin, just as the moon sheds its shadow. The serpent sheds its skin to be born again, as the moon its shadow to be born again. They are equivalent symbols. . . . In the biblical tradition we have inherited, life is corrupt, and every natural impulse is sinful unless it has been circumcised or baptized. The serpent was the one who brought sin into the world. And the woman was the one who handed the apple to man. This identification of the woman with sin, of the serpent with sin, and thus of life with sin, is the twist that has been given to the whole story in the biblical myth and doctrine of the Fall. . . . The Garden is the serpent's place. It is an old, old story. We have Sumerian seals from as early as 3500 BC showing the serpent and the tree and the goddess, with the goddess giving the fruit of life to a visiting male. The old mythology of the goddess is right there." Joseph Campbell, *The Power of Myth,* with Bill Moyers (New York: Anchor Books, 1991), 52–55.

8 **cause of man's fall** Per Campbell, it's ironic that the feminine is pegged as the reason for the Fall, as no goddess mythology teaches separation. As he writes, "With these masculine Semitic mythologies, we have for the first time a separation of the individual from the divine, and this is one of the most important and decisive motifs in the history of mythology: that the eternal life and oneness with the universe are no longer ours. We are separated from God, God is separated from his world, man is turned against nature, nature is turned against man. You do not have this separation in the mythologies of the Great Mother." Campbell, *Goddesses,* 86.

8 **initiated men into the sexual mysteries** As Lucius Apuleius (born A.D. 124) writes: "I am she that is the natural mother of all things, mistress and governess of all the elements, the initial progeny of worlds, chief of the powers divine, queen of all that are in hell, the principal of them that dwell in heaven, manifested alone and under one form of all the gods and goddesses. At my will the planets of the sky, the wholesome winds of the seas, and the lamentable silences of hell are disposed; my name, my divinity is adored throughout the world, in diverse manners, in variable customs, and by many names. For the Phrygians that are the first of all men call me the Mother of the gods of Pessinus; the Athenians, which are spring from their own soil, Cecropian Minerva; the Cyprians, which are girt about the sea, Paphian Venus; the Cretans, which bear arrows, Dictynian Diana; the Sicilians, which speak three tongues, infernal Proserpine; the Eleusians their ancient goddess Ceres; some Juno, others Bellona, others Hecate, others Ramnusie, and principally both sort of the Ethiopians, which dwell in the Orient and are enlightened by the morning rays of the sun; and the Egyptians, which are excellent in all kind of ancient doctrine, and by their proper ceremonies accustomed to worship me, do call me by my true name, Queen Isis." Campbell, *Goddesses,* 252.

8 **instigator of her transgression** Campbell suggests that women are scapegoated because they represent life. "Man doesn't enter life except by woman,

and so it is woman who brings us into this world of pairs of opposites and suffering." Campbell, *Power of Myth*, 55.

8 **(about one-third of the world's population today)** Christians make up 31.2 percent of the world's population, whereas Jews are just 0.2 percent. Conrad Hackett and David McClendon, "Christians Remain World's Largest Religious Group, but They Are Declining in Europe," Pew Research Center, Fact Tank, April 5, 2017, https://www.pewresearch.org/fact-tank/2017/04/05/christians -remain-worlds-largest-religious-group-but-they-are-declining-in-europe/.

9 **did not survive** "Not only do we not have the originals, we don't have the first copies of the originals. We don't even have copies of the copies of the originals, or copies of the copies of the copies of the originals. What we have are copies made later—much later. In most instances, they are copies made many *centuries* later. And these copies all differ from one another, in many thousands of places." It's also important to remember that the Old Testament was originally written in Hebrew, the New Testament in Greek, and that both were then variously translated into Latin, Coptic, Syriac, et cetera. Bart Ehrman, *Misquoting Jesus: The Story Behind Who Changed the Bible and Why* (New York: HarperOne, 2005), 10.

9 **containers for moral turpitude** Karen King, a professor at the Harvard Divinity School who has written many excellent books about Mary Magdalene and other historic figures, offered a succinct overview for *Frontline*. Karen L. King, "Women in Ancient Christianity: The New Discoveries," *Frontline*, April 1998, https://www.pbs.org/wgbh/pages/frontline/shows/religion/first/women .html.

10 **carried forward by the "first apostle," Peter** Calling Peter the first apostle is problematic because it's not true. As Pagels explains, "For nearly 2,000 years, orthodox Christians have accepted the view that the apostles alone held definitive religious authority, and that their only legitimate heirs are priests and bishops, who trace their ordination back to that same apostolic succession. Even today the pope traces his—and the primacy he claims over the rest—to Peter himself, 'first of the apostles,' since he was 'first witness of the resurrection.'" Elaine Pagels, *The Gnostic Gospels* (1979; repr., New York: Vintage, 1989), 11. Yet in all four canonical gospels in the New Testament, it's confirmed that Mary Magdalene was the first to see the resurrected Christ, though the male disciples (*particularly* Peter) expressed skepticism she would be so honored. Here's Mark, for context: "Now when *Jesus* was risen early the first *day* of the week, he appeared first to Mary Magdalene, out of whom he had cast seven devils. And she went and told them that had been with him, as they mourned and wept. And they, when they had heard that he was alive, and had been seen by her, believed not" (Mark 16:9–11). I use the King James Version here in part because it has this passage, which did not actually appear in many early manuscripts. Hal Taussig, who edited *A New New Testament: A Bible for the 21st Century Combining Traditional and Newly Discovered Texts* (2013; repr., New York: Mariner, 2015), a much more inclusive translation of the New Testament that includes many Gnostic Gospels, did not include this passage in the version he—and nineteen other spiritual leaders—put forth. But for most Christians, this is the version of the Bible they've known and read.

10 **extinguish goddess worship almost completely** According to religious scholar Elaine Pagels, the sidelining and denigration of Mary Magdalene align with what was happening to the status of women in the first centuries after Jesus presumably lived and died. "In Greece and Asia Minor, women participated with men in religious cults, especially the cults of the Great Mother and of the Egyptian goddess Isis. While the leading roles were reserved for men, women took part in the services and professions. Some women took up education, the arts, and professions such as medicine. In Egypt, women had attained, by the first century A.D., a relatively advanced state of emancipation, socially, politically, and legally." Pagels, *Gnostic Gospels*, 62.

10 **many of which were feminist** The chastity-focused Cathars venerated Mary Magdalene—and women often assumed leadership roles among them. They were the first targets of the Inquisition. Adriana Valerio, *Mary Magdalene: Women, the Church, and the Great Deception*, trans. Wendy Wheatley (New York: Europa Editions, 2020), 63.

10 **Jesus himself did not write** "Because Jesus himself did not write, all our portraits of him reflect the perspectives of early Christians. Since the end of the eighteenth-century, historians have been asking how these portraits developed. After long and painstaking investigation, they have constructed the following picture: Jesus said and did some things that were remembered and passed down orally. People did not repeat everything he said and did, but only what was particularly memorable or distinctive, especially what was of use in the early churches for preaching, teaching, ritual practices, and other aspects of community life. His parables and his saying (called aphorisms) were often so striking, so pithy and memorable, that they were repeated again and again. A saying like 'Blessed are the poor,' for example, would surely have struck people as remarkable." Karen L. King, *The Gospel of Mary of Magdala: Jesus and the First Woman Apostle* (Santa Rosa, Calif.: Polebridge Press, 2003), 93–94.

10 **her cultural reputation—proves pivotal** While it's easy to get excited about the Gnostic Gospels and Mary Magdalene's gospel, Episcopalian priest and author Cynthia Bourgeault holds that those who read the New Testament closely should know not to underplay the Magdalene's importance there. She writes, "It's true that these recently recovered ancient texts do round out the portrait of Mary Magdalene in significant ways. But in no way do they actually *contradict* the picture already available in the familiar canonical gospels (Matthew, Mark, Luke, and John). Even if we only have these four texts to work with, there is still more than enough material here to warrant a complete revisioning of Mary Magdalene. The question is not about information; it's about how we hear and process it." Cynthia Bourgeault, *The Meaning of Mary Magdalene: Discovering the Woman at the Heart of Christianity* (Boulder, Colo.: Shambhala, 2010), 5.

11 **impossible to control** Campbell, *Goddesses*, 16.

12 **(7) Vainglory, and (8) Pride** According to Professor David Brakke, books like this were quite common. He explains, "Ancient people created anthologies of excerpts from written works for a variety of purposes, including private study, research for one's work, and self-improvement. Christians created anthologies of excerpts from the Bible or 'testimonies' primarily for apologetic reasons, to defend Christological and ecclesiological claims, and for moral exhortation, to

encourage virtue and discourage vice." David Brakke, introduction to *Talking Back (Antirrhêtikos): A Monastic Handbook for Combating Demons,* by Evagrius of Pontus, trans. David Brakke (Collegeville, Minn.: Liturgical Press, 2009), 7.

12 **avarice, gluttony, lust** Pope Gregory I, *Moralia on Job* 31.87, Lectionary Central, http://www.lectionarycentral.com/GregoryMoralia/Book31.html.

12 **anoints Jesus's feet with oil** There's no reference to the sinful woman mentioned in the New Testament as being a prostitute either. In their preface to Leloup's translation of Mary's gospel, David Tresemer and Laura-Lea Cannon write: "It is interesting to note that the Greek word interpreted as 'sinner' in the verse of Luke to which Pope Gregory referred was *harmartolos,* which can be translated several ways. From a Jewish perspective, it could mean one who has transgressed Jewish law. It might also mean someone who, perhaps, did not pay his or her taxes. The word itself does not imply a streetwalker or a prostitute. The Greek word for harlot, *porin,* which is used elsewhere in Luke, is not the word used for the sinful woman who weeps at Jesus' feet. In fact, *there is no direct reference to her—or to Mary—as a prostitute anywhere in the Gospels.*" David Tresemer and Laura-Lea Cannon, preface to *The Gospel of Mary Magdalene,* translation from the Coptic and commentary by Jean-Yves Leloup, English translation and notes by Joseph Rowe (Rochester, Vt.: Inner Traditions, 2002), xvi–xvii.

12 **"if not all the vices?"** Pope Gregory I expounds further about Mary: "It is clear, brothers, that this woman previously used the unguent to perfume her flesh in forbidden acts. What she therefore displayed more scandalously, she was now offering to God in a more praiseworthy manner." Ouch. Quoted from King, *Gospel of Mary of Magdala,* 151.

12 **"clearly an anomaly and threat"** Bourgeault, *Meaning of Mary Magdalene,* 22–23.

13 **perceived as ignominious and base** In the Gospel of John, Christ, during his ascension, says to Mary, "Noli me tangere"—or that's the translation in Latin the church fathers made, which means "Don't touch me." And that is how Mary Magdalene is frequently represented in religious art: clinging to Christ, like the penitent prostitute she's presumed to be, trying to drag him down to her position of baseness. But some religious scholars argue this is a mistranslation from the original Greek, that he's really saying that she shouldn't hold on to him while he is in an in-between state. These theologians think Christ was telling her he was still in the process of his journey back home—he was not castigating her, just telling her to let his physical body go. In their preface, Tresemer and Cannon write, "These words have been interpreted as confirmation that Mary Magdalene still carries some of the taint from her sins. In other words, some perceive Jesus Christ's words as 'Stay away from me, you soiled woman.' Indeed, many statues with the inscription, *Noli me tangere* depict a transcendent Jesus Christ and a woman below him, groveling in the ultimate shame of rejection. Were Mary Magdalene still soiled from her past, however, then we would have to conclude that Jesus Christ was not really an effective healer—that he hadn't really done the job of cleansing her of her demons. If we look at Christ's words in the original Greek, the meaning translates a little differently. '*Me mou aptou*' uses the imperative mood of the verb (h) aptein, 'to fasten.' A better translation would then be, 'Don't hold onto me' or

'Don't cling to me.'" Tresemer and Cannon, preface to Leloup, *Gospel of Mary Magdalene,* xx.

13   **necessitated this type of absolution** This happened at the Fourth Lateran Council in 1215.

14   **a rush of religious art emerged** As Leonard Shlain writes, "Pope Gregory the Great (590–604) confronted a vexing problem. How could he, as the chief priest presiding over a vast empire, ensure that Christian doctrine would be disseminated in a society where people could not read and illustrations were forbidden. Over the strident objections of many strict literalists, but the immense relief of future art lovers, the Pope declared the Second Commandment null and void. 'Painting,' he said, 'can do for the illiterate what writing does for those who can read.'" Leonard Shlain, *The Alphabet Versus the Goddess: The Conflict Between Word and Image* (New York: Penguin Compass, 1998), 266.

15   **turning against one's own** Professor Anne Barstow cites the work of historian R. I. Moore, author of *A Persecuting Society,* explaining, "R. I. Moore demonstrated how the European state became an organ of persecution, how, in the eleventh and twelfth centuries, European governments began, for the first time, to identify groups as enemies of the state—heretics, Jews, lepers, homosexuals—and to *create the myths* that would enable rulers to destroy those groups. Observing that there have been two major periods of persecutions in Europe since, the sixteenth and seventeenth centuries (the witchcraze) and the twentieth (the Holocaust), Moore states that intolerance 'became part of the character of European society,' and that in each case it was the rulers, not the people, who originated and carried out the pogroms. In short, the chief motive behind European racism and bigotry was the drive for political power. Even though none of the victims were powerful enemies, they served as an excuse for governments to use powerful weapons against their own people." Anne Llewellyn Barstow, *Witchcraze: A New History of the European Witch Hunts* (New York: HarperOne, 1995), 39.

15   **assure salvation and access to heaven** This preoccupation is evident through the fourteenth and fifteenth centuries in literature and art, exemplified best by Hieronymus Bosch's *Table of the Seven Deadly Sins,* 1505–1510.

15   **morally suspect targets** See Barstow, who cites the work of professor Richard Dunn: "Given that in about 1560 Europe began to experience population saturation, food scarcity, and runaway inflation, its ruling class 'had a desperate need for scapegoats to meliorate the impact of social disasters for which they had no remedy: poverty, disease, crime, famine, plague, wartime carnage, and revolutionary upheaval, all characteristic of [this] troubled society.' Taking a primarily economic approach, Dunn concludes that 'it was no accident that the great witchcraft hysteria, one of the most distinctive phenomena in the age of religious wars, began in the 1560s.' Other historians stress as triggers for the witch hunts the pressure put on commoners by absolutist central governments and reform-minded churches." Barstow, *Witchcraze,* 57.

16   **being burned at the stake** "These hunts, deserving of the name *witchcraze,* could not have happened unless a major legal change had taken place: the adoption by secular courts of inquisitorial procedures. Secret sessions, withholding of the source of charges, denial of counsel, acceptance of evidence from prejudiced sources, lack of cross-examination, passing of indeterminate

sentences, assumption of guilt—all these were justified to protect the church from heretics and society from witches. The judge was both prosecutor and confessor, trying to condemn the defendant as a follower of Satan but to do so in such a way as to save her soul. Undeniably the most influential change brought in by the inquisitional procedure, however, was the use of torture to force confession and the naming of accomplices." Barstow, *Witchcraze*, 49.

16 **women (and some men)** Records indicate that 82 percent of targets were women except in a few countries, like Russia, where more men were charged (60 percent to 40 percent). There was very little witch-hunting in Russia, though, along with countries along the periphery of Europe; a majority of the hunting was focused in the center of the Holy Roman Empire, in Germany and France. Barstow, *Witchcraze*, 75, 80.

16 **had no options to do so** Barbara Walker, *The Crone: Woman of Age, Wisdom, and Power* (New York: HarperOne, 1985), 30.

16 **healers, prophets, and midwives** As Walker explains, "Magic, prophecy, healing, fertility, birth, death, seasonal ceremonies, and sacred literature were largely the province of women in pre-Christian Europe. During centuries of patriarchal conquest, new laws were set against the old systems of mother-right and matrilineal property inheritance, to take property away from the female family heads recognized by paganism, and place it in the hands of men, according to the church's idea of father-right. Predictably, women often refused to abandon the older customs, which had given them spiritual, economic, and social prominence. Many of them realized that the church sought to reduce women's significance, to mock their sacred songs and stories as 'old wives' tales,' to diabolize their deities, to condemn their magic, even to blame them for all the world's sins." Walker, *Crone*, 53. Meanwhile, Eisler writes, "It is a world in which 'men of God' declare that the half of humanity from whose bodies life ensues is carnal and sinful, and 'witches' are burnt alive at the stake for the crime of healing through 'sorcery' (that is, through folk medicine such as herbs rather than through bleeding and other 'heroic' remedies prescribed by the new Church-trained and licensed male physicians). It is a world in which 'heretics' and 'traitors' who dare to question absolutist dogmas or despotic authority are drawn and quartered, and even stealing a loaf of bread can be a capital offense; where the mass of people live in poverty and filth while the ruling classes hoard gold, silver, and other riches; and where 'spiritual' men preach this must all be patiently accepted, holding out instead the promise of a better afterlife." Riane Eisler, *Sacred Pleasure: Sex, Myth, and the Politics of the Body—New Paths to Power and Love* (New York: HarperOne, 1995), 154.

16 **sanctioned by Pope Innocent VIII** "The attitudes expressed in the *Malleus* explain how Germans justified wiping out a sizable portion of their female population. Germans accused and executed women at the average European rate (82 percent and 82 percent). But because they put to death about 30,000 persons, that means that they destroyed around 24,600 women—a believable figure, given the devastations described above. In one town, Rottenburg, for example, by 1590 at least 150 women had been executed, and worse was to come." Barstow reports that two villages were left with only one woman each and that in one Rhenish village, one person out of every two families was killed. Barstow, *Witchcraze*, 62, 24.

17 **"useful sources of wisdom and knowledge"** Silvia Federici, *Witches, Witch-Hunting, and Women* (Oakland, Calif.: PM Press, 2018), 35, 40; Maria Tatar, *The Heroine with 1,001 Faces* (New York: Liveright, 2021), 121.

17 **forced under torture to denounce each other** Federici, *Witches, Witch-Hunting, and Women,* 40.

17 **across the globe** Barstow, *Witchcraze,* 21.

19 **"privileges to conforming women"** G. Lerner, *Creation of Patriarchy,* 217.

19 **"their gender, among other factors"** Kate Manne, *Entitled: How Male Privilege Hurts Women* (New York: Crown, 2020), 7.

23 **humanity has two great wings** Lynne Twist, "The Soul of Money," interview by Elise Loehnen, *The goop Podcast,* May 30, 2019.

Chapter 2: Sloth

25 **"will protect us from ignorance"** Devon Price, *Laziness Does Not Exist* (New York: Atria, 2021), 106.

25 **the gap is widening** According to the American Psychological Association, the rates are 5.1 for women (out of 10) versus 4.4 for men in 2017; in 2007, they were 6.3 versus 6.0. All these data points are pre-COVID, as assessing the impact of the pandemic has been their primary focus since. "Stress in America: Paying with Our Health," American Psychological Association, February 4, 2015, 11, https://www.apa.org/news/press/releases/stress/2014/stress-report .pdf. The 2017 data can be found in "Stress in America: The State of Our Nation," American Psychological Association, November 1, 2017, https://www .apa.org/news/press/releases/stress/2017/state-nation.pdf.

28 **through hate and judgment** As Kristin Neff explains, "When mothers or fathers use harsh criticism as a means to keep their kids out of trouble ('don't be so stupid or you'll get run over by a car'), or to improve their behavior ('you'll never get into college if you keep getting such pathetic grades'), children assume that criticism is a useful and necessary motivational tool." Kristin Neff, *Self-Compassion: The Proven Power of Being Kind to Yourself* (New York: William Morrow, 2011), 25.

29 **(31.3 percent of women to 22.6 percent of men)** Kim Parker and Eileen Patten, "Caregiving for Older Family Members," Pew Research Center, January 30, 2013, https://www.pewresearch.org/social-trends/2013/01/30 /caregiving-for-older-family-members/; "Volunteering in the United States: 2015," U.S. Bureau of Labor Statistics, press release, February 25, 2016, https:// www.bls.gov/news.release/pdf/volun.pdf.

31 **"the purpose of life is hard work"** Celeste Headlee, *Do Nothing: How to Break Away from Overworking, Overdoing, and Underliving* (New York: Harmony, 2020), xiv.

31 **"during which money was earned"** Headlee, *Do Nothing,* 25.

32 *must* **be spent in the home** Barr, who was raised in the Evangelical tradition, left her church when its elders fired her pastor husband after he asked that women be able to preach to men. She wrote a fascinating book about complementarianism, which she calls "Christian Patriarchy," or the idea that men are the heads of family and wives must submit, according to the Bible. She makes the point that this is a deviation from what Jesus, and even Paul, said, writing,

"What if patriarchy isn't divinely ordained but is a result of human sin? What if instead of being divinely created, patriarchy slithered into creation only after the fall? What if the reason that the fruit of patriarchy is so corrupt, even within the Christian church, is because patriarchy has always been a corrupted system? Instead of assuming that patriarchy is instituted by God, we must ask whether patriarchy is a product of sinful human hands." In terms of the Reformation, on which the modern Evangelical movement is also based, Barr explains that it was terrible for women. In the Catholic tradition, women could espouse virginity and take to cloisters; while barred from preaching, they could teach and guide as mystics and nuns. As she writes, "Women have always been wives and mothers, but it wasn't until the Protestant Reformation that being a wife and a mother became the 'ideological touchstone of holiness' for women. Before the Reformation, women could gain spiritual authority by rejecting their sexuality. Virginity empowered them. Women became nuns and took religious vows, and some, like Catherine of Siena and Hildegard of Bingen, found their voices rang with the authority of men. Indeed, the further removed medieval women were from the married state, the closer they were to God. After the Reformation, the opposite became true for Protestant women. The more closely they identified with being wives and mothers, the godlier they became." Beth Allison Barr, *The Making of Biblical Womanhood: How the Subjugation of Women Became Gospel Truth* (Grand Rapids, Mich.: Brazos Press, 2021), 25, 102–3.

32 **the foundation of capitalism** Max Weber, *The Protestant Ethic and the "Spirit" of Capitalism and Other Writings,* ed. and trans. Peter Baehr and Gordon C. Wells (New York: Penguin Classics, 2002). Weber's original work was published in 1905.

32 **when the mouse lies dormant** According to *The Washington Post,* "The number of large employers using tools to track their workers doubled since the beginning of the pandemic to 60 percent. That number is expected to rise to 70 percent within the next three years." Danielle Abril and Drew Harwell, "Keystroke Tracking, Screenshots, and Facial Recognition: The Boss May Be Watching Long After the Pandemic Ends," *Washington Post,* September 24, 2021, https://www.washingtonpost.com/technology/2021/09/24/remote -work-from-home-surveillance/.

33 **wage for an elementary school teacher** "Occupational Employment and Wages: May 2021," U.S. Bureau of Labor Statistics, accessed July 29, 2022, https://www.bls.gov/oes/current/oes_nat.htm.

34 **"work" much less than that** Headlee cites the research of Laura Vanderkam, who found that women who professed to working sixty-hour weeks actually worked forty-four hours a week, per time logs. Headlee, *Do Nothing,* 50.

36 **less parenting than we do now** Professor Eli Finkel explains that in heterosexual couples there's been a marked increase in parenting, primarily in recent decades, *specifically* for mothers: "From 1965 until the early 1990s, fathers spent four to five hours per week engaged in intensive parenting activities. Then, suddenly, both fathers and mothers sharply increased the time they spent in such activities; by 2008, fathers were up to eight to ten hours per week, and mothers up to fifteen to twenty hours per week. These effects were stronger among more-educated than among less-educated Americans, which dovetails

with the sociologist Annette Lareau's suggestion that highly educated Americans are especially likely to adopt a *concerted cultivation* approach to childhood, in which parents facilitate their children's development via organized activities, language training, and active school involvement." Eli Finkel, *The All-or-Nothing Marriage: How the Best Marriages Work* (New York: Dutton, 2018), 135. Philosopher Kate Manne double-clicked into this data, citing the work of sociologists who looked at hetero couples where both partners work. "Moreover, much of the new work that fathers *did* take on in these situations was the comparatively 'fun' work of engagement with their children—for example, playing with the baby. Fathers did this for four hours per week, on average, while dropping their number of hours of housework by five hours per week during the same time period. Mothers decreased their hours of housework by only one hour per week—while adding about twenty-one hours of child-rearing labor, including fifteen hours of physical child care—for instance, changing diapers and bathing the baby." Kate Manne, *Entitled: How Male Privilege Hurts Women* (New York: Crown, 2020), 121. On the whole, we do less housework now, though expectations of cleanliness and organization have also soared in the last ninety years. "In her book *More Work for Mother,* the historian Ruth Schwartz Cowan shows that when housewives first got access to 'labor-saving' devices like washing machines and vacuum cleaners, no time was saved at all, because society's standards of cleanliness simply rose to offset the benefits; now that you *could* return each of your husband's shirts to a spotless condition after a single wearing, it began to feel like you *should,* to show how much you loved him." Oliver Burkeman, *Four Thousand Weeks: Time Management for Mortals* (New York: Farrar, Straus and Giroux, 2021), 42.

37 **across the animal kingdom** The term *alloparent* was coined by biologist and writer E. O. Wilson. E. O. Wilson, *Sociobiology* (Cambridge, Mass.: Harvard University Press, 1975).

38 **into contemporary consciousness** Sarah Blaffer Hrdy, *Mothers and Others: The Evolutionary Origins of Mutual Understanding* (Cambridge, Mass.: Harvard University Press, 2009).

38 **capture it for posterity** As Montagu writes, "Women, for the first time, were enlisted to replace men in occupations that were formerly the exclusive male preserves. Women became bus drivers, train engineers, truck drivers, ticket collectors, factory workers, farm workers, laborers, supervisors, executive officers, armed services personnel, and a great many other things which almost everyone had believed were beyond female capacity. At first it was claimed the women didn't do as well as men; then it was begrudgingly admitted that they weren't so bad; and by the time the war was over many employers were reluctant to exchange their women employees for men!" Ashley Montagu, *The Natural Superiority of Women* (Lanham, Md.: Altamira, 1999), 54. Meanwhile, Professor Eli Finkel offers a fascinating history of modern marriage and its evolution. He writes about how women were revered as patriots for stepping into the workforce during World War I, then faced resentment when men came home and wanted their jobs back—the onset of the Great Depression didn't help. Then, post–World War II, the G.I. Bill happened, which was updated in 1948 "so that married men could get a substantial tax break only if their wife earned little or no money. Given the conservative cultural zeitgeist

and these sorts of policies, it is not surprising that most women sought fulfillment through domestic life, nor that 60 percent of women who enrolled in colleges or universities left without graduating—either to get married (the so-called M.R.S. *degree*) or out of fear that a college degree would hurt their marriage prospects." Finkel, *All-or-Nothing Marriage,* 60.

39 **"we also didn't have a choice"** Brigid Schulte, "The Culture of Busyness," interview by Elise Loehnen, *The goop Podcast,* May 7, 2020.

39 **"This unspoken business contract is broken"** Heather Boushey, *Finding Time: The Economics of Work-Life Conflict* (Cambridge, Mass.: Harvard University Press, 2016), 5–6.

40 **"women's has shrunk"** Soraya Chemaly, *Rage Becomes Her: The Power of Women's Anger* (New York: Atria, 2018), 67–68.

40 **performing yardwork (59 percent to 10 percent)** Megan Brenan, "Women Still Handle Main Household Tasks in U.S.," Gallup, January 29, 2020, https://news.gallup.com/poll/283979/women-handle-main-household-tasks.aspx.

41 **"than those whose wives did not"** Chemaly, *Rage Becomes Her,* 81.

42 **"It went something like this"** Brigid Schulte, "Ending the Mommy Wars," interview by Elise Loehnen, *goop,* May 8, 2014.

42 **oxytocin can soar** Lee T. Gettler, Patty X. Kuo, Mallika S. Sarma, Benjamin C. Trumble, Jennifer E. Burke Lefever, and Julia M. Braungart-Rieker, "Fathers' Oxytocin Responses to First Holding Their Newborns: Interactions with Testosterone Reactivity to Predict Later Parenting Behavior and Father-Infant Bonds," *Developmental Psychobiology* 63, no. 5 (April 16, 2021): 1384–98, http://doi.org/10.1002/dev.22121.

44 **according to a 2019 study** Brad Harrington, Tina Tawler McHugh, and Jennifer Sabatini Fraone, "Expanded Paid Parental Leave: Measuring the Impact of Leave on Work and Family," Boston College Center for Work and Family, 2019, https://www.bc.edu/bc-web/schools/carroll-school/sites/center-for-work-family/research/work-life-flexibility1.html.

44 **In one dismaying study** "Parental Leave Study," Deloitte, 2016, https://www2.deloitte.com/content/dam/Deloitte/us/Documents/about-deloitte/us-about-deloitte-paternal-leave-survey.pdf.

45 **needs the paycheck and health insurance** I had a long conversation on my podcast about Vicky and the economy of care with Angela Garbes, author of the wonderful *Essential Labor: Mothering as Social Change* (New York: Harper Wave, 2022). Angela Garbes, "Understanding Essential Labor," interview by Elise Loehnen, *Pulling the Thread,* May 12, 2022.

45 **"as far to the other end as possible"** Michaela Boehm, "An Introduction to Tantra," interview by Elise Loehnen, *goop* website, December 18, 2014, https://goop.com/wellness/sexual-health/an-introduction-to-tantra/.

45 **fewer times than guys who don't** Sabino Kornrich, Julie Brines, and Katrina Leupp, "Egalitarianism, Housework, and Sexual Frequency in Marriage," *American Sociological Review* 78, no. 1 (2013): 26–50, https://doi.org/10.1177/0003122412472340.

46 **"subtle but essential necessity"** Boehm, "Introduction to Tantra."

48 **"doing other enjoyable activities"** Headlee, *Do Nothing,* 105.

48 **"personal time during working hours"** Headlee, *Do Nothing,* 98.

49 *eleven million bits per second* Srini Pillay, "The Power of the Unconscious

Mind," interview by Elise Loehnen, *The goop Podcast,* December 18, 2018. Pillay also wrote a book called *Tinker Dabble Doodle Try: Unlock the Power of the Unfocused Mind* (New York: Ballantine, 2017).

49   **"Think about Albert Einstein"** Pillay, "Power of the Unconscious Mind."

50   **shifts in physiology** M. Eskinazi and I. Giannopulu, "Continuity in Intuition and Insight: From Real to Naturalistic Virtual Environment," *Scientific Reports* 11, no. 1876 (2021), https://doi.org/10.1038/s41598-021-81532-w.

50   **at least partially sleep disorders** I spoke to Stanford's Rafael Pelayo, MD, about the incidence of ADHD and sleep disorders, as well as journalist James Nestor, who wrote the fascinating book *Breath.* I interviewed both of them on *The goop Podcast,* on July 16, 2020, and November 12, 2020, respectively. For more on ADHD, I also recommend Gabor Maté, *Scattered Minds: The Origins and Healing of Attention Deficit Disorder* (Toronto, Ont.: Vintage Canada, 1999).

50   **"challenged or outraged in the process"** Montagu, *Natural Superiority of Women,* 46.

51   **girls have outperformed boys** Thomas A. DiPrete and Claudia Buchmann, *The Rise of Women: The Growing Gender Gap in Education and What It Means for American Schools* (New York: Russell Sage Foundation, 2013). Girls outpace boys in intelligence and other computational abilities throughout childhood; it is only in adolescence that boys bridge the gap, likely partially because of social factors. Ashley Montagu offers a comprehensive and fascinating list of the increased aptitude of girls for everything from learning foreign languages to linguistic functioning to code-learning tests. Montagu, *Natural Superiority of Women,* 193–94. Similarly, the National Child Development Study (NCDS) in the United Kingdom tracked an entire cohort of children for half a century and found that girls were tested as being slightly more intelligent across the board until the age of sixteen. Satoshi Kanazawa, "Girls Are More Intelligent Than Boys," *Psychology Today,* October 3, 2013, https://www.psychologytoday .com/us/blog/the-scientific-fundamentalist/201010/girls-are-more -intelligent-boys. Meanwhile, women are outperforming men in higher education across the globe: While college campuses were 58 percent male in 1970, now the population of people who identify as women is 56 percent. National Center for Education Statistics, "Total Undergraduate Fall Enrollment in Degree-Granting Postsecondary Institutions, by Attendance Status, Sex of Student, and Control and Level of Institution: Selected Years, 1970 Through 2029," table 303.70, accessed February 8, 2022, https://nces.ed.gov/programs /digest/d20/tables/dt20_303.70.asp.

51   **women with that title** Claire Cain Miller, Kevin Quealy, and Margot Sanger-Katz, "The Top Jobs Where Women Are Outnumbered by Men Named John," *New York Times,* April 24, 2018, https://www.nytimes.com/interactive /2018/04/24/upshot/women-and-men-named-john.html.

51   **particularly women of color** What's even worse, women are 69 percent of the seven million people in the workforce who earn less than $10 per hour. Jasmine Tucker and Kayla Patrick, "Low-Wage Jobs Are Women's Jobs: The Overrepresentation of Women in Low-Wage Work," National Women's Law Center, August 2017, https://nwlc.org/wp-content/uploads/2017/08/Low -Wage-Jobs-are-Womens-Jobs.pdf. Per the U.S. Census Bureau data of 2018, 56 percent of people living in poverty are women—and more women than

men live in poverty across every racial distinction. Robin Bleiweis and Alexandra Cawthorne Gaines, "Basic Facts About Women in Poverty," Center for American Progress, August 3, 2020, https://www.americanprogress.org/article/basic-facts-women-poverty/.

52 (865,000 versus 216,000) Julie Kashen and Amanda Novello, "How COVID-19 Sent Women's Workforce Progress Backward," Center for American Progress, October 30, 2020, https://www.americanprogress.org/article/covid-19-sent-womens-workforce-progress-backward/.

53 "twice the rate among men" Megan Cassella, "The Pandemic Drove Women Out of the Workforce. Will They Come Back?," *Politico*, July 22, 2021, https://www.politico.com/news/2021/07/22/coronavirus-pandemic-women-workforce-500329.

53 According to a 2021 survey Kathleen Gaines, "Male Nurses Earn $5,000 More per Year Than Female Nurses, Study Finds," Nurse.org, August 19, 2021, https://nurse.org/articles/gender-pay-inequality-in-nursing.

53 according to a 1996 report National Center for Education Statistics, "The Patterns of Teacher Compensation," January 1996, https://nces.ed.gov/pubs/web/95829.asp.

54 over the course of their careers Henrik Kleven, Camille Landais, and Jakob Egholt Søgaard, "Children and Gender Inequality: Evidence from Denmark," *American Economic Journal: Applied Economics* 11, no. 4 (October 2019): 181–209, https://doi.org/10.1257/app.20180010.

Chapter 3: Envy

61 *"feel shame about feeling envy?"* Brené Brown, *Atlas of the Heart: Mapping Meaningful Connection and the Language of Human Experience* (New York: Random House, 2021), 26, 29.

62 "how can I get it?" Lori Gottlieb, "Why You Should Follow Your Envy," interview by Elise Loehnen, *The goop Podcast*, June 20, 2019.

64 "put them back into their cage" Glennon Doyle, *Untamed* (New York: Dial Press, 2020), 285.

65 "others are not foremost on her mind" Rachel Simmons, *Odd Girl Out: The Hidden Culture of Aggression in Girls* (New York: Mariner, 2002), 157.

65 "express competition and jealousy indirectly" Simmons, *Odd Girl Out*, 161.

66 "believe we don't actually have wants" Glennon Doyle, "When You Quit Being Good," interview by Elise Loehnen, *The goop Podcast*, March 5, 2020.

68 "spend a lifetime being silently poisoned" Anne Lamott, *Bird by Bird: Some Instructions on Writing and Life* (New York: Anchor, 1994), 120.

69 " 'private parts of the human soul' " Gordon Marino, "The Upside of Envy," *New York Times*, May 4, 2018, https://www.nytimes.com/2018/05/04/opinion/upside-envy.html.

71 "convey one's inner world" Carol Gilligan, *In a Different Voice: Psychological Theory and Women's Development* (1982; repr., Cambridge, Mass.: Harvard University Press, 1993), xxi.

71 "founded on disconnection from women" Gilligan, *In a Different Voice*, x–xi.

72 "they will be left alone" Gilligan, *In a Different Voice*, 42.

72 "not only for others but for themselves" Gilligan, *In a Different Voice*, 149.

73   **"when other women do the same"** Carol Gilligan and Naomi Snider, *Why Does Patriarchy Persist?* (Medford, Mass.: Polity Press, 2018), 7.

73   **it is *I don't know*** "The turn from healthy protest and political resistance to psychological resistance was signaled in our interview conversations by the appearance of the injunction 'Don't,' an internalized prohibition that for girls came to stand between 'I' and 'know' and for boys between 'I' and 'care.' This internalization of the gender binary that allocates knowing to boys and caring to girls marks an initiation whereby some girls come not to know what in fact they know and some boys not to care about both who and what in truth they care about deeply. The move from relationship into feminine self-silencing and masculine detachment—not knowing and not caring—is necessary for establishing hierarchy, which requires a loss of empathy by those on top and a loss of self-assertion by those below." Gilligan and Snider, *Why Does Patriarchy Persist?*, 41.

74   **"from which to become something more"** Jia Tolentino, *Trick Mirror: Reflections on Self-Delusion* (New York: Random House, 2019), 129.

75   **"the very fact of its existence"** Marion Woodman, *The Pregnant Virgin: A Process of Psychological Transformation* (Toronto, Ont.: Inner City Books, 1985), 118.

76   **"having her as a mother"** Galit Atlas, *Emotional Inheritance: A Therapist, Her Patients, and the Legacy of Trauma* (New York: Little, Brown Spark, 2022), 240.

78   **"envy and resentment of her daughter"** Kim Chernin, *The Hungry Self: Women, Eating and Identity* (New York: Times Books, 1985), 86.

80   **you must put yourself out there** As Epstein explains, "Desire is the crucible within which the self is formed. . . . If we are out of touch with our desires, we cannot be ourselves. In this way of thinking, desire is our vitality, an essential component of our human experience, that which gives us our individuality and at the same time keeps prodding us out of ourselves. Desire is a longing for completion in the face of the vast unpredictability of our predicament." Mark Epstein, *Open to Desire: The Truth About What the Buddha Taught* (New York: Gotham, 2005), 9.

82   **"then I can do that too"** Lacy Phillips and Jessica Gill, "Episode 77: EXPLAINED A Deep Dive into Expanders," *The Expanded Podcast,* January 10, 2020. Lacy and I had a conversation about expansion and envy as well. Lacy Phillips, "Manifesting What We Actually Want," interview by Elise Loehnen, *Pulling the Thread Podcast,* March 4, 2022.

Chapter 4: Pride

86   **"I just really needed a dress"** Arienne Thompson, "Anne Hathaway Finally Explains THAT Pink Oscar Dress," *USA Today,* October 9, 2014, https://www.usatoday.com/story/life/entertainthis/2014/10/09/anne-hathaway-finally-explains-that-pink-oscar-dress/77324896/.

86   **"called out on it, big time"** Benjamin Lee, "Anne Hathaway: 'Male Energy Is Very Different from Toxic Masculinity,'" *The Guardian,* October 20, 2016, https://www.theguardian.com/film/2016/oct/20/anne-hathaway-male-energy-different-from-toxic-masculinity-colossal.

86   **"slightly manic and hyper cheerleadery"** Matthew Belloni and Stephen

Galloway, "THR's Actress Roundtable: 7 Stars on Nightmare Directors, Brutal Auditions, and Fights with Paparazzi," *Hollywood Reporter*, November 19, 2012, https://www.hollywoodreporter.com/movies/movie-news/anne-hathaway -amy-adams-marion-391797/.

86 **"sleepy-eyed multi-hyphenate"** Karina Longworth, "Oscars 2011: The Most Embarrassing Academy Awards Ever?," *LA Weekly*, February 27, 2011, https:// www.laweekly.com/oscars-2011-the-most-embarrassing-academy-awards -ever/.

87 **Timberlake the "Teflon man"** Stephen M. Silverman, "No, Janet Won't Be at the Grammys, After All," *People*, February 4, 2004, https://people.com /awards/no-janet-wont-be-at-grammys-after-all/. At the time, Timberlake re-marked, "I'm frustrated that my character is being questioned. And the fact of the matter is, you know, I've had a good year, a really good year, especially with my music." Sarah Hall, "Janet Nixed from Grammys," *E! Online*, February 5, 2004, https://www.eonline.com/news/46775/janet-nixed-from-grammys.

87 **we know this cultural cycle well** I loved Constance Grady's analysis of this cycle: Constance Grady, "Anne Hathaway's Love-Hate-Redemption Publicity Cycle Is a Familiar (and Sexist) One," *Vox*, April 10, 2017, https://www.vox .com/culture/2017/4/10/15179082/anne-hathaway-publicity-cycle -hathahaters-jennifer-lawrence-taylor-swift.

88 **accused of actual wrongdoing** Maureen O'Connor, "The Twenty Most Hated Celebrities: Why We Hate Them," *The Cut*, April 22, 2013, https:// www.thecut.com/2013/04/20-most-hated-celebrities-why-we-hate-them .html.

88 **"designated as 'theirs'"** Sady Doyle, *Trainwreck: The Women We Love to Hate, Mock, and Fear . . . and Why* (Brooklyn, N.Y.: Melville House, 2016), xviii.

89 **"Why is likable a thing for women?"** Shonda Rhimes and Betsy Beers, "Shonda Rhimes and Betsy Beers on What Makes Partnerships Last," *Bridgerton: The Official Podcast*, May 27, 2021.

90 **"this same opinion of him"** Evagrius Ponticus, *The Praktikos and Chapters on Prayer*, trans. John Eudes Bamberger (Trappist, Ky.: Cistercian Publications, 1972), 20.

90 **pay increases, and votes** While they cited some interesting research, I strug-gled with journalists Katty Kay and Claire Shipman's *New York Times* bestseller *The Confidence Code: The Science and Art of Self-Assurance—What Women Should Know* (New York: Harper Business, 2014), as it put the onus on women. Sim-ilarly, Sheryl Sandberg's bestselling *Lean In: Women, Work, and the Will to Lead* (New York: Alfred A. Knopf, 2013), while an important contribution to women at work, has proven problematic over the years, presenting the idea that the mere presence of women in positions of power will transform society. Both texts essentialize women.

91 **judged the female CEO harshly** Victoria L. Brescoll, "Who Takes the Floor and Why: Gender, Power, and Volubility in Organizations," *Administrative Science Quarterly* 56, no. 4 (March 2012): 622–42, https://doi.org/10.1177 /0001839212439994.

91 **We have been trained not to** Christine Exley and Judd Kessler, "The Gender Gap in Self-Promotion," *Quarterly Journal of Economics* 137, no. 3 (August 2022): 1345–81, https://doi.org/10.1093/qje/qjac003.

91   **"Self-confidence is gender-neutral"** Laura Guillen, "Is the Confidence Gap Between Men and Women a Myth?," *Harvard Business Review,* March 26, 2018, https://hbr.org/2018/03/is-the-confidence-gap-between-men-and-women -a-myth.

92   **she is self-made** Arlan Hamilton, "Adapting Midsentence," interview by Elise Loehnen, *The goop Podcast,* July 7, 2020.

92   **all deserve credit too** "I have to recognize that I've had friends along the way who couldn't put me in a mansion, but they could make sure that I ate that day. And I've had my mother and my brother along for the ride the entire time. So it wasn't like I was there all by myself going through this. They were going through it, too. . . . It's the investors who have believed in me. It's the founders themselves, even though I was putting the money into their companies, they had to believe in me as someone that they wanted along for the ride, because I stand to make money from their success. . . . And it's my teammates at Back-stage Capital and at other companies I run. And it's just something that I wholeheartedly understand and believe. . . . And it's true for a lot of us, it's especially true for these guys who are put up on pedestals. . . . Let's talk about how many people work at these companies. Let's talk about who's taking care of things at home." Arlan Hamilton, "Adapting Midsentence," interview by Elise Loehnen, *The goop Podcast,* July 7, 2020.

92   **"It Finally Caught Up"** Kimberly Weisul, "The Hype Has Always Been Ahead of Arlan Hamilton, and It Finally Caught Up," *Inc.,* March 20, 2019, https://www.inc.com/kimberly-weisul/backstage-capital-champion-under -represented-founders-pivots-hard.html.

94   **"an unattractive quality"** Kate Fagan, *All the Colors Came Out: A Father, a Daughter, and a Lifetime of Lessons* (New York: Little, Brown, 2021), 95.

99   **"higher than it really was"** Ernesto Reuben, Pedro Rey-Biel, Paola Sapi-enza, and Luigi Zingales, "The Emergence of Male Leadership in Competitive Environments," *Journal of Economic Behavior and Organization* 83, no. 1 (June 2012): 111–17, http://doi.org/10.1016/j.jebo.2011.06.016.

100 **"recipe for echoism right there"** Craig Malkin, "What Does Healthy Nar-cissism Look Like?," interview by Elise Loehnen, *The goop Podcast,* April 21, 2020.

101 **"arrogant jerks or sociopaths"** Craig Malkin, *Rethinking Narcissism: The Bad—and Surprising Good—About Feeling Special* (New York: Harper Wave, 2015), 9. As Professor Kristin Neff elaborates, according to research, "Ninety-four percent of college faculty members think they're better teachers than their colleagues and 90 percent of drivers think they're more skilled than their road mates. Even people who've recently caused a car accident think they're supe-rior drivers! Research shows that people tend to think they're funnier, more logical, more popular, better looking, nicer, more trustworthy, wiser, and more intelligent than others. Ironically, most people also think they're above average in the ability to view themselves objectively." Kristin Neff, *Self-Compassion: The Proven Power of Being Kind to Yourself* (New York: William Morrow, 2011), 19–20.

102 **"devastating failure or horrific loss"** Malkin, *Rethinking Narcissism,* 9.

102 **"legacy of false empowerment"** Terrence Real, *Us: Getting Past You and Me to Build a More Loving Relationship* (New York: goop Press, 2022), 72.

103 **"develop a healthy sense of self"** Malkin, *Rethinking Narcissism*, 19.

105 **"what it saw was 'safe'"** Yeshua, Yeshua transmission in Utah, as channeled by Carissa Schumacher, October 2020.

107 **"members understand and share their gifts"** Robin Wall Kimmerer, *Braiding Sweetgrass: Indigenous Wisdom, Scientific Knowledge, and the Teachings of Plants* (Minneapolis, Minn.: Milkweed, 2013), 134.

108 **essential role every one of us plays** Isabel Wilkerson, *Caste: The Origins of Our Discontents* (New York: Random House, 2020), 202–6.

108 **they dial it back up** Therese Huston, *How Women Decide: What's True, What's Not, and What Strategies Spark the Best Choices* (New York: Houghton Mifflin, 2016), 184–85.

108 **"women respond more decisively than men"** Julia Boorstin, *When Women Lead: What They Achieve, Why They Succeed, and How We Can Learn from Them* (New York: Avid Reader Press, 2022), 204.

109 **and not interrupting** As journalist Celeste Headlee writes, "In research dating back to the 1970s, scientists have consistently found that men are more likely than women to interrupt others so they can talk. Other studies have shown that, in meetings, men speak more often and for longer periods than women do. This remains true in online discussions and even on video conference calls. These results were so worrisome that in early 2020, the software company Basecamp limited online meetings and moved toward written communication— only to find that men tend to write more and aggressively challenge others, even in email. Now there's an app for that; businesses (and individuals) that are concerned about equitable communication can make use of an app called Woman Interrupted, which analyzes conversations to detect how often women are interrupted by men." Celeste Headlee, *Speaking of Race: Why Everybody Needs to Talk About Racism—and How to Do It* (New York: Harper Wave, 2021), 131.

110 **"Don't mistake modesty for humility"** Glennon Doyle, "When You Quit Being Good," interview by Elise Loehnen, *The goop Podcast,* March 5, 2020.

111 **"It's not honorable for a woman to, either"** Glennon Doyle, *Untamed* (New York: Dial Press, 2020), 288.

111 **"use them for good in the world"** Kimmerer, *Braiding Sweetgrass,* 239.

112 **"our presence automatically liberates others"** Marianne Williamson, *A Return to Love: Reflections on the Principles of a Course in Miracles* (New York: HarperOne, 1992), 190–91.

Chapter 5: Gluttony

114 **everyone else is deviant** Aubrey Gordon, *What We Don't Talk About When We Talk About Fat* (Boston: Beacon Press, 2020), 8.

116 **six that they evaluated—got worse** A. Gordon, *What We Don't Talk About,* 5.

116 **weighs 350 pounds** Aubrey Gordon, "After Years of Writing Anonymously About Fatness, I'm Telling the World Who I Am," *Self,* December 11, 2020.

117 **"whether we eat, and how much"** A. Gordon, *What We Don't Talk About,* 77.

117 **"ghost of fatness future"** A. Gordon, *What We Don't Talk About,* 80.

117 **"Is my daughter gifted?"** Jessica Nordell, *The End of Bias: A Beginning* (New York: Metropolitan Books, 2021), 194.

117 **more women qualify as obese than men** Bindra Shah, Katherine Tombeau Cost, Anne Fuller, Catherine S. Birken, and Laura N. Anderson, "Sex and Gender Differences in Childhood Obesity: Contributing to the Research Agenda," *BMJ Nutrition, Prevention, and Health* 3, no. 2 (September 9, 2020): 387–90, http://doi.org/10.1136/bmjnph-2020-000074.

117 **"uninterrupted and simply renamed"** A. Gordon, *What We Don't Talk About*, 25.

117 **"failing or sin to account for"** A. Gordon, *What We Don't Talk About*, 10.

117 **rather die ten years early than be fat** Marlene B. Schwartz, Lenny R. Vartanian, Brian A. Nosek, and Kelly D. Brownell, "The Influence of One's Own Body Weight on Implicit and Explicit Anti-fat Bias," *Obesity* 14, no. 3 (March 2006): 440–47, http://doi.org/10.1038/oby.2006.58.

118 **"twenty-five and thirty-four"** A. Gordon, *What We Don't Talk About*, 66. We generally seem to have a pretty dismal self-assessment of our own looks. According to Dove's 2015 global "Choose Beautiful" campaign, only 4 percent of us would "choose beautiful" to describe ourselves.

118 **"abandoned their vigilance even briefly"** A. Gordon, *What We Don't Talk About*, 58.

118 **appearances are rated and judged** N. A. Schvey, R. M. Puhl, K. A. Levandoski, and K. D. Brownell, "The Influence of a Defendant's Body Weight on Perceptions of Guilt," *International Journal of Obesity* 37 (January 8, 2013): 1275–81, https://doi.org/10.1038/ijo.2012.211.

118 **associated with 9 percent lower pay** John Cawley, "The Impact of Obesity on Wage," *Journal of Human Resources* 39, no. 2 (March 2004): 451–74, http://doi.org/10.2307/3559022.

119 **Very keto** Marilyn Monroe's diet was featured in the September 1952 edition of *Pageant* magazine. Ray Siegel, "For the Vegan Weary, Marilyn Monroe's Strange Diet and Exercise Routine," *CR Fashion Book*, December 22, 2019, https://crfashionbook.com/celebrity-a9146775-marilyn-monroe-diet/.

121 **"too greedily, too much"** Rebecca Konyndyk DeYoung, *Glittering Vices: A New Look at the Seven Deadly Sins and Their Remedies* (Grand Rapids, Mich.: Brazos Press, 2020), 166.

122 **"Not Even Close"** Gina Kolata, "One Weight-Loss Approach Fits All? Not Even Close," *New York Times*, December 12, 2016, https://www.nytimes.com/2016/12/12/health/weight-loss-obesity.html.

122 **as many lawmakers already are** Zachary J. Ward, Sara N. Bleich, Angie L. Cradock, Jessica L. Barrett, Catherine M. Giles, Chasmine Flax, Michael W. Long, and Steven L. Gortmaker, "Projected U.S. State-Level Prevalence of Adult Obesity and Severe Obesity," *New England Journal of Medicine* 381, no. 25 (December 19, 2019): 2440–50, http://doi.org/10.1056/NEJMsa1909301.

122 **when it comes to chronic hypertension** The American Cancer Society asserts that being "overweight or obese is clearly linked to an overall increased risk of cancer. According to research from the American Cancer Society, excess body weight is thought to be responsible for about 11% of cancers in women and about 5% of cancers in men in the United States, as well as about 7% of all cancer deaths." *Thought to be* seem like critical words, and they conclude that more research is required. American Cancer Society, "Does Body

Weight Affect Cancer Risk?," accessed February 11, 2022, https://www.cancer
.org/healthy/cancer-causes/diet-physical-activity/body-weight-and-cancer
-risk/effects.html. Here's one study about cancer, obesity, and survival rates:
Ngan Ming Tsang, Ping Ching Pai, Chi Cheng Chuang, Wen Ching Chuang,
Chen Kan Tseng, Kai Ping Chang, Tzu Chen Yen, Jen Der Lin, and Joseph
Tung Chieh Chang, "Overweight and Obesity Predict Better Overall Survival
Rates in Cancer Patients with Distant Metastases," *Cancer Medicine* 5, no. 4
(April 2016): 665–75, https://doi.org/10.1002/cam4.634.

123 **much effort to beat our ancestors** Daniel Lieberman, *Exercised: Why Something We Never Evolved to Do Is Healthy and Rewarding* (New York: Pantheon,
2020), 19.

123 **might be making us fat** Blumberg thinks those environmental plagues are
wreaking havoc in ways we're still only beginning to discern. In his lab, researchers study the long-term impact of endocrine-disrupting chemicals
(EDCs) on our systems, chemicals that he calls obesogenic because of their
ability to encourage weight retention and obesity—scarily, this sometimes
doesn't show up until later generations. There are legions of these loose in our
system—in America, chemicals can be used without safety studies, an ass-
backwards approach. This means there are eighty-four thousand unregulated
chemicals registered with the EPA, used on our food and around us without
our consent, protected by powerful lobbyists. It's an innocent-until-proven-
guilty approach, with environmental and human and animal health on the line.
These chemicals are moved *out* of rotation only when it becomes apparent they
cause harm, and even then, many may linger on in the food supply. It is un-
ethical to run experiments about chemical toxicity on humans; yet it is somehow OK to unleash chemicals into the environment without having any
understanding of their downstream effects. Blumberg's and other scientists'
research into the effects of EDCs is staggering in its scope and repercussions.
What they've discovered suggests that beyond other, unknown effects we are
potentially poisoning future generations with obesity, ensuring they have no
chance to battle expanding waistbands, no matter how many miles they slog at
the gym, no matter how carefully they mete out their meals. Try this on for
size: One of Blumberg's peers, Dr. Mike Skinner, looked at DDT, a widely
used and very toxic insecticide (and EDC). He injected it into mice and found
the first two generations that followed had the expected birth defects but were
of normal weight. In the third generation, 50 percent of the animals were
obese. As Blumberg explains, "Mike began to connect the dots in his head,
considering both the marked rise in obesity rates among US adults over the
past few decades and pregnant women in the 1950s and 1960s who were exposed to DDT. There probably was not a woman who was pregnant in the
1950s and 1960s who was not exposed to DDT. Could the exposures in the
1950s have anything to do with the prevalence of obesity among adults today?"
Bruce Blumberg, *The Obesogen Effect: Why We Eat Less and Exercise More but
Still Struggle to Lose Weight* (New York: Grand Central Life and Style, 2018),
85–86.

123 **were in prior generations** Blumberg, *Obesogen Effect*, 12.

123 **171 pounds, up from 152** Centers for Disease Control, "Body Measure-

ments," accessed February 11, 2022, https://www.cdc.gov/nchs/fastats/body -measurements.htm.

123 **number had almost doubled** The *global* weight loss and weight management diet market is expected to reach $295.3 billion by 2027. Himanshu Vig and Roshan Deshmukh, "Weight Loss and Weight Management Diet Market by Product Type (Better-for-You, Meal Replacement, Weight Loss Supplement, Green Tea, and Low-Calorie Sweeteners) and Sales Channel (Hypermarket/Supermarket, Specialty Stores, Pharmacies, Online Channels, and Others): Global Opportunity Analysis and Industry Forecast, 2021–2027," Allied Market Research, May 2021, https://www.alliedmarketresearch.com/weight-loss-management -diet-market; Julie Bryant, "Fat Is a $34 Billion Business," *Atlanta Business Chronicle,* September 24, 2021, https://www.bizjournals.com/atlanta/stories/2001/09 /24/story4.html; Stefano DellaVigna and Ulrike Malmendier, "Overestimating Self-Control: Evidence from the Health Club Industry," Stanford GSB Research Paper No. 1880, October 2002, http://dx.doi.org/10.2139/ssrn.347520.

124 **"discrimination and internalizing stigma"** A. Gordon, *What We Don't Talk About,* 145. There's a slew of research about weight, stigma, and its downstream impact on health; see Rebecca M. Puhl and Chelsea A. Heuer, "Obesity Stigma: Important Considerations for Public Health," *Journal of Public Health* 100, no. 6 (June 2010): 1019–28, https://doi.org/10.2105/AJPH.2009.159491.

125 **"simply not trying hard enough"** Marisa Meltzer, *This Is Big: How the Founder of Weight Watchers Changed the World—and Me* (New York: Little, Brown, 2020), 141.

126 **more than they had originally lost** Traci Mann, Janet Tomiyama, Erika Westling, Ann-Marie Lew, Barbra Samuels, and Jason Chatman, "Medicare's Search for Effective Obesity Treatments: Diets Are Not the Answer," *American Psychologist* 62, no. 3 (2007): 220–33, https://doi.org/10.1037/0003-066X.62 .3.220.

126 **"you always have a goal"** Geneen Roth, *Women Food and God: An Unexpected Path to Almost Everything* (New York: Scribner, 2010), 29.

127 **"would imply that she was perfect"** Rachel Simmons, *Odd Girl Out: The Hidden Culture of Aggression in Girls* (New York: Mariner, 2002), 164–65.

127 **"stylish anorexia"** Pythia Peay, "A Meeting with Marion Woodman," *The San Francisco Jung Institute Library Journal* 11, no. 1 (1992).

129 **"The chaos stays away"** Roth, *Women Food and God,* 148.

129 **health problems, including obesity** Child Welfare Information Gateway, "Adverse Childhood Experiences (ACEs)," U.S. Department of Health and Human Services, accessed February 11, 2022, https://www.childwelfare.gov /topics/preventing/overview/framework/aces/.

130 **"knew too much about their contempt"** Roxane Gay, *Hunger: A Memoir of (My) Body* (New York: Harper Perennial, 2017), 13.

134 **"full portion of pleasure"** James Gordon, *Transforming Trauma: The Path to Hope and Healing* (New York: HarperOne, 2021), 137.

135 *Self* **magazine** Cynthia R. Bulik and Lauren Reba-Harrelson, "Three Out of Four American Women Have Disordered Eating, Survey Suggests," *ScienceDaily,* April 23, 2008, www.sciencedaily.com/releases/2008/04/080422202514.htm.

135 **"embrace my body at any size"** Gay, *Hunger,* 148.

136 **"solved on the physical level"** Roth, *Women Food and God,* 176–77.

Chapter 6: Greed

138 **his days controlling his passions** John Eudes Bamberger, introduction to *The Praktikos and Chapters on Prayer,* by Evagrius Ponticus (Trappist, Ky.: Cistercian Publications, 1972), xxxix.

138 **small amounts of bread and oil** Bamberger, introduction to *Praktikos,* xliii.

139 **"necessities of life from others"** Evagrius Ponticus, *Praktikos,* 17.

139 **"hardnesses of heart against compassion"** Pope Gregory I, *Moralia on Job* 31.88, Lectionary Central, http://www.lectionarycentral.com/GregoryMoralia /Book31.html.

139 **about 4 billion euros** Philip Pullella, "Vatican Releases Financial Figures, Promises Transparency," Reuters, October 1, 2020, https://www.reuters.com /article/us-vatican-finances/vatican-releases-financial-figures-promises -transparency-idUSKBN26M5XD.

139 **(Matthew 19:24)** Hal Taussig, ed., *A New New Testament: A Bible for the 21st Century Combining Traditional and Newly Discovered Texts* (2013; repr., New York: Mariner, 2015), 47.

140 **"tightfisted grip on money as 'mine'"** Rebecca Konyndyk DeYoung, *Glittering Vices: A New Look at the Seven Deadly Sins and Their Remedies,* rev. ed. (Grand Rapids, Mich.: Brazos Press, 2020), 114.

140 **"smart, careful stewardship"** Martin Luther, "The First Sunday After Trinity," in *The Complete Sermons of Martin Luther,* ed. Eugene F. A. Klug, vol. 6 (Grand Rapids, Mich.: Baker, 1996), 223–40.

141 **had any spiritual value** For a deeper read on Martin Luther and his attitude toward greed, I recommend Kathryn D'Arcy Blanchard, "'If You Do Not Do This You Are Not Now a Christian': Martin Luther's Pastoral Teachings on Money," *Word and World* 26, no. 3 (Summer 2006): 299–309, https://wordand world.luthersem.edu/content/pdfs/26-3_Mission_Congregation/26-3 _Blanchard.pdf.

141 **from $33.5 billion to $232.7 billion** Forbes editors, "Real Time Billionaires," *Forbes,* accessed February 22, 2022, https://www.forbes.com/real-time -billionaires.

141 **226 inherited their wealth** Rachel Sandler, "The Top Richest Women in the World 2022," *Forbes,* April 5, 2022, https://www.forbes.com/sites/rachelsandler /2022/04/05/the-top-richest-women-in-the-world-2022.

142 **signed on for the pledge** Kelsey Piper, "The Giving Pledge, the Campaign to Change Billionaire Philanthropy, Explained," Vox, July 10, 2019, https:// www.vox.com/future-perfect/2019/7/10/18693578/gates-buffett-giving -pledge-billionaire-philanthropy.

142 **61 percent of the dollars donated** Daisy Grewal, "How Wealth Reduces Compassion," *Scientific American,* April 10, 2012, https://www.scientificamerican .com/article/how-wealth-reduces-compassion/; Lilly Family School of Philanthropy, "Women Give 2020 Report—New Forms of Giving in a Digital Age: Powered by Technology, Creating Community," accessed October 18, 2022, https://philanthropy.iupui.edu/institutes/womens-philanthropy-institute /research/women-give20.html.

142 **percent of his total net worth** Michael Hiltzik, "Elon Musk Is Giving $150 Million to Charity. What a Cheapskate," *Los Angeles Times,* April 26, 2021,

https://www.latimes.com/business/story/2021-04-26/elon-musk-150 -million-charity.

142 **twice as much as men** Barclays, "Tomorrow's Philanthropist," 2009, https:// home.barclays/content/dam/home-barclays/documents/citizenship/Reports -Publications/tomorrows-philanthropist.pdf.

142 **legacies rather than their own** Valeriya Safronova, "How Women Are Changing the Philanthropy Game," *New York Times,* January 30, 2021, https:// www.nytimes.com/2021/01/30/style/mackenzie-scott-prisclila-chan -zuckerberg-melinda-gates-philanthropy.html.

145 **"American way of life"** Lynne Twist, *The Soul of Money: Transforming Your Relationship with Money and Life* (New York: W. W. Norton, 2003), 211.

145 **"only 41% of men"** "Buying Power," Catalyst, April 27, 2020, https://www .catalyst.org/research/buying-power/.

147 **"have or make too much"** Sallie Krawcheck, "What We're Taught About Money," interview by Elise Loehnen, *The goop Podcast,* September 17, 2019.

148 **"even with tough markets"** Sallie Krawcheck, "How to Manage Money Through a Crisis," interview by Elise Loehnen, *The goop Podcast,* April 8, 2020.

148 **materialize without effort** According to research, "The average woman keeps 68% of her portfolio in cash . . . , compared to 59% of the average man." Meanwhile, despite research indicating women are better investors than men, 54% of women report having a high level of knowledge about the market, compared with 71% of men, and only 34% of women feel comfortable making decisions about investments, versus 49% of men. Maurie Backman, "Women and Investing: 20 Years of Statistics Summarized," The Motley Fool, March 9, 2022, https://www.fool.com/research/women-in-investing-research/.

148 **within our own brokerage accounts** Ron Lieber, "Women May Be Better Investors Than Men. Let Me Mansplain Why," *New York Times,* October 29, 2021, https://www.nytimes.com/2021/10/29/your-money/women-investing -stocks.html.

156 **perhaps as part of a hazing cycle** Mori Taheripour, "The Human Side of Negotiation," interview by Elise Loehnen, *The goop Podcast,* June 9, 2020.

158 **"being 'difficult' or 'spoiled'"** Jennifer Lawrence, "Why Do I Make Less Than My Male Co-Stars?," *Lenny Letter,* December 5, 2017, https://www .lennyletter.com/story/jennifer-lawrence-why-do-i-make-less-than-my-male -costars.

160 **"no one for you to care for"** Robin Wall Kimmerer, *Braiding Sweetgrass: Indigenous Wisdom, Scientific Knowledge, and the Teachings of Plants* (Minneapolis, Minn.: Milkweed, 2013), 307.

161 **"control and success on diets"** Sendhil Mullainathan and Eldar Shafir, *Scarcity: The New Science of Having Less and How It Defines Our Lives* (New York: Picador, 2013), 41–42.

161 **a world of "you-*and*-me"** Twist, *Soul of Money,* 213.

162 **"average net worth of American households"** Celeste Headlee, *Do Nothing: How to Break Away from Overworking, Overdoing, and Underliving* (New York: Harmony, 2020), 187–88.

163 **"those who are holding onto it"** Twist, "Soul of Money."

165 **fared much better across every measure** CNBC reporter Julia Boorstin summarized the following: "New Zealand, under the leadership of President

Jacinda Ardern, lost only *five* people per million in the year following March 11, 2020, when the World Health Organization's director general named covid-19 as a pandemic. The United Kingdom, on the other hand, lost 1,845 per million and the United States lost 1,599 per million. The gender advantage extended beyond those two island countries to others. As of March 11, 2021, Sweden, with a male leader, had had 1,298 covid-related deaths per million, while its neighboring three countries, led by women, had lost just a fraction of that: Denmark had 411 deaths per million, Finland 140, and Norway 117. Germany, with a female leader, had 872 deaths per million, far less than the losses of three nearby countries with male leaders: Spain (1,541 per million), France (1,369 per million) and Italy (1,673 per million)." Julia Boorstin, *When Women Lead: What They Achieve, Why They Succeed, and How We Can Learn from Them* (New York: Avid Reader Press, 2022), 205.

166 **needs had always been met** Twist, *Soul of Money,* 103–4.

166 **they suffer** Andrew T. Jebb, Louis Tay, Ed Diener, and Shigehiro Oishi, "Happiness, Income Satiation and Turning Points Around the World," *Nature Human Behavior* 2, no. 1 (January 2018): 33–38, https://doi.org/10.1038/s41562 -017-0277-0.

167 **"it is belonging that we crave"** Kimmerer, *Braiding Sweetgrass,* 308.

Chapter 7: Lust

170 **even that is contested** As Robert Gnuse explains, "There are seven texts often cited by Christians to condemn homosexuality: Noah and Ham (Genesis 9:20–27), Sodom and Gomorrah (Genesis 19:1–11), Levitical laws condemning same-sex relationships (Leviticus 18:22, 20:13), two words in two Second Testament vice lists (1 Corinthians 6:9–10; 1 Timothy 1:10), and Paul's letter to the Romans (Romans 1:26–27). . . . These do not refer to homosexual relationships between two free, adult, and loving individuals. They describe rape or attempted rape (Genesis 9:20–27, 19:1–11), cultic prostitution (Leviticus 18:22, 20:13), male prostitution and pederasty (1 Corinthians 6:9–10; 1 Timothy 1:10), and the Isis cult in Rome (Romans 1:26–27)." Robert K. Gnuse, "Seven Gay Texts: Biblical Passages Used to Condemn Homosexuality," *Biblical Theology Bulletin: Journal of Bible and Culture,* prepublished April 22, 2015, https://doi.org/10.1177/0146107915577097.

170 **"I surrendered to my lust"** Augustine, *Confessions,* trans. R. S. Pine-Coffin (New York: Penguin, 1961), 43.

170 **"movement they had not previously known"** This is in Augustine's *The Literal Meaning of Genesis,* which he spent fifteen years writing. Professor Stephen Greenblatt explains that it was Augustine's undesired desiring that pushed him to formulate this theory—it was a disavowal of his own urges. As Greenblatt explains, "In Paradise, Augustine argued, Adam and Eve would have had sex without involuntary arousal: 'They would not have had the activity of turbulent lust in their flesh, however, but only the movement of peaceful will by which we command the other members of the body.' Without feeling any passion—without sensing that strange goad—'the husband would have relaxed on his wife's bosom in tranquility of mind.' . . . This was how it was all meant to be for Adam and Eve. But, Augustine concludes, it never happened, not

even once. Their sin happened first, 'and they incurred the penalty of exile from paradise before they could unite in the task of propagation as a deliberate act undisturbed by passion.'" Stephen Greenblatt, "How St. Augustine Invented Sex," *New Yorker,* June 12, 2017, https://www.newyorker.com/magazine /2017/06/19/how-st-augustine-invented-sex. As sex therapist Ian Kerner explains of Augustine, "He sounds like a lot of my patients wrestling with out-of-control sexual behaviors." I'm guessing Kerner would feel similarly about Jerome (see below). Ian Kerner, *So Tell Me About the Last Time You Had Sex: Laying Bare and Learning to Repair Our Love Lives* (New York: Grand Central, 2021), 93.

171 **moral institution of the Roman state** Fittingly, others within its ranks were also struggling with their sexuality. Saint Jerome, just ten years older than Augustine, was charged with synthesizing the New Testament from its various Greek translations into the Latin Vulgate Bible. Jerome joined an ascetic order to escape women, writing, "And yet he who, in fear of hell, had banished himself to this prison, found himself again and again surrounded by dancing girls! My face grew pale with hunger, yet in my cold body the passions of my inner being continued to glow. This human being was more dead than alive; only his burning lust continued to boil." So says the New Testament's state-sanctioned translator. His views about women and sexuality must have infiltrated his interpretation of canon. Quoted in Leonard Shlain, *Alphabet Versus the Goddess: The Conflict Between Word and Image* (New York: Penguin Compass, 1998), 245.

171 **"through co-option or suppression"** Riane Eisler, *Sacred Pleasure: Sex, Myth, and the Politics of the Body—New Paths to Power and Love* (New York: HarperOne, 1995), 30.

171 **"eunuchs," focused on the Kingdom of Heaven** This is the passage, which begins with Jesus condemning divorce: " 'If that,' said his followers, 'is the position of a man with regard to his wife, it is better not to marry.' 'It is not everyone,' he replied, 'who can accept this teaching, but only those who have been enabled to do so. Some men, it is true, have from birth been made eunuchs, while others have been made eunuchs by people, and others again have made themselves eunuchs for the sake of the realm of heaven. Let him accept it who can" Matthew 19:10–12; Hal Taussig, ed., *A New New Testament: A Bible for the 21st Century Combining Traditional and Newly Discovered Texts* (2013; repr., New York: Mariner, 2015), 47. According to religion professor Jennifer Wright Knust, author of *Unprotected Texts: The Bible's Surprising Contradictions about Sex and Desire* (New York: HarperOne, 2011), "There's a fantastic passage in Matthew where Jesus says to his disciples that some people should be eunuchs for the kingdom of heaven. So the way this gets received by early Christians is that Jesus is recommending celibacy which would make sense, given that he says elsewhere that we shouldn't get married, that we should be focusing our attention on spreading the gospel. . . . Some Christians took this literally and there were some cases of early Christians castrating themselves for the purpose of celibacy." Jennifer Wright Knust, " 'Unprotected Texts': The Bible on Sex and Marriage," interview by Terry Gross, *Fresh Air,* March 10, 2011, NPR.

171 **"adultery with her in his heart"** Taussig, *New New Testament,* 31.

172 **refused to condemn her** This is John 8:3–11. Taussig, *New New Testament,* 199.

172 **"people must not separate"** We've also really screwed up the concept of virginity and the Virgin Birth, which mythologists like Joseph Campbell suggest was code for a spiritual birth, having nothing to do with intercourse. Mother Mary would have been a teenager—typically Jewish women were married off at age thirteen or fourteen. There wasn't a cultural focus on virginity simply because there was no opportunity or precedent for premarital sex (adultery was another thing). Because of this, the Old Testament has been revised in the past decade to more properly reflect what was meant by the word *almah* in Hebrew, which had been encoded as "virgin"—it is now translated as "young woman," divorced from sexual standing. (A few mentions of virgins— *betulah*—remain in the Hebrew Gospel.) Here's where things get really twisted. According to professor and biblical scholar Bart Ehrman, whoever wrote the Gospel of Mark got this wrong, making virginity central to the Jesus-as-Messiah prophecy fulfillment. As he writes, "In the Hebrew Bible, Isaiah indicates that a 'young woman' will conceive and bear a son, a prediction not of a future Messiah but of an event that was soon to take place in Isaiah's own day. When the Hebrew Bible was translated into Greek, however, Isaiah's 'young woman' (Hebrew *alma;* there is a different Hebrew word for 'virgin') came to be rendered by the Greek word for 'virgin' (*parthenos*), and that is the form of the Bible that Matthew read. And so he thought that Isaiah was predicting something not about his own day but about the future Messiah (though the term *Messiah* does not occur in Isaiah 7). So Matthew wrote that Jesus was born of a virgin because that's what he thought Scripture predicted." Whoops. Bart Ehrman, *Jesus, Interrupted: Revealing the Hidden Contradictions in the Bible (and Why We Don't Know About Them)* (New York: HarperOne, 2009), 74. I used Taussig's translation of the New Testament (*New New Testament,* 47).

173 **"compared with 20% of boys"** Joyce Endendijk, Anneloes van Baar, and Maja Dekovic, "He Is a Stud, She Is a Slut!," *Personality and Social Psychology Review* 24, no. 2 (May 2020): 163–90, https://doi.org/10.1177/1088868319891310.

173 **"resulting from low self-esteem"** In this study, women and men rated peers said to have different levels of sexual permissiveness (two or twenty past sexual partners) on how highly they would value them for friendship. Women were penalized for sexual permissiveness; men, celebrated. Zhana Vrangalova, Rachel Bukberg, and Gerulf Rieger, "Birds of a Feather? Not When It Comes to Sexual Permissiveness," *Journal of Social and Personal Relationships* (May 2013): https://doi.org/10.1177/0265407513487638.

173 **which further isolates these women** The researcher quoted was Zhana Vrangalovva. Peter Scowen, "Gasp! Women Think Other Sexually Promiscuous Women Don't Make Good Friends, Study Finds," *Globe and Mail,* June 5, 2013, https://www.theglobeandmail.com/life/the-hot-button/gasp-women-think-other-sexually-promiscuous-women-dont-make-good-friends-study-finds/article12360443/.

175 **"sex between two consenting adults"** Madonna, *Nightline,* December 3, 1990, ABC News.

176 **"without a strong father figure"** James Bradley (@JamesBradleyCA), Twitter, August 7, 2020.

177 **"American psychological cliterodectomy"** Peggy Orenstein, "Taking Control of Our Sexual Experience," interview by Elise Loehnen, *The goop Podcast,* January 22, 2020.

177 **sex could and would kill** I first had this revelation while reading Ada Calhoun's *Why We Can't Sleep: Women's New Midlife Crisis* (New York: Grove, 2020). I was immediately reminded that the horror film that most marked my youth wasn't *A Nightmare on Elm Street,* it was Larry Clark's *Kids,* which tracks an HIV-positive New York City teen as he has sex with virgins during one long, drug-fueled night. Ada Calhoun, "The New Midlife Crisis," interview by Elise Loehnen, *The goop Podcast,* February 11, 2020.

178 **"rather than agents of sexuality"** Orenstein, "Taking Control."

178 **lesbians have never had sex** Orenstein says one young lesbian she interviewed decided sex for her was when she had an orgasm with a partner; it didn't matter what was required or involved for that outcome. Orenstein, "Taking Control."

178 **high school kids have had intercourse** What's particularly interesting about this stat is that it shows a marked decrease: in 1991, the percentage was 54.1 percent, in 2013 it was 46.8 percent. Centers for Disease Control, "Youth Risk Behavior Surveillance System," last reviewed October 27, 2020, https://www.cdc.gov/healthyyouth/data/yrbs/index.htm.

178 **"I'm sexy but not sexual"** Orenstein, "Taking Control."

179 **procreative, relational, or recreational** Ian Kerner, "Understanding Our Sexual Potential," interview by Elise Loehnen, *Pulling the Thread Podcast,* February 3, 2022.

179 **"harassing brothers disappeared"** Maria Tatar, *The Heroine with 1,001 Faces* (New York: Liveright, 2021), 127.

180 **wife to concubine to slave** As Lerner writes, "The distinction between a free married woman and a slave was expressed within degrees of unfreedom. The class difference between a wife living under the patriarchal dominance/protection of her husband and a slave living under the dominance/protection of the master was mainly that the wife could own a slave, male or female, and other property. The slave could not even own herself." Gerda Lerner, *The Creation of Patriarchy* (New York: Oxford University Press, 1986), 96.

180 **social station and acceptance** Gerda Lerner explains: "Domestic women, sexually serving one man and under his protection, are here designated as 'respectable' by being veiled; women not under one man's protection and sexual control are designated as 'public women,' hence unveiled" (*Creation of Patriarchy,* 135). The Middle Assyrian Law Codes, which followed Hammurabi's Code in recency (ca. 1300 B.C.) were similarly terrible for women. In terms of sexual purity, one reads: "If the wives of a man or the daughters of a man go out into the street, their heads are to be veiled. The prostitute is not to be veiled. Maidservants are not to veil themselves. Veiled harlots and maidservants shall have their garments seized and 50 blows inflicted on them and bitumen poured on their heads."

180 **tried to befriend richer girls** Elizabeth A. Armstrong and Laura T. Hamilton, "'Good Girls': Gender, Social Class, and Slut Discourse on Campus," *Social Psychology Quarterly,* prepublished May 28, 2014, https://doi.org/10.1177/0190272514521220.

180 **"concealing her sexual history"** Olga Khazan, "There's No Such Thing as a

Slut," *The Atlantic,* May 18, 2014, https://www.theatlantic.com/health/archive /2014/05/theres-no-such-thing-as-a-slut/371773/.

181   **men (10.3 percent) outpaced women (7 percent)** Janna A. Dickenson, Neil Gleason, and Eli Coleman, "Prevalence of Distress Associated with Difficulty Controlling Sexual Urges, Feelings, and Behaviors in the United States," *JAMA Network,* November 9, 2018.

183   **"desirable but not desiring"** Deborah Tolman, *Dilemmas of Desire: Teenage Girls Talk About Sexuality* (Cambridge, Mass.: Harvard University Press, 2002), 115.

183   **memory offers new perspectives** Psychotherapist Galit Atlas explains that Freud "viewed memory as a fluid entity that was constantly changing and being reworked over time," meaning that "early traumatic events are layered with new meanings throughout life. Freud was especially focused on sexual abuse as an event that would be reworked retrospectively as the child got older and reached certain developmental phases. Sexual abuse in childhood isn't always registered by the child as traumatic. The child is overwhelmed with something they cannot process or even make sense of. As time passes, the traumatic experience is reprocessed. In every developmental phase the child will revisit the abuse from a different angle and with different understanding. When that abused child becomes a teenager and then an adult, when they have sex for the first time or have children, when their child reaches the age they were when the abuse happened—in each moment the abuse will be reprocessed from a slightly different perspective. The process of mourning keeps changing and accrues new layers of meaning. Time will not necessarily make the memory fade; instead, the memory will appear and reappear in different forms and will be experienced simultaneously as real and unreal." Galit Atlas, *Emotional Inheritance: A Therapist, Her Patients, and the Legacy of Trauma* (New York: Little, Brown Spark, 2022), 56–57.

184   **develop the motor skills** Helen Singer Kaplan talked about this in her book *The New Sex Therapy: Active Treatment of Sexual Dysfunctions* (London: Psychology Press, 1974), cited in Eisler, *Sacred Pleasure,* 300.

185   **"child sexual abuse accusations as true"** *Allen v. Farrow,* directed by Amy Zierling and Kirby Dick, HBO, 2021, four episodes.

186   **"killed by their current or former partners"** Katherine Rowland, *The Pleasure Gap: American Women and the Unfinished Sexual Revolution* (New York: Seal Press, 2020), 52.

187   **from a non-tribal member** André B. Rosay, "Violence Against American Indian and Alaska Native Women and Men," National Institute of Justice, May 2016, https://nij.ojp.gov/topics/articles/violence-against-american-indian-and -alaska-native-women-and-men. Another good resource: "The Facts on Violence Against American Indian/Alaskan Native Women," Futures Without Violence, accessed February 12, 2022, https://www.futureswithoutviolence .org/userfiles/file/Violence%20Against%20AI%20AN%20Women%20Fact %20Sheet.pdf. I interviewed the executive director of the National Indigenous Women's Resource Center (NIWRC) about this issue and "man camps" as well. Lucy Rain Simpson, "Ending the Violence Against Indigenous Women and Children," interview by Elise Loehnen, *The goop Podcast,* November 4, 2020.

187 **were reported missing** "Missing & Murdered Indigenous People: Statewide Report Wyoming," University of Wyoming, https://wysac.uwyo.edu/wysac /reports/View/7713.

187 **Black men rape Black women, et cetera** As Sarah Deer, a professor and leading advocate and lawyer for Indigenous women (and member of the Muscogee nation), explains, "AI/AN women . . . report that the majority of assailants are non-Native. The original 1999 Bureau of Justice Statistics report concluded that about nine in ten American Indian victims of rape or sexual assault had white or black assailants. Another report indicated that over 70 percent of the assailants were white." Sarah Deer, *The Beginning and End of Rape: Confronting Sexual Violence in Native America* (Minneapolis: University of Minnesota Press, 2015), 7. For intraracial versus interracial crime statistics, see Rachel E. Morgan, "Race and Hispanic Origin of Victims and Offenders, 2012–15," U.S. Department of Justice, Special Report, October 2017, https:// bjs.ojp.gov/content/pub/pdf/rhovo1215.pdf.

187 **perceived as traitorous** There's no more public example of this than Anita Hill, who accused now Supreme Court justice Clarence Thomas of sexual harassment. As she recounts in her memoir, over the years she has frequently heard questions like "Would you speak to the racist undertones in sexual harassment and how your testimony against a Black man dislodged the unspoken rule of not speaking against a brother and opened the possibility of addressing abuse across all racial barriers?" and comments like "Thank you for breaking an African American cultural taboo by speaking out in the public arena against a Black male." Anita Hill, *Believing: Our Thirty-Year Journey to End Gender Violence* (New York: Viking, 2021), 231.

187 **horrific tools of oppression** As activist Angela Davis writes, "It would be a mistake to regard the institutionalized pattern of rape during slavery as an expression of white men's sexual urges, otherwise stifled by the specter of white womanhood's chastity. That would be far too simplistic an explanation. Rape was a weapon of domination, a weapon of repression, whose covert goal was to extinguish slave women's will to resist, and in the process, to demoralize their men." Angela Davis, *Women, Race and Class* (New York: Vintage, 1983), 23–24.

187 **primary collateral damages of war** Unfortunately and tragically, rape seems to be a perpetual by-product of conflict. Some psychologists theorize that it's because it bonds men together. As the war in Ukraine unfolds, rape is one of its signals, and Human Rights Watch is documenting these war crimes, which are being widely reported. "Ukraine: Apparent War Crimes in Russia-Controlled Areas: Summary Executions, Other Grave Abuses by Russian Forces," *Human Rights Watch*, April 3, 2022, https://www.hrw.org/news/2022 /04/03/ukraine-apparent-war-crimes-russia-controlled-areas.

187 **approximately 975 perpetrators walk free** Deborah Tuerkheimer, "Why Don't We Believe Women?," interview by Elise Loehnen, *Pulling the Thread*, December 16, 2021.

188 **"for any other crime"** Soraya Chemaly, *Rage Becomes Her: The Power of Women's Anger* (New York: Atria, 2018), 135.

189 **"be about us, not them"** Rebecca Traister, *Good and Mad: The Revolutionary Power of Women's Anger* (New York: Simon & Schuster, 2018), 164–65.

189 **men over their female victims** All of Kate Manne's work on "himpathy" is worth studying, but this particular passage about Brock Turner, the Stanford swimmer, perfectly articulates what happens to the women as a result. Manne writes: "The excessive sympathy that flows to perpetrators like Brock Turner both owes and contributes to insufficient concern for the harm, humiliation, and (more or less lasting) trauma they may bring to their victims. And it both owes to and contributes to a tendency to let historically dominant agents get away with murder—proverbially and otherwise—vis-à-vis their historical subordinates. In the case of male dominance, we sympathize with him first, effectively making him into the victim of his own crimes. For, if someone sympathizes with the rapist initially, insofar as he loses his appetite or swimming scholarship, then *he* will come to figure as the victim in the story. And a victim narrative needs a villain, or victimizer. . . . Now consider: who is the 'but-for' cause of the rapist ending up in this situation? None other than the person who testified against him: his victim may hence be recast as the villain." Kate Manne, *Down Girl: The Logic of Misogyny* (New York: Oxford University Press, 2018), 201.

189 **placed on our shoulders as well** Tangentially but related, not only do women transition from victim to victimizers in people's minds, but per Gabor Maté, the brilliant family doctor, "Our society reinforces men's sense of being entitled to women's care in a way that almost escapes being put into words." This is the automatic mothering we provide, as well as the prioritization of other people's care over our own survival. Maté notes how British author Caroline Criado Perez, author of *Invisible Women: Data Bias in a World Designed for Men* (New York: Abrams Press, 2019), describes "implicit male-oriented bias in virtually all aspects of social, economic, cultural, academic, and even medical life. She gives a fascinating example of the asymmetrical apportioning of chores between men and women: 'We have long known that women (in particular women under fifty-five) have worse outcomes than men following heart surgery. But it wasn't until a Canadian study came out in 2016 that researchers were able to isolate women's care burden as one of the factors behind this discrepancy, noticing that women who have bypass surgery tend to go right back into their caregiving roles, while men were more likely to have someone to look after them.'" Gabor Maté, *The Myth of Normal: Trauma, Illness, and Healing in a Toxic Culture,* with Daniel Maté (New York: Avery, 2022), 338.

190 **"different times in his or her life"** Wendy Maltz, *The Sexual Healing Journal: A Guide for Survivors of Sexual Abuse* (New York: William Morrow, 2012), xvi–xvii.

190 **people we know and sometimes love** "Perpetrators of Sexual Violence: Statistics," Rape, Abuse & Incest National Network (RAINN), 2022, https://rainn.org/statistics/perpetrators-sexual-violence.

191 **delimit our lives today** As Gerda Lerner writes, "The impact on the conquered of the rape of conquered women was twofold: it dishonored the women and by implication served as a symbolic castration of their men. Men in patriarchal societies who cannot protect the sexual purity of their wives, sisters, and children are truly impotent and dishonored. The practice of raping the women of a conquered group has remained a feature of warfare and conquest from the second millennium B.C. to the present. It is a social practice,

which, like the torture of prisoners, has been resistant to 'progress,' to humanitarian reforms, and to sophisticated moral and ethical considerations. I suggest this is the case because it is a practice built into and essential to the structure of patriarchal institutions and inseparable from them. It is at the beginning of the system, prior to class formation, that we can see this in its purest essence." Lerner, *Creation of Patriarchy*, 80.

192 **" 'Thank you for taking care of yourself' "** Melissa Febos, *Girlhood* (New York: Bloomsbury, 2021), 203.

192 **"I didn't have a choice"** Febos, *Girlhood*, 211.

192 **"refrigerator that does not open"** Febos, *Girlhood*, 266.

193 **and did not want** Lacy Crawford, "Systems of Silencing," interview by Elise Loehnen, *The goop Podcast*, December 10, 2020.

196 **the experiences don't evaporate** Brené Brown, *Dare to Lead: Brave Work, Tough Conversations, Whole Hearts* (New York: Random House, 2018), 254.

196 **"bodies are free to forget"** Atlas, *Emotional Inheritance*, 119.

197 **interested in the primates** Meredith Chivers, Michael Seto, Martin Lalumière, Ellen Laan, and Teresa Grimbos, "Agreement of Self-Reported and Genital Measures of Sexual Arousal in Men and Women: A Meta-analysis," *Archives of Sexual Behavior* 39 (January 2010): 5–56, https://doi.org/10.1007/s10508-009-9556-9; Jackie Huberman and Meredith Chivers, "Examining Gender Specificity of Sexual Response with Concurrent Thermography and Plethysmography," *Psychophysiology* 10 (October 2015): 1382–95, https://doi.org/10.1111/psyp.12466. For a more in-depth read about the research, this piece made me laugh: Daniel Bergner, "What Do Women Want?," *New York Times Magazine*, January 22, 2009, https://www.nytimes.com/2009/01/25/magazine/25desire-t.html.

199 **"ravishment has to do with love"** Marion Woodman, *Addiction to Perfection: The Still Unravished Bride* (Toronto, Ont.: Inner City Books, 1982), 134.

199 **"not the other way around"** Michael Bader, *Arousal: The Secret Logic of Sexual Fantasies* (New York: Thomas Dunne Books, 2002), 6.

200 **where consent is clearly established** Jaiya, "What's Your Map to Arousal?," interview by Elise Loehnen, *The goop Podcast*, July 30, 2020.

200 ***"feel guilty about doing unto others"*** Bader, *Arousal*, 119.

201 **experience of surrender and awe** If you want a wild but fascinating read, I recommend *The Magdalen Manuscript*, channeled by Tom Kenyon, 2nd ed. (Boulder, Colo.: SoundsTrue, 2006). In it, Mary Magdalen purportedly explains how she was an initiate in the cult of Isis (as was Mother Mary) and states that she and Yeshua engaged in a version of Kundalini sex yoga to charge his *Ka* or etheric body so that upon his descent before his ascension, he could blaze trails of light for the rest to follow.

201 **described as the "maternal matrix"** I love this sentiment from Jungian therapists Marion Woodman and Elinor Dickson: "The freedom we seek does not lie in the patriarchal control we so desperately attempt to maintain. Rather it lies in letting go and descending into the chaos of the maternal matrix where the seeds of new life are waiting to be fertilized. Letting go is embracing the Black Goddess, she who will open our eyes to our illusions, she who will make us see that our treasure lies in the repressed feminine energies that we once

labeled weak, irrational, disorganized, supersensitive, and all the other thought-less labels—naïve, stupid, slow, melodramatic. Descending into her territory demands the death of a rigidly controlled life. Dancing with her means finding a new discipline that allows the new life to sprout and grow." Marion Wood-man and Elinor Dickson, *Dancing in the Flames: The Dark Goddess in Transfor-mation of Consciousness* (Boulder, Colo.: Shambhala, 1996), 181.

202 **happened on their chart** Woodman and Dickson write of this chart and its promised era, distinguishing Jesus from patriarchal Christianity: "It could equally be argued that we are living in a *pre*-Christian era, in that the revolu-tionary message of Christ, though preserved over the years among a few, has never been widely put into practice under the power-as-strength mindset of the patriarchal paradigm. The basic principles of Christianity—compassion, forgiveness, repentance, love for one's enemies, tolerance, meekness—are a leap beyond what patriarchy stands for." Woodman and Dickson, *Dancing in the Flames,* 207–8.

Chapter 8: Anger

206 **filed the pdf away** "The Riso-Hudson Enneagram Type Indicator," Ennea-gram Institute, taken July 12, 2019, https://tests.enneagraminstitute.com/.

207 **contained all knowledge** Don Richard Riso and Russ Hudson, *The Wisdom of the Enneagram: The Complete Guide to Psychological and Spiritual Growth for the Nine Personality Types* (New York: Bantam, 1999), 20.

207 **passionate thoughts (*logismoi*)** Evagrius did not invent the idea of *logismoi* (passionate thoughts) but built them into a system of descriptive psychology. As one of his translators, John Eudes Bamberger, explains, "He found in the desert tradition already a considerable body of teaching concerning the various passions and *logismoi* (passionate thoughts) which was the fruit of a practical experience of many years on the part of the more experienced monks. But he was the first to classify them into an ordered series of eight types of passionate thoughts." John Eudes Bamberger, introduction to *The Praktikos and Chapters on Prayer,* by Evagrius Ponticus, trans. John Eudes Bamberger (Trappist, Ky.: Cistercian Publications, 1972), lxviii.

208 **"remains a mystery"** "The Traditional Enneagram," Enneagram Institute, ac-cessed March 3, 2022, https://www.enneagraminstitute.com/the-traditional -enneagram.

209 **frequently referred to as wrathful** According to anthropologists Carel van Schaik and Kai Michel, "There are no fewer than 390 documented instances of and 130 verbal references to [God's wrath] in the Old Testament." Carel van Schaik and Kai Michel, *The Good Book of Human Nature: An Evolutionary Read-ing of the Bible* (New York: Basic Books, 2016), 74.

209 **(Proverbs 15:1)** King James Version.

209 **(Matthew 5:38–39)** Hal Taussig, ed., *A New New Testament: A Bible for the 21st Century Combining Traditional and Newly Discovered Texts* (2013; repr., New York: Mariner, 2015), 31.

209 **"attacked by poisonous wild beasts"** Evagrius, *Praktikos,* 17.

210 **biographer believes he's describing depression** Evagrius, *Praktikos,* 22.

210 applied correctly and with restraint Rebecca Konyndyk DeYoung, *Glittering Vices: A New Look at the Seven Deadly Sins and Their Remedies*, rev. ed. (Grand Rapids, Mich.: Brazos Press, 2020), 140–41.

210 "resentment and grudge holding" DeYoung, *Glittering Vices*, 146.

211 "place the blame on a woman—his mother!" Harriet Lerner, *The Dance of Anger: A Woman's Guide to Changing the Patterns of Intimate Relations* (New York: William Morrow, 2014), 2.

212 "at odds with maintaining relationships" Carol Gilligan and Naomi Snider, *Why Does Patriarchy Persist?* (Medford, Mass.: Polity Press, 2018), 83.

212 "one of those angry women" Harriet Lerner, "What Our Anger Teaches Us," interview by Elise Loehnen, *Pulling the Thread Podcast*, November 4, 2021.

212 "circumscribe white male dominion" Rebecca Traister, *Good and Mad: The Revolutionary Power of Women's Anger* (New York: Simon & Schuster, 2018), 43.

213 "interests of other women" Mary Beard, *Women and Power: A Manifesto* (New York: Liveright, 2017), 16.

213 making way for new life As anthropologist Marija Gimbutas explains, "The main theme of Goddess symbolism is the mystery of birth and death and the renewal of life, not only human but all life on earth and indeed in the whole cosmos. Symbols and images cluster around the parthenogenetic (self-generating) Goddess and her basic functions as Giver of Life, Wielder of Death, and, not less importantly, as Regeneratrix, and around the Earth Mother, the Fertility Goddess young and old, rising and dying with plant life. She was the single source of all life who took her energy from the springs and wells, from the sun, moon, and moist earth." Marija Gimbutas, *The Language of the Goddess: Unearthing the Hidden Symbols of Western Civilization* (New York: Harper and Row, 1989), xix.

213 "color of death, of bones" Gimbutas, *Language of the Goddess*, xix.

214 "whole field of the culture system" Joseph Campbell, *Goddesses: Mysteries of the Feminine Divine* (Novato, Calif.: New World Library, 2013), 22.

214 one-half of the goddess Gimbutas, *Language of the Goddess*, 207.

214 Trump posed as Perseus Beard, *Women and Power*, 76.

214 "investment in nonwhite people" Traister, *Good and Mad*, 7.

215 allegiance to this system As Seyward Darby explains, "The slogan referred to the privileges of being a wife and mother, protected by men, unsullied by the unladylike muck of feminism. . . . STOP was both a battle cry hurled at feminists and a clarion call to white men—a bid to maintain social status by simultaneously fending off upstart forces and demonstrating solidarity with more powerful ones." Seyward Darby, *Sisters in Hate: American Women on the Front Lines of White Nationalism* (New York: Little, Brown, 2020), 121.

215 rather than "fight or flight" Shelley E. Taylor, Laura Cousino Klein, Brian P. Lewis, Tara L. Gruenewald, Regan A. R. Gurung, and John A. Updegraff, "Biobehavioral Responses to Stress in Females: Tend-and-Befriend, Not Fight-or-Flight," *Psychological Review* 107, no. 3 (2000): 411–29, https://doi.org/10.1037/0033-295X.107.3.411.

216 "often labeled selfish" Marshall Rosenberg, *Nonviolent Communication: A Language of Life* (Encinitas, Calif.: Puddlejumper, 2015), 196.

216 **"their needs are unimportant"** Rosenberg, *Nonviolent Communication*, 55–56.

217 **happy, sad, and pissed off** Marc Brackett, "Permission to Feel," interview by Brené Brown, *Unlocking Us Podcast*, April 14, 2020.

217 **begin analyzing and judging** Rosenberg, *Nonviolent Communication*, 143.

217 **"burn it down in two hours"** Elise Loehnen, "The Tibetan Bon Meditation Tradition," *goop* website, December 26, 2019, goop.com.

218 **"simply too tired to be angry"** Thích Nhât Hanh, *Anger: Wisdom for Cooling the Flames* (New York: Riverhead, 2001), 118.

219 **personality or lifestyle needs** John Gottman, *The Seven Principles for Making Marriage Work* (New York: Harmony, 2015), 137–40.

219 **unclear how to instigate change** Sybil Carrère and John Gottman, "Predicting Divorce Among Newlyweds from the First Three Minutes of a Marital Conflict Discussion," *Family Process* 38, no. 3 (Fall 1999): 293–301, https://doi .org/10.1111/j.1545-5300.1999.00293.x.

221 **"nothing-to-see-here" existence** Adam Grant, "The Unexpected Sparks of Creativity, Confrontation and Office Culture," interview by Elise Loehnen, *The goop Podcast,* March 29, 2018.

222 **"celebration of manipulation"** Terry Real, "Healing Male Depression," interview by Elise Loehnen, *Pulling the Thread Podcast,* October 21, 2021.

222 **"will he change along with her?"** H. Lerner, "What Our Anger Teaches Us."

223 **devour her as depression** Gilligan and Snider, *Why Does Patriarchy Persist?,* 87.

224 **"compliant with external authorities"** Dr. Maté explains that despite the cancer diagnosis, these patients still couldn't express their needs: "While anxious about their disease progression, their worries were focused in a specifically outward direction, away from themselves and toward the effect their illness was having on their families. Such self-abnegation was too well typified in an article I once read in the *Globe and Mail*, written by a woman just diagnosed with breast cancer. 'I'm worried about my husband,' she immediately told her physician. 'I won't have the strength to support him.'" Gabor Maté, *Myth of Normal: Trauma, Illness, and Healing in a Toxic Culture,* with Daniel Maté (New York: Avery, 2022), 99.

224 **"on victimized targets"** Rachel Simmons, *Odd Girl Out: The Hidden Culture of Aggression in Girls* (New York: Mariner, 2002), 3.

225 **"triggered by physical pain"** Amanda Ripley, *High Conflict: Why We Get Trapped and How We Get Out* (New York: Simon & Schuster, 2021), 71.

225 **share the burden and offer support** Simmons, *Odd Girl Out,* 80.

226 **"voices in a hostile culture"** Simmons, *Odd Girl Out,* 220.

226 **focuses on white, middle-class ones** "Minority and low-income girls are often stereotyped as aggressive, loud, and disruptive, and therefore 'at risk.' 'Those loud black girls' is a term used to demean the brassy presence of African American female youth. . . . What little we know about girls' relationships is based mostly on studies of white, middle-class girls. . . . That the girls who engage in direct conflict may have little real social power is a sad irony, to say the least. The assertiveness shown by some minority girls may reflect not self-confidence but their vulnerability in the larger society." Simmons, *Odd Girl Out,* 242–43.

228 **"carry on anyway"** Brittney Cooper, *Eloquent Rage: A Black Feminist Discovers Her Superpower* (New York: Picador, 2018), 4.

229 **school shootings, to Bill Cosby** "American Rage: The Esquire/NBC News Survey," *Esquire,* January 3, 2016, https://www.esquire.com/news-politics /a40693/american-rage-nbc-survey/.

229 **the results were the same** As Soraya Chemaly reports, "This postelection poll showed that 53 percent of respondents were angrier about the state of the world than they were a year prior. No surprises there. Again, women were angrier than men, with 74 percent versus 69 percent saying they encountered, for example, enraging information at least once a day in the news. White women were also, again, persistently angrier than black women, a finding that refutes, as writer and political commentator Professor Melissa Harris-Perry wrote at the time, angry black women mythologizing. This time, liberal and progressive women, 76 percent of whom said they were angrier year-over-year, had the most pronounced response." And when it came to a direct response to Trump, women dramatically led the charge. Chemaly again: "An April 2017 poll of just under thirty thousand people showed that 86 percent of those who had taken steps to protest his administration and its policies were women; 28 percent were between the ages of thirty and forty-five; and 50 percent were between forty-six and sixty-five." Soraya Chemaly, *Rage Becomes Her: The Power of Women's Anger* (New York: Atria, 2018), 241, 247.

230 **"more able to regulate it"** Kristin Neff, *Fierce Self-Compassion* (New York: Harper Wave, 2021), 66.

231 **"might otherwise make known"** Traister, *Good and Mad,* 145.

233 **"claim and want granted"** In a fascinating discussion, Dolly Chugh explains that studies indicate we'll even pay to have our identity affirmed. Dolly Chugh, *The Person You Mean to Be: How Good People Fight Bias* (New York: Harper Business, 2018), 4–7.

234 **what they're trying to say** Rosenberg breaks "emotional liberation" into three stages. In the first, which he calls emotional slavery, "we believe ourselves responsible for the feelings of others. We think we must constantly strive to keep everyone happy. If they don't appear happy, we feel responsible and compelled to do something about it." He describes stage two as the "obnoxious stage," because we typically become angry as over-responsibility begins to feel like a burden. He writes, "When we notice how much of our lives we've missed and how little we have responded to the call of our own soul, we may get angry." Only in stage three do we reach emotional liberation, where we might decide to meet the needs of others via our compassion, but never out of shame, guilt, or fear. Rosenberg, *Nonviolent Communication,* 57–60.

235 **"won't have changed one iota"** Cooper, *Eloquent Rage,* 35.

237 **" 'thoughts about what happens' "** Byron Katie, *Loving What Is: Four Questions That Can Change Your Life* (New York: Harmony, 2002), viii.

237 **"I could be free"** Katie, *Loving What Is,* 37.

241 **seeds of shame and blame** I owe much of my thinking about this to Carissa Schumacher and a Yeshua transmission she gave in October 2021. For those who are concerned about the implications of "You reap what you sow," she offered that people need not be scared: It's simply a time of transparency and accountability.

Chapter 9: Sadness

245 **"drench her in sadness"** Evagrius Ponticus, *The Praktikos and Chapters on Prayer,* trans. John Eudes Bamberger (Trappist, Ky.: Cistercian Publications, 1972), 17.

246 **10 percent of the population** Jeffrey Rediger, *Cured: The Life-Changing Science of Spontaneous Healing* (New York: Flatiron, 2020), 194.

248 **"regardless of our personal wishes"** Barbara Walker, *The Crone: Woman of Age, Wisdom, and Power* (New York: HarperOne, 1985), 28.

248 **"recovery of life's joy"** Joseph Campbell, *The Power of Myth,* with Bill Moyers (New York: Anchor Books, 1991), 188.

251 **done with all that sad stuff** Professor and therapist Pauline Boss writes about both Freud's and Kübler-Ross's evolving understanding of grief in her essential read *The Myth of Closure.* She also explains her framework for "Ambiguous Loss," a term she coined, in which people ping back and forth between different stages, which are, in no particular order: Adjust Mastery, Find Meaning, Reconstruct Identity, Discover New Hope, Revise Attachment, Normalize Ambivalence. Pauline Boss, *The Myth of Closure: Ambiguous Loss in a Time of Pandemic and Change* (New York: Norton, 2021), 98.

251 **expected to get over it** This sentiment came from poet Prageeta Sharma, written about in Cathy Park Hong's *Minor Feelings: An Asian American Reckoning* (New York: One World, 2020), 47.

254 **"Belief clings, but faith lets go"** Alan Watts, *The Wisdom of Insecurity: A Message for an Age of Anxiety* (New York: Vintage, 2011), 24.

254 **"causality even when there is none"** Kate Bowler, "Does Everything Happen for a Reason?," interview by Elise Loehnen, *The goop Podcast,* April 30, 2020.

255 **"mattered more than our own lives"** Elaine Pagels, *Why Religion? A Personal Story* (New York: Ecco, 2018), 67–68.

255 **"into our human nature"** Pagels, *Why Religion?,* 103.

256 **"first two years of bereavement"** George Bonanno, *The Other Side of Sadness* (New York: Basic Books, 2019), 58.

256 **long-term singledom, or illness** Pauline Boss writes, "Of all the losses experienced in personal relationships, ambiguous loss is the most devastating because it remains unclear, indeterminate." Pauline Boss, *Ambiguous Loss: Learning to Live with Unresolved Grief* (Cambridge, Mass.: Harvard University Press, 1999), 5–6.

257 **"as I said I did"** Nora McInerny, *No Happy Endings* (New York: Dey Street, 2019), 3.

258 **now-finite pool of memories** Lucy Kalanithi, "What Matters in the End," interview by Elise Loehnen, *The goop Podcast,* August 2, 2018.

260 **"relationship becomes conflicted and stressful"** Harriet Lerner, *The Dance of Anger: A Woman's Guide to Changing the Patterns of Intimate Relations* (New York: William Morrow, 2014), 50.

261 **"subtly—or forcibly—pushed out of it"** Terrence Real, *I Don't Want to Talk About It: Overcoming the Secret Legacy of Male Depression* (New York: Scribner, 1997), 123.

261 **"wanted to reward them"** bell hooks, *The Will to Change: Men, Masculinity, and Love* (New York: Washington Square Press, 2004), 6.

262 **6.2 percent for men** "Statistics| Major Depression," National Institute of Mental Health, last updated January 2022, https://www.nimh.nih.gov/health /statistics/major-depression.

263 **substance abuse and personality disorders** Real, *I Don't Want to Talk About It*, 84.

263 **"defending your home"** Sam Gringlas, "Daniel Defense, the Maker of the Gun Used in Uvalde, Is Accused of Marketing to Teens," *Weekend Edition*, June 5, 2022, NPR, https://www.npr.org/2022/06/05/1103144998/daniel -defense-the-maker-of-the-gun-used-in-uvalde-is-accused-of-marketing-to-te.

263 **social isolation and unkindness** Constance Hammen and Stefanie Peters, "Differential Responses to Male and Female Depressive Reactions," *Journal of Consulting and Clinical Psychology* 6 (1977): 994–1001, https://doi.org/10.1037 /0022-006X.45.6.994.

264 **"ease to discuss her problems"** Real, *I Don't Want to Talk About It*, 82.

264 **"our own and other people's"** Marc Brackett, *Permission to Feel: Unblocking the Power of Emotions to Help Our Kids, Ourselves, and Our Society Thrive* (New York: Celadon, 2019), 24.

264 **being the most recent example** Harriet Washington, *A Terrible Thing to Waste: Environmental Racism and Its Assault on the American Mind* (New York: Little, Brown Spark, 2019), 106.

265 **sons about anger** Eisenberg has led dozens of studies on this topic; the most cited is Nancy Eisenberg, Adrienne Sadovsky, and Tracy Spinrad, "Associations of Emotion-Related Regulation with Language Skills, Emotion Knowledge, and Academic Outcomes," *New Directions for Child and Adolescent Development* 109 (Fall 2005): 109–18, https://doi.org/10.1002/cd.143.

265 **"about the age of two"** Real, *I Don't Want to Talk About It*, 131.

266 **"it must be destroyed"** Real, *I Don't Want to Talk About It*, 137.

266 **"mask it with indifference or rage"** hooks, *Will to Change*, 64–65.

267 **"bred from just such circumstances"** Real, *I Don't Want to Talk About It*, 109.

269 **feelings of loss and despair** Real uses his own story as typical of this pattern. The child of an abusive, disaffected father, Terry was full of rage and despair. He turned to drugs, almost died, and then clawed his way into college, where he went into therapy and recovered. As with most of the men he treats, his experience adhered to a pattern: trauma, wrapped in covert depression and addiction. He pulled the pin and crossed the wasteland, at a time when he was equipped, with the support of his therapist, to allow his sadness to come. As he writes, "Depression freezes, but sadness flows. It has an end. The thing I had spent so much time avoiding had just swept through me—and I was fine. In the healing safety of [my therapist's] company, my covert depression had become overt. My overt depression had transmuted into grief. And grief, I would come to understand, is depression's cure." Real, *I Don't Want to Talk About It*, 285.

269 **"wants to be legitimate fortune"** I first heard this Max Weber quote from Professor Nell Irving Painter on "Seeing White," an incredible podcast series on race hosted by Professor John Biewen out of Duke University and co-hosted by Chenjerai Kumanyika. It is season 2 of the podcast *Scene on Radio*. I learned a lot as well from the third season on misogyny ("Men"), co-hosted by Celeste Headlee.

Conclusion: Realignment

273 **sources that then disappeared** As the translator and historian John Eudes Bamberger explains, Evagrius was the first to compile and classify the *logismoi* into a system, though he did not invent them. As he writes, "He occupied himself with making the most accurate observations and descriptions of their dynamisms and operations. He was careful to describe the patterns of activity which characterized them and to indicate their inter-relations among themselves. His work in this area became the classic and when John Cassian wished to teach the western monks the desert doctrine on the *logismoi* he could find no better source than the writings of Evagrius." John Eudes Bamberger, introduction to *The Praktikos and Chapters on Prayer*, by Evagrius Ponticus, trans. John Eudes Bamberger (Trappist, Ky.: Cistercian Publications, 1972), lxviii.

274 **Jesus exorcised seven "demons"** I love the suggestion in the preface to Jean-Yves Leloup's *The Gospel of Mary Magdalene,* written by David Tresemer and Laura-Lea Cannon, that when Jesus cast out seven demons from Mary Magdalene, he was clearing her chakra system, i.e., the seven wheels of power that predate all of religion substantially, moving from India to Babylon, Assyria, and ultimately Egypt. As the preface authors explain, "If her purification is viewed in this way, it makes her the most thoroughly sanctified person mentioned in the New Testament. Imagine being completely cleansed of prejudices and old grudges, fogs of illusion, hereditary obstacles to health, all desires. Once healed, she can truly see the spiritual truth that works in all things. She can see the barbarity of other human beings, as well as the transcendent beauty of Jesus Christ's teachings. In modern terms, her heart and energetic centers are open." David Tresemer and Laura-Lea Cannon, preface to *The Gospel of Mary Magdalene,* by Jean-Yves Leloup, trans. Joseph Rowe (Rochester, Vt.: Inner Traditions, 2002), xviii.

275 **"lest you be confined by it"** Interestingly, some theologians read this as Christ rejecting Jewish law, or the Torah, and therefore part of the reason that a pronounced chasm developed between Judaism and Christianity (and its corresponding anti-Semitism). Other theologians assert that Christ, who maintained his Judaism (and never claimed to be the Messiah) insisted on Jewish law, only claiming that he came to evolve it. As Jesus explains, "Do not think that I have come to do away with the Law or the prophets; I have not come to do away with them, but to make them full. For I tell you for sure, until the heavens and the earth disappear, not even the smallest letter, nor one stroke of a letter, will disappear from the Law until all is done. Whoever, therefore, breaks one of these commandments, even the least of them, and teaches others to do so, will be called the least in the realm of heaven; but whoever keeps them, and teaches others to do so, will be called great in the realm of heaven" (Matthew 5:17–20). Hal Taussig, ed., *A New New Testament: A Bible for the 21st Century Combining Traditional and Newly Discovered Texts* (2013; repr., New York: Mariner, 2015), 30.

275 **(Mary 4:1–11)** Taussig, *New New Testament,* 224.

275 **"being out of alignment"** Cynthia Bourgeault, *The Meaning of Mary Magdalene: Discovering the Woman at the Heart of Christianity* (Boulder, Colo: Shambhala, 2010), 137.

276 **"to restore it to its root"** Hal Taussig, "The Gospel of Mary," in his *New New Testament*, 224–25.

276 **needing to be redeemed** Leloup, *Gospel of Mary Magdalene*, 48.

276 **our point of origin** As Karen King elaborates, "The Gospel of Mary defines sin as the adulterous relationship of the soul to the body. When the soul becomes attached to the body, it is overcome by the frailties and passions of the material nature, leading to sickness and death. By turning away from the body and recognizing one's true self as a spiritual being, the self can find the child of true Humanity within and conform to that Image." Karen L. King, *The Gospel of Mary of Magdala: Jesus and the First Woman Apostle* (Santa Rosa, Calif.: Polebridge Press, 2003), 65.

276 **(Mary 9:18–26)** Taussig, *New New Testament*, 225.

276 **"climates" in fascinating depth** Leloup defines the first three climates as *Darkness or Absurdity* ("a nauseating climate where our identification with matter engenders the experience of our nothingness and meaninglessness"), then *Craving* ("a tense and stressful climate of complaints and demands"), then *Refusal of Knowledge* ("a climate of stupor, close-mindedness, complacence, and vanity"), and then, finally, the Fourth Climate of *Sevenfold Wrath*. He believes that it is this climate "that adds its violence to the other climates, bringing them to climaxes of jealousy, possessiveness, pride, and the madness of profane wisdom." Leloup, *Gospel of Mary Magdalene*, 130.

276 **alienated and** *possessed* Leloup, *Gospel of Mary Magdalene*, 139.

276 **"seven forms"** Carissa expands on these prodigiously and offers that the seven demons Jesus ostensibly cast out of Mary Magdalene were simply a rebalancing. Yeshua, *The Freedom Transmissions,* as channeled by Carissa Schumacher (New York: HarperOne, 2021), 37–60.

280 **"balance is again restored"** Anna Lembke, "Navigating an Addictive Culture," interview by Elise Loehnen, *Pulling the Thread Podcast,* November 11, 2021. Lembke wrote an excellent book on addiction called *Dopamine Nation: Finding Balance in the Age of Indulgence* (New York: Dutton, 2021).

INDEX

Elise Loehnen is the host of *Pulling the Thread*. She has co-written twelve books, five of which were *New York Times* bestsellers. She was the chief content officer of goop, the lifestyle and e-commerce company, and she co-hosted *The goop Podcast* and *The goop Lab* on Netflix. Previously, she was the editorial projects director of *Condé Nast Traveler*. Elise lives in Los Angeles with her husband and two sons.

eliseloehnen.com

Instagram: @eliseloehnen

Twitter: @eloehnen